GW00361046

THE JACK THE RIPPER A TO Z

Also by Paul Begg
Into Thin Air: People Who Disappear
Jack the Ripper: The Uncensored Facts

Also by Martin Fido
Bodysnatchers
Charles Dickens
The Crimes, Detection and Death of Jack the Ripper
Murder Guide to London
Murders After Midnight
The Peasenhall Murder (with Keith Skinner)

Also by Keith Skinner
The Ripper Legacy (with Martin Howells)
The Peasenhall Murder (with Martin Fido)

THE JACK THE RIPPER
RIPPER
A to Z

Paul Begg, Martin Fido
and Keith Skinner

HEADLINE

Copyright © 1991 Paul Begg, Martin Fido, Keith Skinner

The right of Paul Begg, Martin Fido and Keith Skinner to be identified
as the Authors of the Work has been asserted by them in accordance
with the Copyright, Designs and Patents Act 1988.

First published in 1991
by HEADLINE BOOK PUBLISHING PLC

10 9 8 7 6 5 4 3 2 1

Map by Peter McClure

All rights reserved. No part of this publication may be
reproduced, stored in a retrieval system, or transmitted,
in any form or by any means without the prior written
permission of the publisher, nor be otherwise circulated
in any form of binding or cover other than that in which
it is published and without a similar condition being
imposed on the subsequent purchaser.

British Library Cataloguing in Publication Data

Begg, Paul
    The Jack the Ripper A-Z
    1. Murderers   2. London (England)
    I. Skinner, Keith   II. Fido, Martin
    364.1523092

    ISBN 0–7472–0424–1

Typeset by Intype, London

Printed and bound in Great Britain by
Richard Clay Ltd, Bungay, Suffolk

HEADLINE BOOK PUBLISHING PLC
Headline House
79 Great Titchfield Street
London W1P 7FN

This book is for
Judy and Siobán Begg
and
Laurie
and
Coral

Acknowledgements

We repeat our gratitude to those acknowledged in our previous books on the subject: *The Crimes, Detection and Death of Jack the Ripper*, Fido, 1987 and 1989; *The Ripper Legacy*, Howells and Skinner, 1987; *Jack the Ripper: The Uncensored Facts*, Begg, 1988.

In addition, we are indebted to: Mr Leonard Archer; Terry Bown; the British Library Science Reading Room; Louise Brodie; Kevin Broome (computer software advice); Frances Collinson (Museum of London); Bill Eckert; Stewart Evans; Michael and Jana Ferguson; Jean Overton Fuller; Robin Gillis and the staff of the Archives Dept, Metropolitan Police (much appreciation); Melvin Harris; Andrew Hewson of John Johnson Literary Agency (much appreciation); Caroline Hill; John Hoye (Operating Theatre Company); Sarah Jane Hughes; LBC Radio; Mrs G. Meredith; May Moore-Anderson; New Scotland Yard; Larry O'Rourke; Ernie Ostrowsky; Linda Richards (Museum of London); Mary Penny; Jonathan Perry; Molly Rumbelow; Ann Stewart; R. N. Stone; David Streatfield; Mr V. Tambling; J. C. Taylor; Dick Totty; John Triffit; Roger Tyrrell; Peter Underwood; Paula Van Langen; Bill Waddell and John Ross of the Metropolitan Police Crime ('Black') Museum; Nick Warren; Mrs Sheila Wolfe; Simon Wood.

For police history and photographs we are particularly indebted to Richard Sharp, Ken Stone and Paul Williams of the Metropolitan Police Museum.

And we are specially grateful to Melvyn Fairclough for discussing his work with us, trusting us neither to plagiarise nor disparage it before it had even been made public.

Foreword
by Donald Rumbelow

Only in fiction have the Jack the Ripper murders been solved. No matter that the solution flies in the face of reason (which it usually does), so long as the old story has new treatments and wildly improbable endings it seems to satisfy some primitive atavistic urging for a world that never existed. Jack can murder his way through the galaxy in a *Star Trek* episode. His women can be American Indians in a television serial. He can be chased by H. G. Wells in the Time Machine to modern-day San Francisco. He can be Sherlock 'Jack the Ripper' Holmes. With a change of sex he can become Jill the Ripper, Sister Hyde or The Nun of Calais. And, the ultimate fantasy, as mad Brigadier General Jack D. Ripper he can bring universal destruction in an Armageddon of nuclear bombs.

The reality and brutality of the Whitechapel murders should not tolerate such indulgences, but even in the work of the most careful researcher there are moments when the imagination soars and the fiction is apt to creep in. Guarding against it and trying to remain objective has always been a problem, which is why a book such as this has long been overdue. *The Jack the Ripper A to Z* has to be the anchor of future Jack the Ripper studies. It is a must for anyone seriously interested in the subject, not least because it has brought together everything that is known. This does not mean that the book is overloaded with unnecessary detail. On the contrary, as the authors and myself know, all of us having published books of our own on the subject, new material has appeared, but equally material has disappeared.

Why the Jack the Ripper murders should exert such fascination remains something of a mystery to many people. Globally there have been instances of far greater tallies of serial killings – eighty plus in some parts of the world – which makes Jack's head count of five seem especially meagre. Some writers have tried to enhance his profile by claiming figures as high as thirteen and twenty, even though this means casting the net wide and counting, in one instance at least, the same victim twice! Nor does the case have the glamour and trial drama of the Brideshead years with such titans of the English bar as Marshall Hall and Birkett appearing for the defence and the British public cheering them on to rescue their clients from the public hangman. The reality of the Whitechapel murders is one of deprivation, degradation and distress, a procession of tired, broken-spirited women trudging the streets in men's hob-nailed boots, their only homes the clothes on their backs, their few possessions kept in their skirt pockets, offering gin-puffed lips and tired flesh to any man who wants it for fourpence, twopence or a loaf of stale bread.

But the name is a buzz word. Mention Jack the Ripper or Sherlock Holmes and you evoke the same response. Images crowd the mind of fog, hansom cabs, gaslit cockney pubs, crumpets for tea, top hats, red silks, scarlet women and romance for a guinea – with change at the end of the evening! It is a totally fictitious world but for aficionados of the Jack the Ripper murders it is the world they want to read about and the world they want to enter. Useless to tell them that there was not any fog and that one of the murders was done in early daylight. They won't believe you. They will still cling to the old images.

What surprises people is how much is already known about the murders. The credit for much of the new material must go to the authors of this book who believe that, given two years and enough finance, they could solve the mystery once and for all. This book is their springboard to that solution. Putting such a huge amount of material on the market is tantamount to giving every 'ripperologist' a head start. It is obviously going to shake a lot of cherished illusions, but equally it is going to be the starting point for a lot of new inquiries. Most books on the subject either tailor the facts to the theory or leapfrog their way to a conclusion over a succession of assumptions and suppositions. The only way to resolve the Ripper's identity once and for all is to stay anchored to the known facts for fear of losing the really vital and important clues. One of the strengths of this book is that readers and writers won't have to constantly hack away at the ever expanding undergrowth of nonsense that continues to be published before an objective look can be given at the so-called evidence that has justified the new material's publication. Hopefully this book might even stop some more meretricious Ripper books from being published!

Contrary to what is sometimes argued, the preoccupation with the Ripper is not anti-feminist. Most people's interest is not in the murders themselves but in the puzzle and in the identity of the murderer. For no other murders is there a list of suspects that ranges from a future King of England to a back-street abortionist and includes two poisoners, a Jewish slaughterman, a royal tutor, a royal surgeon, an artist and a mad coachman as well as a policeman and a wife-killer. Nor is this list complete. To complicate matters there is generally some vast conspiracy embracing royalty, Freemasons, the Establishment and police against a background of magic, catholicism and sometimes a killer using a cloak of invisibility! Such theorising has only been possible because of the generally assumed lack of raw material on which to build. Rebutting such theories has often been time-consuming because of this in-built resistance to changing the way that the murders are perceived.

Thank heavens for this book!

At last we can get rid of some of the nonsense. Clearly, there is new material still waiting to be found. What is so heartening about this book, though, is the way that the writers have pooled their resources (and friends' resources, as I know from the way that my files have been ransacked) to get us nearer to the definitive answer. And they have come up with some real goodies. One of the core documents is the Macnaghten Memoranda listing three suspects – Druitt, Kosminski and Ostrog. Dan Farson identified Druitt back in the late fifties. More recently Martin Fido identified Kosminski, although both his co-authors and myself disagree with him as to Kosminski's actual role. Collectively the three of them have now identified Ostrog, which in itself is a major feat as he was using almost thirty aliases at the time! Two or three years ago it was thought that there was little else to be discovered in the way of fresh documentation, least of all photographs of four of the victims – Nichols, Chapman, Stride and Kelly. Some have now surfaced, though. Coincidentally, at about the same time Mary Kelly's post mortem report was found, which enabled researchers to rebut theories that she had been murdered because she was pregnant but left them with an even bigger problem – to explain away why her heart was missing.

The apparent lack of documentary material over the years has led to sinister accusations of Scotland Yard and Home Office cover-ups of names in high-places. This is highly unlikely. From my own experiences, as a serving police officer I would say that the most likely explanation is that documents went missing as a result of a mixture of indifference, carelessness and theft. Unfortunately, the destruction of police records is always assumed to have a sinister explanation because of the nature of the organisation involved. Happily, one does not have to look very far to see what has happened in other organisations. Last year (1990) it was reported that 12,000 records relating to national buildings and monuments such as Stonehenge had been inadvertently burned by the Department of the Environment on the instructions of a junior at English Heritage. Losses such as this are tragic but what is totally unforgivable is when papers are looted from the national archives. At the time of writing, a systems engineer has just been convicted of stealing over 15,000 documents from the Public Record Office by cutting them from files and smuggling them out under his jacket. Claims that he was doing this to protect the papers from the morons who were looking after them must be regarded with some cynicism when one learns that some of the documents were sold for cash and that files and papers are still missing. The Public Record Office says that this is a growing concern. Not surprisingly, the Mepol papers, where the Jack the Ripper papers are stored, have had folios taken. Living and working in Yorkshire, Paul Begg, before he began his own book, had all the files photocopied as he was unable to do research work in London. From comparisons he knows that over one hundred documents have gone missing recently – that is on top of the Suspects file which disappeared some time ago. What remains has been put on microfilm, but the disappearances rouse the long-held fear that the missing files will either be sold, kept until the purloiner dies or, worse, that they will be destroyed by someone unaware of their significance. What this particular book does in some sense is plug the gap as it gives not only everything that is known but also a useful summation of the documentary evidence and a breakdown of the missing items that are known to have been removed from the files.

Contemporaries used to think of Jack the Ripper as some sort of super-villain or monster. Some, obviously readers of Poe's *Murders in the Rue Morgue*, thought that he must have been an orangutan to account for his almost supernatural disappearances; others thought that he might have been a thuggee from India or the actor playing Mr Hyde in the first stage presentation of *Dr Jekyll and Mr Hyde*, so overwhelming was his presentation of evil. Most people, I think, would be quite disappointed by the real Jack the Ripper. Probably they would be surprised by the ordinariness of the man. Having written my own book on the subject I had my own images of him. The nearest I ever got to the reality was when I went to the trial of Peter Sutcliffe, the Yorkshire Ripper. Sutcliffe had created a reign of terror over a longer period and far greater area than the Whitechapel murderer had ever done; he had murdered thirteen women and nearly killed seven more. In court, it was his ordinariness that was surprising. As he walked to the witness box to be cross-examined, one noted the head of wiry hair, the drooping moustache and – that touch of vanity – the cuban high heels to give him that extra bit of height. Watching him being chased by the Attorney-general through a long cross-examination there were moments when I thought I could almost hear him think, usually just before he said something outrageous as if in proof of his insanity. In those moments before utterance he would hyper-ventilate and the whole court would freeze in expectation to hear what he was about to say. Despite seeing and hearing him, though, I could not say what he was like. There was a molten core inside the man the depths of which I could not even begin to gauge. Most people have a fund of shared experiences which makes it possible for them to empathise even with total strangers. Here there was nothing like that. It was impossible to feel, let alone understand, a rage so great that it could make this man jump from his car and batter and mutilate a woman walking quietly home.

What is the face that we shall see when the mystery of Jack the Ripper is finally solved? Probably something not so very dissimilar from our own.

And I have no doubt that the mystery *will* be solved.

With the amount of newly discovered material now available and the hope of more to come, this book guarantees it.

DONALD RUMBELOW
March 1991

Authors' Note

Ten new books in four years and still public interest in the semi-legendary figure of Jack the Ripper seems to increase rather than diminish. Letters regularly received by the authors and Scotland Yard show that many people want facts and theories clarified, or want information about ancestors involved in the case. General historians and educationists are recognising that crime in general – and the Ripper cases in particular – are valuable and largely untapped sources of social history. But for all these concerned people it is vital that history be separated from legend, that the canards be swept away and the facts established. The Ripper case has suffered more than most from imaginative theorising and wild speculation, and it has become clear that an authoritative, comprehensive, unbiased, and easy-to-use reader/researcher's companion and reference book has long been needed; the more so in view of the quantity of new information which has emerged from aggressive research over the last four years. We have tried to supply such a book.

This book contains a great deal of new factual information. We have identified and described hitherto undiscovered Metropolitan Police suspect Michael Ostrog and have traced the early police suspect John Sanders. Unlike the police in 1888, we also know where he was at the time of the murders. We include a number of photographs which have never been published before and details of many participants in the investigation, including some previously unnoted but important witnesses.

We have not, however, offered a definitive answer to the enduring question: Who was Jack the Ripper? We have described the suspects advanced over the years and in important cases we have noted the arguments for and against. We have also issued caveats against arguments which seem to disregard or alter established facts or are based on peculiar and unhistorical methods. We have given the facts and the data by which to measure the conclusions of others. We have given the surviving medical reports on the victims and quoted the vital historical documents emanating from the policemen engaged on the case who knew more about it than anyone else. And, in answer to many enquiries, we have provided a descriptive breakdown of the Scotland Yard and Home Office files on the Whitechapel murders, showing what is and is not to be found in these famous papers.

Simon Wood has remarked that the Ripper case is a thousand times more confused today than it was in 1888. We hope we have supplied some guidance through the labyrinth. It would be folly to claim that this book is free of error, however, so we would welcome corrections, advice on omissions and any information and/or photographs from descendants of the people involved.

Note on Terms

Cross-references are printed **bold** in the text. To reduce unnecessary page-turning, however, the recurrently named victims are only emboldened when specific information of importance to the question in point is to be found under their entries.

We have employed a descriptive terminology as tabulated below:

Author: One who repeats the familiar story of Jack the Ripper, largely from secondary sources.

Crime Historian: One whose writing on Jack the Ripper is part of an output involving other writing on crime.

Researcher: One who has added new facts or corrected old errors by his study of the Ripper.

Theorist: One who has advanced an argument favouring a particular suspect.

Suspect (if unmodified by any adjective): One who was suspected at the time of the murders or shortly afterwards by responsible people in a position to know what they were talking about.

Alleged suspect: One proposed at or around the time of the murders by under-informed or irresponsible speculation.

Non-contemporaneously alleged suspect: Proposed by theorist in the early part of the twentieth century.

Recently alleged suspect: Proposed by subsequent (usually post-war) theorist/s.

Informant: Someone from whom anybody – police, press, or a modern theorist – received relevant information.

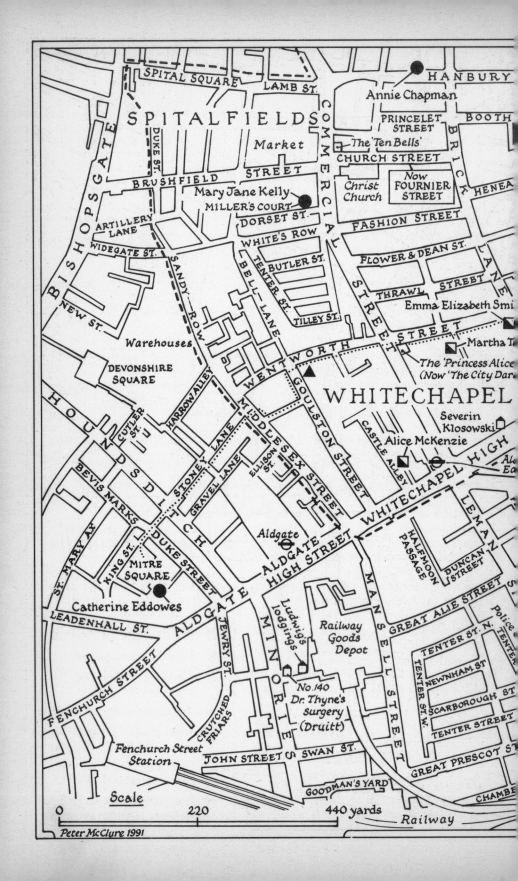

SPITAL SQUARE

LAMB ST.

HANBURY

Annie Chapman

PRINCELET
STREET

BOOTH

SPITALFIELDS

DUKE ST.

The 'Ten Bells'

Market

CHURCH STREET

HENEA

BRUSHFIELD

STREET

Christ
Church

Now
FOURNIER
STREET

BRICK

Mary Jane Kelly

FASHION STREET

MILLER'S COURT

ARTILLERY
LANE

DORSET ST.

FLOWER & DEAN ST.

WIDEGATE ST.

WHITE'S ROW

THRAWL

STREET

LANE

BISHOPSGATE

NEW ST.

BUTLER ST.

BELL LANE

TENTER ST.

Emma Elizabeth Smi

SANDY ROW

TILLEY ST.

Martha T

Warehouses

WENTWORTH

GOULSTON STREET

STREET

The 'Princess Alice
(Now 'The City Dar

DEVONSHIRE
SQUARE

HARROW ALLEY

WHITECHAPEL

HOUNDSDITCH

CUTLER
ST.

STONEY LANE

GRAVEL LANE

MIDDLESEX STREET

ELLISON ST.

Severin
Klosowski

CASTLE ALLEY

Alice McKenzie

Ale
Ea

BEVIS MARKS

WHITECHAPEL HIGH

ST. MARY AX

Aldgate

HALFMOON
PASSAGE

LEMAN

ALDGATE
HIGH STREET

DUNCAN
STREET

KING ST.

DUKE STREET

MITRE
SQUARE

GREAT ALIE STREET

Police
Tenter

Catherine Eddowes

MANSELL STREET

TENTER ST. N.

LEADENHALL ST.

ALDGATE

JEWRY ST.

MINORIE

Ludwig's
lodgings

Railway
Goods
Depot

NEWNHAM ST.

TENTER ST. W.

SCARBOROUGH ST.

FENCHURCH STREET

No.140
Dr. Thyne's
Surgery
(Druitt)

TENTER STREET

CRUTCHED FRIARS

GREAT PRESCOT ST

Fenchurch Street
Station

JOHN STREET

SWAN ST.

CHAMBE

GOODMAN'S YARD

Scale

Railway

0

220

440 yards

Peter McClure 1991

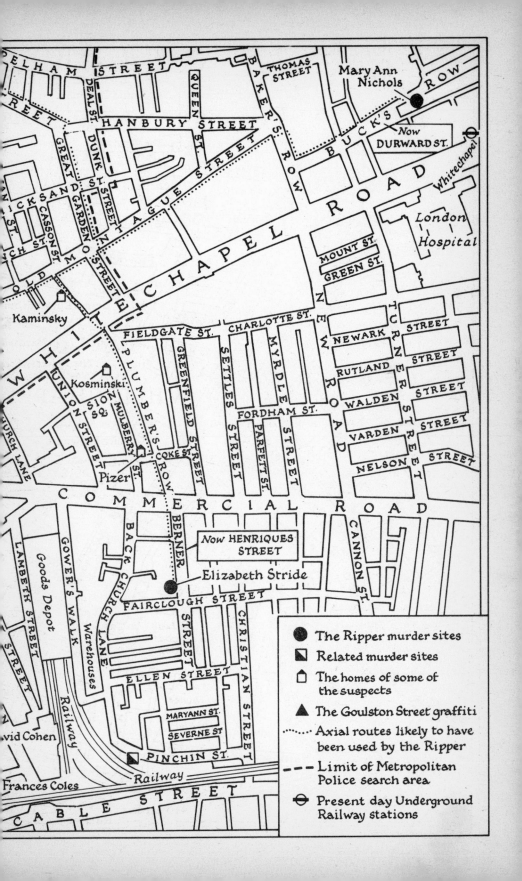

Introduction

In the 1880s the East End of London was the skid-row of the Metropolis. Writing just over a decade later, the American author Jack London called it 'the Abyss'.

There was an industrious local community engaged in many trades which served the rest of the capital, plus labourers who worked at London docks or in the markets, but high unemployment and low wages made for a large transient population. These people occupied the great many common lodging houses, or doss houses, where a bed could be hired for fourpence a night.

Amid the poverty, homelessness and utter desperation there was immorality, drunkenness, crime and violence. Robberies and assaults were common, there were frequent street fights, intimidation by the several gangs who dominated certain streets or district (see **Emma Elizabeth Smith**, a victim of mindless street brutality; also **'Leather Apron'**, who was alleged to extort money from prostitutes) and murder. The cry at night of 'Murder!' was reportedly so common that no one took notice of it.

This was the milieu of Jack the Ripper, a serial killer who selected his victims from local prostitutes and inflicted extensive post-mortem mutilations. His crimes horrified the local population, shocked the nation in general and became an international sensation.

Nobody knows for certain how many women were murdered by Jack the Ripper. It is generally agreed that there were only five victims (printed in bold below), but Robert Anderson, the Head of the CID at the time of the murders, seems to have accepted that there were six and included Martha Tabram. Others had added Alice McKenzie. The press included the almost certainly fictitious 'Fairy Fay', Emma Smith, the Pinchin Street torso and Frances Coles. With the exception of 'Fairy Fay', all were included in the Metropolitan Police 'Whitechapel Murders' file, although there was never any real doubt that Smith, the Pinchin Street victim and Coles were not killed by the Ripper.

The following list gives the date of each murder, the name of the victim (the canonical five in bold) and the place where the body was found.

VICTIMS

26 December 1887	'Fairy Fay'	Somewhere off Commercial Street
3 April 1888	Emma Elizabeth Smith	Osborn Street
7 August 1888	Martha Tabram	37 George Yard
31 August 1888	**Mary Ann Nichols**	Buck's Row
8 September 1888	**Annie Chapman**	29 Hanbury Street
30 September 1888	**Elizabeth Stride**	Berner Street

	Catharine Eddowes	Mitre Square
9 November 1888	Mary Jane Kelly	Miller's Court, Dorset Street
21 November 1888	Annie Farmer	19 George Street; alleged attempted murder
20 December 1888	Rose Mylett	Clarke's Yard, Poplar High Street; alleged murder
17 July 1889	Alice McKenzie	Castle Alley
10 September 1889	unidentified woman, possibly prostitute Lydia Hart	Pinchin Street
13 February 1891	Frances Coles	Swallow Gardens

At various times it has been suggested that Stride, Eddowes or Kelly was not a victim of the Ripper, but a good case can only be made against Stride.

Although the mutilation of the victims, the close proximity of the murders in both geography and time, and the apotheosis of horror of the so-called 'double event' (the murder of Stride and Eddowes within an hour on the same night) generated considerable fear in the East End, the crimes were used initially by certain segments of the press to attack both the Government and the police, and later as part of a circulation battle. The crimes therefore achieved far greater prominence and notoriety than might otherwise have been the case. But there can be little doubt that they are largely remembered today because a letter memorably signed 'Jack the Ripper' was widely believed to have been written by the murderer. This icy soubriquet entered the public consciousness and has remained there ever since. The letter was almost certainly written by a journalist whose identity was known or at least accepted by senior Scotland Yard officers.

The crimes should not be viewed in isolation and thereby given undue significance, but they nevertheless contributed to social reforms in the East End of London and are comparatively important in the history of the development of the Metropolitan CID. The Ripper also presaged the advent of the serial killer, a late twentieth-century phenomenon which is today the subject of considerable study by psychologists and law enforcement agencies, particularly in the United States, where serial killing has been described as epidemic.

The crimes have also proved valuable to modern social historians, who have found that the intensive press interest at the time has left a singular insight into the day-to-day life of the lowest social group of people in one of the poorest parts of what was then the heart of a great empire.

There can be little doubt, however, that modern interest in the case is generated by the mystery of and speculation about the killer's identity. International attention was attracted by the claim that the Ripper was royalty – Prince Albert Victor (Duke of Clarence) – and later by the story that the murders were committed by a group of Freemasonic conspirators led by Dr Sir William Gull and sanctioned by the Government. In the case of the former, the Prince was demonstrably not in London at the time of the murders, and the latter hypothesis lacks supporting evidence.

Whilst it is possible that the killer's identity will never be known, hopes were raised in 1959 when author Daniel Farson brought to public attention a police report written in 1894 in which three suspects were named: Montague John Druitt, Michael Ostrog, and an immigrant called Kosminski.

In 1987 it was learned that some notes on the case had been left by Chief Inspector Donald Swanson, who had overall charge of the investigation. Referring to a suspect claimed by Robert Anderson to have unquestionably been the Ripper, Swanson named that suspect as 'Kosminski' (see **Macnaghten memoranda; Aaron Kosminski, Aaron Davis Cohen**).

Apart from raising hopes that the Ripper may yet be identified with sufficient certainty to convince all but the most hardened sceptic, these discoveries – which are only the most important of a great many pieces of information to have come to light in recent years – show that there is still information 'out there'. The future may therefore see a steady decline in the number of theories which argue from secondary sources and have little or no evidential support. Instead we should see the fruits of solid historical research which, even if it ultimately fails to bring us any nearer to knowing who the Ripper was, will at least add to our knowledge of late Victorian London.

A

ABBERLINE, INSPECTOR FREDERICK GEORGE (1843–1929)
Metropolitan Police Inspector in charge of detectives on the ground in
Whitechapel murders investigation. Often wrongly described as the officer
in charge of the case (see **Dr Robert Anderson**; Chief Inspector **Swanson**).
Born in Blandford, Dorset, Abberline was the son of Edward Abberline, a
saddler who as Sheriff's Officer and Clerk of the Market was also involved
in local government activities, and Hannah (née Chinn), who, on Edward's
death in 1859, kept a shop and raised three children, Harriett, Edward and
Frederick. Frederick worked as a clocksmith before joining the Metropolitan Police in 1863 (Warrant no. 43519). In 1865, he was promoted to
Sergeant. He spent the whole of 1867 in plain clothes investigating **Fenian**
activities. In March 1868 he married labourer Tobias Mackness's 25-year-
old daughter Martha, but she died of consumption in May 1868 at Elton,
Northamptonshire.

In 1873 Abberline was promoted to Inspector and transferred to H
Division (Whitechapel), where he remained for the next fourteen years. He
married in 1876 Emma Beament, daughter of merchant Henry Beament.
Two years later, 1878, he was promoted to Local Inspector (Head of H
Division CID), and in 1887 was transferred to Scotland Yard at the special
request of **James Monro** and **Frederick Williamson**. Promoted Inspector
First Class in 1888 and Chief Inspector in 1890. He retired on a full pension
in 1892 and worked as a private enquiry agent, including three seasons at
Monte Carlo, and in 1898 accepted the European agency of Allen Pinker-
ton's famous detective company. In 1904 he retired to Methuen Road,
Bournemouth, moving in 1911 to nearby Holdenhurst Road, where he died
in 1929. He was buried in an unmarked grave (no. Z259N) in Wimborne
Cemetery (cf. **Montague John Druitt**). His wife, Emma, died in 1930.

Theorists have sometimes argued for a suspicious significance in Abberline's retirement when aged only forty-nine, so soon after his promotion to
Chief Inspector, and especially as he investigated both Jack the Ripper and
the **Cleveland Street Scandal**. However, the 1890 Police Bill (see **Henry
Matthews** and **James Monro**) provided for early retirement with improved
pension opportunities and, although only intended in the first instance for
officers injured or debilitated by their duties, it created a lucrative opportunity – still enjoyed by the police today – to enjoy a well-paid leisure and
the freedom to earn additional money. Abberline was only one of many to
seize the opportunity.

Very little is known about Abberline. No photograph of him has as yet
been discovered. However, towards the end of his life he compiled a
press-cutting book for a friend, **Walter Green**, in which he made brief
handwritten annotations. He observed that at the time of his retirement he
had received 84 commendations and awards, something which he felt was

near to a record and in which he clearly took great pride. He also explained that at the time of his retirement the authorities objected to officers writing their memoirs, which, he agreed, tended to reveal police methods to the criminal classes. He nevertheless did start writing his 'Reminiscences', of which there are 28 handwritten pages concerning a 'missing person' case and a further 12 recounting his recollections of Monte Carlo. In neither the press-cutting book nor the 'Reminiscences' does he say anything about or even allude to what are today regarded as his most important cases.

What is known about Abberline, what all accounts agree on, is that he was signally able and efficient, and possessed a more intimate knowledge of the East End and its underworld than any police contemporary. **Walter Dew**, though he believed that the day-to-day investigation was in the charge of Chief Inspector **Henry Moore**, stressed that Abberline's knowledge of the district made him one of the most important members of the Whitechapel Murders case team.

Because of the importance placed on his part in the investigation, particularly by theorists, Abberline's thoughts on the Ripper case deserve detailed consideration. But it is probable that he was not as well informed as has long been supposed (see **Scotland Yard Files**). Note also that when asked by the press what organs had been removed from Annie Chapman, Abberline stated that he had not seen the medical report. This seems a remarkable example of under-information, but one not inconsistent with other evidence.

Cassells Saturday Journal, 22 May 1892, reported Abberline as observing: 'Theories! We were almost lost in theories; there were so many of them.'

The *Journal* also expressed surprise at Abberline's assertion that Mary Kelly was the last victim and called this 'a new theory'.

In the spring of 1903 Abberline gave two extremely important interviews to the *Pall Mall Gazette*. These were in response to suggestions made in some morning papers (and contradicted authoritatively by **G. R. Sims**) that the Ripper was **Severin Klosowski**, who had recently been convicted of murder under the name of George Chapman. The journalist reportedly found Abberline 'surrounded with a sheaf of documents and newspaper clippings' dealing with the Whitechapel murders, and in the process of writing to **Sir Melville Macnaghten** about 'how strongly [he] was impressed with the opinion' that Chapman was the Ripper.

'I have been so struck with the remarkable coincidences in the two series of murders,' [Abberline] continued, 'that I have not been able to think of anything else for several days past – not, in fact, since the Attorney-General made his opening statement at the recent trial, and traced the antecedents of Chapman before he came to this country in 1888. Since then the idea has taken full possession of me, and everything fits in and dovetails so well that I cannot help feeling that this is the man we struggled so hard to capture fifteen years ago.'

Abberline gave as his reasons for believing Klosowski to be the Ripper that: He arrived in London shortly before the murders began, and they stopped after he went to America; he had studied medicine and surgery in Russia, and the 'series of murders was the work of an expert surgeon'; Klosowski's 'wife' Lucy Baderski had said that whilst in America he had attacked her with a long knife; **Dr Phillips** said that the medical skill in Annie Chapman's murder was directed to the extraction of her womb, that coroner **Wynne Baxter** had revealed how an American was known to have been seeking to purchase wombs, and Abberline claimed that similar murders in America had taken place when Klosowski went there, as though the market was still open; Klosowski lived in George Yard where Martha Tabram was killed; he resembled descriptions of the murderer as to height, foreign appearance, and peaked cap; he resorted to poison in the 'George Chapman' stage of his career because the women were 'of different classes, and obviously call[ed] for different methods of despatch'.

Abberline's only reservation was that witnesses described the suspicious man talking to Ripper victims as being thirty-five or forty, whereas Klosowski was twenty-three in 1888. But these witnesses, he said, saw a rear view, from which it was difficult to assess age (cf. **Mrs Darrell**, but compare **Joseph Lawende** and **Israel Schwartz**).

The interview caused something of a small debate with G. R. Sims, who under the name 'Dagonet' wrote a column in the Sunday *Referee* and confidently asserted that the Ripper was a young medical student who was found drowned in the Thames. The *Pall Mall Gazette* reinterviewed Abberline and reported:

'You can state most emphatically,' said Mr Abberline, 'that Scotland Yard is really no wiser on the subject than it was fifteen years ago. It is simple nonsense to talk of the police having proof that the man is dead. I am, and always have been, in the closest touch with Scotland Yard, and it would have been next to impossible for me not to have known about it. Besides, the authorities would have been only too glad to make an end out of such a mystery, if only for their own credit.'

To convince those who have any doubts on the point, Mr Abberline produced recent documentary evidence which put the ignorance of Scotland Yard as to the perpetrator beyond the shadow of doubt.

'I know,' continued the well-known detective, 'that it has been stated in certain quarters that "Jack the Ripper" was a man who died in a lunatic asylum a few years ago, but there is nothing at all of a tangible nature to support such a theory.' [Cf. **A. D. Cohen, W. G. Grainger, M. Ostrog, J. Sanders, G. W. B. Smith**.]

As for the medical student drowned in the Thames (cf. **Montague John Druitt**), Abberline stated:

'I know all about that story. But what does it amount to? Simply this. Soon after the last murder in Whitechapel the body of a young doctor was found in the Thames, but there is absolutely nothing beyond the fact that he was found at that time to incriminate him. A report was made to the Home Office about the matter, but that it was "considered final and conclusive" is going altogether beyond the truth . . . the fact that several months after December 1888, when the student's body was found, the detectives were told to hold themselves in readiness for further investigations seems to point to the conclusion that Scotland Yard did not in any way consider the evidence as final.'

Finally, **H. L. Adam** wrote in his introduction to *The Trial of George Chapman* (1930):

Chief Inspector Abberline, who had charge of the investigation into the East End murders, thought that Chapman and Jack the Ripper were one and the same person . . . Abberline never wavered in his firm conviction that Chapman and Jack the Ripper were one and the same person. When **Godley** arrested Chapman, Abberline said to his confrère, 'You've got Jack the Ripper at last.'

H. L. Adam acknowledges the assistance of George Godley in the writing of the book, so there is probably a basis for this statement, but Abberline had told the *Pall Mall Gazette* that his suspicions regarding Klosowski were only aroused following the opening of the trial, which suggests that Abberline could not have made the above statement to Godley at the time of Klosowski's arrest.

Crime historians have seriously questioned Abberline's conclusions, many being wholly unable to accept that the Ripper would have resorted to poison, and noting that, apart from the killing of a vagrant woman known as 'Old Shakespeare', there were no Ripper-like murders in either New York or New Jersey during Klosowski's residence there in the early 1890s. As for Abberline's certainty that Scotland Yard did *not* know the identity of the Ripper, this is or seems to be in direct conflict with contrary statements by Sir Robert Anderson, Chief Inspector Swanson and, to some extent, with Sir Melville Macnaghten, at least two of whom were presumably in a better position to know the facts than was Abberline, despite the positive assertions of the latter. Nevertheless, Abberline's comments should not be overlooked.

(See **Dr Dutton** for the claim that Abberline suspected Klosowski in 1888 and for suggestion that Klosowski exchanged identities with **Dr Pedachenko**; also see **Nigel Morland** for the allegation that Abberline proposed a radically different conclusion at the end of his life, claiming not only that the identity of the Ripper was known but that he was to be found among the upper classes of society.)

Joseph Gorman Sickert's latest version of the **Freemasons**' conspiracy behind the Ripper crimes rests on cryptic entries in a diary for 1896 which he claims Abberline wrote. As **Melvyn Fairclough** has observed, however, the signature 'G. F. Abberline' is puzzlingly included. See *The Ripper and the Royals*.

ABERCONWAY, CHRISTABEL MARY MACLAREN, 2ND BARONESS (d. 1974)

Younger daughter of **Sir Melville Macnaghten**. Married (1910) Henry Duncan MacLaren, suc. Baron Aberconway, 1911. Transcribed copy of **Macnaghten memoranda** from original manuscript which had passed from her mother to her elder sister, **Mrs Julia Donner**.

In 1959 Lady Aberconway showed these notes to **Daniel Farson**, thereby initiating serious post-war study of the Whitechapel Murders. In a letter to the *New Statesman* at the end of that year she denied the likelihood of her father's burning any Ripper documents (but see under **Melville Macnaghten**). Until 1965 she insisted that the names of suspects in the memorandum not be published.

ACCOMPLICES OF THE RIPPER (HANSARD)

Inferentially alleged by **Henry Matthews** to exist. 23 November 1888, Home Secretary Matthews observed when answering a Parliamentary question on the offer of a reward for information, 'In the case of [Mary Jane] Kelly there were certain circumstances which were wanting in the earlier cases, and which make it more probable that there were other persons who, at any rate after the crime, had assisted the murderer.'

These circumstances are unknown. It is possible that they refer to the liability that the murderer would have been excessively bloodstained after

Kelly's murder and so his household were assumed to have concealed his cleaning himself up. (Cf. **Anderson**'s mention of 'his people', though this refers to deductions reached after the double murder.) It is known that **Dr Phillips** was influential in procuring this offer of a **pardon**.

ADAM, HARGRAVE LEE
True-crime writer. Publications include *Police Work from Within* (1914), *The Police Encyclopaedia*, with Introduction by Sir Robert Anderson (1920), *The Trial of George Chapman* (ed. 1930), *C.I.D.: Behind the Scenes at Scotland Yard* (1931).

Acquaintance of **Dr Robert Anderson, Sir Charles Warren** and **Sir Melville Macnaghten**, Adam has left important descriptions of each. He also remarked in the introduction to *The Trial of George Chapman* that Anderson, Macnaghten and **Major Henry Smith** had all assured him that the Ripper's identity was known to the police. Macnaghten wrote *Days of My Years* at Adam's instigation.

In Volume VI of the *Police Encyclopaedia* he observed that most prostitute murders were by men who imagined themselves to have been venereally infected by their victims, and said it was 'generally believed' that this was the motive in the Whitechapel case. This may reflect the opinions of all or any of the policemen above.

ALBERICCI, FREDERICO
Alleged Ripper co-conspirator. Identified by **Melvyn Fairclough** in *The Ripper and the Royals* as an Italian-American footman employed at 78 Brook Street, the West End residence of **Sir William Gull**, in the early 1880s. Subsequently declined to a life of crime in the East End, where he was known as 'American Freddy' or '**Fingers Freddy**'. It is suggested that he was employed to assist Gull and **Lord Randolph Churchill** in 1888 when they initiated and executed the alleged **Freemasons**' conspiracy to preserve the secret of **Prince Albert Victor**'s illegal marriage.

ALBERT EDWARD, PRINCE OF WALES (1841–1910)
King Edward VII, 1901–10. Alleged in recent oral tradition to have been Jack the Ripper or a leading suspect. There is obvious confusion with his son **Prince Albert Victor**, whose family nickname was 'Eddie'. (Albert Edward's was 'Bertie'.)

ALBERT VICTOR CHRISTIAN EDWARD, PRINCE (1864–92)
From 1891 Duke of Clarence and Avondale.

Recently alleged Ripper suspect. Grandson of Queen Victoria and Heir Presumptive to the throne. Trinity College, Cambridge, 1883. Hon. LLD, 1888. Aide-de-camp to Queen Victoria, 1889. Duke of Clarence and Avondale and Earl of Athlone, 1891. Engaged to Princess May of Teck (subsequently Queen Mary), December 1891, but died in January 1892 of pneumonia complicating influenza contracted in epidemic.

The allegation that he was the Ripper was first made by **Dr Thomas Stowell** and was subsequently repeated by **Frank Spiering**. The surmise was that the Prince suffered from 'syphilis of the brain' which led him to commit the murders, and a successful cover-up by the authorities concealed this from the public. Additional arguments were that, as a deer-hunter, he would have possessed the requisite skill to disembowel bodies; and his appearance was similar to that of suspect **M. J. Druitt**.

Apart from that alleged by Spiering, no historical evidence in support of this theory has ever been adduced, and it is conclusively disproved by the following evidence taken from Court Circulars, diaries, journals, etc.:

29 August–7 September 1888: The Prince was staying with Viscount Downe at Danby Lodge, Grosmont, Yorkshire. (Nichols murdered 31 August.)

7–10 September 1888: The Prince was at the Cavalry Barracks in York. (Chapman murdered 8 September.)

27–30 September: The Prince was at Abergeldie, Scotland, where Queen Victoria recorded in her journal that he lunched with her on 30 September. (Stride and Eddowes murdered between 1.00 and 2.00 a.m., 30 September.)

1 November: Arrived in London from York.

2–12 November: The Prince was at Sandringham. (Kelly murdered 9 November.)

Prince Albert Victor also plays a major role in the story concerning Jack the Ripper purveyed by **Joseph Sickert** and presented to the public as fact by the late **Stephen Knight**. This claims that Prince Albert Victor secretly and illegally married Mr Sickert's grandmother, **Annie Elizabeth Crook** – a potential scandal which the authorities sought to suppress by incarcerating Annie in a lunatic asylum. The murders occurred because victim Mary Jane Kelly, who had been engaged as a nursemaid by the Prince and his secret wife, told her cronies and tried to blackmail the Government with her knowledge. This supposedly led **Sir William Gull** to use **Freemasonic** ritual punishments to disembowel the blackmailers.

No historical evidence to support this narrative has ever been found, although there is some evidence that elements of the story were circulating prior to 1950. (See **Melvyn Fairclough, Jean Overton Fuller, Florence Pash**.) Claims that the Prince secretly survived the pneumonia of 1892, or that his death was clandestinely hastened, are without foundation. (See **Stowell, Spiering, Fairclough**; also **Michael Harrison's** *Clarence* (1972) for an account of the Prince's life and death.)

ALBROOK, LIZZIE (b. 1868)

Friend of Mary Jane Kelly. Lived in Miller's Court and worked at a lodging house in Dorset Street. Visited Kelly on the night of her murder and was there when **Joseph Barnett** called on Kelly between 7.30 and 7.45 p.m. (See also **Maria Harvey**.) Speaking of Kelly, Albrook said,

> About the last thing she said was, 'Whatever you do don't you do wrong and turn out as I have.' She had often spoken to me in this way and warned me against going on the streets as she had done. She told me, too, that she was heartily sick of the life she was leading and wished she had money enough to go back to Ireland where her people lived. I do not believe she would have gone out as she did if she had not been obliged to do so to keep herself from starvation.

ALLEN, ELIZABETH

Informant. Denizen of Crossingham's Lodging House cited in press. Described in the *Echo* (20 September 1888) as giving the police information pointing to a suspect. This may have a bearing on '**Leather Apron**'. (Cf. **Eliza Cooper**.)

ALLEN, POLICE CONSTABLE JOSEPH, 423H
Seen by **Police Constable Walter Andrews** during the patrol on beat duty
in which he found the body of Alice McKenzie. Allen had eaten a snack
under the lamp-post where the body was found twenty minutes later. He
spoke to Andrews in Wentworth Street on leaving **Old Castle Street**, and
was subsequently summoned by **Sergeant Badham** from **Commercial
Street** and despatched to the police station.

ANDERSON, DAVID (1944–)
Researcher, specialising in **M. J. Druitt** and history of Chiswick. Has come
up with important material, including (as accredited by **Daniel Farson**)
samples of Druitt's handwriting and a press account of his inquest.

ANDERSON, DR (LATER SIR) ROBERT (1841–1918)
Assistant Commissioner, Metropolitan Police CID; officer in charge of
Whitechapel Murder Investigation from 6 October 1888 until closure of the
file in 1892. Stated several times in writing that the identity of the Ripper
was known. Born in Dublin, Ireland, the son of Crown Solicitor Matthew
Anderson. Educated at Trinity College, Dublin, he took his BA in 1862
and in 1863 was called to the Bar at King's Inn, Dublin. His elder brother,
Samuel, Solicitor-General in the viceregal administration, secured him
work reviewing Fenian activities.

In 1876 the Government formed in London an intelligence branch to
combat Fenianism and Anderson was brought over as deputy to the Head,
an intelligence colonel named Fielding, but the branch was soon closed.
Anderson stayed on at the Home Office as 'Advisor in Matters Relating to
Political Crime' and as the spymaster controlling **Thomas Miller Beach**
(known as Henri Le Caron), who had penetrated the **Fenian** movement in
the United States, and other spies.

In 1870 Anderson was called to the Bar at Middle Temple and in 1873 he
married Agnes Alexandrina Moore. There were five children, the eldest of
whom, Arthur Moore-Anderson, in 1947 wrote a biography of his parents.
In 1886 Anderson found himself in trouble with **Hugh Childers**, the Home
Secretary, and was relieved of his duties, except for his relations with Le
Caron, who refused to deal with anyone else. From July 1887 to August
1888 he was Secretary to the Prison Commissioners. In August 1888
Anderson succeeded **James Monro** as Assistant Commissioner, CID, a
post he held until his retirement in 1901, when he was awarded a knight-
hood.

In retirement Anderson devoted himself to charitable work and writing.
A prolific author, he produced nearly two dozen books on theology,
numerous articles for various journals, a book on penology (*Criminals and
Crime*), and an autobiography (*The Lighter Side of My Official Life*). His
last years were spent in isolation caused by deafness. This depressed
him, as did endless nights of insomnia and the deaths of numerous
friends from earlier years. On 15 November 1918 he spent the evening
writing and reading his Bible. At 10.30 p.m. he went to bed and died a few
minutes later.

As a policeman Anderson was described by **Major Arthur Griffiths**
(*Mysteries of Police and Crime*) as:
>   an ideal detective officer, with a natural bias for the work . . . of the
>   quickest apprehension, with the power of close, rapid reasoning from

facts, suggestions or even impressions. He seizes on the essential point almost by intuition . . . he is the most discreet, the most silent and reserved of public functionaries. Someone said he was a mystery to himself . . . he has perhaps achieved greater success than any other detective of his time.

H. L. Adam (*CID*) wrote that Anderson was 'a curious combination of theologian and man-of-the-world. What he did not know about crime was scarcely knowledge.'

A slight damper on such glowing testimonials, particularly in view of the source, was published in the *Police Review* on Anderson's retirement:

Turning to the repute in which Dr Anderson was held in his immediate official circle, his tenure of office was considered to be characterised by the comfortable placidity for which the majority of our public functionaries are remarkable. Moreover, his temperament, so admirably adapted to his social and religious proclivities, was not such as best fits one for the work of the CID. A Biblical scholar of repute, and a literary recluse, such as he is, would hardly be the man to take an active part in fighting the criminal classes of London. Discreet, silent, and reserved though he was, according to Major Arthur Griffiths's estimate, he lacked one inestimable quality to success as the Director of the Detective staff of the most important Police Force in the world, and that was just the requisite kind of knowledge of the world and of men. An acknowledged authority on our penal system, it was, perhaps, hardly a looked-for choice on the part of Mr Home Secretary Matthews . . .

A recent estimate of Anderson's character and personality by Bernard Porter (*Origins of the Vigilant State*) described him as:

no doubt an irritating and opinionated man, inclined – as pious people are – to maintain that an action was morally justified because his principles debarred him from committing an immoral one . . . Anderson was one of those who clearly loved being taken for a man of mystery and power; one who knew more of vital importance than it was possible for him in the national interest to divulge . . .

Anderson was obviously a complex character, but for the Ripper researcher trying to assess his important statements about the identity of Jack the Ripper, it is his honesty which is of overall importance. After his retirement Anderson was involved in an incident which called his honesty into question.

In May 1887 *The Times* published a series of articles which caused public uproar and resulted in a Parliamentary Commission of Enquiry in 1889. One of the articles included information given to Anderson by Henri Le Caron and Anderson was accused of handing over Government papers without authority. It was even privately suggested that Anderson should be removed as the head of the CID. Anderson, however, stated that it was part of a long-standing agreement that the letters were Le Caron's property, were to be returned to him whenever requested, and had never been in a Government department. Anderson's involvement was completely overshadowed by the exposure of the forger Pigott, who had provided other material and committed suicide after a withering cross-examination. The furore was revived when Anderson revealed in his autobiography: 'To the present hour I do not know whether the Home Secretary was then aware of my authorship of *The Times* articles of 1887 on "Parnellism and Crime", for in relation to that matter I acted with strict propriety in dealing with Mr

Monro and not with the Secretary of State.'

Monro, however, quickly responded with a letter in which he said that 'no such authority was asked by Mr Anderson, and none was given by me . . . A long time afterwards, Mr Anderson informed me that he had written one or more of the articles, and I felt much annoyed.' On hearing of Monro's denial an Irish MP, Mr Macreagh, stated in the House of Commons, 'Then the statement of Sir Robert Anderson that he had official permission to write these articles is another edition of Anderson's Fairy Tales.'

The reference to the fairy-tale writer and collector Hans Christian Andersen was a joke, not a suggestion that Anderson had a record of economy with the truth, but although the controversy eventually subsided, it leaves open the question of whether Anderson lied or not. The truth will probably never be known, but it is thought unlikely that Anderson lied even by impartial observers such as J. A. Cole (Le Caron's biographer; *Prince of Spies*), who argued that Monro probably agreed in principle that the idea of the newspaper article was a good one and that Anderson misunderstood this to be a sanction for it. And among some Home Office papers there is a letter from James Monro containing inferential evidence that this was indeed the case.

There therefore seems to be no hard reason for thinking that Anderson was a liar, although several 'revelations' in his autobiography – all, when tested, proving to be true – seem to conflict with the repeated references to his discretion. Here again, though, there are statements in his writings from which it can be inferred that he did not consider it indiscreet to reveal secrets once the need for secrecy had passed, particularly when he believed that the public benefited from the knowledge. There is therefore little or no reason to doubt that he fully believed what he had to say about Jack the Ripper.

Anderson took up his post at Scotland Yard on the day of Mary Ann Nichols' murder. He described it in his memoirs as 'the Second of the crimes', which suggests that he regarded **Martha Tabram** as the first victim. Anderson had been prescribed a month's sick leave by Dr 'Gilbart Smith' (see **Dr. S. J. Harvey**), so he assigned the case to Chief Inspector **Donald Swanson**. In a memo appointing Swanson he wrote:

I am convinced that the Whitechapel murder case is one which can be successfully grappled with if it is systematically taken in hand. I go so far as to say that I could myself in a few days unravel the mystery provided I could spare the time to give undivided attention to it.

Thus, supremely confident that the case would soon be solved, Anderson left for Switzerland – on the very day Annie Chapman was murdered. Anderson returned to England on 6 October, after the double event, and was told by both Home Secretary **Henry Matthews** and Commissioner **Sir Charles Warren** that they held him 'responsible to find the murderer'. Anderson, perhaps not now so confident, replied, 'I will hold myself responsible to take all legitimate means to find him.'

Anderson made a few recommendations. One, that all known prostitutes found on the streets of the East End after midnight should be arrested, was rejected, and Anderson instead let it be known that prostitutes could not and would not be protected by the police. He later commented that, 'However the fact may be explained, it is a fact that no other street murder occurred in the "Jack-the-Ripper" series.' It is not clear, however, whether this means that he issued the warning after the murder of Mary Kelly, or whether, with precisian accuracy, he distinguished her murder indoors from the murders on the streets.

In his memoirs Anderson wrote that he spent a day and a half on his return from the continent examining the evidence, presumably meaning pertinent statements, police reports, and summaries, either written or orally presented by Chief Inspector Swanson, and he says that 'we' reached certain conclusions (see below) which eventually proved correct in every respect. However, it does not appear that at this time he had any idea who the Ripper was, for on 23 October he wrote to the Home Office, 'That five successive murders should have been committed without our having the slightest clue of any kind is extraordinary . . .' (One might observe that here again he seems to include Martha Tabram among the Ripper's victims.)

Anderson liaised closely with James Monro (who at this time was a Home Office adviser on political crime, the Ripper crimes therefore technically being beyond his jurisdictional brief), who, along with Chief Inspector Swanson, may have been one of the 'we' mentioned above. Anderson was also greatly influenced by the reports of Dr Thomas Bond, whom he specifically asked to review the autopsy notes and advise on whether or not the Ripper appeared to have anatomical knowledge or surgical skills.

Anderson's position as Head of the CID and the concomitant knowledge he must have possessed of the case make his observations on the Ripper exceptionally important, particularly in view of statements claiming that the identity of the Ripper was known. His first public observation on the Ripper case was made in 1901 in a short article on penology, but it attracted no attention beyond Home Office civil servants who added the item to a file concerning what they perceived as Anderson's habit of publishing official information. In the same year the *Pall Mall Gazette*, in an article on Anderson's retirement, wrote of the Ripper murders: 'The mystery surrounding those crimes has never been (publicly) solved, though the police have an explanation which they believe satisfactory.'

In *Criminals and Crime* (1907), he repeated the statements made earlier in the 1901 article:

No amount of silly hysterics could alter the fact that these crimes were a cause of danger only to a particular section of a small and definite class of women, in a limited district of the East End; and that the inhabitants of the Metropolis generally were just as secure during the weeks the fiend was on the prowl, as they were before the mania seized him, or after he had been safely caged in an asylum.

In 1910 Anderson's memoirs, *The Lighter Side of My Official Life*, were published, first in serialised form in *Blackwood's Magazine*, and subsequently as a book, in which certain changes were made to his comments on the Ripper. In *Blackwood's* he wrote:

One did not need to be a Sherlock Holmes to discover that the criminal was a sexual maniac of a virulent type; that he was living in the immediate vicinity of the scenes of the murders; and that, if he was not living absolutely alone, his people knew of his guilt, and refused to give him up to justice. During my absence abroad the Police had made a house-to-house search for him, investigating the case of every man in the district whose circumstances were such that he could go and come and get rid of his blood-stains in secret. And the conclusion we came to was that he and his people were low-class Jews, for it is a remarkable fact that people of that class in the East End will not give up one of their number to Gentile Justice.

And the result proved that our diagnosis was right on every point. For I may say at once that 'undiscovered murders' are rare in London, and the 'Jack-the-Ripper' crimes are not in that category. And if the police here had powers such as the French police possess, the murderer would have been brought to justice . . . I will only add here that the 'Jack the Ripper' letter which is preserved in the Police Museum in Scotland Yard is the creation of an enterprising London journalist.

In a footnote he added:

Having regard to the interest attaching to this case, I should almost be tempted to disclose the identity of the murderer and of the pressman who wrote the letter above referred to, provided that the publishers would accept all responsibility in view of a possible libel action. But no public benefit would result from such a course, and the traditions of my old department would suffer. I will only add that when the individual whom we suspected was caged in an asylum, the only person who had ever had a good view of the murderer at once identified him, but when he learned that the suspect was a fellow-Jew he declined to swear to him.

In the book edition of these memoirs Anderson made certain changes. He added the qualifiers 'certain' before 'low-class' and 'Polish' before 'Jews'; he incorporated the footnote in the main text and omitted the reference to the publisher accepting liability in the event of libel; he also made a significant alteration to the last sentence, which now read:

I will merely add that the only person who had ever had a good view of the murderer unhesitatingly identified the suspect the instant he was confronted with him, but he refused to give evidence against him.

It should be noted that Anderson here omitted the reference to the suspect having been 'caged in an asylum' and the comment that both suspect and witness were Jewish, and changed the soft 'declined to swear to him' to the harder 'refused to give evidence against him'.

Anderson also added a new paragraph:

In saying that he was a Polish Jew I am merely stating a definitely ascertained fact. And my words are meant to specify race, not religion. For it would outrage all religious sentiment to talk of the religion of a loathsome creature whose utterly unmentionable vices reduced him to a lower level than that of the brute.

Major Smith of the City Police in his own memoirs had commented on the serialisation of Anderson's autobiography and accused Anderson of representing the whole East End Jewish population as accessories to the crimes, and some researchers have also argued that Smith's words contain an accusation of anti-Semitism. Whether or not Smith's words influenced Anderson to make the changes for the volume edition, it seems clear that the changes were made in an effort to qualify and redefine the statements about the Jews, and to make clear that the race, not the religion, of the suspect was at the core of his remarks, and that those remarks were founded on fact, not speculation.

One alteration which may have an additional and important significance in light of the **Swanson marginalia**, however, is the reference to the identification having taken place 'when the individual whom we suspected was caged in an asylum'. Anderson's assertion that the identification was

after the suspect had been committed to an asylum is flatly contradicted by
Swanson, who says that it took place *before*.

Both the serialisation and the volume versions of the memoirs also
contain an important footnote concerning the number of murders. As
already noted, Anderson seems to have regarded Martha Tabram as the first
in the series, and he says specifically that the last was that of Mary Kelly. In
a footnote to the serialisation he wrote:

I am here assuming that the murder of Alice M'Kenzie on 17th July 1889
was by another hand. I was absent from London when it occurred, but
the Chief Commissioner investigated the case on the spot. It was an
ordinary murder and not the work of a sexual maniac.

In the volume edition he wrote:

I am here assuming that the murder of Alice M'Kenzie on the 17th of
July 1889, was by another hand. I was absent from London when it
occurred, but the Chief Commissioner investigated the case on the spot
and decided it was an ordinary murder, and not the work of a sexual
maniac. And the Poplar case of December, 1888, was a death from
natural causes, and but for the 'Jack the Ripper' scare, no one would
have thought of suggesting that it was a homicide.

Again the researcher must question the significance of the alterations.
Was Anderson, with precisian accuracy, saying that he had no personal
involvement with the McKenzie investigation and therefore could not
presume to speak with authority on the conclusions? Or does his attribution
of the conclusion to Commissioner Monro suggest that Anderson suspected
that McKenzie could have been a Ripper victim? If Anderson believed that
McKenzie *could* have been murdered by the Ripper then this suggests that
either the eye-witness identification was not as certain as Anderson elsewhere would have us believe, or that the identification took place after July
1889.

In 1920, two years after Anderson's death, Anderson's last statement
about the Ripper was printed in an introduction to H. L. Adam's *Police
Encyclopedia*:

So again with the 'Whitechapel Murders' of 1888. Despite the lucu-
brations of many an amateur 'Sherlock Holmes', there was no doubt
whatever as to the identity of the criminal, and if our London 'detectives'
possessed the powers, and might have recourse to the methods, of
Foreign police forces, he would have been brought to justice. But the
guilty sometimes escape.

Anderson always refers to the Ripper by way of illustrating what he
recognises as the just constraints placed upon the British police in comparison with the almost total freedom of action permitted foreign forces, and in
reply to critics who fail to take this into account when comparing the
success of the British police with their foreign counterparts. Among the
constraints Anderson seems to have had in mind was the absence abroad of
the writ of *habeas corpus*, which in Britain protected the innocent by forcing
the police to release a suspect within a given period if charges could not be
brought. He might also have had in mind the comparative freedom of the
foreign police to enter and search private premises.

It is perhaps also worth noting that in volume IV of the *Police Encyclopedia*, H. L. Adam wrote:

A great deal of mystery still hangs about these horrible Ripper outrages,
although in a letter which I have just received from Sir Robert Anderson,

he intimates that the police knew well enough at the time who the miscreant was, although unfortunately, they had not sufficient legal evidence to warrant them laying hands upon him . . .

Despite the centrality of his position, the certainty of his charges, and the strength of his integrity, Anderson presents the historian with several problems, not the least of which is his conflict with Swanson, with whom he worked closely and harmoniously, and whose story his own should have paralleled. However, despite these problems, the combined testimony of Anderson and Swanson weighs heavily towards the identity of the Ripper having been known (but see **Anderson's suspect** for the problem surrounding even this conclusion).

(Also see **Melvyn Fairclough, Stephen Knight**, and **Joseph Sickert** for the suggestion that Anderson was an accessory to the murders and shielded the murderer.)

ANDERSON'S SUSPECT
Dr Robert Anderson does not name the man who, he claims as 'a definitely ascertained fact', was positively identified as Jack the Ripper. Yet as he was the man in charge of the case and the only policeman to say decisively that it had been solved, it seems vital to identify his suspect. He says that the man was a poor Polish Jew from the immediate vicinity of the murders who was sent to an asylum, after which a witness identified him as the murderer.

Two names have been proposed: **Aaron Kosminski** and **David** (or **Aaron Davis**) **Cohen**.

Kosminski is named by **Chief Inspector Swanson** in his **marginalia** glossing Anderson's cursory remarks. Kosminski's name is also given by **Melville Macnaghten** in his **memoranda** naming three police suspects. Like Anderson's suspect, Kosminski was a poor Polish Jew from Whitechapel who was sent to an asylum. He was taken to Mile End Workhouse Infirmary on 4 February 1891 and transferred to Colney Hatch Lunatic Asylum on 7 February 1891; transferred again to Leavesden Asylum for Imbeciles in April 1894, and died there on 24 March 1919. Swanson states correctly that Kosminski resided with his brother, and notes that he was sent to Colney Hatch Asylum. He states that the identification took place before Kosminski entered the asylum, and cites the ending of the murders after the identification as circumstantial evidence against him. He asserts that Kosminski died shortly after entering the asylum. Macnaghten believed Kosminski to have been incarcerated in March 1889, and to be alive in an asylum in February 1894.

David or Aaron Davis Cohen was the first Jewish patient to be sent to a London public asylum after the murder of Mary Jane Kelly, and the only one whose incarceration coincides with the murders' cessation. He was a foreign Jew, from Whitechapel. He was arrested on 7 December 1888, transferred from Whitechapel Workhouse Infirmary to Colney Hatch Asylum on 21 December, and died there 20 October 1889.

ANDERSON'S WITNESS
Dr Robert Anderson says that the (unnamed) witness who identified his suspect was 'the only person who ever had a good view of the murderer'. It would therefore be useful to identify this witness from the several people alleged to have seen suspicious men with victims shortly before they were murdered.

Chief Inspector Swanson independently confirms Anderson's statement that the witness was male and Jewish. This reduces the known possibilities to two: **Joseph Lawende** and **Israel Schwartz**. (Paul Begg suggests that **Joseph Hyam Levy** might be a third.)

Joseph Lawende saw Catharine Eddowes in company with a man outside Mitre Square at a time which makes it virtually certain he was her killer. Lawende (unlike his two companions) saw the man's face and noted his clothing. He gave the City Police a description they regarded as satisfactory, and at the inquest the Police Solicitor gained the coroner's permission for Lawende's description of the man's face to be withheld. **Major Henry Smith** expressed general approval of Lawende as a witness and the validity of his description. On the other hand, Lawende stated that he did not believe he would recognise the man if he saw him again.

Schwartz saw Elizabeth Stride thrown to the ground on the pavement outside Dutfield's Yard in Berner Street at 1.45 a.m., an estimated fifteen minutes before her freshly killed body was found inside the yard. He had followed her assailant from Commercial Road, and turned back to look at the incident, running away when the assailant shouted 'Lipski!' apparently at him, and another man who came out of a pub began to follow him down the road. Evidence was presented to the inquest that Stride had been seen in a different place at 1.45 a.m. (See **James Brown**.) No newspaper reported Schwartz as a witness at Stride's inquest.

Police notes in the margins of their interview with Schwartz none the less indicate that they believed his testimony. **Dr Robert Anderson**, drafting the preamble for a report of Inspector Abberline's to be sent to the Home Office, used the words, 'the evidence of Schwartz at the inquest in Eliz. Stride's case . . .' This is the only documentary suggestion that Schwartz was called as a witness.

(See also **W. G. Grainger, Unidentified Witnesses at Mitre Square**.)

ANDREWS, INSPECTOR WALTER (b. 1847)
Warrant no. 52192. Metropolitan Police CID. Joined force, 1869. Retired, 1889. **Walter Dew** lists Andrews along with Chief Inspector **Moore** and **Inspector Abberline** as having been seconded to Whitechapel from Scotland Yard to take charge of the investigation. Dew describes him as 'a jovial, gentlemanly man, with a fine personality and a sound knowledge of his job'.

The *Pall Mall Gazette*, 31 December 1888, reported:
Inspector Andrews, of Scotland Yard, has arrived in New York from Montreal. It is generally believed that he has received orders from England to commence his search in this city for the Whitechapel murderer. Mr Andrews is reported to have said that there are half a dozen English detectives, two clerks, and one inspector employed in the same chase . . . [T]he fact that a man suspected of knowing a good deal about this series of crimes left England for this side of the Atlantic three weeks ago, has, says the *Telegraph* correspondent, produced the impression that Jack the Ripper is in that country.

Andrews had escorted a man named R. G. I. Barnet to Montreal, where he was accused of helping to wreck the Central Bank.

ANDREWS, POLICE CONSTABLE WALTER
Discovered the body of Alice McKenzie in Castle Alley. Probably b. 1858,

Heveningham, Suffolk. Joined Metropolitan Police, 1880. Retired, 1906. Warrant no. 64735. On his beat circuit from Old Castle Street to Goulston Street he was checked by Sergeant Badham. Their frequently alleged 'conversation' took the form:

'All right?'

'All right, sergeant.'

Andrews also spoke to **PC Joseph Allen**, who had just eaten a snack in Castle Alley. Twenty minutes later Andrews found the body.

ANTI-SEMITISM

Nineteenth-century anti-Semitism derived spurious social justification from the charge that dispersed Jews owed a higher allegiance to their race than to the societies in which they lived. In the Russian empire, especially, this led to severe terror campaigns against unoffending Jewish communities, and a massive emigration of Jews seeking shelter in more tolerant countries, particularly England and America.

Thousands of Jews poured into Britain every year throughout the 1880s. It was the great wish of all Englishmen of good will, Jew or Gentile, to avoid the growth of calculated anti-Semitism in England, and this aim had a powerful influence on events when the Ripper murders broke out in the heart of the Jewish settlement in London: Whitechapel and Spitalfields.

The influx of destitute immigrants to a district already poor and over-crowded had inevitable social consequences. The existing population feared their jobs were put at risk by competitors who would accept lower wages. They feared that housing would become inaccessible as the newcomers pressed for accommodation within the square mile to the east of the old synagogues in Duke's Place and Bevis Marks. They feared that the visible poverty of the newcomers and their overcrowded living conditions threatened dirt and disease. They feared that their cultural traditions would be swamped by a group which spoke Yiddish and wore foreign clothes.

When the Metropolitan Police investigating the Whitechapel Murders announced that they suspected the unknown Jewish immigrant '**Leather Apron**', they provoked instant anti-Semitism at street level. East End ruffians committed assaults on innocent Jews with cries that, 'No English-man would commit murders like these!' The upheaval was only signifi-cantly reduced when the police announced that they had found Leather Apron and he was innocent. (See **John Pizer**.)

Thereafter the police showed every sign of wishing to avoid a renewal of the racial tension. The Met instantly erased the **Goulston Street graffito** and were congratulated by the *Jewish Chronicle* and the radical press for so doing. **Sir Charles Warren** issued the public statement that JUWES did not mean Jews in any known language, though neither he nor Dr Adler, the Chief Rabbi, who thanked him for this, could really have doubted that the word was a misspelling of Jews. **Major Smith** had the traditional knives of a shochet (Jewish ritual butcher) compared with the wounds on Catharine Eddowes and sent the pathologist's report that they could not have inflicted them to the *Jewish Chronicle*, which was duly grateful.

ARNOLD, SUPERINTENDENT THOMAS (b. 1835)

Head of H Division (Whitechapel) at the time of the murders. Absent on leave prior to the double murders. (See **Acting Superintendent West**.) Joined Metropolitan Police in 1855, but resigned, volunteering for the

Crimea. Returned to England, 1856, and rejoined the police. Warrant no. 35059. Served his entire career in the East End, except for a brief posting to B Division. He was involved in many of the district's most celebrated criminal cases, including the **Lipski** murder.

On 30 September 1888, it was Arnold, as the man responsible for preserving the peace in Whitechapel and Spitalfields, who was most anxious to have the **Goulston Street graffito** erased. He had sent an inspector with a wet sponge to await orders to wipe it out when **Sir Charles Warren** visited the site at dawn and concurred that it should be removed.

He commented on the Whitechapel murders in an interview in the *Eastern Post* in February 1893:

I still hold to the opinion that not more than four of these murders were committed by the same hand. They were the murders of Annie Chapman in Hanbury Street, Mrs Nicholls [*sic*] in Buck's Row, Elizabeth Stride in Berner Street, and Mary Kelly in Mitre Square.

We do not know whether by 'Mary Kelly in Mitre Square' Arnold is discounting Kelly or Eddowes as a Ripper victim.

It is clear from the remainder of the interview that Arnold neither knew nor suspected the identity of the murderer.

AUTUMN OF TERROR

Book by **Tom Cullen** (1965). US title *When London walked in Terror*. Paperback as *The Crimes and Times of Jack the Ripper* (1973).

This was the first publication to use the **Macnaghten memoranda** and make **Montague John Druitt**'s full name known. Cullen accepted Macnaghten's identification of Druitt as the Ripper. He established some biographical details about Druitt's schooldays and suggested that his chambers in the Temple were used as a residence. He also postulated a social motivation, drawing attention to Toynbee Hall and the University Settlements movement, with the suggestion that Druitt might have intended to call public notice to the squalid conditions prevailing in the East End.

While the subsidiary arguments in support of the Druitt theory were not very persuasive, Cullen's book was generally and rightly admired for the serious effort he made to establish a full and, as far as possible, accurate account of the murders. He supplied a great deal of new data. Much of it, unfortunately, came from his very wide study of newspaper reports and showed a tendency to accept rather uncritically what they proposed as fact. Thus Cullen endorses the idea of a murdered '**Fairy Fay**'; and some of his other facts have not been successfully traced to source by subsequent researchers. But no researcher doubts that Cullen definitely had sources for all his statements, albeit some were unreliable.

Autumn of Terror is generally regarded as the first good post-war book on Jack the Ripper, and one which set the standard for measuring subsequent writing on the subject for ten years.

AVENGERS, THE (1969, Great Britain)

TV series starring Patrick MacNee and Linda Thorson; cult 1960s show with bizarre plots; Thorson succeeded Honor Blackman and Diana Rigg; episode 'Fog'.

B

BACHERT, WILLIAM ALBERT (b. 1860)
Engraver, resident Newnham Street. By 1890, Chairman of **Vigilance Committee** formed during the murders to urge official action. Frequently misspelled Backert.

Early in September 1888, he wrote to the *Evening News* expressing horror at the murders. 2 October, Bachert was reported as having seen a dark man in a morning coat with a shiny bag and a black hat in The Three Tuns, Aldgate (frequently misdescribed in the press as 'The Three Nuns'). The man furtively asked questions about streetwalkers and expressed hostility to prostitution. When an old match-seller looked in, however, he made a speedy appointment to go up Northumberland Alley off Fenchurch Street with her.

Donald McCormick learned from **Dr Thomas Dutton** that in March 1889 Bachert was badgering the police about the murders and was confidentially told by the police that the murderer had died by drowning at the end of 1888. Dutton's source is unknown, but if his statement is true the information reinforces belief in police suspicion of **M. J. Druitt**. March 1889 coincides curiously with the date **Macnaghten** gives in error as the date of **Kosminski**'s incarceration.

15 February 1891 Bachert was called as a reserve juror at Frances Coles' inquest. Coroner **Wynne Baxter** refused to let him be empanelled, despite Bachert's loud protest that he was being deliberately excluded because he would 'enquire too closely'.

It seems possible, despite age differences as reported in the press, that he was the 'engraver and agitator' of Tower Hamlets who became secretary of the Unemployed Relief Committee, but was also charged with uttering counterfeit florins in 1889 (acquitted), and fraudulent theft of bread and flour in 1893 (convicted and sentenced to 3 months hard labour).

BADHAM, SERGEANT EDWARD, 31H (b. 1862)
Warrant no. 65001. Second policeman at scene of Alice McKenzie's murder. Uniformed policeman on duty inspecting beat constables on 17 July 1889. He spoke briefly to **Police Constable Walter Andrews** in Castle Alley, but on proceeding to the next constable's beat was recalled by Andrews' whistle on discovery of Alice McKenzie's body.

Badham's name is frequently misspelled Bedham, and some sources mention a Sergeant Betham accompanying **Inspector Beck** to see Mary Jane Kelly's body. This probably refers to Badham. (See also **Sgt Barry.**)

BALFOUR, ARTHUR JAMES (1848–1930)
Prime Minister, 1902–06. Chief Secretary for Ireland, 1887–91, earning the

nickname 'Bloody Balfour' in September 1887 by his rigorous suppression of disturbances.

The late **Douglas G. Browne** wrote in *The Rise of Scotland Yard*, 'A third head of the CID, **Sir Melville Macnaghten**, appears to identify the Ripper with the leader of a plot to assassinate Mr Balfour at the Irish Office'. This extraordinary claim, unsupported by any extant writing of Macnaghten's, cannot be casually dismissed. Browne had access to the **Scotland Yard files** and **Home Office files** on the Ripper at least twenty years before they were opened to the public and presumably saw documents which have since gone missing. There *were* **Fenians** aspiring to assassinate Balfour. So although Macnaghten is not known to have played any part in detecting Irish terrorism, he may have heard and recorded suspicion of a Fenian as the Ripper, prior to hearing the information that convinced him the Ripper was **Druitt**.

Suggestive details emerge in the private manuscript memoir written by Monro in 1903 and secret files deposited in the Home Office archives by Anderson.

In 1887 Monro and Anderson were jointly involved in foiling the plot to explode a bomb in Westminster Abbey during Queen Victoria's Jubilee celebrations (21 June 1887). This was prevented by scaring the principal conspirator back to America from France. But after that had been done, H Division drew the Secret Department's attention to a suspicious man lodging in Whitechapel who paid clandestine visits to a sick man in Lambeth. The visitor, a known Fenian named Harkins, was arrested and found to be carrying a newspaper cutting announcing a forthcoming visit to Birmingham by Mr Balfour, though he claimed to be illiterate and ignorant of its content. The sick man's identity was uncertain; he was known variously as 'Cohen' or 'Brown'. On his death it transpired that he had been financing the gang, and Harkins and another confederate named Callan were embarrassed by lack of funds. Monro brought them into the open at 'Cohen's' inquest, and in February both drew long sentences for possession of explosives.

The following year, according to Monro, the Fenians determined on a campaign of assassinations, aimed especially at killing Balfour. A prominent Fenian known as General Millen travelled to France to control the operation, and there he was confronted by a Scotland Yard man and decided not to enter England. His Irish subordinate Roger McKenna was also seen in Paris and given to understand that his movements were watched. Through him the leading perpetrator in England, a man called Walsh, was uncovered. The plot came to nothing.

Sir Robert Anderson's filed notes, presumably written close to the time, state that **Superintendent Williamson** went to France and frightened off the organiser of the Jubilee Bomb Plot. **James Monro**'s manuscript reminiscence, written fifteen years later, ascribes that journey to Inspector Melville, and says that Williamson scared off General Millen the following year. Millen was, in any case, a double agent acting for HM Government.

Somewhere among these events may lie the facts which Macnaghten apparently used to support his suspicion that a would-be assassin of Balfour was also the Ripper.

BARBER, ROGER

Theorist. Author of 'Did Jack the Ripper Commit Suicide?' in the *Criminologist*, Autumn 1990.

Noting a preponderant medical opinion that a sexual serial murderer would commit suicide if he were not caught, Barber further noted the lack of evidence corroborating **Melville Macnaghten**'s suspicion of **M. J. Druitt**, and looked for appropriate suicides in the East End roughly contemporaneous with the ending of the murders. He proposes **Edward Buchan** as the Ripper.

BARNARDO, DR THOMAS (1845–1905)

Alleged suspect. Entered **London Hospital** as student, 1866, and began East End street preaching. 1867, opened first shelter for destitute boys. **Dr Robert Anderson** was associated with his work from the outset and remained on the council of Barnardo's Homes until his death.

During the murders, Barnardo visited doss-houses urging prostitutes to place children in his care for the time being rather than risk their suddenly being orphaned. In 32 Flower and Dean Street he talked in the kitchen to a woman whom he later recognised as Elizabeth Stride when he saw her body in St George's-in-the East mortuary.

Because of the preponderant **'Doctor' theories**, Barnardo (FRCS, 1879), a well-known doctor who visited doss-houses, came under local suspicion, as noted by Gillian Wagner in her biography of him.

BARNETT, MRS HENRIETTA OCTAVIA (1851–1936)

Social reformer. Wife of **Samuel Barnett**. Mrs Barnett's contribution to the Ripper agitation was drafting the Petition of the Women of East London which was sent to Queen Victoria with over 4,000 signatures appended. It promised to try to make men feel the wickedness of sins of impurity which led to such crimes, and urged the Queen to have the police close all brothels.

BARNETT, JOSEPH

Born 1858 and died 1926 according to death certificate postulated as his by **Bruce Paley**, or born 1860 and died 1927 according to **Paul Harrison**. **Mary Jane Kelly**'s lover. Recently alleged suspect. London-born of Irish descent, riverside labourer and market porter, licensed to work at Billingsgate Fish Market. Nicknamed **'Danny'** according to press report. Met Kelly in Commercial Street on Good Friday, 8 April 1887. They met again the following day, and lived together thereafter at various East End addresses, culminating in 13 Miller's Court.

Some time in 1888 Barnett lost his job and after a dispute with Kelly on 30 October he left and took lodgings in Buller's Boarding-House, Bishopsgate. After the separation, Barnett visited Kelly almost daily and gave her money. On Thursday 8 November he called at Miller's Court between 7.30 p.m. and 8.00, finding her with 'a female who lived in the same court', whose name he apparently did not know. (See **Lizzie Albrook, Maria Harvey**.) He said he left her room at about 8.00 p.m. Thereafter returned to Buller's for the remainder of the evening. **Maurice Lewis** claimed to have seen him and **'Julia'** drinking with Kelly in **The Horn of Plenty**. After the murder, Barnett moved to live with his sister in Portpool Lane, Gray's Inn.

Bruce Paley has suggested that Barnett might have been the Ripper. He adduces no facts in support of the theory: only the postulation that he might have committed the other murders to frighten Kelly off the streets, finally killing her when this failed. He also suggests that Barnett might have retained a key to the room, missing the fact that it was spring-locked. The suggestion finds no favour with most researchers, who note that police appeared satisfied after questioning Barnett for four hours and examining all his clothing. **Paul Harrison**, reproducing Paley's theory of motivation without acknowledgement (so possibly coincidentally) asserts subjectively that Barnett was the Ripper, identifying him positively with another Joseph Barnett who died in Old Ford Road in 1927.

BARNETT, REVEREND SAMUEL AUGUSTUS (1846–1904)
Rector of St Jude's, Whitechapel, 1873–94. Well-known East End social reformer. Wrote frequently to the press during the murder scare, suggesting that the rich should pay for improved street lighting, and the poor should treat their womenfolk better; that philanthropical capitalists might buy up slum property and rebuild it as cheap model housing; and that the police might exert themselves to put down vice in the 'wicked quarter-mile' around Dorset Street, Flower and Dean Street, and Thrawl Street, rather than hunting for the murderer. He particularly wanted women stopped from stripping to the waist for fights.

BARRETT, POLICE CONSTABLE THOMAS, 226H
Possibly b. 1857, Sherborne. Joined H Division, Metropolitan Police, 1883. Warrant no. 67481. Retired, 1908. Saw a soldier he said was a Grenadier Guardsman, aged 22–26, 5ft 9ins tall, fair complexion, dark hair, small brown moustache turned up at ends, loitering in Wentworth Street at 2.00 a.m. on 7 August 1888. The soldier told Barrett he was 'waiting for a chum who had gone with a girl'. (See **Martha Tabram**.) Barrett was summoned to scene of Tabram's murder by **John Saunders Reeves**, and despatched another constable for **Dr Killeen**.

BARRY (or BERRY) SERGEANT, 31H
Reported as conveying Annie Chapman's body to mortuary on ambulance and took description dictated by **Sergeant Thick**. But probably **Sergeant Badham** misdescribed.

BATCHELOR, J. H.
Private detective hired by *Evening News* and **Vigilance Committee** to make investigations after Elizabeth Stride's murder. See under **Mr Grand**.

BATES, THOMAS
Witness at Elizabeth Stride's inquest. Watchman at 32 Flower and Dean Street. Testified that he knew Stride as 'Long Liz' and she tried to make her living charring. He repeated her story about the *Princess Alice* (vessel) disaster. Said she left lodging house about 7.30 p.m., seeming cheerful.

BAXTER, WYNNE EDWIN (1844–1920)
Coroner presiding over inquests on Mary Ann Nichols, Annie Chapman, Elizabeth Stride, Rose Mylett, Alice McKenzie and Frances Coles. Born and resident in Lewes, whereof Junior Headborough (1868), Junior High Constable (1878), Senior High Constable (1880) and first Mayor (1881).

Solicitor, practising largely in London, and during 1880s held two deputy coronerships. Publications included standard work on *Judicature Acts and Rules*.

In 1887 he won a very bitter election as coroner for East London and Tower of London against **Dr Roderick MacDonald**. Baxter was accused of electoral improprieties. Supported by the Conservatives, he carried Hackney and Stoke Newington resoundingly, though the Radical Dr MacDonald was far more strongly favoured in Whitechapel and Spitalfields. In less than a year the district was subdivided and ironically Baxter was given the South-Eastern Division, which had largely voted against him.

Baxter was a flamboyant coroner, notably dressy and garrulous. He used 'Inquest, London' as his telegraphic address. He seemed critical of the police at Mary Ann Nichols' inquest held in the Whitechapel Working Lads' Institute (next to the present Whitechapel Underground station) on 1 September (reconvened 3, 17, 23 September). He criticised them for failing to observe the abdominal mutilations before taking the body to the mortuary, and for not having ordered the washing of the body under their own observation. **Inspector Helson**'s claim that the mortuary had acted without regard to police instructions was rebutted by pauper **James Hatfield**, who had laid the body out. When a juror pointed out that Hatfield's memory was so poor that he had denied the body wore stays, although he had personally shown them to the jury when they visited the mortuary, Baxter snappishly defended Hatfield.

Annie Chapman's inquest in the Working Lads' Institute (12, 13, 14, 19, 26 September) saw the zenith of Baxter's public standing in the Ripper affair. In summing up, he suggested that the motive was the extraction of the missing uterus for sale to an American doctor who, he had been informed, had been offering large sums of money for specimens to enclose with subscription copies of a monograph he was writing. He was praised in the press for drawing attention to this abuse with its danger of reviving Burking, and contrasted favourably with Scotland Yard. But the **British Medical Journal** corrected Baxter, who did not repeat the theory at Elizabeth Stride's inquest (1, 2, 3, 5, 23 October in the Vestry Hall, Cable Street).

Rose Mylett's inquest (21 December 1888; 3, 9 January 1889, in Poplar Coroner's Court) evoked Baxter's strongest attack on the police.

At his last appearance in a Ripper-related case, on 15 February 1891, he refused to let **Mr Albert Bachert** appear as a reserve juror at Frances Coles' inquest. The police had decided this was not a Ripper crime and Bachert would almost certainly have questioned their conclusion.

Baxter's frequent friction with the Metropolitan Police led **Stephen Knight** to claim that he was trying to investigate the murders seriously, and so came in conflict with the **Freemasons**' plot to cover up the truth, engineered largely by **Sir Charles Warren** and **Dr Robert Anderson**. It seemed obvious to Knight that Baxter was not a Freemason. Knight was wrong. Baxter was a prominent Freemason in South Sussex Lodge. His conflicts with the police were undoubtedly the result of his combative personality, combined with the typical Victorian coroner's touchy concern for the dignity of his office. But neither he nor they were involved in any attempt to help a guilty murderer escape justice.

Baxter's short-lived theory of the sale of organs to the American anatomist misled **Inspector Abberline**. The example of his over-long inquests may have encouraged MacDonald to the undesirable brevity with which he conducted Kelly's.

Despite searches in Lewes, Stoke Newington, and the Middlesex and Greater London Archives, no traces of Baxter's inquest papers have surfaced.

BAYLEY, JOSEPH and THOMAS
Packing-case makers operating from 23a **Hanbury Street** (the yard of The Black Swan public house). A piece of crumpled paper, saturated with blood, was found in their yard on 11 September and believed to prove that the murderer had followed the route indicated by **Laura Sickings'** bloodstain in no. 25. But police asserted the paper had not been there on the day of the murder. See also **James Green, James Kent**.

BEACH, THOMAS MILLER (MAJOR HENRI LE CARON)
(1841–94)
Informant. Spy, controlled by Dr Robert **Anderson**. Infiltrated **Fenian** movement in America. Published *Twenty-five Years in the Secret Service* (1892), which praises Anderson highly.

BECK, INSPECTOR WALTER (b. 1852)
Probably first policeman at site of **Mary Jane Kelly**'s murder. Joined Metropolitan Police, 1871. Warrant no. 53559. Resigned 1896. On duty as Station Inspector, Commercial Road Police Station, 9 November 1888.

Beck deposed at the inquest, 'I was the first police officer called to 13 Miller's Court by **McCarthy** . . . [I]t was shortly after 11 o'clock when I was called.' **Abberline** noted that Beck went to the scene with constables on duty. No mention is made in contemporary police reports of the presence of **Walter Dew, Sergeant Godley,** or **Sergeant Badham**, who were all at one time or another described by themselves or others as first at the scene.

BEDHAM, SERGEANT
See **Sergeant Badham**.

BELL, DONALD
Theorist. Canadian author and journalist. Published, 'Jack the Ripper – The Final Solution' in the *Criminologist*, Summer 1974.

Argues that **Thomas Neill Cream** might have bribed his way out of Joliet Prison, or escaped in 1888, and committed the Whitechapel Murders. Supporting evidence is **Derek Davis**'s claim that Cream's writing matches that of two Ripper letters. **Donald Rumbelow** has disposed of this theory conclusively by discovering affidavits from Cream's uncle and sister-in-law and a letter from Cream himself which show beyond question that Cream was incarcerated at the time of the murders.

BELLORD, EDMUND JOSEPH (1857–1927)
A founder and leading committee member of **Providence Row Night Refuge**. Solicitor and, according to **Stephen Knight**, partner in Perkins and Bellord, estate agents of Cleveland Street. Admitted to the Roll, 1881; practised in Queen Victoria Street, 1881–93.

Knight claims that when the tobacconist at 22 Cleveland Street needed an assistant, Walter Sickert approached 'a lawyer who ran an East End refuge for poor working women' who brought Mary Jane Kelly to Cleveland Street. This is apparently a reference to Bellord.

BELLOSELSKI, PRINCE SERGEI
Informant. Russian exile. Showed **Donald McCormick** copy of the *Ochrana Gazette* for January 1909 containing request for return of files on **Vassily Konovalov**.

If, as described, this item did give **Alexei Pedachenko** as Konovalov's alias, it supplies the only known link between Konovalov and Pedachenko (who is otherwise known to us from **William Le Queux**).

BERNER STREET (today **HENRIQUES STREET**)
Elizabeth Stride's murder site. Residential street at the northern edge of St George's-in-the-East parish, abutting on Whitechapel. Berner Street ran north-south from Commercial Road to Ellen Street (terminating today at Boyd Street). Beyond Ellen Street lay the Swedish church, from which Stride received alms occasionally.

On the western side of the street, in 1888, four houses north of the Fairclough Street crossroad, a relatively narrow entry sealed by double gates with a wicket led into Dutfield's Yard. The two-storey wooden building to the north of the yard was the **International Workingmen's Educational Club**. Four cottages stood at the south of the yard. The western end was sealed by Dutfield's coachworks and a small sack-making factory. Opposite the yard, on the eastern side of Berner Street, a Board School stood on the corner with Fairclough Street. Stride's body was found just inside the entry to Dutfield's Yard, on the north side, just past the open gate. On the same side as the yard, a public house stood on the corner with Fairclough Street: next to it was **Matthew Packer**'s greengrocer's shop.

Today, most of the eastern side of the street north of Fairclough Street, including the site of Dutfield's Yard, has been swallowed up by a primary school. The Board School was replaced by the Bernhard Baron Community Centre, now converted to residential flats. Very few buildings from the 1880s remain standing.

BEST, –
Journalist. Alleged author of '**Jack the Ripper**' letters.

Dr Robert Anderson, Donald Swanson and **Melville Macnaghten** all independently mention Scotland Yard's belief that the '**Dear Boss**' letter was a hoax by an identifiable journalist.

A writer in *Crime and Detection* for August 1966 describes using the 'very spry and clear-minded' seventy-year-old ex-journalist Best as a contact in 1931:

Returning homewards with me, Best discussed murders, the Whitechapel murders in particular. With much amplifying detail he talked of his days as a penny-a-liner on the *Star* newspaper. As a freelance he had covered the Whitechapel murders from the discovery of Tabram. He claimed that he, and a provincial colleague, were responsible for *all* the 'Ripper' letters, to 'keep the business alive . . . [I]n those days it was far easier to get details, and facts from the police, than today.' Best did not mind me having these facts so many years later, and said a close reading of the *Star* of the time might be informative, and that an experienced graphologist with an open mind would be able to find in the original letters 'numerous earmarks' of an experienced journalist at work; the pen used was called a 'Waverly Nib' and was deliberately battered to achieve the impression of semi-literacy and 'National School' training! Best scoffed at the notion that the 'Ripper' had written a single word about his crimes.

We may note that Best was probably unaware of the full total of 'Ripper' letters sent to the police and held on file. But his confidence suggests that he claimed responsibility for the most widely reported missives, including the 'Dear Boss' letter and postcard sent to the Central News Agency, and possibly the 'From Hell' letter sent to George Lusk with half a kidney.

BEST, J.

Witness at Elizabeth Stride's inquest. Labourer, residing 82 Lower Chapman Street. With **John Gardner**, saw a woman whom he later identified as Stride leave The Bricklayers' Arms in Settles Street with a man shortly before 11.00 p.m. on 29 September 1888. The couple were sheltering from a rainstorm when Best and Gardiner started 'chipping' them, saying, 'That's **Leather Apron** getting round you'. The man they saw was about 5ft 5ins tall, with a black moustache, weak, sandy eyelashes, and wore a morning suit and billycock hat. He was definitely English. (Cf. **William Marshall**.)

BIRRELL, EMILY

Vagrant, friend of Catharine Eddowes.

Emily Birrell, with her man, met Catharine Eddowes and **John Kelly** on their return from hop-picking in Kent, September 1888. Emily gave Eddowes a London pawnbroker's ticket for a man's shirt, since she and her man were going to Cheltenham. The ticket in her name was subsequently found in the mustard tin beside Eddowes' body, and on reading press reports of the name 'Birrell', Kelly came forward and identified Eddowes.

BLACK THE RIPPER (1975, USA)

Film directed by Frank R. Saletri. Stars Hugh van Patten, Bole Nikoli, Renata Harmon.

BLACKWELL, DR WILLIAM P. (1851–1900)

Doctor called to pronounce Elizabeth Stride dead. LRCP, LRCS (Edin.), 1882. Arrived at the murder scene at 1.16 a.m. precisely, and determined Stride had been dead no more than twenty minutes. He believed she had been killed standing up, her head being dragged back by the silk handkerchief around her neck, and her throat cut. He believed her blood-smeared right hand indicated a struggle. **Dr Bagster Phillips**, who carried out the post-mortem, disagreed.

BLAVATSKY, HELEN PETROVNA (1831–91)

Non-contemporaneously alleged suspect. Influential student of comparative and eastern religions who co-founded the Theosophical Society.

John Symonds, **Aleister Crowley**'s literary executor, cites an unpublished untitled essay in which Crowley wrote, 'It is hardly one's first, or even one's hundredth guess, that the Victorian worthy in the case of Jack the Ripper was no less a person than Helena Petrovna Blavatsky.' This pointless remark, which appears, syntactically, to say that Crowley did *not* suspect her, is presumably an example of his peculiar humour.

BLENKINSOP, JAMES

Informant. Nightwatchman, overseeing roadworks in St James's Place (adjacent to and accessible from Mitre Square). Told the *Star* (1 October 1888) that at about 1.30 a.m., 30 September 1888, a respectably dressed man approached him and asked, 'Have you seen a man and a woman go through here?' Blenkinsop replied that he had seen some people pass, but had not taken any notice. It seems inconceivable that this story was not fully investigated by the City Police. Blenkinsop was not called to the inquest. (Cf. **Unidentified witnesses at Mitre Square.**)

BLOODHOUNDS

Agitation for the use of bloodhounds in hunting the murderer began with correspondence in *The Times* in October 1888. **Edwin Brough**, a breeder of Scarborough, was invited to bring two dogs, Burgho and champion Barnaby, to London. Police trials in Regent's Park on 9 October were very successful; in Hyde Park the following day, less so. **Sir Charles Warren** sportingly offered himself as 'fox' for the second trial, for which he was ridiculed, though it is not true that the dogs bit him. (This legend appears to have been started by an innuendo in *Police Review* for 29 October 1897.)

On 19 October a canard appeared in the press to the effect that Barnaby and Burgho had been taken on training in Tooting and were lost. In fact Burgho was in the care of Mr Edward Taunton, being trained at Hemel Hempstead. Barnaby had been returned to Mr Brough. Experiment had shown the dogs could not follow trails through crowded city streets, and the police decided against buying them. Nevertheless, this decision was so far from being made known to the CID in Whitechapel that **Abberline, Reid** and **Arnold** delayed entering Mary Jane Kelly's room for two hours in case Scotland Yard should want the dogs to be first on the murder scene.

BOND, DR THOMAS (1841–1901)

Police surgeon to A Division (Westminster). Submitted reports on Mary Jane Kelly, Alice McKenzie and Rose Mylett; also a general report on the Ripper murders for **Dr Robert Anderson**'s benefit. Educ. King's College and King's College Hospital. MRCS, 1864; MB, 1865; FRCS, 1866. Served with Prussian army, 1866. Surgeon to A Division, Metropolitan Police, 1867. Assistant Surgeon, Westminster Hospital, 1873; Surgeon, 1897. Committed suicide, throwing himself from bedroom window, after a long period of insomnia and depression followed by a painful illness.

His report on Mary Jane Kelly, recovered by Scotland Yard in 1987, follows:

Position of body

The body was lying naked in the middle of the bed, the shoulders flat, but the axis of the body inclined to the left side of the bed. The head was turned on the left cheek. The left arm was close to the body with the forearm flexed at a right angle & lying across the abdomen. The right arm was slightly abducted from the body & rested on the mattress, the elbow bent & the forearm supine with the fingers clenched. The legs were wide apart, the left thigh at right angles to the trunk & the right forming an obtuse angle with the pubes.

The whole of the surface of the abdomen & thighs was removed & the abdominal Cavity emptied of its viscera. The breasts were cut off, the arms mutilated by several jagged wounds & the face hacked beyond recognition of the features. The tissues of the neck were severed all round down to the bone.

The viscera were found in various parts viz: the uterus & Kidneys with one breast under the head, the other breast by the Rt foot, the Liver between the feet, the intestines by the right side & the spleen by the left side of the body. The flaps removed from the abdomen and thighs were on a table.

The bed clothing at the right corner was saturated with blood, & on the floor beneath was a pool of blood covering about 2 feet square. The wall by the right side of the bed & in a line with the neck was marked by blood which had struck it in a number of separate splashes.

Postmortem examination

The face was gashed in all directions the nose, cheeks, eyebrows and ears being partly removed. The lips were blanched & cut by several incisions running obliquely down to the chin. There were also numerous cuts extending irregularly across all the features.

The neck was cut through the skin & other tissues right down to the vertebrae the 5th & 6th being deeply notched. The skin cuts in the front of the neck showed distinct ecchymosis

The air passage was cut at the lower part of the larynx through the cricoid cartilage.

Both breasts were removed by more or less circular incisions, the muscles down to the ribs being attached to the breasts. The intercostals between the 4th, 5th & 6th ribs were cut through & the contents of the thorax visible through the openings.

The skin & tissues of the abdomen from the costal arch to the pubes were removed in three large flaps. The right thigh was denuded in front to the bone, the flap of skin, including the external organs of generation & part of the right buttock. The left thigh was stripped of skin, fascia & muscles as far as the knee.

The left calf showed a long gash through skin & tissues to the deep muscles & reaching from the knee to 5 ins above the ankle.

Both arms & forearms had extensive & jagged wounds.

The right thumb showed a small superficial incision about 1 in long, with extravasation of blood in the skin & there were several abrasions on the back of the hand moreover showing the same condition.

On opening the thorax it was found that the right lung was minimally adherent by old firm adhesions. The lower part of the lung was broken & torn away.

The left lung was intact: it was adherent at the apex & there were a few adhesions over the side. In the substances of the lung were several nodules of consolidation.

The Pericardium was open below & the Heart absent.

In the abdominal cavity was some partly digested food of fish & potatoes & similar food was found in the remains of the stomach attached to the intestines.

We may note especially that Bond makes the error of describing the body as naked, though it actually wore the remains of a chemise. The extraction of the heart through the severed diaphragm suggests to some researchers a degree of medical skill. The missing heart was never reported in the press and remained information the police chiefs kept to themselves. Likewise, **Abberline** was apparently unaware of the discovery of the uterus. Bond's report corrects various exaggerations reported in the press and repeated by subsequent writers, viz no viscera were draped on nails in the walls; the uterus was neither stolen nor gravid (i.e. she was not pregnant).

Bond's general report to Anderson on the five Ripper cases is more speculative and, generally, less useful:

I beg to report that I have read the notes of the four Whitechapel Murders, viz:–

1. Buck's Row
2. Hanbury Street
3. Berner's [sic] Street
4. Mitre Square.

I have also made a Post Mortem Examination of the mutilated remains of a woman found yesterday in a small room in Dorset Street –

1. All five murders were no doubt committed by the same hand. In the first four the throats appear to have been cut from left to right. In the last case owing to the extensive mutilation it is impossible to say in what direction the fatal cut was made, but arterial blood was found on the wall in splashes close to where the woman's head must have been lying.

2. All the circumstances surrounding the murders lead me to form the opinion that the women must have been lying down when murdered and in every case the throat was first cut.

3. In the four murders of which I have seen the notes only, I cannot form a very definite opinion as to the time that had elapsed between the murder and the discovering of the body. In one case, that of Berner's [sic] Street, the discovery appears to have been made immediately after the deed – In Buck's Row, Hanbury Street, and Mitre Square three or four hours only could have elapsed. In the Dorset Street Case the body was lying on the bed at the time of my visit, two o'clock, quite naked and mutilated as in the annexed report –

Rigor Mortis had set in, but increased during the progress of the examination. From this it is difficult to say with any degree of certainty the exact time that had elapsed since death as the period varies from 6 to 12 hours before rigidity sets in. The body was comparatively cold at 2 o'clock and the remains of a recently taken meal were found in the stomach and scattered about over the intestines. It is, therefore, pretty certain that the woman must have been dead about twelve hours and the partly digested food would indicate that death took place about 3 or 4 hours after the food was taken, so 1 or 2 o'clock in the morning would be the probable time of the murder.

4. In all the cases there appears to be no evidence of struggling and the attacks were probably so sudden and made in such a position that the women could neither resist nor cry out. In the Dorset Street case the corner of the sheet to the right of the woman's head was much cut and saturated with blood, indicating that the face may have been covered with the sheet at the time of the attack.

5. In the four first cases the murderer must have attacked from the right side of the victim. In the Dorset Street case, he must have attacked in front or from the left, as there would be no room for him between the wall and the part of the bed on which the woman was lying. Again, the blood had flowed down on the right side of the woman and spurted on to the wall.

6. The murderer would not necessarily be splashed or deluged with blood, but his hands and arms must have been covered and parts of his

clothing must certainly have been smeared with blood.

7. The mutilations in each case excepting the Berner's Street one were all of the same character and showed clearly that in all the murders the object was mutilation.

8. In each case the mutilation was inflicted by a person who had no scientific nor anatomical knowledge. In my opinion he does not even possess the technical knowledge of a butcher or horse slaughterer or any person accustomed to cut up dead animals.

9. The instrument must have been a strong knife at least six inches long, very sharp, pointed at the top and about an inch in width. It may have been a clasp knife, a butcher's knife or a surgeon's knife. I think it was no doubt a straight knife.

10. The murderer must have been a man of physical strength and of great coolness and daring. There is no evidence that he had an accomplice. He must in my opinion be a man subject to periodical attacks of Homicidal and erotic mania. The character of the mutilations indicate that the man may be in a condition sexually, that may be called satyriasis. It is of course possible that the Homicidal impulse may have developed from a revengeful or brooding condition of the mind, or that Religious Mania may have been the original disease, but I do not think either hypothesis is likely. The murderer in external appearance is quite likely to be a quiet inoffensive looking man probably middle-aged and neatly and respectably dressed. I think he must be in the habit of wearing a cloak or overcoat or he could hardly have escaped notice in the streets if the blood on his hands or clothes were visible.

11. Assuming the murderer to be such a person as I have just described he would probably be solitary and eccentric in his habits, also he is most likely to be a man without regular occupation, but with some small income or pension. He is possibly living among respectable persons who have some knowledge of his character and habits and who may have grounds for suspicion that he is not quite right in his mind at times. Such persons would probably be unwilling to communicate suspicions to the Police for fear of trouble or notoriety, whereas if there were a prospect of reward it might overcome their scruples.

Bond's deductions are of limited intrinsic value, since he argues for instantaneous and silent killing in every case, despite the defence wounds on Mary Jane Kelly's hands which he had observed. He accepts circumstantially impossible times of death for the cases on which he had read notes. But he sets up immediate conflict with **Dr Phillips**, who argued that the five murders were *not* by the same hand, and that skill *was* shown in Chapman's, Stride's and Kelly's cases, though not, apparently, in that of Eddowes. Since the report was addressed specifically to Anderson, we may assume that Anderson paid special heed to Bond's opinion – a view supported by Anderson's insistence that Bond submit reports on Rose Mylett and Alice McKenzie.

In Mylett's case, Bond at first confirmed the opinion of previous doctors that she had been strangled with a piece of string, but after a second visit opined that she had choked to death on her collar after falling down drunk.

In Alice McKenzie's case he again disputed Bagster Phillips' findings:
I see in this murder evidence of similar design to the former Whitechapel Murders viz: sudden onslaught on the prostrate woman, the throat skilfully & resolutely cut with subsequent mutilation, each mutilation indicating sexual thoughts & a desire to mutilate the abdomen & sexual organs.

I am of opinion that the murder was performed by the same person who committed the former series of Whitechapel Murders.

This time his conclusions were not accepted, possibly because Anderson had gone on leave by the time his report was considered.

BOOKS – NON-FICTION

Books about Jack the Ripper, once out of print, are collectors' items with high asking prices.

The following chronological list is comprehensive:

Anon, *The Whitechapel Murders: or The Mysteries of the East End*. London: Purkiss, 1888.

Richard Kyle Fox, *The History of the Whitechapel Murders: A Full and Authentic Narrative of the Above Murders with Sketches*. New York: Fox, 1888.

W. J. Hayne, *Jack the Ripper: or the Crimes of London*. 1889. (Listed by Alexander Kelly – see below – as catalogued by Library of Congress, but untraceable there or elsewhere.)

Anon, *The Latest Atrocities of Jack the Ripper*. Stuttgart, 1889.

Anon, *Jack lo Squartatore*. Venice, 1889.

Carl Muusmann, *Hvem var Jack the Ripper?*. Copenhagen: Hermann-Petersen, 1908.

Leonard Matters, *The Mystery of Jack the Ripper*. London: Hutchinson, 1929. Pbk, London: Arrow, 1964.

Jean Dorsenne, *Jack l'Éventreur*. Paris: Les Éditions de France, 1935.

Edwin Thomas Woodhall, *Jack the Ripper: or When London Walked in Terror*. London: Mellifont Press, 1935.

William Stewart, *Jack the Ripper: A New Theory*. London: Quality Press, 1939.

Alan Barnard (ed.), *The Harlot Killer: the Story of Jack the Ripper in Fact and Fiction*. New York: Dodd Mead, 1953.

Donald McCormick, *The Identity of Jack the Ripper*. London: Jarrolds, 1959. Pbk, revised, London: Pan, 1962. Revised again, London: John Long, 1970.

Tom Cullen, *Autumn of Terror: Jack the Ripper. His Crimes and Times*. London: Bodley Head, 1965. Reissued as *The Crimes and Times of Jack the Ripper*, same publisher, 1973. US title: *When London Walked in Terror*. Boston: Houghton Mifflin, 1965.

Robin Odell, *Jack the Ripper in Fact and Fiction*. London: Harrap, 1965. Revised pbk, London: Mayflower, 1966.

Daniel Farson, *Jack the Ripper*. London: Michael Joseph, 1972. Revised pbk, London: Sphere, 1973.

Michael Harrison, *Clarence: the Life of HRH the Duke of Clarence and Avondale 1864–1892*. London: W. H. Allen, 1972. US title: *Clarence: Was he Jack the Ripper?*, 1974.

Michell Raper, *Who was Jack the Ripper?* London: Tabaret Press, 1975.

Elwyn Jones and John Lloyd, *The Ripper File*. London: Arthur Barker, 1975. Pbk, London: Futura, 1975.

Donald Rumbelow, *The Complete Jack the Ripper*. London, W. H. Allen, 1975. Revised ed., 1979. 2nd revised ed, 1987. Pbk of 2nd revised ed. with addenda, London: Penguin, 1988.

Stephen Knight, *Jack the Ripper: The Final Solution*, London: Harrap, 1976. Pbk, London: Panther, 1981. Revised ed., London: Treasure Press, 1984.

Richard Whittington-Egan, *A Casebook on Jack the Ripper*. London: Wildy, 1976.

Frank Spiering, *Prince Jack: The True Story of Jack the Ripper*. New York: Doubleday, 1978.

Arthur Douglas, *Will the Real Jack the Ripper?* Chorley, Lancs: Countryside Publications, 1979.

Martin Fido, *The Crimes, Detection and Death of Jack the Ripper*. London: Weidenfeld, 1987. Revised Pbk, same publisher, 1989.

Melvin Harris, *Jack the Ripper: The Bloody Truth*. London: Columbus, 1987.

Martin Howells and Keith Skinner, *The Ripper Legacy*. London: Sidgwick and Jackson, 1987. Pbk, London: Sphere, 1988.

Terence Sharkey, *Jack the Ripper: 100 years of Investigation*. London: Ward Lock, 1987.

Peter Underwood, *Jack the Ripper: One Hundred Years of Mystery*. London: Blandford Press, 1987. Pbk, London: Javelin, 1988.

Colin Wilson and Robin Odell, *Jack the Ripper: Summing up and Verdict*. London: Bantam, 1987. Pbk, London: Corgi, 1988.

Anon, *Aleister Crowley and Jack the Ripper*. Cambridge: privately printed, 1988. (100 copies only.)

Paul Begg, *Jack the Ripper: The Uncensored Facts*. London: Robson, 1988. Pbk, same publisher, 1989.

Winston Forbes-Jones, *Who was Jack the Ripper?* Redhill: Pipeline Promotions, 1988.

Melvin Harris, *The Ripper File*. London: W. H. Allen, 1989.

Jean Overton Fuller, *Sickert and the Ripper Crimes*. Oxford: Mandrake, 1990.

Paul Harrison, *Jack the Ripper: The Mystery Solved*. London: Robert Hale, 1991.

Melvyn Fairclough, *The Ripper and the Royals*. London: Duckworth, 1991.

Also:

Tom Robinson: *The Whitechapel Horrors: Being an Authentic Account of the Jack the Ripper Murders*. Manchester: Daisy Bank Publications, n.d.

And of special importance to all collectors and researchers, the indispensable:

Alexander Kelly, *Jack the Ripper: A Bibliography and Review of the Literature* with Introduction by **Colin Wilson**. London: Association of Assistant Librarians, 1972. Revised, 1984.

BOOTH, 'GENERAL' WILLIAM (1829–1912)

Erroneously alleged theorist. Evangelist; founder of Christian Mission in Whitechapel, 1865 (renamed Salvation Army, 1878). Confused by **Colin Wilson**, when working from memory, with **Commissioner Lamb** of the Salvation Army, who did suggest a suspect. Booth is not known to have held any views on the identity of the Ripper.

BOUGOIN, STEPHANE

Writer, translator, popular culture researcher and collector. A former professional footballer who opened the first specialist crime book store in Paris, *Le Troisième Oeuil*, Stephane Bougoin is the leading living authority on filmed and fictional treatments of Jack the Ripper. He has for some time been compiling a definitive book on the subject.

BOULTBEE, WALTER ERNEST (1853–97)
Marital connection of **Druitt** family. Private secretary to **Sir Charles Warren, James Monro** and **Sir Edward Bradford** successively. Married, 1885, Ellen Baker, niece of Alfred Mayo, a lasting friend and distant relative of Thomas Druitt (d. 1891). In fact, the interrelated Druitt, Mayo and Elton families, all with members who emigrated to Australia, have retained links to the present day, and long shared mutual genealogical interests. It is, at the very least, food for thought that a connection of this clan should have been ensconced in Scotland Yard when **Melville Macnaghten** picked up 'private information' about the family's suspicions of **Montague John Druitt**.

BOUSFIELD, MRS MARY (alias Luckhurst)
Witness at Martha Tabram's inquest. Formerly Martha's landlady at 4 Star Street, where she lived with her husband, woodcutter William Bousfield. Martha left leaving her rent unpaid about three weeks before her death. According to Mrs Bousfield, Martha sold matches for a living. MEPO **Files** 3/140/4 and the press give her name as Bousfield; MEPO file 3/140/3 gives it as Luckhurst.

BOWYER, THOMAS, 'INDIAN HARRY'
Discoverer of Mary Jane Kelly's body. An Indian army pensioner, residing at 37 Dorset Street, he worked for **John McCarthy**, and was sent to collect Kelly's arrears of rent at 10.45 a.m. on 9 November 1888. Unable to get an answer or open the spring-locked door, he pulled back the coat and curtain hanging behind the broken window pane and saw the mutilated body on the bed. See also **Unidentified man seen by Thomas Bowyer**.

BRADFORD, COLONEL SIR EDWARD RIDLEY COLBORNE, BT (1836–1911)
Metropolitan Police Commisioner during last part of public Ripper scare. Educ. Marlborough. Madras Cavalry, 1853; served Persia, 1856–7, and through latter part of Indian Mutiny. 1860, Col. i/c 1st Indian Horse, and Political Assistant in West Malwa. 1867, lost left arm to a tigress in shooting incident. 1874–78, general supervisor of operations against thugee (Kali-worshipping highwaymen murderers) and dacoiti (bandits). 1878, Gov-General's Agent, Rajputana, and Chief Commissioner, Ajmir. KCSI, 1885. 1887, Secretary to Secret and Political Dept, India Office, London. 1889–90, conducted **Prince Albert Victor** on tour around India. 1890–1903, Metropolitan Police Commissioner. Bt, 1902.

An easy man to get on with, and a very successful commissioner after the short unhappy terms of **Warren** and **Monro**. It is probable that he was informed when the Ripper file was closed in 1892, and he would know why.

BRICK LANE/OSBORN STREET
Emma Elizabeth Smith's murder site. Well-known Spitalfields thorough-fare, running north-south from Whitechapel High Street to Columbia market, Shoreditch. The southern end, from Wentworth Street to White-chapel High Street, is Osborn Street. Named after sixteenth-century brick

and tile manufactory nearby. Laid out by John Stott in 1660, when the Black Eagle Brewery was built there. Nos 65–79 built 1705–6 by brewer Joseph Truman.

Emma Smith is variously described as being killed in Osborn Street and Brick Lane. Most reports agree that she was killed 'opposite' Taylor Bros Mustard and Cocoa Mill which stood on the north-east corner of the Wentworth Street/Old Montague Street crossroads.

At the Shoreditch/Bethnal Green northern end, Brick Lane ran into 'the Nichol', a criminal slum surrounding Old Nichol Street and made notorious as 'the Jago' in Arthur Morrison's late nineteenth-century social novels. South of Hanbury Street and the sprawling premises of Truman, Hanbury Buxton's brewery, the road was a centre of Jewish settlement and shopping, including the Jewish Steam Baths and the old Huguenot chapel which has been successively a Baptist chapel, a mission centre of the Society for the Propagation of the Gospel among Jews, an orthodox synagogue, and (today) a mosque.

Church Street, Fashion Street, Flower and Dean Street, and Thrawl Street all ran from the east of Brick Lane to **Commercial Street. The Frying Pan** (converted to an Indian restaurant, 1991) stood on the corner of Brick Lane and Thrawl Street. **Jill the Ripper** (midwife/abortionist) reputedly lived in or around Brick Lane.

Today the thoroughfare is the centre of Bangladeshi settlement, with many fine Indian restaurants, groceries and sari shops, though there are still two excellent bagel shops at the Bethnal Green Road end.

Cf. **Dr Killeen, Jill the Ripper, Mary Ann Nichols**.

BRIDGE ACROSS TIME (ARIZONA RIPPER, TERROR AT LONDON BRIDGE) (1985, USA)

Film directed by E. W. Swackhamer. Stars David Hasselhoff, Stephanie Kramer. Spirit of Ripper resumes killing following restoration of missing brick to London Bridge – on which British police of 1888 gunned him down! – in Arizona. *Knight Rider* and *Baywatch* Hasselhoff investigates. TV movie. (Video available.)

BRITANNIA, THE

Public house, at north corner of Commercial Street and Dorset Street, frequented by Mary Jane Kelly. Licensed to Walter Ringer (who also kept a paint and oil shop in adjacent Brushfield Street). Occasional references to it in testimony as 'the Ringers" or 'Mrs Ringers" suggest that his wife was more frequently behind the bar. Though an imposing building, it was only licensed as a beershop, for which reason it was not entered on contemporary OS maps as a public house, and several researchers have confused its location with **The Horn of Plenty** at the other end of Dorset Street.

The Britannia was demolished in the extension of Spitalfields Market, 1928.

See also **Caroline Maxwell**.

BRITISH MEDICAL JOURNAL, THE

Professional organ for doctors; less radical than *The Lancet* in the nineteenth century.

In an important report on 6 October 1888, it discredited **Wynne Baxter's**

heory that the victims' wombs had been stolen for sale to an American
doctor:

It is true that enquiries were made at one or two medical schools
[contemporary press reports indicate that these were University College
Hospital and the Middlesex Hospital] early last year by a foreign physician, who was spending some time in London, as to the possibility of
securing certain parts of the body for the purpose of scientific investigation. No large sum, however, was offered. The person in question was
a physician of the highest reputability and exceedingly well accredited to
this country by the best authorities in his own, and he left London fully
eighteen months ago. There was never any real foundation for the
hypothesis, and the information communicated, which was not at all of
the nature the public has been led to believe, was due to the erroneous
interpretation by a minor official of a question which he had overheard
and to which a negative reply was given. This theory may be dismissed,
and is, we believe, no longer entertained by its author.

Despite this quite conclusive refutation, which silenced Mr Baxter on
he subject, **Abberline** still believed the theory fifteen years
ater.

BRITTAIN, CHARLES

Slaughterman. Joined **Tomkins** and **Mumford** to look at Mary Ann Nichols' body.

BROUGH, EDWIN (fl. 1890)

Provided **bloodhounds** for police trials during the Ripper scare. Breeder
and trainer of bloodhounds in Scarborough. Wrote to *The Times*, 8 October
1889, praising English bloodhounds, though expressing some reservations
as to their effectiveness in city streets. He must already have been engaged
to send Burgho and champion Barnaby down to London for police trials.

After the trials in the parks, Brough was indignant to learn from Mr
Edward Taunton, who had care of the dogs, that the police had taken one
of them to the scene of a burglary to see whether he could track the
criminal. The dog proved incapable of following scent through the city
streets, but Mr Brough feared that vengeful villains might try to injure his
valuable and uninsured animal. He demanded its immediate return: hence
the widely reported absence of the animals when they were wanted and
supposed to have been lost on Tooting Bec. In *The Bloodhound and Its Use
in the Tracking of Criminals* (1904), however, Brough claimed that the six-
week gap between the double murder and the murder of **Mary Jane Kelly**
could be put down to Barnaby and Burgho's presence in London.

BROWN, DR FREDERICK GORDON (1843–1928)

City Police surgeon responsible for report on Catharine Eddowes. Also
accompanied **Dr Phillips** to inspect Alice McKenzie's body *in situ*. Educ.
Merchant Taylors, St Thomas's Hospital and Paris. City Police Surgeon,
1886–1914. A very prominent **Freemason**, at one time Grand Officer of the
Grand Lodge of England.

His excellent post-mortem report is preserved at the Corporation of
London Records. It is imperfectly punctuated, as it is in the form of notes
taken verbatim by **Coroner Langham**. For convenience, we have added
correct punctuation. We have not inserted the coroner's questions which

(particularly toward the end) determine the brief comments and rep
etitions.

The body was on its back, the head turned to left shoulder. The arms b
the side of the body as if they had fallen there. Both palms upwards, th
fingers slightly bent . . . Left leg extended in a line with the body. Th
abdomen was exposed. Right leg bent at the thigh and knee . . .

The throat cut across . . .

The intestines were drawn out to a large extent and placed over th
right shoulder – they were smeared over with some feculent matter. /
piece of about two feet was quite detached from the body and place
between the body and the left arm, apparently by design. The lobe an
auricle of the right ear was cut obliquely through.

There was a quantity of clotted blood on the pavement on the left sid
of the neck round the shoulder and upper part of arm, and fluid blood
coloured serum which had flowed under the neck to the right shoulder
the pavement sloping in that direction.

Body was quite warm. No death stiffening had taken place. She mus
have been dead most likely within the half hour. We looked for super
ficial bruises and saw none. No blood on the skin of the abdomen c
secretion of any kind on the thighs. No spurting of blood on the bricks c
pavement around. No marks of blood below the middle of the body
Several buttons were found in the clotted blood after the body wa
removed. There was no blood on the front of the clothes. There were n
traces of recent connection.

When the body arrived at Golden Lane [mortuary] some of the bloo
was dispersed through the removal of the body to the mortuary. Th
clothes were taken off carefully from the body. A piece of deceased's ea
dropped from the clothing.

I made a post mortem examination at half past two on Sunday after
noon. Rigor mortis was well marked; body not quite cold. Green dis
coloration over the abdomen.

After washing the left hand carefully, a bruise the size of a sixpence
recent and red, was discovered on the back of the left hand between th
thumb and first finger. A few small bruises on right shin of older date
The hands and arms were bronzed. No bruises on the scalp, the back c
the body or the elbows.

The face was very much mutilated. There was a cut about a quarter c
an inch through the lower left eyelid, dividing the structures completel
through. The upper eyelid on that side, there was a scratch through th
skin on the left upper eyelid, near to the angle of the nose. The righ
eyelid was cut through to about half an inch.

There was a deep cut over the bridge of the nose, extending from th
left border of the nasal bone down near to the angle of the jaw on th
right side of the cheek. This cut went into the bone and divided all th
structures of the cheek except the mucous membrane of the mouth.

The tip of the nose was quite detached from the nose by an oblique cu
from the bottom of the nasal bone to where the wings of the nose join o
to the face. A cut from this divided the upper lip and extended throug
the substance of the gum over the right upper lateral incisor tooth. Abou
half an inch from the top of the nose was another oblique cut. There wa
a cut on the right angle of the mouth as if the cut of a point of a knife
The cut extended an inch and a half, parallel with lower lip.

There was on each side of cheek a cut which peeled up the skin, forming a triangular flap about an inch and a half.

On the left cheek there were two abrasions of the epithelium . . . under the left ear.

The throat was cut across to the extent of about six or seven inches. A superficial cut commenced about an inch and a half below the lobe below (and about two and a half inches below and behind) the left ear, and extended across the throat to about three inches below the lobe of right ear. The big muscle across the throat was divided through on the left side. The large vessels on the left side of the neck were severed. The larynx was severed below the vocal chord. All the deep structures were severed to the bone, the knife marking intervertebral cartilages. The sheath of the vessels on the right side was just opened. The carotid artery had a fine hole opening. The internal jugular vein was opened an inch and a half – not divided. The blood vessels contained clot. All these injuries were performed by a sharp instrument like a knife, and pointed.

The cause of death was haemorrhage from the left common carotid artery. The death was immediate and the mutilations were inflicted after death.

We examined the abdomen. The front walls were laid open from the breast bone to the pubes. The cut commenced opposite the enciform cartilage. The incision went upwards, not penetrating the skin that was over the sternum. It then divided the enciform cartilage. The knife must have cut obliquely at the expense of the front surface of that cartilage.

Behind this, the liver was stabbed as if by the point of a sharp instrument. Below this was another incision into the liver of about two and a half inches, and below this the left lobe of the liver was slit through by a vertical cut. Two cuts were shewn by a jagging of the skin on the left side.

The abdominal walls were divided in the middle line to within a quarter of an inch of the navel. The cut then took a horizontal course for two inches and a half towards right side. It then divided round the navel on the left side, and made a parallel incision to the former horizontal incision, leaving the navel on a tongue of skin. Attached to the navel was two and a half inches of the lower part of the rectus muscle on the left side of the abdomen. The incision then took an oblique direction to the right and was shelving. The incision went down the right side of the vagina and rectum for half an inch behind the rectum.

There was a stab of about an inch on the left groin. This was done by a pointed instrument. Below this was a cut of three inches going through all tissues making a wound of the peritoneum [sc. perineum] about the same extent.

An inch below the crease of the thigh was a cut extending from the anterior spine of the ilium obliquely down the inner side of the left thigh and separating the left labium, forming a flap of skin up to the groin. The left rectus muscle was not detached.

There was a flap of skin formed from the right thigh, attaching the right labium, and extending up to the spine of the ilium. The muscles on the right side inserted into the frontal ligaments were cut through.

The skin was retracted through the whole of the cut in the abdomen, but the vessels were not clotted. Nor had there been any appreciable bleeding from the vessels. I draw the conclusion that the cut was made after death, and there would not be much blood on the murderer. The cut was made by some one on right side of body, kneeling below the middle of the body.

I removed the content of the stomach and placed it in a jar for further examination. There seemed very little in it in the way of food or fluid, but from the cut end partly digested farinaceous food escaped.

The intestines had been detached to a large extent from the mesentery. About two feet of the colon was cut away. The sigmoid flexure was invaginated into the rectum very tightly.

Right kidney pale, bloodless, with slight congestion of the base of the pyramids.

There was a cut from the upper part of the slit on the under surface of the liver to the left side, and another cut at right angles to this, which were about an inch and a half deep and two and a half inches long. Liver itself was healthy.

The gall bladder contained bile. The pancreas was cut, but not through, on the left side of the spinal column. Three and a half inches of the lower border of the spleen by half an inch was attached only to the peritoneum.

The peritoneal lining was cut through on the left side and the left kidney carefully taken out and removed. The left renal artery was cut through. I should say that someone who knew the position of the kidney must have done it.

The lining membrane over the uterus was cut through. The womb was cut through horizontally, leaving a stump of three quarters of an inch. The rest of the womb had been taken away with some of the ligaments. The vagina and cervix of the womb was uninjured.

The bladder was healthy and uninjured, and contained three or four ounces of water. There was a tongue-like cut through the anterior wall of the abdominal aorta. The other organs were healthy.

There were no indications of connexion.

I believe the wound in the throat was first inflicted. I believe she must have been lying on the ground.

The wounds on the face and abdomen prove that they were inflicted by a sharp pointed knife, and that in the abdomen by one six inches long.

I believe the perpetrator of the act must have had considerable knowledge of the positions of the organs in the abdominal cavity and the way of removing them. The parts removed would be of no use for any professional purpose. It required a great deal of medical knowledge to have removed the kidney and to know where it was placed. Such a knowledge might be possessed by some one in the habit of cutting up animals.

I think the perpetrator of this act had sufficient time, or he would not have nicked the lower eyelids. It would take at least five minutes.

I cannot assign any reason for the parts being taken away. I feel sure there was no struggle. I believe it was the act of one person.

The throat had been so instantly severed that no noise could have been emitted. I should not expect much blood to have been found on the person who had inflicted these wounds. The wounds could not have been self-inflicted.

My attention was called to the apron. It was the corner of the apron, with a string attached. The blood spots were of recent origin. I have seen the portion of an apron produced by Dr Phillips and stated to have been found in Goulston Street. It is impossible to say it is human blood. I fitted the piece of apron which had a new piece of material on it which had evidently been sewn on to the piece I have, the seams of the borders of the two actually corresponding. Some blood and, apparently, faecal matter was found on the portion found in Goulston Street. I believe the wounds on the face to have been done to disfigure the corpse.

This is one of the most important yet contentious of all documents in the history of Jack the Ripper.

The post mortem was observed by Drs **Sequeira, Sedgwick Saunders** and **Bagster Phillips**. The two former gave evidence at the inquest suggesting that they did not think much expertise was evinced by the murderer, and stated that in this they agreed with Dr Brown. Phillips did not contradict Coroner **Wynne Baxter**, who described the Mitre Square murderer as an unskilled imitator. Brown responded to the coroner's repeated questions as to whether the murderer had surgical *skill* with the reply that he had *anatomical knowledge*, enabling him to identify and remove the kidney. He did not at any time volunteer information on this subject.

The kidney remains another point of controversy. **Richard Whittington-Egan**, the only crime historian with medical training and experience of dissecting cadavers, concluded that the murderer was unskilled and the kidney extracted by chance. He consulted leading renal authorities before publishing this conclusion. But **N. P. Warren**, the only practising surgeon to have made a substantial contribution to the history of the Ripper, demurs. He believes, from experience, that the kidney is so difficult to expose from the front of the body that the murderer must have had some anatomical experience, and he draws attention to Brown's remark that the kidney had been 'carefully' extracted.

The authors are not medically trained, and cannot say conclusively whether the medical evidence suggests that the Ripper was skilled or not, as doctors disagree today as they did at the time. There is no dispute, however, that N. P. Warren is correct in saying this report does show clear signs of Bright's disease in the right kidney. (See **Major Smith, Lusk kidney** for relevance.)

Other points of interest are the sexual focus, indicated by ripping the victim upward, from the pubes to the breastbone, and then concentrating on some very detailed cutting in the genital area which extracted the womb and almost detached one side of the external genitalia.

It is interesting that Brown reports no trace of sexual connection, and refers to the absence of secretion of any kind on the thighs, pointing to his possible expectation that premature ejaculation or masturbation over the body might have occurred. This (like **Bond**'s report and **Anderson**'s remarks) points to a surprisingly confident and accurate recognition of the practices of sadistic **serial murderers**; a sophisticated knowledge which was not possessed by the press or the junior police of the period, who looked for rational motives or hallucinatory religiose madness to explain the crimes.

The portion of the ear which fell off in the mortuary does not indicate any attempt to remove the ears, as promised in the **'Dear Boss' letter**.

The throat was cut as deeply as Annie Chapman's and Mary Ann Nichols'; like theirs, too, it had been cut across twice. The abrasions on the cheek below the left ear are reminiscent of the bruising on Nichols and Chapman. The small bruise on the back of the hand suggests an intercepted attempt at defence blocked by a hand or fist rather than the knife. (See under **Elizabeth Stride, Mary Jane Kelly, M.O.** for relevance.)

BROWN, JAMES
Witness at **Elizabeth Stride**'s inquest. Testified that at 12.45 a.m. he was passing along Fairclough Street on his way home to no. 35, and saw Stride with her back to the wall of the Board School, talking to a stoutish man, about 5ft 7ins tall, wearing a long coat which almost reached his heels. He had his arm against the wall, as if to stop her from leaving, and she was saying, 'No, not tonight. Maybe some other night.' Brown did not see the man's face or notice his cap. He did not observe the flower on Stride's dress. About fifteen minutes later, before he had finished his supper, he heard cries of 'Murder' as members of the **International Workingmen's Educational Club** went to find the police.

His reported sighting coincides exactly with the time at which **Israel Schwartz** said he saw Stride being thrown to the pavement outside Dutfield's Yard. If both men correctly identified Stride, one of them was wrong about the time.

The *Evening News* learned that a courting couple was in a road crossing Berner Street at the time, and it has been suggested that Brown might have mistaken them for Stride and a man. Brown was self-confessedly not very observant.

BROWNE, DOUGLAS G. (1884–1963)
Author of *The Rise of Scotland Yard* (1956). Pp. 205–9 discuss the Ripper case. Educ. Westminster. MC, 1918.

The book was completed by Browne after the original author, Ralph Straus's death. In the introduction Browne says he 'had the generous help of the authorities at New Scotland Yard in being given access to the records without which such a work as he contemplated could not have been undertaken'. In five passages the book uses words drawn directly from the **Home Office** and **Scotland Yard Files**, and not known to occur anywhere else. It follows that Browne, Straus or both had access to the files prior to 1956; certainly twenty years before any other researcher.

Since folios were constantly purloined from the files until the PRO put them on microfilm, it seems probable that Straus or Browne found documentary evidence for the remarkable statement, 'Sir **Melville Macnaghten** appears to identify the Ripper with the leader of a plot to assassinate Mr **Balfour** at the Irish Office.' (See **Arthur Balfour** for discussion.)

See also **Jack the Ripper's knife**.

BROWNFIELD, DR MATTHEW
K Division Metropolitan Police Surgeon. The first doctor to examine **Rose Mylett**. He concluded that a faint mark on her neck showed that she had been strangled with a ligature like a piece of string.

BRUCE, ALEXANDER CARMICHAEL (1850–1926)
Assistant Commissioner, Metropolitan Police, 1884–1914. Kt, 1908. Visited Buck's Row and Hanbury Street murder sites. Educ. Brasenose, Oxon. Called to bar, Lincoln's Inn, 1875.

BUCHAN, EDWARD (1859–1888)
Recently alleged suspect. Marine store dealer (said in one newspaper report to have been a shoemaker) of Robin Hood Lane, Poplar, who committed suicide on 19 November 1888. Advanced as suspect by Roger Barber in

'Did Jack the Ripper Commit Suicide' (*Criminologist*, Autumn 1990) on the basis that the sudden cessation of the crimes following the murder of Kelly is most likely explained by the suicide of the killer.

BUCHSE DER PANDORA, DIE (PANDORA'S BOX)
(1928, Germany)
Film directed by Georg Wilhelm Pabst. Stars Louise Brooks, Gustav Diesel. It by no means belittles Pabst's direction to say that sensuous Brooks carries this hypnotic study of self-destruction based on Wedekind plays in which amoral woman ends up a victim of Ripper (Diesel). Full version was restored 1983. (Video available.)

BUCK'S ROW (today Durward Street)
Mary Ann Nichols' murder site. A street to the east of Whitechapel parish, close to Bethnal Green, running east-west from Brady Street to Baker's Row (today's Vallance Road). About halfway along its length, parallel Winthrop Street running east–west from Brady Street converges, and the remainder of Buck's Row is extremely broad. An 1870s Board School (condemned after lying empty and being burned out in the 1980s) stood at the point of convergence.

The narrow section of Buck's Row comprised a recently built terrace of residential houses on the south side in 1888, and a number of warehouses (known as wharves because they formerly fronted a canal) to the north. A stable yard lay between the Board School and the terrace, facing the handsome ornamented-brick manager's house of Essex Wharf (demolished 1990). Nichols' body was found lying in front of the yard gate with its head to the east.

After the murder (and in consequence of it), the name Buck's Row was changed to Durward Street. The street line remains today, but most surrounding buildings have been demolished.

BUKI, MRS
Former landlady of Mary Jane Kelly. According to the *Star* of 12 November 1888, Mrs Buki was the 'lady' living in one of the roads off St George's Street (the western end of The Highway) with whom, according to **Mrs Carthy**, Kelly lodged on first coming to the East End. Mrs Buki accompanied Kelly to Knightsbridge, where they recovered a number of Kelly's clothes from another lady's house.

A single newspaper report gives us no guarantee that the name was correctly heard and spelled.

BURNS, ELIZABETH
Prostitute. On 18 September 1888 she took **Charles Ludwig** under a railway arch off the Minories, but ran out screaming when he threatened her with a knife, and reported him to a policeman in Aldgate. According to the Press Association she was 18 years old, and had one arm, so she may well have been **'One-Armed Liz'**.

BURY, WILLIAM HENRY (1859–89)
Alleged suspect. Wife-murderer, hanged in Dundee, April 1889. Told police his wife had committed suicide. Her body was found in a box in his basement flat with strangulation marks and deep, Ripper-like abdominal

stabs. Chalked on a door to the tenements was 'Jack the Ripper is at the back of this door', and beside the stairs leading down to Bury's flat were the words, 'Jack the Ripper is in this sellar' [sic]. Bury had come to Dundee from Bow in January. The *New York Times*, 12 February 1889, suggested that he was the Ripper and murdered his wife because she suspected him.

See **Euan Macpherson**.

BUTLER, DETECTIVE CHIEF SUPERINTENDENT ARTHUR
Theorist. Joined Metropolitan Police 1938; retired 1968. In 1972 Butler contributed articles to the *Sun* which embellished William Stewart's theory of a midwife-abortionist '**Jill the Ripper**'. Butler said she lived near Brick Lane; mutilated bodies to disguise failed abortions; was blackmailed by Emma Elizabeth Smith and an accomplice named '**Fingers Freddy**'; wheeled bodies to their dumping-spots in a perambulator.

Butler claimed his source was oral tradition from people whose uncles and aunts personally remembered the details. Subsequently the entire 'Jill the Ripper' theory has collapsed with the discovery of **Dr Bond**'s medical report, proving that Mary Jane Kelly was not pregnant.

BYFIELD, SERGEANT JAMES GEORGE
Joined City of London Police 1868; City Warrant no. 4171; retired 1895. Station Sergeant at Bishopsgate Police Station, on duty at 8.45 p.m., 29 September 1888, when Catharine Eddowes was brought into the station very drunk. Byfield put her in a cell until she had sobered up. At 1.00 a.m. she gave **Police Constable George Hult** her name as Mary Ann Kelly and her address as Fashion Street before being released.

C

CADOCHE, CADOSCH or **CADOSH, ALBERT** (born c. 1865)
Witness at Annie Chapman's inquest. Young carpenter, resident at 27 Hanbury Street, next door to murder site. Testified that at 5.30 a.m. on 8 September he went into the yard of his house and heard from the yard of no. 29 a voice say, 'No!' A few minutes later he heard what he believed to be something falling against the wooden fence dividing the yards. He heard nothing more and his suspicions were not aroused. He went to work passing Spitalfields church at 5.32, and saw no one in Hanbury Street as he left his house.

Coroner **Wynne Baxter**, summing up nine days later, said that Cadoche had mistakenly reported hearing the cry at 5.15 – fifteen minutes before **Mrs Darrell** saw Annie Chapman alive on the street. In fact, if *The Times* reports are accurate, it was Mr Baxter who was confusing the witnesses' times.

CAMERON, PROFESSOR JAMES (1930–)
Pathologist. Opinions cited by **Donald Rumbelow**. Like **Francis Camps**, he believes the Ripper throttled victims before using a knife. He has also suggested that the London Hospital drawings and photographs of Catharine Eddowes indicate a right-handed murderer from the drag to the right of the abdominal incision.

Professor Cameron has further suggested that the victims might have been killed by strangulation from behind as they pulled up their skirts and presented themselves anally to a supposed client. (See under **M.O.** for discussion.)

CAMPS, FRANCIS (1905–1972)
Pathologist. Publications include: *The Investigation of Murder* (with Richard Barber, 1966); *Camps on Crime*, 1973.

In *The Investigation of Murder*, Camps pointed out that contemporary pathologists all assumed that the Ripper killed his victims quickly and cleanly with a knife. But modern experience shows that sadistic sexual murderers most frequently strangle their victims. Throat-cutting would not have been quick, clean and quiet compared with strangulation. Camps was thus probably the first person since **Wynne Baxter** at Annie Chapman's inquest to point toward today's impression of the Ripper's **M.O.**

Wrote 'More About Jack the Ripper' for *London Hospital Gazette* to accompany drawings and diagrams supplied to **Mr Langham** for Catharine Eddowes' inquest, which Camps's assistant Sam Hardy discovered in London Hospital basement.

CANSBY, INSPECTOR WILLIAM (b. 1852)

Warrant no. 52772. With **Sergeant Thick**, organised a line-up in which **Emmanuel Violenia** identified **John Pizer** as the man he had seen with Annie Chapman shortly before her murder.

CARTHY, MRS

Informant. Landlady, from Breezer's Hill, Ratcliff Highway. Told press that Mary Jane Kelly had lodged with her after a period lodging with a woman in St George's Street (the western end of the Ratcliff Highway) when she left the West End. Claimed the St George's Street landlady had accompanied Kelly to a French 'lady's' residence in Knightsbridge to reclaim her box and expensive dresses. This is the only known corroboration for Kelly's reported claim to have worked in a 'gay house' with French connections in the West End.

   Mrs Carthy said that Kelly left Breezer's Hill in late 1886 and went to live with a man who was connected with the building trade. (Possibly **Joseph Fleming**.) **Joseph Barnett** called Mrs Carthy's 'a bad house'.

   See also **Mrs Phoenix**, **Mrs Buki**.

CARTWRIGHT, POLICE CONSTABLE

Directed by **Inspector Spratling** to conduct a thorough search of the scene of **'Polly' Nichols'** murder and the surrounding neighbourhood.

CASEBOOK ON JACK THE RIPPER, A

Book by **Richard Whittington-Egan** (1975). This and **Donald Rumbelow**'s *The Complete Jack the Ripper* comprised the first full-length accounts of the case which did not attempt to identify the murderer.

   Whittington-Egan's concise but very important study concentrated on presenting accurate facts and correcting legendary accretions. Among the essential historical revisions presented were: recognition of the postmark on the 'dear old boss' postcard (see **'Jack the Ripper' letters**), proving that it was mailed *after* the press had described the double murders, and not before; establishing that there was no pile of coins and rings at Annie Chapman's feet; correctly identifying Wentworth Model Dwellings as the site of the **Goulston Street graffito**; casting serious doubt on the probability of the **Lusk kidney**'s having come from Catharine Eddowes' body.

   Whittington-Egan also discovered the letter from **Dr Benjamin Howard** to the **Spectator** which refuted his alleged involvement in covering-up **Sir William Gull**'s guilt. (Cf. **Stephen Knight**.)

CASTLE ALLEY (today part of Old Castle Street)

Alice McKenzie's murder site. Former almost enclosed alley running north-south between Old Castle Street and Whitechapel High Street. Today absorbed by the southern end of Old Castle Street.

   The alley was entered by a very narrow covered entry from Whitechapel High Street. The north end, with Public Baths and a Board School on the western side, was sealed by two bollards to prevent wheeled traffic from passing between Old Castle Street and Castle Alley. The body was found about halfway along the 180-yard alley, on the western side, outside the back door into David King's contractors' premises. The opposite side of the alley was lined with residential house backs, whose ground floor was protected from passing pedestrians by a wooden hoarding extending across the pavement. The alley was used at night to hold costermongers' carts and barrows.

In consequence of the murder, the narrow entry was demolished and the street widened as an extension of Old Castle Street.

CAUNTER, SERGEANT ELI (b. 1852)
Warrant no. 55750. Traced 'Pearly Poll' (see **Mary Ann Connolly**) when she had gone into hiding with her cousin. **F. P. Wensley** described him as a valued colleague in H Division, Nicknamed 'Tommy Roundhead'.

CHALKED MESSAGE, THE
See **Goulston Street graffito**.

CHANDLER, INSPECTOR JOSEPH LUNISS (b. 1850)
First senior policeman to handle the finding of Annie Chapman's body. Joined Metropolitan Police 1873. Warrant no. 56638. Demoted to Sergeant for drunkenness on duty, 1892; retired, 1898.

He was on duty at Commercial Street Police Station at 6.02 a.m., 8 September 1888, when he saw men running up Hanbury Street. Told of the murder, he went to the site: sent for **Dr Phillips**; sent to the Station for an ambulance; and notified Scotland Yard. He cleared the passage in 29 Hanbury Street of people, and covered the body with sacking.

12 September he was reported in the *Star* as saying 'with a laugh' that the alleged bloodstains on the fence of 25 Hanbury Street seen by **Laura Sickings** were sprinkles of urine.

Much is made by **John Morrison** of the fact that Mrs Belloc Lowndes names a police inspector Joseph Chandler in her novel *The Lodger*, but there is no reason to suppose she had received inside information from the Commercial Street Station Inspector, let alone that she bought it for thirty shillings [£1.50] at 6.30 p.m. on 9 November 1888, as Morrison asserts.

CHAPMAN, ANNIE (1841–88)
Second Ripper victim. Born Eliza Anne Smith in Paddington. Father, George Smith, a Lifeguardsman, married her mother, Ruth Chapman, 1842, and family moved to Windsor, 1856. 1869, married **John Chapman** at All Saints Church, Knightsbridge. Lived West London until 1881, when moved back to Windsor. Two daughters (one died 1882), one (crippled) son. Shortly before her daughter Emily's death, Annie abandoned her family and returned to London, receiving sporadic allowances from Chapman until his death in 1886. Allegedly her alcoholism and immorality broke up the marriage. But acquaintances described her as only occasionally drunk. (Cf. **John Chapman**'s death.) Thereafter lived variously by hawking her own crochet work, selling matches or flowers, living off men friends, and occasionally prostituting herself. During 1886 she lived at 30 Dorset Street with a sievemaker named or nicknamed Jack Sivvey. From about May 1888 she lived mainly at **Crossingham's Lodging House**, 35 Dorset Street.

She stood 5ft tall, was stout, had dark wavy brown hair, blue eyes and a thick nose. Police and press said front teeth were missing from her lower jaw; **Dr Bagster Phillips** said her front teeth were perfect. Phillips also reported that at the time of her death she was undernourished, with chronic diseases of the lungs and brain membranes which would before long have killed her.

During the first week of September she fought with **Eliza Cooper**. According to Annie's friends the dispute arose because Annie told 'Harry the Hawker' she saw Eliza steal a florin from him, replacing it with a halfpenny. According to Eliza, the provoking halfpenny had been thrown at her by Annie in lieu of the return of her soap, which had been borrowed for the use of **Ted Stanley**. Both accounts agree that a halfpenny and a man who appeared to be sharing the ladies' favours lay behind the fight, which was variously described as taking place on 1, 2, 4, 5 and 6 September, and in **The Britannia**, in the kitchen at Crossingham's, or starting in one and resuming in the other. Annie suffered a black eye and bruising about the chest from this fight, and complained to **Amelia Palmer** that she would have to go to the Infirmary. No woman matching her description was admitted to Whitechapel or Spitalfields Workhouse Infirmaries at this time, but she may have collected some medication.

At 11.30 p.m., 7 September, **Timothy Donovan**, deputy of Crossingham's, let her into the kitchen. **William Stevens** saw her there at 12.12 a.m., slightly the worse for drink. She took a box of pills from her pocket and when the box broke, put the pills in a torn piece of envelope taken from the mantelpiece. It bore the crest of the Sussex Regiment, the letter M in a man's handwriting, and a postmark 'London, 28 August, 1888'. She probably left the lodging house then, and went for a drink shortly afterwards. (See **Frederick Stevens**.) By 1.35 a.m. she had returned. Donovan said he found her drunk and eating a baked potato in the kitchen, and asked for her doss money, to which she replied, 'I haven't got it. I am weak and ill and have been in the infirmary.' She left, saying, 'Don't let the bed. I'll be back soon.'

John Evans the watchman reported that she had just returned to Crossingham's, and told him she had been to see one of her sisters in Vauxhall and had just slipped out for a pint of beer. She also said to him, 'I won't be long, Brummy. See that Tim keeps the bed for me.' West saw her go into Paternoster Row in the direction of Brushfield Street.

It is probable that Donovan, Stevens and West all mistook Chapman's general ill-health for intoxication. (See under **Dr Phillips**.)

She was reportedly seen in **The Ten Bells** opposite Spitalfields Market soon after it opened at 5.00 a.m., but this was a mistake in identity (see **Edward McKenna**). Around 5.30, **Elizabeth Darrell** saw a woman whom she identified as Chapman on the pavement outside 29 Hanbury Street, talking to an apparently foreign man, a little taller than herself, who said to her, 'Will you?' to which Chapman replied, 'Yes'. Very shortly afterwards, **Albert Cadoche** possibly overheard the murderous assault in the back yard of no. 29.

Shortly before 6.00 a.m. **John Davis** went into the back yard of 29 Hanbury Street and found Chapman's body lying on her back parallel to the fence (which was on her left), with her head close to the house back door steps. Her dress was pulled above her knees exposing her striped stockings, and her intestines lay across her left shoulder. (See **Dr Bagster Phillips** for detailed injuries; **M.O.** for discussion of their significance.)

A small crowd gathered in the passage running from the Hanbury Street door of no. 29 to the back door (see **Henry Holland, James Green, James Kent, Mrs Hardyman**) and **Inspector Chandler** took charge shortly after

6.00 a.m. The immediate police search discovered the piece of torn envelope and two pills in a screw of paper. There was also a folded and saturated leather apron about two feet away from the standpipe in the yard. (See **'Leather Apron'** for significance.)

Dr Bagster Phillips arrived at about 6.30. After examining the body he ordered it to be taken to Whitechapel Workhouse Infirmary Mortuary in Eagle Street, off Old Montague Street. He then discovered the contents of Annie Chapman's pocket (which had been cut open) lying in a surprisingly neat or deliberate pile: a piece of coarse muslin, two combs, and almost certainly two farthings, which may have been brightly polished. (See **Inspector Reid**, **Major Henry Smith**.) The coins were described in press reports the following day; were not mentioned in reports of the inquest; but reappeared in newspaper stories two weeks later, accompanied by or incorporating an alleged 'pile' of Annie Chapman's rings. This was a canard. Chapman had been wearing three brass rings when she left Crossingham's and they were missing from her body. Abrasions on her ring finger showed where one had been torn off, probably by her murderer. The rings were never traced, despite widely publicised police enquiries. **Martin Howells** has privately remarked to the authors that they might have been stolen by mortuary attendants.

The body was washed and laid out by **Mary Simonds** and Frances Wright, to the annoyance of Bagster Phillips when he came to carry out the post mortem. At 11.30 a.m. Annie was identified by Amelia Palmer. On Monday 10 September, **Emmanuel Violenia** was shown the body in the mortuary.

On Friday, 14 September Annie Chapman was buried secretly at Manor Park. Members of her family attended the funeral.

CHAPMAN, FREDERICK RICHARD (1851–88)
Alleged suspect. Real name of **'Dr Merchant'**, pseudonymously identified by **B. E. Reilly** as the only Brixton doctor whose death coincided with the ending of the murders, and therefore probably **Police Constable Robert Spicer**'s suspect. MB and CM, 1874 (Glasgow). MO, Brixton District. Former MO, Fever and Smallpox Hospital, Hull; and Surgeon, Hull and Sculcoates Dispensary. Born in Poona, India; son of an army NCO. Came to London from provincial practice, 1886. Wrote pamphlets on medical subjects and letters to professional press. Died of septic tubercular abscess, conspicuously poor, probably because of long illness.

CHAPMAN, GEORGE (1865–1903)
Alleged suspect. See **Severin Klosowski**.

CHAPMAN, JOHN (1843–86)
Husband of **Annie Chapman**. Domestic head coachman. A relative of her mother, Ruth Chapman, he married Annie on 1 May 1869.

1870, the couple lived in Bayswater; 1873, in a Mews off Berkeley Square. **Timothy Donovan** alleged that Mrs Pearcer of Hackney, a friend of Annie's, told him Chapman lost his post as valet to a gentleman in Bond Street because of Annie's dishonesty.

By 1881 he was working for Josiah or Joseph Weeks at St Leonard's Mill Farm Cottage, Windsor. In 1882 the marriage broke down. According to the police this was because of Annie's 'drunken and immoral ways'. He paid her 10/- [50p] a week, though not, apparently, absolutely regularly, until his death at Grove Road, Windsor, on Christmas Day, 1886. He died of cirrhosis of the liver and dropsy, which throws a question over *Annie*'s supposed alcoholism as causing the marital breakdown.

Amelia Palmer alleged, incorrectly, that he was a veterinary surgeon.

CHAPPELL, MARY
Friend of **Mrs Fiddymont** who, like her, saw a strange man with a bloodstained hand in the Prince Albert Tavern. Chappell left the pub by a different door and pointed the man out to Joseph Taylor.

CHEEKS, MARGARET 'MOG'
Prostitute fellow-lodger of Alice McKenzie who was missed from her lodgings on the night of McKenzie's murder, 17 July 1889. Estranged wife of Charlie Cheeks. Mog was missing for two days after the discovery of McKenzie's body, leading to a short-lived fear that she, too, had been murdered. In fact she had been staying with her sister.

CHILDERS, RIGHT HONOURABLE HUGH CULLING EARDLEY (1827–96)
Gladstonian Home Secretary. MP for Pontefract, 1860–85; for Edinburgh, 1886. First Lord of the Admiralty, 1868–71; Chancellor of the Duchy of Lancaster, 1872–3; Secretary of State for war, 1880–2; Chancellor of the Exchequer, 1882–5; Home Secretary, 1886. As Home Secretary, he appointed **Sir Charles Warren** Metropolitan Police Commissioner.

CHRIST CHURCH, SPITALFIELDS
Parish church of **Spitalfields**. Commissioned under the Fifty New Churches Act of 1711 and paid for through a coal tax, it was designed by Nicholas Hawksmoor. Struck by lightning in 1841. Some alterations were made, but it is still seen as a Hawksmoor masterpiece. Now only occasionally used for worship, but concerts are held there and it is the venue for the well-attended Spitalfields Festival. The crypt is used as a rehabilitation centre for alcoholics. The small park beside the graveyard was known as 'Itchy Park' because vagrants and derelicts slept there.

The Ten Bells stands opposite the church.

CHRONICLES OF CRIME, THE
Three handwritten books of notes and observations on various crimes compiled by **Dr Thomas Dutton**. **Donald McCormick** saw them in 1932 and uses them extensively in *The Identity of Jack the Ripper*. In 1935, on Dutton's death, a Miss Hermione Dudley stated that she had been given them 'some time ago'. Their whereabouts today is unknown.

CHURCHILL, LORD RANDOLPH HENRY SPENCER (1849–94)
Recently alleged suspect. Conservative statesman. Son of Sixth Duke of Marlborough and father of Sir Winston Churchill. After Disraeli's death, promoted the Primrose League and the cause of a colourful radical Toryism. Secretary of State for India, 1885–6. Chancellor of the Exchequer, 1886; resigned office the same year in protest over financial demands of ministers for the army and navy, effectively terminating his political career. He published articles on his travels in South Africa in 1891, but thereafter

faded from the public eye. He died of syphilis, contracted, according to Frank Harris's unreliable memoirs, from a squalid and impoverished prostitute smuggled into his bed as a practical joke by companions on a youthful drinking spree.

His passionate partisan nature led Lord Randolph to throw himself energetically into the violent personal quarrel between his brother, the Marquess of Blandford, and **Albert Edward**, Prince of Wales (arising in 1876 from the Prince's tactless attempt to force a marriage between Blandford and his own former mistress, Lady Aylesford). Lord Randolph went so far as to threaten the Prince with blackmail, using letters from Lady Aylesford which had come into his possession. This reckless action led to his banishment from court circles and temporary social ostracism.

In spite of this, according to **Joseph Sickert** and **Melvyn Fairclough**, Churchill felt bound to take the lead in protecting the Prince's eldest son's good name and the position of the crown when, allegedly, East End prostitutes centring on Mary Jane Kelly attempted to use their knowledge of **Prince Albert Victor**'s supposed secret marriage to **Annie Elizabeth Crook** for blackmailing purposes. Sickert and Fairclough say that Churchill was the very highest **Freemason** in the land in 1888, and therefore organised the conspiracy of Freemasons in which **Sir William Gull**, assisted by **John Netley**, **Frederico Albericci** and, possibly, **J. K. Stephen**, murdered the women. They note that (apart from the shabby-genteel appearance) Churchill fits the description of the man **George Hutchinson** saw accost Mary Jane Kelly on the night of her death. And they find the name of Churchill, with most of the other co-conspirators, listed with cryptic clues in torn pages from the 1896 diary which Mr Sickert says was given to his father by **Inspector Abberline**.

See *The Ripper and the Royals*; also *Jack the Ripper: The Final Solution* and *Joseph Gorman Sickert* for variant stories emanating from Mr Sickert.

CIMARRON CITY (1958, USA)
TV series (26 x 50 min.) starring George Montgomery. Western about peace-keeping mayor; episode 'Knife in the Darkness'; Ripper kills dance-hall girls.

CITY OF LONDON POLICE
Founded 1839, following success of Robert Peel's Metropolitan Police Force, which the City of London had refused to accept in replacement of its tried and tested constables. Responsible to the Corporation of the City of London, its jurisdiction covers the administrative area of the City (roughly the square mile lying north of London Bridge).

Catharine Eddowes was the only Ripper victim murdered in the City. The force was expected to liaise with the **Metropolitan Police** once involved in the Whitechapel Murders investigation. According to **Walter Dew**, cooperation between the two forces was very good throughout the case. But see **Henry Matthews**, **James McWilliam**.

In 1888–9 the City Commissioner was **Sir James Fraser**; his deputy was Major **Henry Smith**, and James McWilliam was head of the CID.

CLAPP, GEORGE
Witness at Catharine Eddowes' inquest. Caretaker at no. 5 Mitre Street,

whose bedroom overlooked Mitre Square. Heard nothing of the murder.

CLARENCE, DUKE OF
See **Albert Victor, Prince**.

CLARKE, GEORGE
Builder's merchant who kept materials in the yard between 106 and 108 Poplar High Street, where Rose Mylett's body was found.

CLEVELAND STREET SCANDAL
Notorious incident of 1889, when investigation of missing postal orders incidentally uncovered a number of Post Office boys who supplemented their wages by working in a male brothel, run by Charles Hammond, in 19 Cleveland Street.

When the brothel was raided and its proprietor's associates prosecuted, they made allegations against a number of society gentlemen who had been among their clients. Lord Arthur Somerset, bachelor equerry to the Prince of Wales, discreetly retired to Dieppe rather than face the enquiry. Lord Euston faced it, claiming that he had been misled into expecting an exhibition of posed female nudes when he visited the premises. The authorities were distinctly perturbed by the suggested implication of a Very Important Person, designated 'P.A.V.' in official memoranda. Strenuous and successful efforts were made to keep his name out of the hearings. This personage was almost certainly **Prince Albert Victor**.

Since **Joseph Sickert**'s tale of the Prince's secret and illegal marriage makes play with various Cleveland Street locations (for the shop where **Annie Elizabeth Crook** allegedly worked, the studio where **Walter Sickert** allegedly introduced the lovers, and the love-nest from which Annie was allegedly kidnapped by Special Branch men), it has been suggested that the notorious Cleveland Street scandal has contributed details (like the Special Branch raid) to Mr Sickert's story.

Abberline was prominent in the Cleveland Street investigation. **Swanson**, proceeding determinedly against rent boys in the later 1890s, noted Lord Euston (as well as several of the witnesses at Oscar Wilde's trial) still participating in West End homosexual functions or being blackmailed.

Cf. *The Ripper and the Royals*.

COHEN, AARON DAVIS (1865–89)
aka **David Cohen**. Recently alleged suspect. Brought before Thames Magistrates Court, 7 December 1888, by **Police Constable J. Patrick** 91H as a lunatic wandering at large. Named as Aaron Davis Cohen. Sent by court to workhouse infirmary for observation. His hearing minuted with those of **Gertrude Smith**, **Mary Jones** and **Ellen Hickey**. Delivered to Whitechapel Workhouse Infirmary by PC Patrick at 5.00 p.m. the same day under the name of David Cohen. Age given as 23; address, 86 Leman Street. No known relatives.

Dr Larder, the workhouse medical superintendent, reported that Cohen was supposed to have attempted suicide; that he was violent, noisy and difficult to manage, and threatened other patients. Henry Williams, infirmary attendant, reported that he damaged infirmary fittings, and shouted and danced about if unrestrained. On 21 December Cohen was discharged to Colney Hatch Lunatic Asylum.

Brought to Colney Hatch under restraint, Cohen threw himself on the ground on arrival. The asylum noted his occupation as tailor and that he was a foreign Jew. As he had done in the infirmary, he refused and spat out food at first. He was fed by tube, and put in strong dress to prevent him from tearing his clothes, though at no time was he straitjacketed.

28 December he was separated from other patients as dangerous, and on the same date was noted as physically ill. Throughout the next nine months he was restless, dirty, aggressive, mischievous and destructive. But on 15 October 1889 he became enfeebled and was confined to bed, where, 20 October, he died of exhaustion of mania and pulmonary phthisis.

Martin Fido argues that he was **Anderson's suspect** and Jack the Ripper, stating that a comprehensive search through London asylum, infirmary and pauper lunatic records for 1888–90 reveals no other inmate who fits Anderson's description and whose incarceration coincides with the termination of the murders. He also notes that Cohen, uniquely in the period, died prematurely after transfer to Colney Hatch, as the **Swanson marginalia** claim happened to the suspect. He suggests that the name of a lunatic at large suffering from raving mania with no known relatives was unlikely to have been accurately established, and that the address 86 Leman Street must be inaccurate as it was a Protestant Boys' Club. This has not seemed persuasive to other researchers.

The case against Cohen as the Ripper is that Swanson unequivocally names Anderson's suspect as **Kosminski,** and this name is corroborated in the only other police source to name a Polish Jewish suspect – the **Macnaghten memoranda.** Nor is there any documented reason to doubt the general data on Cohen's name, occupation, etc. recorded by the court and asylum. It is further noted that the CID were still on the alert after Cohen's death, and, according to Swanson, the identification of Anderson's suspect also took place after Cohen had died. For the attempt to reconcile Cohen's guilt with the Swanson marginalia and Macnaghten memoranda, see **Nathan Kaminsky,** *The Crimes, Detection and Death of Jack the Ripper.*

COHEN, DAVID (1865–89)
See **Aaron Davis Cohen.**

COHEN, JACOB
Lay witness for certification of **Aaron Kosminski.** Resided 51 Carter Lane, EC. Said Kosminski refused food from others, and went about the streets picking up bread from the gutters and drinking from standpipes. Refused to be washed and had not worked for years. Took up a knife and threatened his sister's life.

COHEN, N.
Should have appeared to charge **Ellen Hickey** with assault before Thames Magistrates Court at the same time and under the same Minute of Attendance as **Aaron Davis Cohen.** Hickey was discharged as N. Cohen did not appear.

COHN, DR (or Koch)
Recently alleged suspect. Named by **Inspector Keaton.** Nothing more is presently known.

COINS AND RINGS, pile of
See under **Annie Chapman**.

COLES, FRANCES (1865–91)
aka 'Carrotty Nell', Frances Hawkins, Frances Coleman.
Final alleged Ripper victim. Good-looking daughter of a respectable former bootmaker whom she frequently visited in Bermondsey Workhouse. Employed as wholesale chemist's packer until c.1884 when she went on the streets.

At 2.20 a.m., 14 February 1891, **Police Constable Thompson** 240H found her lying in Swallow Gardens: a narrow alley running under the railway arches between Chambers Street and Rosemary Lane (today's Royal Mint Street). Her throat had just been cut and was bleeding profusely, but her eyes were open and she was still alive. As he attended to her, he heard footsteps running away toward Rosemary Lane. Frances Coles died on the stretcher produced to take her to hospital. Her left ear was 'torn' but completely healed over as if an earring had been ripped out some years in the past. Her black crêpe hat lay in the roadway beside her. There was another hat pinned to the folds of her dress.

The threat of a revived 'Ripper' scare in the newspapers brought **Superintendent Arnold, Inspector Reid**, Chief Constable **Melville Macnaghten** and Assistant Commissioner **Robert Anderson** to the scene of the crime the following morning, and the site of crime was very carefully examined. Blood was taken for analysis, and 2/- [10p], presumed to be the woman's earnings (cf. '**Rosy**'), found hidden behind a lamp-post or gutterpipe at the end of the alley. Early enquiries produced a witness called William 'Jumbo' Friday who said he had seen Coles standing near Swallow Gardens with a stocky man who looked foreign and like a ship's fireman. Enquiries in the docks revealed that Coles had spent most of the previous two days with **Thomas James Sadler**, an extremely violent and volatile ship's fireman from the *Fez*, presently moored at London Docks. He had bought her the new hat which led her to pin her old one under her dress.

On 13 February he had quarrelled with her after being mugged. Twice in the evening he had turned up at the common lodging house where they had stayed, the second time covered with blood. Police arrested Sadler, and presented a very thorough case at the inquest (conducted by Coroner **Wynne Baxter** at the Working Lads' Institute, Whitechapel, on 15, 16, 20, 23 and 27 February) hoping he would be sent forward for trial. The Seamen's Union paid for Sadler to have proper legal representation, and in consequence it was established that 'Jumbo' Friday had actually seen a local couple who knew him and had recognised him (Kate McCarthy and Thomas Fowles); and that Sadler really had been in a fight that had nothing to do with Frances Coles when he turned up bloodstained at her lodgings. The jury found 'Murder by a person or persons unknown' and Sadler was discharged. Three years later, however, in the **Macnaghten memoranda**, Melville Macnaghten hinted his unshaken conviction of Sadler's guilt.

COLICOTT –
Criminal sadist. In the Kennington district, during January or February 1891, according to fugitive references in the **Macnaghten memoranda**, Colicott stabbed about six young women from behind. He was arrested, but discharged because of faulty identification. Macnaghten believed that

Thomas Cutbush was imitating Colicott when he stabbed Miss Johnson a few weeks later. Articles in the *Sun* in 1894 confused Cutbush with Colicott.

COLLARD, INSPECTOR EDWARD (1846–92)
Witness at Catharine Eddowes' inquest. Joined City of London Police, 1868. Died, 1892, as Chief Inspector, Bishopsgate Division. Station Inspector on duty in Bishopsgate, 30 September 1888. He was called to Mitre Square to see the body and timed his arrival as 2.03 a.m. He organised a search of the district immediately, and house-to-house interviews the following day.

For some reason, *The Times* ascribed his evidence at the inquest to **Superintendent James McWilliam**.

COLLIER, EDWARD
Deputy coroner for the South Eastern Division of Middlesex, conducted inquest on Martha Tabram.

COLLINS, POLICE CONSTABLE EDWARD ALBERT, 426H
Collins was fetched, in company with **Police Constable Lamb**, by **Morris Eagle** after the discovery of **Elizabeth Stride**'s body. Collins immediately went to summon Dr Blackwell, returning with Blackwell's assistant Dr Kay at 1.16 a.m. precisely (exactly the time Blackwell gave for his own arrival). At 5.30 a.m. Collins washed away all traces of blood from Dutfield's Yard.

COLWELL, MRS SARAH
Informant. Resident of Brady Street (at eastern end of Buck's Row) who claimed to have been awakened during the small hours of 31 August by the noise of a running woman screaming. It appeared to Mrs Colwell that the woman was being struck as she ran, but there was no sound of pursuing footsteps. The following morning, Mrs Colwell and certain journalists believed they saw spots of blood in Brady Street, and some newspapers speculated that Mary Ann Nichols might have been killed there and removed to Buck's Row. The police discounted this entirely and doubted the presence of the blood spots. No other witness heard anything untoward in Brady Street.

COMMERCIAL ROAD
Arterial road, running east-west from Aldgate to Limehouse, lined by houses, shops, tenements, small factories and warehouses. Plumber's Row, Mulberry Street and Settles Street ran into it from the north; **Berner Street** from the south, immediately facing Plumber's Row. Constructed by the Commercial Road Company in the first decade of the nineteenth century. Extended from Back Church Lane to Whitechapel High Street, 1870.

Not to be confused with **Commercial Street**.

COMMERCIAL STREET
Major highway running north–south from Shoreditch to Whitechapel High Street, passing between Christ Church, Spitalfields, and Spitalfields Market.

From **Christ Church** to **Whitechapel** was built in 1845 with the intention of demolishing slum alleys and courts that had sprung up around Christ Church. The aim was not really successful, and the slum denizens swarmed into the adjacent streets around **Dorset Street, Flower and Dean Street**, and Thrawl Street. The extension from Christ Church to Shoreditch was opened in 1858.

Dorset Street runs into Commercial Street from the west, facing Christ Church graveyard and its abutting garden ('Itchy Park', where the homeless slept rough). **The Britannia** stood on the corner of Dorset Street and Commercial Street. On the other side of the road, a little further north, **The Ten Bells** stands. Further north again, **Hanbury Street** branches off, running south-east. Corbett's Court, where **Robert Paul** worked, lay on the northern side of the corner of Hanbury Street and Commercial Street. North again, on the western side of the road, stood the Commercial Street Police Station (now converted into housing association apartments).

Church Street (today's Fournier Street) ran to the east between The Ten Bells and the church. South of Itchy Park, on the eastern side of the street, the **Queen's Head** stood on the corner of Fashion Street. South again, Flower and Dean Street and Thrawl Street ran off to the east before Wentworth Street crosses Commercial Street. **The Princess Alice** (today The City Darts) stands on the corner with Wentworth Street. **George Yard** and **Goulston Street** ran south of Wentworth Street, one block away from Commercial Street to the east and west respectively.

Cf. **George Hutchinson, Dr Pedachenko.**

COMPLETE JACK THE RIPPER, THE
Book by **Donald Rumbelow** (1975). The first, and still the outstanding, attempt to present an overview of the whole case in its historical context, together with a survey of theories that have been put forward as to the Ripper's identity, and the use made of the figure of the Ripper in the arts and popular culture.

It is distinguished by the massive amount of important new information Rumbelow has brought to his study of the case, from the reprinting of **Dr Bond**'s general report on all the medical evidence in the first edition, to new information from Sweden about Elizabeth Stride included in the 1987 reissue.

It is a strength that Rumbelow has updated the book with new information from his own and others' researches, although the mass of material covered means that some early exploded canards have survived in later editions to mislead the unwary.

None the less, this book has deservedly stood as the standard work on Jack the Ripper since its publication.

CONNOLLY, MARY ANN (b. 1838)
Aka 'Pearly Poll'. Witness at Martha Tabram's inquest. Unmarried prostitute; in August 1888 had known Tabram (as Emma Turner) for four to five months and resided at **Crossingham's Lodging House** for two months. Big woman, with low, husky voice, drink-reddened face.

Testified that she and Tabram were together in the company of a guardsman and a corporal from c. 10.00 p.m., 7 August. Met the soldiers in **The Two Brewers**. Drank together in several pubs until c. 11.45 p.m., when Connolly took the corporal up Angel Alley, while Martha Tabram took the guardsman up **George Yard** (today's Gunthorpe Street). Left the corporal at the corner of George Yard c. 12.15 a.m.

After police questioning, Connolly disappeared and was only traced by **Sergeant Caunter** to her cousin's (Mrs Shean of 4 Fuller's Court, Drury Lane) some days later. She was taken to an identity parade of Scots Guards at the Tower of London, but failed to recognise the men she and Martha had been with. She now claimed the soldiers had white cap bands, which the police said indicated the Coldstream Guards, so she was taken by police to Wellington Barracks, Birdcage Walk, where she picked out Guardsmen George and Skipper from a parade of Coldstreams. Both established firm alibis, and police concluded Connolly did not intend to help them.

The *Echo* (20 September 1888) reported there were detectives working on 'a slight clue given them by Pearly Poll' which 'was not thought much of the time', but now supported by **Eliza Cooper** and **Elizabeth Allen** seemed to point suspicion at 'a man actually living not far from Buck's Row'. It is not known what the clue was, but it may have something to do with 'Leather Apron'.

CONVALESCENT POLICE SEASIDE HOME
Alleged site of identification of **Anderson**'s suspect. The **Swanson marginalia** say that the suspect was 'identified at the Seaside Home where he had been sent by us with difficulty in order to subject him to identification'.

By 1910, when Swanson was writing, 'the Seaside Home' was normal police vernacular for the Convalescent Police Seaside Home. The first of these had been opened at 51 Clarendon Villas, West Brighton, in March 1890. In 1893 a purpose-built police Seaside Home was opened, and subsequently the establishment moved to several different addresses. Thus, if Swanson was correct, the identification took place at least eighteen months after the original sighting, and sixteen months after the last Ripper murder. (Cf. Swanson's observation, 'And after this identification which suspect knew, no other murder of this kind took place in London.')

Any attempt to address this difficulty has to meet the certainty that Swanson is remembering *something* that happened. Hypothetical solutions include the suggestion that Swanson referred to an identification in one of the various privately owned homes to which Metropolitan Policemen were sent on convalescence between December 1887, when the Police Convalescent Home Fund was started, and 1890, when the home for exclusive police use was opened; that Swanson unwittingly referred to a different identification of a different suspect, not realising that **Dr Robert Anderson** had previously mentioned the identification as taking place after the suspect was in an asylum; or that Swanson's memory was absolutely accurate, meaning that the entire Scotland Yard chiefs' belief that they knew the Ripper's identity is questionable.

CONWAY, THOMAS
Husband, probably common-law, of Catharine Eddowes. Former private in 18th Royal Irish Foot from which he drew a pension under the name of Thomas Quinn. Cohabited with Eddowes from c. 1864 in Wolverhampton. She bore him three children, had his initials tattooed on her arm, and claimed that they were legally married. According to Wolverhampton press the couple lived by selling chapbooks written by Conway.

The marriage broke down c. 1880. **Annie Phillips** blamed Eddowes' drinking and frequent absconding. **Elizabeth Fisher** blamed Conway's drinking and wife-beating. By the time of her murder they had not seen each other for some years.

COOK, ELIZABETH (1820–93).
Resident of no. 6 Cleveland Street, 1888–93. Confused by **Stephen Knight** with **Annie Elizabeth Crook**.

COOPER, ELIZA
Witness at Annie Chapman's inquest. Resident of **Crossingham's Lodging House;** probable prostitute. Quarrelled and fought with Chapman in the week before her murder (see under **Annie Chapman** for details). With **Elizabeth Allen**, she was cited by the *Echo*, 20 September 1888, as the source of information leading police to suspect 'a man actually living not far from Buck's Row'. This may have been connected with **'Leather Apron'**. (See also **John Pizer, Mary Ann Connolly**.)

COPSEY, MR AND MRS
Residents in 29 Hanbury Street (Annie Chapman's murder site). Cigar-makers, occupying the second-floor back room. In one press report described as **The Misses Huxley**.

CORAM, THOMAS
Witness at Elizabeth Stride's inquest. Labourer in coconut-fibre factory. Resident of Plumber's Row. Returning home from Bath Gardens off Brady Street at 12.30 a.m. on 29 September 1888, he found a dagger-shaped knife with a 9–10in blade, its handle wrapped in a bloodstained handkerchief, on the doorstep of Mr Christmas's laundry at 252 Whitechapel Road (north side). He summoned Police Constable Drage and went with him to Leman Street Police Station.
   The knife was completely irrelevant. The blade was round-ended, and could not have caused the injuries to the Ripper's victims; moreover it was in Coram's hands before Stride and Eddowes were killed.

CORONER, MARIA (b. 1867)
Hoaxer. Mantle-maker's employee of Bradford, said to be respectable. Charged, 21 October 1888, with causing a breach of the peace by sending letters signed 'Jack the Ripper' to the Chief Constable and a local paper, declaring the murderer's intention of coming to Bradford to 'do a little business'. She is the only auther of a **'Jack the Ripper' letter** who can be positively named.

COWDRY, SAMUEL AND SARAH (b. 1827 and 1828 respectively)
Clerk of Works in Police Department, and his wife. Employers of Mary Ann Nichols, who worked for these devout teetotallers at Ingleside, Rose Hill Road, Wandsworth, in May and July 1888, describing them to her father as 'very nice people'. She then absconded, stealing clothing valued at £3.10s.0d. (See under **Mary Ann Nichols** for her full description.)

COX, MARY ANN (born c. 1857)
Witness at Mary Kelly's inquest. 'A widow and an unfortunate', in her own words, residing at 5 Miller's Court. She gave important evidence about Kelly's return home drunk around midnight in the company of a blotchy-

faced man with a carrotty moustache; her singing; and footsteps leaving Miller's Court at dawn (see under **Mary Jane Kelly**). Mrs Cox accepted that the footsteps might be those of the beat policeman.

An inaccurate report of Mrs Cox's recollections, gathered from her niece by **Daniel Farson**, is a fascinating piece of oral history, showing the hold of the top-hatted toff Ripper image, and the tendency to improve Mrs Cox's own image from that she gave (above) at the inquest:

The night of the murder of Mary Kelly my aunt was very young, just married with one child. She was standing at her door and waiting for her husband who was a bit of a boozer. She saw Mary coming through the iron gate with this gentleman, a real toff. Mary was always bringing home men, mostly seamen from a pub called The Frying Pan, singing and holding their arms, with a bottle of gin under her arm. This night as they got under the lamp in the court they stopped. Mary's words was, 'All right, love. Don't pull me along.' My aunt said they were only a few yards away from her at the door; she said she saw him as plain as looking at her hand. He was a fine looking man, wore an overcoat with a cape, high hat, not a silk one, and Gladstone bag. As they went into the house, Mary called out 'Good night,' to my aunt.

Mrs Cox appeared in Thames Magistrates Court in August 1887 and January 1888 on assault charges. For the first, which may have been an assault on the arresting Police Constable Batten, she was sentenced to a month's imprisonment. For the second, an assault on Eliza Smith, she was fined five shillings after two remands. We take her estimated age from the court records.

COX, SARAH
Resident of 29 Hanbury Street, Annie Chapman's murder site. An old woman, allowed to stay in a third floor back room as a charity by **Mrs Richardson**.

CRAWFORD, HENRY HOMEWOOD (1850–1936)
City of London solicitor, acting for police at Catharine Eddowes' inquest. Educ. Thanet College. Admitted solicitor, 1872; practised in partnership with Samuel Chester at 90 Cannon Street, EC until 1935. Freemason and amateur actor. At Eddowes' inquest he requested the withholding of **Joseph Lawende**'s description of the man outside Church Passage with Eddowes, saying, 'I have special reason for not giving details as to the appearance of this man.'

CREAM, DR THOMAS NEILL (1850–92)
Alleged suspect. Poisoned four prostitutes in Lambeth, 1891–2. Arrested and convicted largely because of his obsessive habit of writing incriminatory letters over false names to the authorities. Allegedly overheard by hangman Billington to say, 'I am Jack the . . .' on the scaffold. But was definitely not the Ripper, as he was incarcerated in Joliet Prison, Illinois, during the end of 1888 for the murder of a man called Stott. (See **Donald Bell**, Derek Davis.)

CRIME MONTHLY: WHO WAS JACK THE RIPPER?
LWT TV special documentary, broadcast (London area only) in 1990. Advanced **Aaron Kosminski** as the Ripper. Rehearsed the major pieces

of historical police evidence (**Macnaghten memoranda** and, especially, **Swanson marginalia**) and argued that Kosminski must be the Ripper. LWT photographed Kosminski's grave for the first time.

CRIMES AND TIMES OF JACK THE RIPPER
See *Autumn of Terror*.

CRIMES, DETECTION AND DEATH OF JACK THE RIPPER, THE
Book by Martin Fido (1987). Despite its admirable research, this book has not won over many informed adherents. It is generally accepted that it correctly identified the suspect **Kosminski** named in the **Macnaghten memoranda**, and some researchers have agreed that its serious historical investigation of the credibility of the police in the case was an improvement on the previous unthinking repetition of partisan political attacks on them. It is austerely presented, with sketch-maps of the murder sites as the sole illustrations, and a type which obscures the punctuation from many readers.

But it is the final argument which has disappointed or defeated almost all. The book noted that twenty-three-year-old Whitechapel immigrants of central European extraction recurred among the names unearthed along the trail of Kosminski, and proposed that two or three of these had been confused: partly because **Nathan Kaminsky** might have tried to hide his identity, and partly because the City and Metropolitan police might have suspected Kosminski and **David Cohen** respectively during their enquiries, subsequently concluding (wrongly) that the two men were one and the same '23-year-old Polish Jew in Colney Hatch'.

The argument has proved incomprehensible to most readers and persuasive to no researchers.

CRIMINALS AND CRIME: SOME FACTS AND SUGGESTIONS
Book by **Sir Robert Anderson** (1907). His remarks on the Ripper case in this book (see under **Anderson**) illustrate his conviction that the public habitually mistakes sensational crimes for important crimes.

CROOK, ALICE MARGARET (1885–1950)
Alleged daughter of **Prince Albert Victor**. According to **Joseph Sickert** and **Stephen Knight**, sole offspring of the liaison and illegal marriage between the prince and **Annie Elizabeth Crook**. Allegedly two attempts were made to eliminate Alice in road accidents in 1888 and 1892. For the former, see **Lizzie Madewell**. The latter, according to **Jean Overton Fuller**, took place in the presence of **Florence Pash**.

Knight stated that Alice was brought up by **Walter Sickert** in Dieppe, leaving him when she was eighteen, and subsequently marrying William Gorman but returning to become Sickert's mistress for twelve years when Gorman proved impotent. In fact, Alice and William Gorman lived together until his death, acknowledging five children. Joseph Sickert (one of the five) claims to be the result of a renewed liaison between his mother and Sickert which did not end her marital relations with Gorman, though he claims that Alice and Sickert had one previous child before her marriage.

All that can be substantiated of this story is that some parts of it were apparently known to Florence Pash prior to 1948.

See also *The Ripper and the Royals*.

CROOK, ANNIE ELIZABETH (1862–1920)
Alleged secret wife of **Prince Albert Victor**. Actual grandmother of **Joseph Sickert**, who has claimed that the Ripper murders were an establishment cover-up to preserve the secret. Daughter of William Crook (d. 1891) and Sarah Ann Crook (1838–1916). In 1885 gave birth to an illegitimate daughter, **Alice Margaret Crook** (father unknown), at St Marylebone workhouse. At this time she worked as a confectionery assistant and lived at 6 Cleveland Street. The following year the building was demolished. One of the flats thereafter erected on the site was occupied 1888–93 by an Elizabeth Cook, who has sometimes been confused with her.

In January 1891, Annie Elizabeth was living at 9 Pitt Street, Tottenham Court Road. Various subsequent addresses are known, and she spent much of her later life in workhouses. She died in the Lunacy Ward of Fulham Road Workhouse. She had never been certified, but probably would have been had she survived.

Contrary to Joseph Sickert's story, she was not resident at 6 Cleveland Street in April 1888 when he alleges Special Branch men kidnapped her. Nor was she incarcerated for the remainder of her life. Nor was she a Roman Catholic. Her alleged secret marriage would have been illegal under the Royal Marriages Act (1772) as contracted without the sovereign's permission, and no elaborate plot would have been necessary to have it discreetly set aside.

See also *The Ripper and the Royals*.

CROSS, CHARLES
(Forename variously mistranscribed **George**, etc., by contemporary press and some authors.) Witness at Mary Ann Nichols' inquest and the person who discovered her body. Carman, resident Doveton Street, Cambridge Heath Road, Bethnal Green, employed by Pickford's in Broad Street. At 3.45 a.m. saw the body lying opposite Essex Wharf, Buck's Row, and went to examine it, thinking at first it was an abandoned tarpaulin. Joined by **Robert Paul**, Cross concluded the woman was dead, and the two went on to Hanbury Street, where they found **Police Constable Mizen** and told him there was a woman lying lifeless in the gutter in Buck's Row.

CROSSINGHAM'S LODGING HOUSE
35 Dorset Street, Spitalfields. Opposite Miller's Court, where Mary Kelly was murdered. Managed by deputy **Timothy Donovan**. Frequented by a very large number of people associated with the Ripper case. See **Elizabeth Allen, Annie Chapman, Eliza Cooper, Mary Ann Connolly, George Hutchinson, 'Leather Apron', – West**.

CROSSMAN'S LODGING HOUSE
Alternative name of The Round House, Holloway, where **John Pizer** was staying on the night of Mary Ann Nichols' murder.

CROW, ALFRED GEORGE (born c. 1864)
Witness at Martha Tabram's inquest. Drove cab no. 6.600, and resided at George Yard Buildings where he saw a body, presumably Tabram's, on the first floor landing at 3.30 a.m., 7 August 1888, but paid no attention, it being common to find people sleeping there.

CROWLEY, EDWARD ALEXANDER (ALEISTER) (1875–1947)

Alleged theorist. Professional occultist. He made several claims to know the identity of Jack the Ripper (see under **Helena Blavatsky, Leonard Gribble, Robert Donston Stephenson**) but it is unlikely that he possessed any original information about the murders.

See also **W. W. Westcott**.

CULLEN, TOM

American journalist, resident in England. Publications include *The Prostitutes' Padre* (1975), *Autumn of Terror* (1965), *Crippen, The Mild Murderer* (1977).

Cullen is deeply esteemed by most writers on Jack the Ripper. It is a matter for regret that he no longer has the notes and sources he used for his work twenty-five years ago, when publishers were unwilling to include source material in true crime books, and journalist authors like Cullen had not recognised the advantage to posterity of doing so. But no one questions that Cullen faithfully reproduced material he found in a very wide range of newspapers over a broad span of time, albeit he did not distinguish between primary and secondary source material.

CUNNINGHAM, INSPECTOR JAMES HENRY (b. 1868)

Joined C Division, 1888 (warrant no. 73958), and was drafted to patrols in Whitechapel during the Ripper scare. Also frequently escorted **G. R. Sims** 'through some of the worst slums in London' (probably later in life) collecting material for articles.

CUSINS, MARY

Informant. Lodging-house keeper of Little Paternoster Row, Dorset Street. Reported that **Joseph Isaacs** stayed in her house for three or four days prior to Mary Kelly's murder. She had heard him pacing in his room at nights, and he left suddenly after the murder, leaving a violin bow in his room.

Police asked her to look out for him and report back. On 7 December he returned for the bow, and she followed him to Julius Levenson's pawnshop, hoping to find a policeman. None was about, and when Isaacs came running out of Levenson's she could do nothing but lay the information at a police station. Her description ensured his subsequent arrest.

CUTBUSH, SUPERINTENDENT CHARLES HENRY (1844–96)

Uncle of **Thomas Cutbush**. Executive Superintendent, Scotland Yard (in charge of Supplies and Pay). Shot himself in his own kitchen in his daughter's presence following some years of depression, severe headaches and mild paranoid delusions, apparently resulting from a blow to the head.

CUTBUSH, THOMAS HAYNES (1866–1903)

Alleged suspect. Resident of Albert Street, Kennington. Believed to have contracted syphilis c.1888, whereupon he began to suffer paranoid delusions. Abandoned his job canvassing for a directory (having formerly worked for a tea firm in The Minories), and took to rambling about at night, reputedly often returning home with muddy clothes. His whereabouts at the time of the Ripper murders was never ascertained.

On 5 March 1891 he was detained as a lunatic in Lambeth Infirmary, but escaped within hours. Taking a knife he had bought in Houndsditch a week or so previously, he stabbed Florence Grace Johnson and attempted to wound Isabelle Frazer Anderson in Kennington. Both assaults were made from behind, apparently in imitation of **Colicutt**.

He was arrested on 9 March and charged with malicious wounding. He died in Broadmoor.

The *Sun*, on 13 February 1894 and following dates, suggested that he was Jack the Ripper. Cutbush's occupational connection with the East End, and the events of 1888, made this an attractive suggestion. The police themselves seem to have weighed the idea carefully, putting **Inspector Race** and **Sergeant McCarthy** to investigate him, and finally Chief Constable **Melville Macnaghten** prepared his memorandum to disprove the theory. He showed that Cutbush's knife was not the Ripper's, and indicated the absurdity of supposing that the frenzied disemboweller of 1888 would lie dormant for two years and then re-emerge stabbing women in the bottom. The valuable remainder of the memoranda describes the more plausible Ripper suspects **Druitt**, **Kosminski** and **Ostrog**.

We may note suggestions of hereditary paranoid tendency in **Superintendent Cutbush**.

D

DAM, HARRY
Journalist. Alleged by **Lincoln Springfield** to be responsible for the accusation that **John Pizer** was 'Leather Apron'. Springfield also claimed that Pizer was persuaded not to issue a libel writ by payment of £10. Since Dam worked for the *Star*, which gave more sensational coverage to the 'Leather Apron' scare than any other paper, Springfield's story carries some conviction.

'DANNY'
Nickname of **Joe Barnett**, according to a Press Association report, 10 November 1888. (And see under **Maurice Lewis**.) **Bruce Paley** believes Joe Barnett had a brother named Daniel.

DARRELL OR DURRELL, MRS
Alternative name of **Elizabeth Long**.

Described in the *Guardian*, 12 September 1888, and other papers of 13 September as having seen a man and a woman talking on the pavement outside 29 Hanbury Street at 5.30 a.m. on the morning of Annie Chapman's murder. On 12 September Mrs Darrell identified the body in the mortuary. Described as Mrs Long when testifying at the inquest. A note on police files calls her the woman 'Darrell or Long'.

DAVIES –, (died c. 1882)
Alleged husband of Mary Jane Kelly, who told **Joe Barnett** she had married Davies, a collier, c. 1879, and he died in a mine explosion two or three years later. Since she had been brought up in Wales, and moved to Cardiff on being widowed, the marriage presumably took place in Wales. No trace of this marriage has been found on the indexes.

DAVIES, DR MORGAN (1854–1920)
Alleged suspect's alleged suspect. Born in Whitechapel. MB, MRCS, 1879 (London); LRCP, 1880 (London). FRCS, 1882. MD, 1884 (Aberd). House Phys., House Surg., and Resident Accoucheur, London Hospital. Private residence, 10 Goring Street, Houndsditch.

He was accused by **Robert Donston Stephenson**, who claimed that while under treatment in London Hospital he had witnessed Dr Davies give a graphic performance of the way he believed the Ripper to have killed and sodomised his victims. Stephenson alleged this convinced him Davies was unbalanced, and when (as he claimed) he learned from W. T. Stead that medical reports showed the victims had been sodomised (they didn't), he realised Davies must be the Ripper and started to spy on him.

Melvin Harris claims Stephenson deliberately made himself notorious to police with this story in order to distract attention from his own guilt. Although papers now missing from Scotland Yard files referred to Stephenson, there was no reference in them to any questioning of Dr Davies.

DAVIS, JOHN
Witness at Annie Chapman's inquest. Discovered her body. A stooped, elderly carman employed in Leadenhall Market, he had occupied the third floor front room of 29 Hanbury Street with his wife and three sons for about two weeks when the murder occurred. After a restless night, awake from 3.00 a.m. to 5.00, then dozing for about half an hour, he got up at 5.45 a.m. (timed by Spitalfields Church clock bell) and went to the back yard where he saw the body. He called James Green and James Kent who went to look for police. Davis went to Commercial Street Police Station, and returned to 29 Hanbury Street.

DAY, SEAN P.
Theorist. Contributes seven-page entry to Peter Underwood's *Jack the Ripper: One Hundred Years of Mystery*, describing the lost unpublished manuscript of his book on the Ripper which would have named his own choice for 'the face behind the mask' with corroborative data. Mr Day does not reveal who this was to be. He does argue that Martha Tabram was a Ripper victim.

DAYS OF MY YEARS
Book by Sir Melville Macnaghten (1914). Memoirs of retired Assistant Commissioner, CID, who joined Scotland Yard in June 1889 as Assistant Chief Constable, CID, and, as Chief Constable, wrote the important Macnaghten memoranda in 1894. Published just one year after he had told the press that he had no intention of writing his memoirs. The book recounts major cases and describes well-known colleagues, fully justifying his reputation for affability. It relies upon memory and so contains various slips and errors. One chapter deals with Jack the Ripper. See under Melville Macnaghten, Macnaghten memoranda for discussion.

'DEAR BOSS' LETTER
See under Jack the Ripper letters.

DEARDEN, DR HAROLD (1883–1962)
Narrator of brother-officer's theory. Author of 'Who was Jack the Ripper' in *Great Unsolved Crimes* (ed. A. J. Hale, 1935).

On 9 November 1918, a companion in trenches on the Somme told Dearden this was the second time his birthday had been ruined, the other being the occasion of his tenth birthday. His father had been proprietor of a private lunatic asylum on the outskirts of London. At dinner time a noisy and violent lunatic was brought in, disturbing the boy's birthday party. The lunatic was the son of one of his father's oldest friends, and later, when calmed down, became a smiling and gently demented companion for the boy, with a great talent for drawing. By the time the boy was old enough to ask questions, his father was dead.

'But,' said Dearden's comrade, 'the last murder was on the night of

November 8th, remember. Looks queer, doesn't it?' Searches in Dearden's regimental records have not as yet identified the brother officer.

DEEMING, FREDERICK BAILEY (1853–92)
Alleged suspect. Murdered: wife and four children in Rainhill, Liverpool, 1891; second wife, in Melbourne, Australia, 1892; possibly other victims. A plumber and fitter, as well as confidence trickster, he cemented his victims' bodies under kitchen hearthstones. After conviction in Australia, Deeming was reported to have confessed to the 'last two' Ripper murders. His solicitor strenuously denied that he made any confession whatsoever. See also *The East End Murderer. I Knew Him.*

DEW, WALTER, CHIEF INSPECTOR (1863–1947)
As Detective Constable, H Division, actively engaged on Ripper case. Joined Metropolitan Police, 1882, Warrant No. 66711. Posted to X Division (Paddington Green). Transferred to H Division (Whitechapel) CID, 1887. Nicknamed 'Blue Serge' from a suit he habitually wore. From 1889 enjoyed steady promotion until Chief Inspector, 1906. Resigned, 1910, and set up as 'confidential agent', resident in Wandsworth. His highly publicised pursuit and capture of Hawley Harvey Crippen made him the first Scotland Yard 'superstar', and he published his memoirs, *I Caught Crippen*, in 1938.

Despite some inaccuracies, the memoirs give a convincing first-hand account of police work on the ground. The frequent errors in the third of the book devoted to the Ripper case are of the kind one would expect from an honest man reminiscing without recourse to documents. He misspells a great many names. He makes several mistakes over Elizabeth Stride's murder. He wrongly believed that **Robert Paul** never came forward to corroborate **Charles Cross**'s evidence. He believed that Emma Smith and Martha Tabram were Ripper victims. In common with practically every other policeman, he dismissed the **'Dear Boss' letter** as a hoax; he also believed the **Goulston Street graffito** was not the Ripper's work. He believed the man seen by **Matthew Packer** was Elizabeth Stride's murderer.

Dew confirms that the streets of Whitechapel were exceptionally heavily patrolled by uniformed and plainclothes policemen, including some disguised as women. He suggests that Stride might have accepted a client despite the scare if he was respectably dressed, and notes that while unusually presentable pedestrians were automatically stopped and questioned, local middle-class residents, being known by sight to H Division police, came and went unchallenged. Subsequently, however, Dew reverses his opinion, observing that police patrols drafted from other divisions stopped all unusual passers-by unselectively.

His memory of **Chief Inspector Moore** as the senior officer handling the case is compatible with his status as a divisional CID constable, uninformed about the controlling activities of **Swanson** and **Anderson** in Scotland Yard. It is the more relevant that he knew **Abberline** was not in charge. He protested that the police chiefs made an unnecessary enemy of the press by withholding information from them (while recognising the need for some confidentiality). But he felt that 'The police at this time were terribly buffeted. In some cases they did not receive the support they had a right to expect.'

He remembered being sent to search an escape route from 29 Hanbury Street to Spitalfields Market: east along the street to Brick Lane; south on Brick Lane as far as Princelet Street; west along Princelet Street back to Spitalfields Market. As the market could have been reached much more directly by going straight up Hanbury Street in the westward direction, this circuit is puzzling, though Dew does not comment on it.

It seems that the only victim Dew saw in situ was Mary Jane Kelly. He found the sight of her body harrowing and hated thinking about the case for ever afterward.

See **Unidentified man seen in Buck's Row**.

DIEMSCHÜTZ, LOUIS

Witness at Elizabeth Stride's inquest. Discovered her body. Steward of **International Workingmen's Educational Club**. Street salesman of cheap jewellery. On Saturday 29 August 1888 he was out all afternoon and evening, peddling his wares at Westow Hill Market, Sydenham. He returned to the club at approximately 1.00 a.m. (timed by tobacconist's clock in Commercial Road) driving his pony and cart, with the intention of leaving goods with his wife before stabling the pony in George Yard (Gunthorpe Street). When the pony turned in to Dutfield's Yard, it pulled to the left in the narrow entrance between the clubhouse and the cottages, and hesitated to go forward. Diemschütz felt something soft behind the gates with his long-handled whip, and descending, struck a match and found it was an unconscious woman. Believing her to be drunk, and momentarily suspecting she might be his wife, he went into the club. There he told several members, and went back to the gate with a group including **Morris Eagle** and **Isaacs Kozebrodsky**. When they found Stride's throat cut, Diemschütz and another member ran off unsuccessfully searching for a policeman, but met **Edward Spooner** at the corner of Fairclough Street and Christian Street. He returned with them to the club, where they examined the body for about five minutes before **Police Constables Lamb** and **Collins** arrived.

The general police and press impression was that Diemschütz's pony had disturbed the Ripper, who ran away before mutilating his victim. (But see under **Elizabeth Stride** for alternative suggestions.) **Melville Macnaghten** seems to have confused Diemschütz with **Joseph Lawende, Joseph Hyam Levy** and **Harry Harris**. (See under **Macnaghten memoranda** for significance.)

Diemschütz told *The Times* the following day that Stride's body held a packet of cachous, some of which had spilled out, in the left hand, and some grape stalks in the right hand. There was a flower pinned to her dress.

In March 1889, Diemschütz was sentenced to three months hard labour for his part in an affray when local residents in Berner Street attacked International Workers' Educational Club members who had been demonstrating against Dr Adler's insistence that Jews could not be socialists. The Club members fought policemen whom they had summoned, believing them to be reinforcements for their assailants, and Diemschütz lost an assault charge he laid against Detective Constable Froest.

DIEMSCHÜTZ, MRS

Wife of **Louis Diemschütz**. Reported in *The Times* (2 October 1888) as saying, 'Just about 1.00 a.m. Sunday I was in the kitchen on the ground floor of the club and close to the side entrance. I am positive I did not hear screams or sounds of any kind.' This was corroborated by a servant who said no sounds were heard from the yard between 12.40 and 1.00 a.m.

DIPLOCK, DR THOMAS BRAMAH (c. 1830–92)

Coroner for West Middlesex and Western Division of the County of London. Conducted inquest on **Montague John Druitt**. Educ. St Andrews and St George's Hospital. MD, 1856. MRCS, 1963. House surgeon at the Lock Hospital, and surgeon to London Friendly Institution. Elected coroner, 1858.

DIRNENMÖRDER VON LONDON, DER (1976, Switzerland)

Film directed by Jesus Franco. Stars Klaus Kinski (Ripper), Josephine Chaplin.

'DOCTOR' THEORIES

All initially derive from firm medical conclusions reached by **Dr Bagster Phillips**, with doubtful support of **Frederick Gordon Brown**. Conversely, **Dr Thomas Bond** and lay observer **Walter Dew** both strongly insisted that the inexpert mutilations of the Ripper's victims were not the work of a trained hand. **Dr Llewellyn**, predictably, did not express an opinion, since Mary Ann Nichols' murder on its own did not invite such speculation. **Dr Blackwell** could not usefully have commented, as Elizabeth Stride's abdomen was unmutilated.

Modern medics also disagree: **N. P. Warren** and **Robin Odell** believe some skill is indicated; **Richard Whittington-Egan** and the **FBI** demur. The authors are medically untrained, and cannot say conclusively whether the medical evidence really points to the Ripper's having any surgical skill. We cautiously suggest that the balance of opinion is slightly against it.

The case for skill rests upon: the precision of the lower cut severing Chapman's uterus; the difficulty of securing Eddowes' kidney from the front of the body; the difficulty of extracting Kelly's heart through the diaphragm; the fact that all these operations were performed in great haste and abysmal light. The case against rests upon the random nature of most of the injuries; the apparent failed attempts to decapitate Chapman and Kelly; Dr Phillips' conviction that Catharine Eddowes was the victim of an unskilled imitator; the belief that the apparent marks of skill were all the result of chance.

The widely publicised notion that the Ripper was a doctor took instant hold on public and police in 1888. Three medical students, including **John Sanders**, were among the early suspects investigated by the Metropolitan Police. Two of the suspects named in the **Macnaghten memoranda** were described as doctors – **Druitt** and **Ostrog**. **Spicer** believed the doctor he arrested in Heneage Street was the Ripper. **Leeson** claimed that suspicion of 'a certain doctor' was felt throughout H Division CID. **Abberline** argued that **Klosowski**'s elementary surgical training formed part of the case against him.

All the above suspects are historical: they genuinely existed and were suspected by some reasonably competent person at or soon after the time of the murders. The following list comprises other medical personnel who were either suspected by other contemporaries or emerged from later rumours or theorising: **Dr Barnardo, Dr Morgan Davies, 'Dr D'Onston',**

Sir William Gull, 'Jill the Ripper' (midwife and nurse variants), Dr Pedachenko, 'Dr Stanley'.

DONNER, GERALD MELVILLE (1907–68)
Grandson of **Sir Melville Macnaghten**.

Early in the 1950s, **Philip Loftus** saw an original framed 'Jack the Ripper' letter, which he thought he recognised as a facsimile, on Donner's wall. (This suggests it was the **'Dear Boss' letter**: the only one to be reproduced, with the 'saucy Jacky' postcard, by the police.) Donner said it was the original and proceeded to show Loftus Sir Melville's notes on the case. See under **Macnaghten memoranda** for details and discussion.

Subsequently Donner went to Madras, where he had three framed letters hanging on his wall. He returned to England in 1957/8, having expressed his intention of bringing his Ripper material with him. If he did so, it was assumed he would sell the documents. As they have never appeared in salerooms, the authors doubt whether this occurred. Donner died in India, leaving all his possessions to his wife (d.1970). Searching enquiries strongly suggest that she did not possess any Ripper material.

The original 'Dear Boss' letter was returned anonymously by post to Scotland Yard, with other Ripper and Crippen documents, in 1987.

DONNER, MRS JULIA (1881–1938)
Elder daughter of **Sir Melville Macnaghten**. Inherited the version of **Macnaghten memoranda** from which **Lady Aberconway** transcribed her surviving copy. Present whereabouts of Mrs Donner's copy unknown, but it seems likely to have passed to her son **Gerald Melville Donner**, and might just be the version he showed to **Philip Loftus** in 1950.

DONOVAN, TIMOTHY
Witness at **Annie Chapman**'s inquest. The deputy (manager) of **Crossingham's Common Lodging House**, 35 Dorset Street, where he saw her eating a baked potato and, in his opinion, the worse for liquor at 1.45 a.m., 8 September 1888. He asked her for her doss-money, which she had not got, and declined her request to let her stay on trust. She then left, saying she would be back soon, and asking him to save her bed.

It has been noted that Donovan's various statements to police, press and inquest steadily softened his severity with her, as if he recognised that it seemed unkind to have driven a homeless woman out to the streets where she was murdered. Donovan also told the press he knew **'Leather Apron'** by sight and had ejected him from Crossingham's for threatening a woman before the murders began.

Donald Rumbelow suggests he might have been the twenty-nine-year-old Timothy Donovan, labourer of 7 Russell Court, St George's-in-the-East, who died 1 November 1888 of cirrhosis of the liver, phthisis and exhaustion. He might equally have been the Timothy Donovan, aged about thirty, who repeatedly appeared before Thames Magistrates Court on assault charges during 1887 and 1888, and who seems to be the same Timothy Donovan, labourer, who was indicted for murdering his wife Mary at 27 Lucas Street, Stepney, in 1904. There is no supporting evidence in either case.

D'ONSTON, DR ROSLYN
See **Robert Donston Stephenson**.

DORSENNE, JEAN
Author of *Jack l'Éventreur*, which contains tantalising hints that he mixed some real information gleaned from a surviving policeman on the case with a great deal of gossip and probable fiction.

DORSET STREET
Mary Jane Kelly's murder site. An infamous road in Spitalfields, running east-west between **Commercial Street** and Crispin Street. At the Commerical Street end it faced Christ Church burial ground; at the Crispin Street End, the **Providence Row Night Refuge and Convent**. Laid out in the 1670s and at one time known as Datchett Street, probably from William Wheler of Datchett who owned much land in the vicinity.

On the north side of the street in 1888, about a third of the way along from Commercial Street, a narrow brick archway led into Miller's Court. Mary Kelly's room was the ground-floor back room of 26 Dorset Street, partitioned off from the remainer of the house, and entered by a door in Miller's Court immediately on the right as the pedestrian came out from under the arch.

There were three pubs on the north side of Dorset Street: **The Britannia** on the corner with Commercial Street; The Blue Coat Boy in the middle; and **The Horn of Plenty** on the corner with Crispin Street. Many of the houses in the street were common lodging houses, including **Crossingham**'s. Locally it was sometimes called 'Dosset Street' in reference to the doss-houses. **John McCarthy**'s chandler's shop (i.e., grocer's) stood on the other side of the Miller's Court entry from no. 26.

The street was believed to be one of the most dangerous in London; police who pursued criminals into it were liable to be seriously assaulted by the denizens. In 1904 it was renamed Duval Street. The northern side, including Miller's Court, was demolished in extensions to Spitalfields Market in 1929. The southern side was replaced with a multi-storey car park in the 1960s, and today the street is an unnamed private road.

DOUGLAS, ARTHUR
Author of *Will the real Jack the Ripper?* (1974). Mr Douglas has also written on the Lancashire Witches.

DR JEKYLL AND SISTER HYDE (1971, Great Britain)
Film directed by Roy Ward Baker. Stars Ralph Bates, Martine Beswick. Ripper is sub-plot in self-explanatory variation of dual personality classic; remarkable likeness of Bates and Beswick has often been commented on.

DREW, THOMAS STUART
Blacksmith, with shop in York Road, Walworth. Allegedly cohabited with Mary Ann Nichols, June–October 1887.

DRÔLE DE DRÂME OU L'ÉTRANGE AVENTURE DE DOCTEUR MOLYNEUX (BIZARRE, BIZARRE) (1937, France)
Film directed by Marcel Carné. Stars Françoise Rosay, Jean Louis Barrault

(Ripper). Superb comedy which holds up well; second film by Carné as director.

DRUITT, ANN (1830/1–90)
Mother of **Montague John Druitt**. Mentioned in letter or papers he left when contemplating suicide because he feared he was 'going to be like mother'. Suffered from depression and paranoid delusions (that she was being electrocuted) following the death of her husband in 1885. Attempted suicide 1888, and in July was sent to the Brooke Asylum, Clapton, where she was attended by Dr William Pavy, an expert on diabetes, and certified insane. In September 1888, she was transferred on leave from asylum to Dr J. R. Gasquet's establishment in Brighton, where her certification lapsed by oversight and was renewed early in 1889 with formal transfer of her incarceration to Brighton where she had remained uninterruptedly since the previous September. In May 1890 she was transferred to the care of the Tuke brothers at Manor House Asylum, Chiswick, where she died six months later.

Diabetes seems to have been a hereditary condition, inducing melancholia and suicidal urges. Her mother committed suicide while insane; her sister attempted it and spent a period in an asylum. Montague John's eldest sister killed herself in old age.

DRUITT, DR LIONEL (1853–1908)
First cousin of **Montague John Druitt** and alleged author of *The East End Murderer – I Knew Him*.

Educ. St David's, London and Edin. MRCS, 1875. LRCP (Lond), MB, Mast. Surg. (Edin), 1877. MD (Edin), 1882. 1879, listed in Medical Register at 140 Minories; surgery of **Dr Thyne**. Also listed in Medical Directory as Assistant House Surgeon, Craiglockhart Poorhouse, Edinburgh. It is not known in which order and for how many months he practised in each of these places. Subsequently at 122 Clapham Road; also frequently but intermittently resident at his father's home in Strathmore Gardens. In 1886 he emigrated to Australia, living at first with his uncle, Archdeacon Thomas Druitt in Cooma, NSW. In 1888 he married Susan Murray in Wagga Wagga. In 1897–8 he lived in Dandenong Road, Melbourne, and in 1903 was living in Drouin. He died in Mentone, Victoria.

Daniel Farson speculates that his presence in The Minories in 1878 or 1879 gave Montague John Druitt his introduction to the East End. See also *The East End Murderer – I Knew Him*.

DRUITT, MONTAGUE JOHN (1857–88)
Suspect. Born Wimborne, Dorset. Educ. Winchester and New College, Oxford. BA, Lit.Hum., Class III, 1880. Successful debater and sportsman (fives and cricket) at school and college; unsuccessful amateur actor (poor performance as Sir Toby Belch in school play). Steward of college junior common room. Employed as schoolmaster, Mr Valentine's school, Blackheath, 1880. Admitted Inner Temple, 1882; called to the bar, 1885, attached to Western Circuit. Joined Arthur Jelf's chambers, 9 King's Bench Walk. Active sportsman: secretary Morden Cricket Club, 1884; hon. sec. and treas., Blackheath Cricket, Football and Lawn Tennis Co., 1885. Special pleader, Western Circuit, 1887. Dismissed by Mr Valentine after being in 'serious trouble at the school', c.30 November 1888. Last

seen alive c.3 December 1888 (but see below).

His body was recovered from the Thames off Thorneycroft's Torpedo Works, Chiswick, by waterman **Henry Winslade**, on 31 December and examined by **PC George Moulson**. It had been immersed for about a month. There were stones in the overcoat pockets. He left a letter for Mr Valentine, alluding to suicide, and a paper addressed to his brother with words to the effect that, 'Since Friday I felt that I was going to be like mother [see **Ann Druitt**], and it would be best for all concerned if I were to die'. (Text composite from two press reports which are not direct quotation.) The inquest, on 2 January 1889, found 'suicide whilst of unsound mind', which permitted burial in consecrated ground, Wimborne cemetery.

The reason for his dismissal by Mr Valentine is unknown, although its serious nature indicates that it might have been a contributory cause of his suicide. Druitt had no financial worries. He was not, as used to be asserted, a failed barrister. Working as a special pleader did not entail courtroom appearances, and was compatible with his teaching and sporting activities. He earned sufficient to leave considerably more money than he had inherited from his father or earned by teaching.

Druitt came to notice in 1959 when **Daniel Farson** discovered the **Aberconway** version of Sir Melville **Macnaghten's memoranda**, naming him as the probable Ripper and describing him as

Mr M. J. Druitt, a doctor of about 41 years of age and of good family, who disappeared at the time of the Miller's Court murder, and whose body was found floating in the Thames on 31 Dec: i.e. 7 weeks after the said murder. The body was said to have been in the water for a month, *or more* – on it was found a season ticket between Blackheath and London. From private information I have little doubt but that his own family suspected this man of being the Whitechapel murderer; it was *alleged* that he was sexually insane.

The preliminary material (mostly concerning **Thomas Cutbush** and describing the murders) also contains observations appertaining to Druitt:

A . . . rational and *workable* theory, to my way of thinking, is that the 'rippers' [*sic*] brain gave way altogether after his awful glut in Millers Court and that he then committed suicide . . .

And:

Personally, after much careful & deliberate consideration, I am inclined to exonerate the last 2 [suspects], but I have always held strong opinions regarding *no. 1*, and the more I think the matter over, the stronger do these opinions become. The *truth*, however, will never be known, and did indeed, at one time lie at the bottom of the Thames, if my conjections [*sic*] be correct.

Farson's preliminary research established that Macnaghten's suspect really existed, and corrected the errors in the memorandum. He also perceived that Druitt was evidently the suspect obscurely described in Macnaghten's published memoirs, *Days of My Years* (1914):

Although . . . the Whitechapel murderer, in all probability, put an end to himself soon after the Dorset Street affair in November 1888, certain facts, pointing to this conclusion, were not in possession of the police till some years after I became a detective officer.

And:

I incline to the belief that the individual who held up London in terror resided with his own people; that he absented himself from home at certain times, and that he committed suicide on or about the 10th of November 1888 . . .

Macnaghten's error about the date of the suicide presumably resulted from his confessed dependence on memory when writing the memoirs.

Druitt was given more prominence when **Tom Cullen** (1965) discovered details about his personality; more still when Farson published his **Jack the Ripper** (1972), with new data on **Lionel Druitt** and other suggested evidence (see *The East End Murderer – I Knew Him*). **Donald McCormick** recognised the importance of the new suspect and incorporated into the revised edition of his *The Identity of Jack the Ripper* oral information from an unidentified 'London doctor who knew [Walter] Sickert and whose father was at Oxford with Druitt'. This man apparently told McCormick that Druitt's mind gave way because a blackmailer had accused him of being the Ripper; and that Walter Sickert had believed that his suspect, the veterinary student, was called Druitt, Drewett or Hewitt. He also alleged that Sickert had told his story to Macnaghten in the Garrick Club, and Macnaghten believed it must describe Montague John Druitt, since, like the veterinary student, he had a mother in Bournemouth. McCormick's explanation remains untested as he says he cannot now help researchers, having passed his notes to someone else and never retrieved them.

The new spate of Druitt information provoked **Philip Loftus** to write privately to Lady Aberconway giving a description of the version of the memoranda he had seen in **Gerald Melville Donner**'s possession. This described 'MICHAEL JOHN DRUITT, a DOCTOR of FORTY ONE years of age . . .' (Loftus's capitals and dots).

The Scotland Yard version of the **Macnaghten memoranda** was described by **Donald Rumbelow** (1975). It added nothing to the Aberconway version except that the allegation was strengthened to a statement that 'He was sexually insane'. The references to Druitt's age and season ticket were omitted.

At this point, Druitt was the most plausible historical suspect ever named. **Stephen Knight** (1976) undermined the cosy consensus backing the Druitt theory by pointing out that Macnaghten himself was clearly not positive, and that his conclusion was unsupported by any other police officer.

Macnaghten's writings are the only documentary evidence against Druitt. The 'certain facts' may have been among documents he allegedly destroyed prior to his retirement. On 2 June 1913 he told the *Daily Mail* that he had joined the Yard six months after the Ripper committed suicide, and said he had a 'very clear idea' who the Ripper was, adding, however, that he would never reveal it and saying, 'I have destroyed all my documents and there is now no record of the secret information which came into my possession at one time or another'.

The only evidence that suspicion of Druitt was shared by other policemen prior to the receipt of the 'certain facts' lies in an article by **G. R. Sims** in the *Referee* in 1902, which observed, 'the name of the man found drowned was bracketed with two others as a possible Jack, *and the police were in search of him alive when they found him dead*' (our italics). In 1903 Sims wrote, 'the body of the man suspected by the chiefs of Scotland Yard, and by his own friends, who were in communication with the Yard, was found in the Thames'.

It is probable that Sims's source for all this information was Macnaghten, whose account of three suspects he follows quite closely in other places. Another recipient of information from Macnaghten, Major **Arthur Griffiths**, adds nothing to his recorded impressions.

The bases for Macnaghten's conclusion are not explained, comprising the unspecified 'private information' and 'certain facts'. It is, perhaps, significant that he refers to Druitt's family (as Sims refers to 'his friends'). Druitt's brother William first heard that he was missing on 11 December 1888, and it may be between then and the end of the month that suspicion fell on Druitt.

There was, moreover, some family connection between the Macnaghtens and the Druitts. Macnaghten's father, the last chairman of the East India Company, appointed Montague's aunt's brother to the board in 1855. (Cf. **W. Boultbee**.) Since Macnaghten was not attached to Scotland Yard until June 1889, however, the 'Scotland Yard chiefs'' suspicion of Druitt cannot easily be laid at the door of family gossip relayed by him. During December 1888, moreover, Macnaghten may be presumed to have been preoccupied with the final illness of his father, who died on the 28th.

Albert Bachert's account of hearing from the police in March 1889 that the Ripper had drowned in the Thames supports the conclusion that Druitt was believed to have been the Ripper prior to Macnaghten's arrival in Scotland Yard. It rests, however, on the unreliable testimony of **Dr Dutton** as quoted by McCormick.

We can be reasonably certain that Macnaghten had seen details of the finding of Druitt's body. The pockets contained: four large stones; £2.17s.2d in cash; a cheque for £50 and another for £16; a silver watch on a gold chain with a spade guinea as seal; a pair of kid gloves; a white handkerchief; a first-class half-season rail ticket from Blackheath to London, and a second-half return from Hammersmith to Charing Cross, dated 1 December. There were said to be no papers or letters of any description, which suggests that the cheques were the source from which his identity was established so that his family in Bournemouth could be notified. Macnaghten correctly described the season ticket between London and Blackheath. The possibility is that he had seen or consulted Moulson's original report, since so much of his other information was at variance with inquest testimony.

The dating of the return half ticket suggests that Druitt committed suicide in Hammersmith or Chiswick on 1 December. The reason for his going there is obscure; his mother did not transfer to the Manor House Asylum, Chiswick Lane, for another eighteen months. The date proposed officially as that on which he was last seen alive, 3 December, appears to be an arithmetical deduction from William Druitt's recollection that he heard on 11 December that Montague had not been seen in chambers for a week.

The essential case for believing Druitt to be the Ripper is that Macnaghten, a colleague of the men who made the fullest investigation at the time, reached this conclusion and placed it on file. The case against is that Anderson and Swanson, the men in charge of the case, recorded a different conclusion. The frequently proclaimed case for believing Druitt to be innocent on the grounds that 'there is not a shred of evidence against him' confuses legal with historical evidence: i.e., it accurately indicates that we do not know what grounds there might have been for bringing charges against him, but irresponsibly extends this to imply that Macnaghten shared our ignorance.

It is the authors' opinion that (unless another suspect's guilt is conclusively proved) Druitt cannot be finally discounted until further research has established the probable nature of the private information which convinced Macnaghten, as well as of the 'certain facts' which he believed proved that the Ripper was a man (presumably Druitt) who had committed suicide shortly after the last murder.

DRUITT, WILLIAM HARVEY (1856–1909)
Montague John Druitt's elder brother, and witness at his inquest. Educ. Clifton and Trinity (Oxon.). A solicitor resident in Bournemouth, he became concerned on learning that Montague had not been seen in his chambers for about a week preceding 11 December 1888. Thereupon he went to London, learned of his dismissal from Mr Valentine's school on 30 November, and found suicide notes in his brother's lodgings. At the inquest he reportedly described himself and his mother as Montague's only relatives. If he said it, this was definitely untrue. (Five other siblings still lived.) Cf. **Andrew Holloway**.

DUDMAN, SERGEANT
City Police officer who, with **Inspector Izzard** and **Sergeant Phelps**, sought to preserve public order after Catharine Eddowes' murder.

DURRELL, MRS
See **Mrs Darrell**.

DUTFIELD, ARTHUR
Owner of small carriage works which sealed off the western end of Dutfield's Yard (entered from the east between 40 and 42 Berner Street), the site of Elizabeth Stride's murder.

DUTTON, DR THOMAS (1854–1935)
Theorist and Aldgate resident. Educ. Bayswater Grammar School, Guy's Hospital, Edinburgh and Durham Universities. LM and LRCS, Edin., 1878; MB, 1880; MD, Durham; MRCP, Edin., 1882. 1881–4 Admiralty Surgeon and Agent (Chichester Division) and MO, Mahood Division, Westhampnett Union, E. Member of Poor Law Medical Officers Assn, Chichester and West Sussex Microscopical Society, and the National League for Physical Education and Improvement. Hon. physician to Uxbridge Road Maternity and Child Welfare Clinic; Hon. Surgeon to the Royal Defence Corps, and Surgeon in the Mercantile Marine, serving on SS *Elysia* and RMS *Tongariro*. Fellow of the Hunterian Soc., Vice President of the Imperial Medical Reform Union, Vice Chairman of the Pure Food Society. From at least 1879–91 listed in directories as at 130 Aldgate High Street. He was thus in the locality at the time of the Whitechapel Murders.

After his death, a Miss Hermione Dudley told the *Sunday Chronicle*:
I knew the doctor when I was quite a young girl . . . By far the most interesting document he compiled was his Chronicles of Crime, three volumes of handwritten comments on all the chief crimes of the past sixty years. My father was one of the few men to whom he showed this

document and owing to my interest in it, Dr Dutton gave it to me some time ago . . .

I am certain that the doctor assisted with the post-mortems on the Jack the Ripper victims. His diary makes this quite clear. Often he told me, and he repeats it in his diary, that he knew the identity of Jack the Ripper. He described him as a middle-aged doctor, a man who had been embittered by the death of his son. The latter had suffered cruelly at the hands of a woman of the streets and the father believed this to be the cause of his brilliant son's death.

Despite this précis of the 'Dr Stanley' theory, Dutton is more familiarly associated with the Dr Pedachenko theory, which he expounded to Donald McCormick in 1932, allowing him to see and take notes from the *Chronicles of Crime*. McCormick suspected that Miss Dudley had read Leonard Matters' exposition of the Stanley theory and confused it with Dutton's views.

It is customary for researchers to disparage the reported views of Dr Dutton. But his career shows that he was a man of wide interests and considerable ability. McCormick, who draws heavily on Dutton, offers a caveat: 'It should be stressed that Dutton's *Chronicles of Crime* were not a single narrative, but rather a collection of impressions and theories which he noted down at various periods.' McCormick quotes Dutton's comments on books published in 1923 (William Le Queux, *Things I Know*) and 1930 (H. L. Adam (ed.), *The Trial of George Chapman*), indicating that Dutton continued making his notes almost to the end of his life. The notes, then, may well contain various theories and changes of opinion.

It should further be noted that by the time McCormick met Dutton, the old man was living a reclusive life in cobwebby surroundings suggesting some geriatric deterioration. And McCormick himself did not refer back to his own notes, taken in 1932, until after the war (at least thirteen years later). Moreover, the Chronicles have not been seen since Miss Dudley declared her possession of them in 1935. *All* we know about them comes from McCormick's recollections and notes. They must, therefore, be treated with great caution at present.

In addition to their crucial material on the Pedachenko theory, the Chronicles (or Dr Dutton's conversation) are reported as claiming: that Abberline was a friend of Dutton's who would dash round to his house for advice on occasion; that Abberline suspected Severin Klosowski as early as 1888 [effectively denied by Abberline in 1903]; that Albert Bachert was told by the police in March 1889 that the Ripper was dead and had been found drowned in the Thames (cf. Druitt); that Dutton used microphotography to determine that 32 of the Jack the Ripper letters were by the same hand [improbable; though microphotography might conceivably indicate similar papers or inks]; that Dutton took a microphotograph of the Goulston Street graffito [effectively denied by police authorities at Catharine Eddowes' inquest] and the prints were destroyed by Sir Charles Warren.

For all the problems he gives the researcher, Dutton's residence in Aldgate (making him a plausible acquaintance of Abberline and Bachert) and his arguable half-awareness of some genuine police information that was generally unknown before 1958 and 1991 mean that the rediscovery of his *Chronicles of Crime* would be a great blessing to Ripper studies, and his statements can never be entirely discounted.

E

EAGLE, MORRIS

Witness at Elizabeth Stride's inquest. Russian immigrant of 4 New Road, Commercial Road. Travelled in jewelry. On 29 September 1888, chaired discussion at the Workers' International Educational Club on the necessity for socialism among Jews. Left at 11.45 p.m. to take his young lady home, returning 12.35 a.m. Going through the passage at the gateway from Berner Street into Dutfield's Yard he saw nothing unusual, but, given the total darkness, could not swear the body was not there. Upstairs in the club he joined a friend in singing a Russian folk song. At about 12.55 a member called Gilleman came upstairs and said there was a dead woman in the passage. Eagle went out with **Kozebrodsky** (Isaacs) and saw the body.

As soon as I saw the blood I got very excited and ran away for the police. I did not touch the body. When I got outside I saw Jacobs and another man [probably **Diemschütz**] going for the police in the direction of Fairclough Street, and I then went to Commercial Street, all the time shouting 'Police!' On getting to the corner of Grove Street I saw two constables [**Lamb** and **Collins**] and told them that a woman had been murdered. They returned with me to the yard. I then noticed several members of the club and some strangers were there.

EAST END MURDERER – I KNEW HIM, THE

Alleged document supposedly written by **Dr Lionel Druitt** and privately published in Australia.

First mentioned in a letter from a Mr A. Knowles to **Daniel Farson**, who had, early in 1959, issued a public request for any information concerning Jack the Ripper for use in a television series. Knowles apparently responded that he had seen a document in Australia written by a Lionel Druitt, Drewett or Drewery, called *The East End Murderer – I Knew Him*, and 'printed privately by a Mr Fell of Dandenong in 1890'.

At this early stage of his research, Farson had not seen the **Macnaghten memorandum** describing **Montague John Druitt** as a doctor, a suicide in December 1888, and Jack the Ripper. So the Knowles letter was filed with other pieces of fugitive information to be followed up if and when appropriate.

The discovery of Druitt's cousin Lionel in medical directories, with the information that he was in Australia in 1887, suddenly alerted Farson and his research team to the importance of the Knowles letter. (They never learned that the doctor actually lived in Dandenong *Road*, Melbourne, from 1897 to 1901.)

By then it was impossible to confirm the letter's details, as Farson's file had been purloined by an unidentifiable visitor to the studio. Appeals for Mr Knowles to come forward failed, possibly because he was Mr Arthur

Knowles of Blackheath who died aged 84 in June 1959.

The existence of an Australian document was also reported by Mr Maurice Gould of Bexleyheath, who wrote to Farson that between 1925 and 1930 two men in Australia had independently told him they knew the identity of Jack the Ripper, and both said they learned it from papers owned by a Mr W. G. Fell, an Englishman, who died in 1935. He had occasionally looked after one of Mr Gould's informants – an elderly man called McCarrity or McGarrity – in Koo-Wee-Rup near Lang Lang (outside the Dandenong Ranges, and over sixty miles away from the town of Dandenong). Mr Gould's other informant was a journalist called Edward MacNamara, who said that Mr W. G. Fell of Dandenong had housed a man called Druitt who left him papers proving the Ripper's identity. Fell, it seemed, owned this document and was willing to sell it for £500. Farson concluded that the Gould/MacNamara material was or included a copy of *The East End Murderer – I Knew Him*.

Rigorous and repeated searches in Australian libraries and archives have totally failed to find any publication whatsoever on the East End or the Whitechapel Murders by Lionel Druitt.

In 1986, Mr John Ruffels, historical researcher of Bondi, wrote up the results of his personal attempts over the previous twelve years to establish the truth. His most exciting discovery was that Gould had known, not one, but two Fells in Australia: a storekeeper called W. G. Fell from Lang Lang, for whom Gould had actually worked in 1930; and a man from Melbourne who was 'some sort of free-lance journalist or printer'. It was the latter, an ex-English guardsman (according to Gould's information to Ruffels), who possessed the document. Mr Ruffels subsequently established that a printer called John James Fell (b. 1888) was employed by the Melbourne *Age* from 1906 to 1937, though he was Australian born and shorter than Mr Gould's ex-guardsman.

Mr Gould said he had first met the printer/journalist Fell in Melbourne; later he met him again in Koo-Wee-Rup where Fell showed him the document and offered to sell it to him. Mr Gould had seen the document, which he described as a 'confession' with a printing type like the old style *Police Gazette*.

In 1986 **Martin Howells** and Keith Skinner also traced Maurice Gould. He did not feel he had been in any way misrepresented in Farson's book. But they did glean from him a somewhat different story from the two reported by Farson and Ruffels. Mr Gould now said (and wrote: the authors have his observations) that MacNamara introduced the name of Fell in the course of a conversation with Gould and another man which had originally concerned **Frederick Bailey Deeming**. Mr Gould's expressed interest in the Ripper case had led to his being offered the exorbitantly priced document, which he now described as two or three sheets of hand-written paper, including the word 'Ripper' somewhere.

Howells and Skinner knew that Deeming (arrested 1892) was widely rumoured to have confessed to 'the last two' Ripper murders. He had used the alias 'Drewen' on coming to Australia, and a manuscript confession in his hand would have had a high cash value in that country, unlike a privately printed document of 1890 alleging knowledge of a previously unknown Ripper suspect. They concluded that the Gould/MacNamara document was, in fact, an alleged Deeming confession, and had nothing to do with Lionel Druitt.

John Ruffels had, however, found a document allegedly identifying Jack the Ripper, printed in the Australian town where Lionel Druitt was living in 1890, the very year the Knowles letter had claimed for *The East End Murderer – I Knew Him*. Genealogist Shirley Richards established that in August 1890 Lionel Druitt had moved to St Arnaud where he lived for at least the next couple of years. The *St Arnaud Mercury* printed a supplement in November 1890 which included a story (reprinted from the *New York World*) about an East End landlady with a lodger she suspected of being the Ripper.

Mr Knowles's association of the document with Fell and Dandenong remains unexplained.

None the less, most researchers agree that Howells and Skinner have unearthed persuasive data plausibly suggesting that the alleged pamphlet by Lionel Druitt never existed, and emerges from garbled recollections of the *St Arnaud Mercury* article and the supposed Deeming confession.

EDDOWES, CATHARINE (1842–88)
Fourth Ripper victim.

Born Wolverhampton, daughter of tinplate worker George Eddowes, who moved with his large family to Bermondsey before she was two. (The spelling 'Catharine' is taken from her birth certificate.)

Educ. St John's Charity School, Potter's Field, Tooley Street, until her mother, Catharine Eddowes, née Evans, died in 1855, when most of her siblings entered Bermondsey Workhouse and Industrial School. Thereafter her movements are uncertain. According to the *Wolverhampton Chronicle* she returned to the care of her aunt in Biston Street, Wolverhampton, and continued her education at Dowgate Charity School. Certainly, some time between 1861 and 1863 she left home with a pensioner named **Thomas Conway**, formerly enlisted in the 18th Royal Irish Regiment under the name Quinn, and drawing a regimental pension under that name. According to the newspapers the couple lived by selling chapbooks (which Conway wrote) in Birmingham and the Midlands. According to Catharine's friends, she claimed that she had legitimately married Conway, and had his initials TC tattooed on her arm. No trace of this marriage has been found on the registers. They had three children: Annie (born c. 1865), George (born c. 1868) and another son (born c. 1873).

In 1880 the Conways separated, Catharine taking custody of Annie, and Conway the boys. Annie said Catharine's habitual drinking and periodic absences caused the breakdown; Catharine's sister Elizabeth Fisher attributed it to Conway's occasional drinking and violence.

In 1881 Catharine joined an Irish porter (probably **John Kelly**, with whom she was still living seven years later) in his lodgings in Flower and Dean Street. Annie married Louis Phillips and she and her husband spent the next few years moving around Bermondsey and Southwark (from King Street to Anchor Street to Dibbon Grove to Southwark Park Road) to avoid her mother's scrounging.

In September 1888, Catharine and Kelly went hop-picking in Kent. They failed to earn much, and at the end of the month they returned on foot with another man and his common-law wife, **Emily Birrell**.

On 28 September Catharine and Kelly reached London, where Kelly earned 6d [2½p]. Eddowes took 2d and went to find a bed in the casual ward at Shoe Lane Workhouse. Kelly took 4d to pay for a bed at Cooney's

Lodging House, 55 Flower and Dean Street. At Shoe Lane, where she was well known, Catharine told the superintendent, 'I have come back to earn the reward offered for the apprehension of the Whitechapel murderer. I think I know him.' He warned her to take care she was not murdered, to which she replied, 'Oh, no fear of that.' (One press report attributed this story to the superintendent of Mile End Casual ward.)

At 8.00 a.m. on 29 September she arrived at Cooney's, having been turned out of Shoe Lane. She and Kelly agreed to pawn a pair of his boots, and she took them to one Smith or Jones in Church Street, receiving 2/6d [12½p] and a ticket in the name of 'Jane Kelly'. The couple bought tea, sugar and food, and ate breakfast in the kitchen at Cooney's between 10.00 and 11.00.

By 2.00 p.m., they were again without money. (2/6d had a purchasing power of around £8, which suggests that they bought liquor as well as breakfast.) They parted at 2.00 p.m. in Houndsditch, Catharine saying she was going to Bermondsey to borrow money from Annie, and would be back by 4.00. Whatever she then did, she did not find Annie, and was not seen again until evening.

At 8.30, City **Police Constable Louis Robinson** found her causing a drunken disturbance outside 29 Aldgate High Street, where, according to **Tom Cullen**, she first attracted a small crowd by imitating a fire engine, and then lay down on the pavement to sleep. With the help of **Police Constable George Simmons**, Robinson took her to Bishopsgate Police Station where she gave her name as 'Nothing', and Station Sergeant **Byfield** locked her in a cell. At 8.50, Robinson looked in and found her asleep and smelling strongly of drink. At 9.45 **Police Constable George Hutt** came on duty and inspected the cells at regular intervals. At 12.15 a.m. Catharine was awake and singing softly to herself. At 12.30 she called out to ask when she could be released. 'When you are capable of taking care of yourself,' Hutt told her. 'I can do that now,' she replied. At 1.00 a.m. he released her and she asked the time. 'Too late for you to get any more drink,' he said. 'I shall get a damn fine hiding when I get home,' she told him. 'And serve you right,' he responded. 'You have no right to get drunk.' She gave her name and address as Mary Ann Kelly of 6 Fashion Street. And Hutt said amiably, 'This way, missus', as he guided her through the passage, and asked her to close the outer door after her. 'All right. Good night, old cock,' were Catharine's last recorded words.

At approximately 1.35 a.m., **Joseph Lawende, Joseph Hyam Levy** and **Harry Harris** saw her standing in the Duke's Place entrance to Church Passage, a covered entry leading into Mitre Square, talking amicably to a man with her hand on his chest. Lawende and Levy identified her by her clothes: neither saw her face.

Very shortly after they had left, at about 1.40 a.m. **Police Constable James Harvey** came along Duke's Place and down Church Passage on his beat. He saw no one and heard nothing from the square, which he did not enter.

At 1.45 (by his estimation) **Police Constable Edward Watkins** came into the square from the opposite side, and found Catharine Eddowes' body in the southwest corner. He immediately summoned **George Morris**, the nightwatchman at Kearley and Tonge's, to his assistance. Morris, running out into Aldgate, found Police Constable Harvey and **Police Constable Holland**. Holland went and fetched **Dr Sequeira** from Jewry Street: he, too, timed his arrival at 1.45 a.m. Station Inspector **Edward Collard** at Bishopsgate Police Station was informed of the discovery at 1.55, and sent for police surgeon **F. Gordon Brown** before going to the square, which he reached at 2.03. Brown arrived within a few minutes, followed by **Superintendent McWilliam** and **Sergeant Foster**. At some subsequent point, **Major Henry Smith** also arrived at Mitre Square.

Beside the body, **Sergeant Jones** found three boot buttons, a thimble and a mustard tin containing the pawn tickets for Emily Birrell's man's shirt, and Kelly's boots. These ultimately established Eddowes' identity.

The body was transferred to Golden Lane Mortuary. For Catharine Eddowes' appearance and injuries, see under **Dr Gordon Brown**. The official police listing of her clothes and possessions, taken at the mortuary, was as follows (we omit phrases detailing cuts and bloodstains caused by the murder):

Black Straw Bonnet trimmed with green & black Velvet and black beads, black strings . . .

Black Cloth Jacket, imitation fur edging round collar, fur round sleeves . . . 2 outside pockets, trimmed black silk braid & imitation fur.

Chintz Skirt, 3 flounces, brown button on waistband . . .

Brown Linsey Dress Bodice, black velvet collar, brown metal buttons down front . . .

Grey Stuff Petticoat, white waist band . . .

Very Old Green Alpaca Skirt . . .

Very Old ragged Blue Skirt, red flounce, light twill lining . . .

White Calico Chemise . . .

Mans White Vest, button to match down front, 2 outside pockets . . .

No Drawers or Stays.

Pair of Mens lace up Boots, mohair laces. right boot has been repaired with red thread . . .

1 *piece of red gauze Silk* . . . found on neck.

1 *large White Handkerchief* . . .

2 *Unbleached Calico Pockets* . . .

1 *Blue Stripe Bed ticking Pocket*, waist band, and strings . . .

1 *White Cotton Pocket Handkerchief*, red and white birds eye border.

1 *pr. Brown ribbed Stockings*, feet mended with white.

12 *pieces of white Rag*, some slightly bloodstained.

1 piece of white Coarse Linen.

1 piece of Blue & White Shirting (3 cornered).

2 Small Blue Bed ticking Bags.

2 Short Clay Pipes (black).

1 Tin Box containing Tea.

1 do do do Sugar.

1 Piece of Flannel & 6 pieces of soap.

1 Small Tooth Comb.

1 White Handle Table Knife & 1 metal Tea Spoon.

1 Red Leather Cigarette Case, white metal fittings.

1 Tin Match Box, empty.

1 piece of Red Flannel containing Pins & Needles.

1 Ball of Hemp.

1 piece of old White Apron.

Press reports add part of a pair of spectacles, one mitten, and a printed card for 'Frank Carter, 305 Bethnal Green Road'. They describe the outer chintz dress as having a pattern of chrysanthemums or Michaelmas daisies and lilies. The white apron was so dirty that at first glance it seemed black (**Walter Dew** so described it).

The other piece of the apron (approximately half) was picked up at 2.50 a.m. in the doorway of Wentworth Model Dwellings underneath the **Goulston Street graffito**. Since there was no doubt whatever that the piece was from Catharine's apron (it crossed and matched a repair), this constituted the one physical clue ever left by the Ripper, demonstrating that his escape route from Mitre Square was in the direction of northeast Whitechapel, Spitalfields or Mile End New Town.

The inquest on Catharine Eddowes was conducted by Coroner **Langham**. Although her daughter Annie Phillips testified to her scrounging to such an extent that her husband and children deliberately avoided her, others portrayed a more pleasant, if feckless, character. According to John Kelly, Elizabeth Fisher, another sister, **Eliza Gold**, and the deputy at Cooney's, **Frederick William Wilkinson**, she was very good natured and cheerful, often singing and rarely drunk. None of them claimed to know that she prostituted herself, though Kelly and Wilkinson would have good reason to avoid admitting such knowledge, lest charges of living off immoral earnings or brothel-keeping be brought against them. Still, we have no direct evidence that she did prostitute herself: only the suggestive facts that shortly before she died she was talking to a strange man at a dark corner in a direction leading away from the lodging house where she was staying; and that she had, apparently, no money at 2.00 p.m. on 29 September, but had acquired enough to make a drunken scene six hours later.

Her conversation with the police in Bishopsgate Police Station, coupled with her loyalty to Kelly, and what can be made out of her features beneath the injuries in her mortuary photographs, support the impression that she was probably the liveliest, as she was (just) the oldest of the Ripper's victims. She may not have known her precise age herself: her sister wrongly believed her to be only forty-three when she died.

She was buried in an unmarked grave in Ilford on 8 October, the expenses for an elm coffin and a funeral cortege led by an open-glass hearse being met by the undertaker, **Mr Hawkes**. Crowds lined the streets for the funeral.

EDE, THOMAS

Witness at the inquest on Mary Ann Nichols. Railway signalman. Despite queries as to the relevance, he was permitted by Coroner **Wynne Baxter** to give evidence on 17 September 1888 that he had seen a suspicious man in a two-peaked cap with four inches of knife blade protruding from his pocket outside The Foresters' Arms on 8 September. He returned to the inquest hearing of 22 September to confirm that he had now identified the harmless lunatic **Henry James** as the man he had seen.

ELLIOTT, DETECTIVE CONSTABLE GEORGE (b. 1860)

Warrant no. 65447. One of the policemen coming to the assistance of **Police Constable Ernest Thompson** when he discovered the body of Frances Coles.

ELLISDON, INSPECTOR ERNEST, J Division (b. 1846)
Joined Metropolitan Police, 1868; warrant no. 50657. Left and rejoined in
1872; warrant no. 56308. Resigned 1894. As Divisional Inspector played
little part in the murder investigation, but was responsible for putting
Inspector Reid in charge of the Martha Tabram inquiry.

ENRIGHT, DETECTIVE SERGEANT PATRICK, J Division
(b. 1849)
Warrant no. 58207. Joined Metropolitan Police, 1874; resigned, 1890,
suffering from tubercular infection of the lung. Given temporary charge of
Mary Ann Nichols' body at the mortuary, he left strict instructions that it
should not be touched. These were disregarded, and the full extent of her
injuries was revealed before she had been properly medically examined.
With **Abberline, Helson** and **Godley** he observed Nichols' inquest on
behalf of the CID.
   With **Inspector Reid** and **Sergeant Godley** he was named by the *Echo*
(20 September 1888) as following up a clue given by 'Pearly Poll' (see **Mary
Ann Connolly**) which led the authorities 'to suspect a man actually living
not far from Buck's Row'. (See **John Pizer, 'Leather Apron'**.) On 10
November 1888 he was gazetted in Police Printed Orders as receiving an
award of 5/- [25p] at the same time as **Sergeant Thick** was awarded 7/-.

EVANS, JOHN
Witness at Annie Chapman's inquest. Nightwatchman at **Crossingham's
Lodging House**. An elderly man, nicknamed Brummy. Testified to seeing
Annie at Crossingham's around 1.35 a.m., 8 September 1888. She said she
had just been out for a pint of beer. Also said she had been to Vauxhall to
see one of her sisters. She told Evans she had not enough money for her
bed, but would soon get it. Her last recorded words were to him: 'I won't
be long, Brummy. See that Tim [**Donovan**] keeps the bed for me.' He saw
her go up Little Paternoster Row in the direction of Brushfield Street. It
was his impression that she was the worse for drink.

F

FAIRCLOUGH, MELVYN (1944–)
Researcher and author of *The Ripper and the Royals* (1991). A furniture
restorer and friend of **Joseph Sickert**, Mr Fairclough has patiently worked
out as much as possible of the detailed story emerging from the old
gentleman's piecemeal recollections. He has also seen most, if not all, of his
collection of papers and photographs allegedly connected with the Ripper-
related stories, including the alleged **Abberline** journal of 1896.

'FAIRY FAY' (d. 1887)
Alleged murder victim.
    According to Terence Robertson, writing in *Reynolds News* (29 October
1950), this was the only known name of the Ripper's first victim. Found
murdered in back streets behind Commercial Road on Boxing Night, 1887,
having taken a short cut home from a pub in Mitre Square. **Inspector Reid**
directed the enquiry, and after a few weeks informed Scotland Yard that for
want of information the case had been shelved. The press paid scant
attention.
    With the possible exception of **Tom Cullen**, no subsequent researcher
has found *any* other mention of this incident. There is no trace of Reid's
report in the Scotland Yard files. The death registers show no 'Unknown
Female' dying in the East End on Boxing Night 1887; the only such to die
in Whitechapel that month perished of starvation and exposure. Nor were
Whitechapel women with interestingly similar names (Sarah Fayer, Alice
Farber, Emma Fairy) who died in December 1887 and December 1886
murder victims.

FANTASY ISLAND (1980, USA)
TV series starring Ricardo Montalban, Herve Villechaize; popular series
about self-indulgent wealthy people paying gross national income of a small
country to have their wishes granted on a mysterious island; episode 'With
Affection, Jack the Ripper'.

FARMER, AMELIA
See **Amelia Palmer**.

FARMER, ANNIE (born c. 1848)
Self-alleged Ripper victim.
    Separated wife of a City Road tradesman, Annie Farmer picked up a
shabby-genteel client in a suit at 7.30 a.m. on 20 November 1888, and took
him to Satchell's Lodging House, 19 George Street, Spitalfields, where he
took a bed for the two of them.
    At 9.30 Annie screamed, and the man, fully dressed, raced out of the

doss-house, along George Street and into Thrawl Street, where he shouted to two cokemen, 'What a — cow!' before disappearing into the crowd. Annie's throat was lightly cut, and she claimed the man had attacked her. Police found it was a shallow wound made with a blunt blade, quite unlike the Ripper's deep wounds inflicted with a sharp blade. They also discovered she was hiding coins in her mouth, and concluded that she had tried to rob her client, and devised the ingenious protection of injuring herself and accusing him of being Jack the Ripper.

FARMER SPUDD AND HIS MISSUS TAKE A TRIP TO TOWN
(1915, Great Britain)
Film directed by J. V. L. Leigh. We know little about this film except that the Spudds visit Madame Tussaud's in London and encounter a waxwork of the Ripper.

FARSON, DANIEL (b. 1927)
Theorist. Journalist, photographer, television presenter, author. BA (Cantab.). Journalist and staff photographer on *Picture Post*. Joined Associated Rediffusion Television, 1956, and also ran a pub, *The Waterman's Arms*, in Narrow Street, Limehouse. Many publications include: 'On the Trail of Jack the Ripper' (*TV Times*, 7 November 1959); *Jack the Ripper*, 1972; serialised in the *Evening News*, 18–22 September 1972; revised paperback, 1973; 'The Strange Obsession' (*Men Only*, June 1973).
In 1959 Farson presented television series *Farson's Guide to the British*. Two episodes, 5 and 12 November, revealed the initials of **Montague John Druitt**, whose name he had discovered in the **Aberconway** version of the **Macnaghten memoranda**.
Farson's huge importance in Ripper studies lies in that discovery of the Macnaghten memoranda, previously unknown to the public, and in his undertaking the initial research to establish the historical existence of Montague John Druitt. This was a landmark, establishing at last the identity of the body taken from the Thames and so often alleged by sources emanating from Scotland Yard to be the Ripper. It represents the essential starting point for all serious modern studies of the case.
For his further work in trying to establish Druitt as the Ripper, see: **Montague John Druitt, *Jack the Ripper* (Farson)**, *The East End Murderer – I Knew Him*.

FBI PSYCHOLOGICAL PROFILE OF THE RIPPER
Prepared, 1988, on suggestion of William Eckert of the Milton Helpern Institute of Forensic Sciences, for Cosgrove-Muerer TV Productions, and broadcast internationally by them in the programme *The Secret Identity of Jack the Ripper*.
Salient features of the profile were: a male in his late twenties, locally resident. Employed, since murders were associated with weekends. Free from family accountability, since murders took place between midnight and 6.00 a.m. Low class, since murders evinced marked unfastidiousness. Not surgically or anatomically skilled. Likely to have been in some form of trouble with police prior to murders. Likely to be seen by associates as a loner. Likely to have been abused as a child, especially by or with concurrence of his mother.

FENIANS AND FENIANISM
Nineteenth-century terms for illegal and dubiously legal Irish Nationalist activists and their doings. Important in 1888 because the Irish problem dominated politics, and the Fenians monopolised senior police attention, especially many of those most engaged in the Ripper case. (See **Anderson, Monro, Williamson**.) Recurrent Fenian dynamite campaigns included successful explosion of a bomb in Scotland Yard, and an unsuccessful plot to dynamite Westminster Abbey during the Queen's Jubilee of 1887.

Since the radical press (notably the *Star* and the *Pall Mall Gazette*) favoured the Irish national cause, Scotland Yard suffered from journalistic objections to precautionary measures, which could be construed as unwarranted infringement on freedom of opinion. For this reason (in part) a hostile campaign attacking the Metropolitan Police was already under way when the Whitechapel Murders began, and the radical press willingly used them as a new weapon.

Expectation of the Special Parliamentary Commission on allegations made in *The Times* series 'Parnellism and Crime' also affected Anderson and Monro in 1888, as both had much to lose if it emerged that they had secretly assisted anonymous journalistic attacks on elected MPs.

Sir Charles Warren, a Liberal, had been appointed by Gladstone's Home Secretary **Childers**, and then suffered press abuse for loyally carrying out the anti-Irish Nationalist policies of the subsequent Conservative Government. Nor did Conservative Home Secretary **Henry Matthews** support him against attack.

See under **Balfour** for direct links between police anti-Fenian and Ripper investigations.

FERRETT, INSPECTOR ARTHUR, H Division (b. 1844)
Joined Metropolitan Police 1865; warrant no. 46631. Retired 1891. On 7 December 1888, Ferrett was the officer bringing charges against **Gertrude Smith** and **Mary Jones** for brothel-keeping, heard by Thames Magistrates Court under the same Minute of Adjudication (21451) as **Ellen Hickey** for assaulting **N. Cohen**, and producing **Aaron Davis Cohen** as a lunatic at large. (See under **Mary Jones, David Cohen** for importance.)

In March 1889 when the fracas at the International Workers' Educational Club led to sentences for **Louis Diemschütz** and **Kozebrodsky** (see under **Diemschütz** for details), Diemschütz was refused permission to bring charges against Ferrett for failing to prevent a breach of the peace when the club members summoned police assistance.

FIDDYMONT, MRS
Informant. Landlady of now demolished Prince Albert in Brushfield Street, Spitalfields (known locally as 'the clean house'). Reported that a strange man entered the pub at 7.00 a.m. on 8 September 1888 with spots of blood on the back of his right hand, dried blood between his fingers, and a streak of blood below his right ear. After hurriedly drinking half a pint of beer he left the pub, and Mrs Fiddymont's friend **Mary Chappell** followed him and pointed him out to Joseph Taylor.

An early press report claimed that the police were not interested in Mrs Fiddymont's suspect. This cannot be reconciled with their use of Mrs Fiddymont to view an identification parade including the suspect **Pigott**, another involving **John Pizer**, and Abberline's stated intention of having her see **Issenschmidt** in Bow Infirmary Asylum as soon as his condition permitted. Abberline also reported (19 September): 'Issenschmidt . . . is identical with the man seen in the Prince Albert . . . by Mrs Fiddymont . . .' As the police rapidly lost interest in her, this may be true.

FILES

Many authors have repeated the canard that Scotland Yard's files on the Whitechapel Murders were suspiciously closed until 1992 and contained secret information which would ultimately identify the Ripper.

Actually, there is nothing suspicious about a serious crime file being closed for 75 or 100 years: it was and is normal practice. In fact, the Metropolitan Police and Home Office Files on the case have been open to researchers at the Public Record Office since 1976 and 1986 respectively, and had previously been seen by a number of writers – notably **Douglas Browne, Donald Rumbelow** and **Stephen Knight** – all of whom felt that they contained no material at all which would help scholars identify the murderer. Many serious researchers, however, feel that the version of the **Macnaghten memoranda** deposited in the files is extremely important. And other papers which have been examined give a valuable picture of the police conduct of the case.

Unfortunately, these papers were ruthlessly pillaged by souvenir-hunters until the PRO microfilmed them and denied researchers access to the originals under normal circumstances. Documents that have been seen by living authors (like the detailed report on **Robert Donston Stephenson**) are now missing. And the most important papers on suspects have never, as far as it is known, been seen by living researchers. The 'Suspect File' (HO144/220/49301A) at the Home Office contains such insignificant information that it acknowledges on the binder that it holds 'Absurd Cases Only'.

For the use of researchers we include a detailed listing and brief description of the important files on the murders under **Scotland Yard Files** and **Home Office Files**.

The bulk of the City Police files on the case were, unfortunately, lost in bomb damage.

FILMS AND JACK THE RIPPER

There has never been a factual dramatic reconstruction of the Ripper crimes. *Jack the Ripper* (1988) probably comes the nearest – and this may be taken as a good indication of how far removed into the realms of fantasy most Ripper films have been. Many so-called 'Ripper films' merely use the theme, some so loosely that it is difficult to see the Ripper connection, and others have simply used the name.

We have limited entries to those films in which the Ripper connection is, we hope, obvious. See under film titles (in chronological order): *Farmer Spudd and His Missus Take a Trip to Town*; *Das Wachsfigurenkabinett* (*Waxworks*); *The Lodger: A Story of the London Fog*; *Die Buchse der Pandora* (*Pandora's Box*); *The Lodger* (*The Phantom Fiend*); *Drôle de Drâme ou L'Étrange Aventure du Docteur Molyneux* (*Bizarre, Bizarre*); *The Lodger; Room to Let; Man in the Attic; Jack the Ripper; A Study in Terror; No Orchids for Lulu; Dr Jekyll and Sister Hyde; Hands of the Ripper; Jack el Destripador de Londres; The Groove Room; Black the Ripper; Der Dirnenmorder von London; Lulu* (France); *Lulu* (USA);

Time after Time; Murder by Decree; The Ripper; Bridge Across Time
(*Arizona Ripper; Terror at London Bridge*); **Jack's Back**.

'FINGERS FREDDY'
Recently alleged blackmailing accomplice of **Emma Elizabeth Smith**, and
possible Ripper victim or Ripper co-conspirator.

Described in **Superintendent Arthur Butler**'s articles in the *Sun* (1972)
as a threadbare criminal street entertainer who performed conjuring tricks
while accomplices picked the pockets of his audience. Butler heard that this
man was also Emma Elizabeth Smith's protector and associated with her in
an attempt to blackmail **Jill the Ripper** (midwife) by threatening to
denounce her as an illegal abortionist. Butler claims that Freddy disappeared after Smith's murder. Nobody knew whether he had been murdered
himself by a male accomplice of Jill the Ripper, or fled, knowing his own
life was in danger. Butler claimed to have heard this story so frequently that
he overcame his initial disbelief of it.

Melvyn Fairclough suggests that **Frederico Albericci**, East End criminal co-conspirator of **Lord Randolph Churchill** and **Sir William Gull** in
Joseph Sickert's most recent account of the **Freemasons'** conspiracy to
commit the Ripper crimes, may also have been known by the nickname
'Fingers Freddy'. We note the concomitant possibility that Butler's story is
garbled from Mr Sickert's sources, or vice versa.

FIRES ON THE DOCKS
John Pizer's innocence was in part established by reference to a conversation he held with a Metropolitan policeman in Seven Sisters Road (several
miles away from Whitechapel) on the night of 30–31 August, concerning
the great glow in the sky they could see from a fire on London Docks.

There were, in fact, two fires that night. The first was in the Spirit Quay,
South Dock, and it took from 8.30 p.m. to 11.30 to bring under control as
the intense heat from blazing gin and brandy in the first floor of a warehouse
prevented firemen from approaching close to it at first, while moored
vessels impeded the approach of fire-fighting ships. The other (which
Ellen Holland had been down to watch when she encountered Mary Ann
Nichols) broke out in Messrs Gibbs & Co.'s engineering works in Shadwell
Dry Dock, and destroyed a sailing ship's spars and rigging before spreading
to Gowland's Coal Wharf, where 800 tons of coal burned until late the
following morning.

FISHER, LIZZIE
Spitalfields woman, probably mistaken by another for Mary Jane Kelly.

An unnamed source (probably the same woman as '**Margaret**', who told
the Press Association Kelly had no money and intended to make away with
herself at the time of her death) told the *New York Times* that she had seen
Lizzie Fisher with a well-dressed man at 10.30 p.m. on 8 November 1888;
that Lizzie's little boy spent the night at a neighbour's, and was sent on an
errand by the man who was in his mother's second-floor lodging when he
returned home in the morning.

Since much of the story is identical with 'Margaret's' and inapplicable to
Kelly, it is probable that she too saw Lizzie Fisher and described her in
error as Kelly.

'FITZGERALD, ANNIE'

Alleged alias used by Elizabeth Stride on her appearances in Thames Magistrates Court for drunk and disorderly conduct. According to *The Times* she always denied being drunk and claimed that she suffered from fits. In fact, for the overwhelming majority of her frequent appearances, Stride used her own name. But on 10 June 1887 thirty-two-year-old Mary Ann Fitzgerald was fined 5/- [25p] with the option of five days for drunk and disorderly behaviour and using obscene language. The age and the offences fall within the ranges ascribed on other occasions to Stride.

FLOWER AND DEAN STREET

Held lodging-houses used by Elizabeth Stride, Catharine Eddowes and Mary Ann Nichols. Street running east-west between **Commercial Street** and **Brick Lane**. Laid out by builders John Flower and Gowen Dean, who bought adjacent sites for speculative development in 1655.

Contained many common lodging-houses used by prostitutes in the 1880s. Described in 1883 as 'perhaps the foulest and most dangerous street in the whole metropolis' (James Greenwood, *Strange Company*). Decades of agitation for its improvement culminated in Nathan Meyer Rothschild's purchase of a quarter of the street in 1883, and his construction of Charlotte de Rothschild Dwellings as cheap accommodation for the poor. After and in consequence of the Ripper scare, the remainder of the street was redeveloped, much of it by the Four Per Cent Dwelling Company.

Mr Foster, surveyor for the City of London Police, drew attention to its neighbourhood at the Catharine Eddowes inquest as, in his opinion, the Ripper's probable escape destination as indicated by the apron under the **Goulston Street graffito**.

Today only a short stretch of the western end remains, renamed Lolesworth Close. This is still sometimes used by local prostitutes serving pedestrian clients. The Clement Attlee Adventure Playground covers much of the original Flower and Dean Street, and Flower and Dean Walk runs transversely across the site.

FORENSIC SCIENCE

1888 was too early for forensic science to play a large part in the investigation. Microscopic examination of fragments of material or hair presumed to have come from the murderer had not been developed. **Dr Dutton**'s alleged microphotographs of the **'Jack the Ripper' letters** and **Goulston Street graffito** served no useful purpose, if they were ever taken.

It was a common complaint among police that no material clues had been left. Fingerprinting was suggested by a correspondent to *The Times* from his experience in the Far East, but even he showed the rudimentary state of forensics by remarking that it might be 'almost as useful' a clue as a footprint. Blood could be identified as mammalian, but not yet proved to be human or identified in blood groups.

Forensic medicine was taken seriously. Notably, the Metropolitan Police preferred **Dr Phillips**'s estimates of times of death to the contradictory evidence of **Mrs Darrell**, **John Richardson** and **Caroline Maxwell**. Researchers today are unanimous that the police were correct and Caroline Maxwell was wrong in believing she saw Mary Jane Kelly on the morning of 9 November 1888. Conversely, Dr Phillips is believed to have been mistaken in the case of Annie Chapman. It is noted that estimating time of death is still an imprecise art, depending on taking the internal body temperature (rectally or from the liver) and accurately estimating the likely speed of cooling in the air temperature. All doctors at the Ripper case contented themselves with estimating the body's external temperature by touch, and making further calculations on the (admittedly very imprecise) onset of rigor mortis. The state of digested food in the stomachs of victims would have been useful, except that the times of their last meals could not be established.

Three areas in which forensic medicine was reliable, however, were posthumous bruising; cause of death; and the nature of the weapon used. Bruising had been carefully studied in Edinburgh at the time of Burke and Hare's arrest in 1829, so the doctors could reliably assert that bruising on the victim's throats and necks had been caused before their throats had been cut. They could assert reliably that there were indications of asphyxiation prior to the throat-cutting, and that the cause of death was haemororrhage from the carotid artery; also that the abdominal and facial mutilations were posthumous. Measurement of wounds could accurately determine the maximum breadth and minimum length of the Ripper's knife.

See under **Dr Bond, Dr Brown, Dr Llewellyn, Dr Phillips, MO.**

FOSTER, DETECTIVE SUPERINTENDENT ALFRED LAWRENCE (1826–97)

City Police. Warrant no. 3636. Educ. King Edward's Grammar School, Warwick. Worked in solicitor's office before joining Prison Service, wherein he rose to become Deputy Governor of Clerkenwell House of Detention. 1864, invited by **Colonel Fraser** to serve in City Police as Superintendent. Rose to Chief Superintendent, and resigned, 1892. Married with two daughters and five sons, one of whom became Chief Inspector at Cloak Lane Police Station. A lifelong abstainer and active in the Temperance Movement, Foster was noted for his integrity and extreme courtesy.

Present in Mitre Square soon after the discovery of Catharine Eddowes' body. The *Evening News* reported that he was one of the detectives into whose care **Joseph Lawende** was entrusted during his sequestration. Foster's seniority may hint at the importance attached to this witness. He also informed the press on 1 October that the firemen at the night fire station in St James's Place, adjacent to Mitre Square, had been questioned, and had not noticed anybody around at the time of the murder.

FOSTER, FREDERICK

City Surveyor. Witness at the Catharine Eddowes inquest. Presented plans of Mitre Square, routes to Goulston Street, and location of doorway containing **Goulston Street graffito**. Also made sketches of Eddowes' injuries while the body was in the mortuary.

FOURNIER STREET

Held **Emma Elizabeth Smith**'s lodgings. Street running east-west between **Commercial Street** and **Brick Lane**. Originally called Church Street, it was developed at the time of the construction of **Christ Church**, Spitalfields. The houses, which are today very expensive and undergoing extensive restoration, were occupied by Huguenot silk-weavers who worked in the attics, the windows of which were designed to give maximum light.

On the Commercial Street corner is **The Ten Bells**. On the Brick Lane corner, a large Huguenot chapel built in 1742 has been successively an English nonconformist chapel, a mission for the Society for the Propagation of the Gospel among the Jews, a synagogue, and a mosque. No building's history so manifestly declares the changing history of the neighbourhood.
Cf. **Miss Lyons**.

FRANCE, MURDERS IN
A group of stories, perhaps connected, referring to Ripper-like murders in Paris prior to 1888. The perpetrator/s either came under suspicion as being the Ripper, or lay behind other suspect theories.

Many newspapers of 1888 reported that in 1872 **Nicolai Wassilli** had murdered one or more prostitutes in Paris. He was allegedly released from an asylum in January 1888, and believed to have come to London. Michael Mack may have referred to him when he wrote to *The Times* that he had read a French work in 1887 describing the murder and mutilation of several Paris prostitutes 'many years ago'. Mack, however, believed the perpetrator had been executed.

The *Independence Belge* recalled the murder of a young Parisienne whose dismembered body had been found in front of Montrouge church in November 1886. Her head, legs and right arm had been severed, and her right breast and uterus taken away. The paper said that the torso was wrapped in wax cloth and tied with whipcord of English manufacture. This is apparently the murder attributed by the *Ochrana Gazette* to **Vassily Konovalov**.

FRASER, COLONEL SIR JAMES (1814–92)
Commissioner, City of London Police. Son of Colonel Robert Fraser and Sarah Forbes; entered the army, rising to Colonel of 54th Foot. 1854, resigned his commission and became Chief Constable of Berkshire. Hoped to become Metropolitan Commissioner, but took it with good grace when Sir Edward Henderson was appointed, and accepted Commissionership of the City Police instead in 1863. His relations with the Mayor and Corporation were always excellent. By the time of the Whitechapel Murders he was ready for retirement. He was on leave when Catharine Eddowes' murder in Mitre Square involved the City Force, but does not appear to have objected to **Major Henry Smith**'s continuing to pursue the case vigorously after his return. Fraser retired in 1890.

FREEMASONS AND FREEMASONRY
Men's secret society, demonstrably dating back to late 17th or early 18th century, though members claim it derives directly from the Medieval Guild of peripatetic stonemasons.

From its earliest definitely recorded period, Freemasonry mixed alleged remnants of medieval craftsmen's traditions with the supposed hermeneutic beliefs and 'lore' of Christian Rosenkreutz and similar semi-occult adepts. Despite this highly irrational content, Freemasonry became a focus of anti-clericalism and anti-autocracy during the age of reason, and thereby attracted the condemnation of the Vatican. Many distinguished men, such as Mozart and Voltaire, were Masons or associated with Masonic lodges.

By the late 19th century, English Freemasonry was, as it is today, essentially an organisation supporting charities and practising mutual self-help among members. It was highly pro-establishment, and included several members of the royal family. Its 'secret' activities consisted of certain elaborate rituals conveying instruction in the legendary 'lore' and binding members to secrecy with blood-curdling oaths. Despite all of which, any large public library will contain books revealing the essential secrets of the 'craft' and the liturgy of its basic rituals.

It has come under reasonable suspicion from the general feeling that Masons in certain public bodies (notably the police and local authorities) may extend fraternal help to brother-Masons in ways that would be considered potentially corrupt in any other context, and irrational suspicion from the fear that its rituals and lore conceal anti-christian or occult tendencies. But there seems no justification whatsoever for the suggestion that a conspiracy of Freemasons prompted by **Lord Salisbury** and executed by **Sir William Gull** and **Walter Sickert** carried out the Whitechapel Murders.

This was first proposed by **Joseph Gorman Sickert** and **Stephen Knight**. The only concrete link between the murders and Masonry either proposed was the word 'Juwes' in the **Goulston Street graffito**. This, it was suggested, was the collective noun for Jubela, Jubelo and Jubelum, the mythical murderers of the equally mythical Hiram Abiff, master-mason of Solomon's Temple, as revealed to postulants in early stages of Freemasonry. Unfortunately, Jubela, Jubelo and Jubelum were dropped from English Masonic rites early in the 19th century, and would almost certainly have been completely unknown to English Masons of 1888. Moreover, historians of Freemasonry are not aware of the term 'Juwes' ever having been applied to them in Britain where they were referred to collectively as 'The Three Ruffians'.

Knight and Sickert's allegations are further vitiated by their almost total ignorance of the Masonic affiliation or otherwise of the protagonists in the Ripper case. Their guesses were usually wrong. (See, e.g., **Wynne Baxter, Dr Bagster Phillips, Lord Salisbury**.)

FREINBERG, ALEXANDER
Coffee stall holder of 51 Leman Street, who anglicised his name to Alexander Finlay. Victim of threatened assault by **Charles Ludwig**.

FROM CONSTABLE TO COMMISSIONER: THE STORY OF SIXTY YEARS: MOST OF THEM MISSPENT
Book by Lieutenant-Colonel Sir Henry Smith (1910). Memoirs of the man who, as Assistant City Police Commissioner in 1888, handled much of the Catharine Eddowes case in the absence, on leave, of Commissioner **Colonel Fraser**.

The title exemplifies the normal level of accuracy: Smith joined the police aged forty-four with the immediate rank of Chief Superintendent and the correct anticipation that retirements would ensure his rapid rise to Assistant Commissioner and Commissioner. He was never a constable in his life. The subtitle exemplifies the persistent tone of self-mocking persiflage.

The Scotland Yard library copy contains a handwritten annotation under the author's name:

A good raconteur and a good fellow, but not strictly veracious: most of the book consists of after dinner stories outside his personal experience.

In dealing with matters within his own knowledge he is often far from accurate as my own knowledge of the facts assures me.

G.H.E.

GHE was George H. Edwards, Secretary to the Metropolitan Police, 1925–7, and the book fully bears out his strictures. For its extensive comments on Jack the Ripper, see under **Major Henry Smith**.

FRYING PAN, THE
Public house on the corner of Brick Lane and Thrawl Street where Mary Ann Nichols said she drank away her doss money on the last night of her life.

FULLER, JEAN OVERTON
Theorist and informant. Author of *Sickert and the Ripper Crimes* (1990). Daughter of Captain J. H. M. Fuller and artist Violet Overton Fuller. Educ. London University (BA Eng.). Brief career on stage. Examiner in Postal Censorship during WWII. Poet and author of books, frequently touching tangentially on modern occultists.

Her *The Magical Dilemma of Victor Neuberg* (1965) refers to Vittoria Cremers' story that **Robert Donston Stephenson** was Jack the Ripper. *Sickert and the Ripper Crimes*, which suggests that **Walter Sickert** was the Ripper, is most important for its evidence (via **Florence Pash**) that **Joseph Gorman Sickert** and/or member/s of his family were circulating the claim that he was Walter Sickert's son and possibly **Prince Albert Victor**'s grandson as early as 1948.

G

GALLAGHER, POLICE CONSTABLE 221H
Arrested **Charles Ludwig** when summoned by **Alexander Freinberg**.

GANGS IN THE EAST END
Emma Smith was undoubtedly murdered by a group of muggers, probably from 'The Nichol', a criminal slum surrounding Old Nichol Street at the top of Brick Lane.

Other gangs were locally feared and suspected of being involved in the murders. The best-known East End gangs of the period were the Blind Beggar Gang (race track pickpockets), the Hoxton High-Rips, and the Limehouse Forty Thieves.

GARDNER, JOHN
Labourer of 11 Chapman Street. Witness at Elizabeth Stride's inquest. Saw Elizabeth Stride and a male companion at The Bricklayers' Arms, Settles Street, on 29 September 1888. He corroborated the story of his friend, **J. Best**, in every detail. Also added (to *Evening News* reporter) that the woman he had seen had a flower pinned to her dress.

GEORGE YARD (today Gunthorpe Street)
Martha Tabram's murder site. A narrow alley running north-south between Wentworth Street and Whitechapel High Street. Entered by a covered archway from Whitechapel High Street, next to The White Hart. Tabram's body was found on the first floor landing of George Yard Buildings, a tenement on the eastern side of the alley at its northern end where, today, residential flats stand adjacent to the back of Toynbee Hall. **Severin Klosowski** worked in a barber's shop in the basement of The White Hart at the time of the murders.

Cobbled George Yard, with its picturesque arched entry, holds more of the atmosphere of the Ripper's day than any other genuine Ripper-related site in the East End.

GISSING, GEORGE ROBERT (1857–1903)
Alleged suspect. Author of naturalist novels (notably *New Grub Street*) and aesthetic *belles lettres* (notably *The Private Papers of Henry Rycroft*). Named by **Richard Whittington-Egan** in a list of unlikely prominent Victorians suggested occasionally as suspects. Gissing left Owen's College, Manchester, in disgrace after contracting a disastrous marriage with a prostitute. Presumably this scandalous *mésalliance*, coupled with the almost unrelieved gloom of some of his writing, led to the suggestion that he might have been the Whitechapel murderer.

GLADSTONE, RIGHT HONOURABLE WILLIAM EWART
(1809–98)
Alleged suspect.

The high-minded Victorian Prime Minister took a vow, while an undergraduate, to devote his spare time to fighting the social evil of prostitution. He carried this out throughout his life, bravely risking scandal by visiting demi-mondaines, and taking street-walkers home for tea and improving conversation with his wife. This association with prostitution gave rise to the suggestion that the Leader of the Opposition (as he was in 1888) might himself have taken to a more vigorous procedure than exhortation to put an end to vice. It carries no weight whatsoever – among other reasons, one might note that Gladstone's missionary activities were invariably carried out in the West End.

A later gloss was the suggestion that the Ripper carried a little black bag (see **Goldstein, Hutchinson, Police Constable Smith**) and it was notorious that Gladstone bags were named after the statesman. In fact, Mr Gladstone did not carry such a bag himself; the nickname derived from a famous speech in which he demanded that the Turk be driven from the Balkans, 'bag and baggage'.

GODLEY, DETECTIVE SERGEANT GEORGE (1858–1941)
Prominent in the Ripper investigations. Born in East Grinstead, Sussex, he was a sawyer before joining the Metropolitan Police in 1877. Warrant no. 61230. Retired in 1908 with the rank of Detective Inspector.

He was serving in J Division (Bethnal Green) CID in 1888. He observed Mary Ann Nichols' inquest on behalf of the CID, in company with **Abberline**, **Helson** and **Enright**. The *Police Review* said on his retirement: 'Called in each case from his bed while the bodies were still warm, Mr Godley's knowledge of this series of crimes is perhaps as complete as that of any Officer concerned.' The same article says he was first on the scene of the Kelly murder (but see **Walter Beck, Walter Dew**).

Godley is today remembered chiefly as the officer who arrested the poisoner **Severin Klosowski** (George Chapman), after whose trial Abberline allegedly said to him, 'I see you've got Jack the Ripper at last.'

He does not feature prominently in any of the Ripper reports, though the *Echo*, misspelling his name 'Goadby', said that with **Reid** and **Enright** he was engaged in searching for a suspect 'actually living not far from Buck's Row' on 20 September.

GOLD, MRS ELIZA
Catharine Eddowes' sister, and witness at her inquest. Mrs Gold described Catharine as being of sober habits. Said she earned her living as a hawker and had last been living at 55 Flower and Dean Street.

GOLDSTEIN, LEON
Resident of Berner Street vicinity who may have triggered belief in the Ripper's habit of carrying a shiny black bag.

Mrs Fanny Mortimer told police the only person to pass through Berner Street in the fifteen minutes or so she stood outside prior to Elizabeth Stride's murder was a man carrying a shiny black bag who hurried down the street, glancing up at the **International Workingmen's Educational Club** as he passed it. This was subsequently exaggerated in the recollection of **Walter Dew** (at least) to his having hurried *through* Dutfield's Yard, the precise spot where the body was found.

The day after the murder, Goldstein, of 22 Christian Street, presented himself at Leman Street Police Station, and identified himself as the man seen by Mrs Mortimer. He had been going home with a bag full of empty cigarette boxes from a coffee shop in Spectacle Alley.

The only press report on Goldstein known to us is in *Lloyd's Weekly London Newspaper*, 7 October 1888. Inadequate publicity given to his self-identification probably permitted the plethora of suspicious black-bag-carrying men reported thereafter.

GORMAN, JOSEPH
See **Joseph Gorman Sickert**.

GOULDING, POLICE CONSTABLE ROBERT
Discovered the body of Rose Mylett in Clarke's Yard, Poplar, concluding immediately that she had died of natural causes.

GOULSTON STREET GRAFFITO
Alleged clue left by the Ripper.

Chalked words found by **Police Constable Alfred Long** at 2.55 a.m., 30 September 1888, on the black brick fascia edging the open doorway of the staircase and basement door of nos 108–19, Wentworth Model Dwellings, Goulston Street. The graffito was almost immediately above the blood-stained portion of Catharine Eddowes' apron which the murderer had thrown into the doorway in his flight from the scene of the crime. (See under **Catharine Eddowes** for brief description of the apron clue and its topographical importance.) Long said that the apron had not been there when he previously passed the doorway at 2.20, but he did not notice whether the words were or not.

The graffito became a matter of immediate controversy. The Metropolitan Police and the Home Office agreed that the wording was 'The Juwes are the men That Will not be Blamed for nothing', as noted (except for the misspelling 'Juwes') by Police Constable Long. The City Police claimed that it was 'The Juwes are not The men That Will be Blamed for nothing', as noted by **Detective Constable Halse**. Other observers proposed minor variations. The difference could not be resolved, since the Metropolitan Police erased the words at approximately 5.30 a.m. without photographing them, despite City Police requests that they should be photographed.

There has been dispute ever since as to whether the words were or were not written by the murderer; as to whether they were intended to expose, confess, create false suspicion of, or refute Jewish association with the crime; as to whether the word 'Juwes' meant Jews at all.

Chief Inspector Swanson, in a report to the Home Office, stated that the chalk was 'blurred'. **Superintendent Arnold**, who went to the spot, concluded immediately that the graffito had nothing to do with the murder. But he feared that traders coming to Petticoat Lane Market would believe from its position it was a clue, and it would revive the **anti-Semitism** that the earlier **'Leather Apron'** enquiry had provoked. The Wentworth Model Dwellings, erected the previous year, were largely occupied by Jews, and a disturbance might have flared up on the spot. Arnold therefore had an Inspector with a wet sponge in readiness when **Sir Charles Warren** authorised the erasure of the graffito, and he was praised by Warren for his promptitude.

Walter Dew subsequently remarked that the graffito was one among many in the district purporting to be by the murderer, and he did not believe any of them to be genuine.

But **Detective Constable Halse**, one of the first City policemen on the scene, claimed that the words appeared to have been written recently. He said that he had previously passed the doorway at approximately 2.20 and had noticed neither words nor apron. He said that he had urged that they should be photographed, or that all but the top line (containing the word 'Juwes') should be retained, only to be overruled by the Metropolitan Police. **Major Henry Smith** and **Superintendent McWilliam** also claimed to have ordered that they be photographed.

Sir Charles Warren suspected that the words were intended to cast false suspicion on Jewish radicals. When the press suggested that 'Juwes' was Yiddish for Jews, he issued a public statement that the word 'Juwes' did not mean Jews in any known language, and was personally thanked by the Chief Rabbi for this contribution to countering anti-Semitism.

BBC researchers working on *The Ripper Files* suggested that the words 'Juwes' referred to the Masonic-loric figures Jubela, Jubelo and Jubelum (see under **Freemasons and Freemasonry**) and **Stephen Knight** and **Joseph Sickert** accepted this view, claiming the words were written by **Sir William Gull**.

GRAINGER, WILLIAM GRANT (born c. 1858)

Near-contemporaneous suspect. Born Cork. Went to sea, c. 1873. Joined Cork City Artillery, 1883, and trained annually with them until dismissed in 1889 as being of bad character. During 1887–90 he repeatedly stayed in Cork Workhouse; from 1889 there were also interludes in Fulham Workhouse. In February 1891 he spent a month in Banstead Asylum; subsequently returning to Cork, Fulham and St Pancras Workhouses, and twice being sentenced to imprisonment for drunkenness in the East End. Supposedly he frequented the company of loose women, but was frequently cheated and robbed of garments by them, and at least once lost all his clothes in Whitechapel.

In March 1895 he was caught retreating from the junction of Butler Street and the Tenter Ground, Spitalfields, where he had just inflicted a 1½ in. 'rip' in Alice Grahame's abdomen. Under arrest, he remarked that Alice Grahame had been extortionate. Speculation immediately began in the press that he might be Jack the Ripper. He gave his occupation as ship's fireman, though neither he nor his mother could identify any ship on which he had served.

He was sentenced to ten years penal servitude, but was paroled after seven. His solicitor, Mr Kebbel, in the meantime, put it about that he was Jack the Ripper and had died in prison. In 1910 **L. Forbes Winslow** issued a magisterial denial of this claim. He asserted that he had personally taken up the case of Grainger (whom he called Grant). He agreed with Kebbell that Grainger had trained as a medical student, been cast off by his family, and sunk to the position of fireman on a cattleboat. But Winslow knew he could not be the Ripper because he did not fit what Winslow had discovered about **G. Wentworth Bell Smith**, who, Winslow was sure, was the Ripper and had given up his crimes because Winslow scared him off.

One point in the suspicion of Grainger has real importance. The *Pall Mall Gazette* of 7 May 1895 reported that

there is one person whom the police believe to have actually seen the Whitechapel murderer with a woman a few minutes before that woman's dissected body was found in the street. That person is stated to have identified Grainger as the man he saw. But obviously identification after so cursory a glance, and after the lapse of so long an interval, could not be reliable; and the enquiries were at length pulled up in a *cul-de-sac*.

The *Gazette*'s point is self-evidently sound. But the authors note that if the person believed by the police to have seen the Whitechapel murderer was **Anderson's witness**, then considerable doubt is cast upon his earlier identification of **Anderson's suspect**.

GRAND, MR

Private Detective of 283 The Strand, employed with his colleague **J. H. Batchelor** by the Whitechapel Vigilance Committee and certain newspapers (including the *Evening News*) to make enquiries following the night of the double murder.

They learned that **Miss Eva Harstein** and her sister Mrs Rosenfield had seen a blood-caked grapestalk and some flower petals in the entry to Dutfield's Yard before the police washed it down after Elizabeth Stride's murder. Grand and Batchelor recovered a grapestalk from rubbish swept by police into the drain in Dutfield's Yard. They then learned from **Matthew Packer** that he had sold grapes to the man accompanying Stride an hour or more before her death, a fact he had omitted to tell the police in their routine questioning.

The *Evening News* featured these discoveries very prominently, crowing over their success in finding a 'clue' the police had missed, and compelling further questioning of Packer. (See also **Sergeant Stephen White**.)

GRANT, WILLIAM
See **W. G. Grainger**.

GRAPES IN ELIZABETH STRIDE'S HAND
See under **Matthew Packer, Dr Bagster Phillips, Elizabeth Stride** for discussion.

GRAY, ALFRED
Briefly suspected. English vagrant arrested in Tunis, January 1889, with a gang of burglars. Suspected briefly of being the Ripper when a naked woman tattooed on his arm was noticed, and it was learned that he had come from Spitalfields where he lived with an Italian woman.

GREEN, MRS EMMA
Witness at Mary Ann Nichols' inquest. Widow, living with her daughter and two sons in New Cottage, Buck's Row, the end house of the terrace adjoining Brown's stable yard gate, where the body was found. Although Mrs Green's and her daughter's bedroom window almost overlooked the murder site, and she was a light sleeper, neither heard anything unusual until the police began their investigation of the newly-discovered body. Her son washed the blood away from the gutter after the body had been removed.

GREEN, JAMES
Witness at Annie Chapman's inquest. A man of medium height, with short, neatly plastered-down hair, he lived at 36 Acton Street, Burdett Road, and worked for **John and Thomas Bayley**, the packing-case manufacturers of 23a Hanbury Street. With **James Kent**, he was summoned by **John Davis** immediately on discovery of the body.

GREEN, WALTER
Resided with the retired Inspector and Mrs **Abberline** in Bournemouth, possibly as lodger or paying guest. It was for his benefit that Abberline compiled a collection of his press-cuttings with annotations on the cases which most interested him.

GREEN HORNET, THE (1966, USA)
TV series (26 × 25 min) starring Van Johnson and Bruce Lee; comic book heroes à la Batman; episode 'Alias the Scarf'.

GRIBBLE, LEONARD
Author. Publications include: many books of true crime and crime fiction; entry 'Jack the Ripper' in *Chambers Encyclopaedia* (1966); 'Was Jack the Ripper a Black Magician?' in *True Detective*, March 1973; 'The Man They Thought Was Jack the Ripper' in *True Detective*, March 1977.

'Was Jack the Ripper a Black Magician?' retails a secondhand version of the **'Dr Stanley'** story, adding that the doctor used so-called black arts to protect himself. It also suggests that **Aleister Crowley** knew the Ripper's identity. 'The Man They Thought Was Jack the Ripper' examines and dismisses **Severin Klosowski**.

GRIFFITHS, MAJOR ARTHUR HENRY (1838–1908)
Crime historian, publicising opinions of **Melville Macnaghten**. Born Poona, India. Educ. King William's College, Isle of Man. Entered army 1855 and served in the Crimea, and at Gibraltar (1864–70) where, among other duties, he had temporary charge of the convict establishment. On return to England, became, successively, deputy Governor of Chatham Prison (1870–2), Millbank (1872–4), and Wormwood Scrubs (1874–81). Also Inspector of Prisons 1878–96. Acknowledged authority on London and European prison systems and history, he wrote extensively on the subject, in both factual and fictional forms.

Publications include: *Mysteries of Police and Crime* (3 vols, 1898–1903); *Fifty Years in Public Service* (1904).

In *Mysteries of Police and Crime*, he wrote:
The general public may think that the identity of . . . Jack the Ripper was never revealed. So far as actual knowledge goes, this is undoubtedly true. But the police, after the last murder, had brought their investigations to the point of strongly suspecting several persons, all of them known to be homicidal lunatics, and against three of these they held very plausible and reasonable grounds of suspicion. Concerning two of them the case was weak, although it was based on certain colourable facts. One was a Polish Jew, a known lunatic, who was at large in the district of Whitechapel at the time of the murders, and who, having afterwards developed homicidal tendencies, was confined in an asylum. This man was said to resemble the murderer by the one person who got a glimpse

of him – the police-constable in Mitre Court. The second possible criminal was a Russian doctor, also insane, who had been a convict both in England and Siberia. This man was in the habit of carrying about knives and surgical instruments in his pockets; his antecedents were of the very worst, and at the time of the Whitechapel murders he was in hiding, or, at least, his whereabouts were never exactly known. The third person was of the same type, but the suspicion in his case was stronger, and there was every reason to believe that his own friends entertained grave doubts about him. He was also a doctor in the prime of life, was believed to be insane or on the borderland of insanity, and he disappeared after the last murder, that in Miller's Court, on 9 November 1888. On the last day of the year, seven weeks later, his body was found floating in the Thames, and was said to have been in the water for a month. The theory in this case was that after his last exploit, which was the most fiendish of all, his brain entirely gave way, and he became furiously insane and committed suicide.

Griffiths is here referring to **Kosminski, Ostrog** and **M. J. Druitt**, the three suspects named in the **Macnaghten memoranda**. Indeed, Griffiths so closely parallels Macnaghten that it may be taken as certain he is recapitulating information received from him. He echoes, for example, Macnaghten's unique reference to a City police constable witness in the vicinity of Mitre Square.

He gives some important expansion of Macnaghten's information: notably the fact that the three named suspects emerged as the most 'plausible and reasonable' from a group under consideration. (Cf **G. R. Sims**.) We note his extraordinary remark that the Polish Jew developed homicidal tendencies *after* committing a series of atrocious murders.

GROOVE ROOM, THE (WHAT THE SWEDISH BUTLER SAW, CHAMPAGNE GALLOP, and possibly other titles) (1973, Sweden)

Film directed by Vernon P. Becker. Stars Sue Longhurst, Ole Soltoft, Diana Dors, Martin Ljung (Ripper). We understand that this is a pornographic comedy with Ripper theme as sub-plot!

GULL, SIR WILLIAM WITHEY (1816–90)

Recently alleged suspect. Eminent clinical physician. MD (London), 1846; FRCP, 1848. Medical Tutor and Lecturer, Guy's Hospital, and Fullerian Professor of Physiology (1847–9). FRS, 1869. Honorary doctorates: Oxford, Cambridge and Edinburgh. 1871, treated **Albert Edward, Prince of Wales** for typhus. Created baronet the following year. 1887–90, physician-in-ordinary to Queen Victoria. Suffered a minor stroke in 1887 which left him slightly paralysed on the right side. Thereafter suffered three epileptiform attacks and two further strokes, dying one month after the last of these.

Despite claims that he was the unnamed physician allegedly psychically identified by **Robert James Lees**, and the possibility that he was the unnamed 'royal surgeon' who avenged his venereally infected son, in the story related to **Michael Harrison** when he was a child (cf. **'Dr Stanley'**), the first published naming of Gull in connection with the Whitechapel Murders was made by **Dr Thomas Stowell** in his article in the *Criminologist* in 1970.

As the former junior partner and close friend of Gull's son-in-law, Dr

Theodore Dyke Acland, Stowell had learned from Gull's daughter, Caroline Acland, a good deal about her father. There seemed to be some possible validity in the claim that R. J. Lees thought he had identified Gull as the Ripper, since Lady Gull had once allegedly been infuriated by a visit from a psychic medium and a policeman who asked impertinent questions; moreover, it was suggested that Gull had occasional 'lapses of memory' after his stroke in 1887, and once found blood on his shirt.

Stowell's basic theory accused **Prince Albert Victor**, Duke of Clarence and Avondale, of the murders. But he associated Gull with this as the family doctor who might have followed, exposed and incarcerated his royal patient. In support of this, he remarked that 'It was said that on more than one occasion Sir William Gull was seen in the neighbourhood of Whitechapel on the night of a murder'. He does not say by whom this was said, and the authors are unaware of any evidence for the claim.

Frank Spiering's *Prince Jack* in essence repeats Stowell's story, claiming that it is supported by a diary entry of Gull's deposited in the New York Academy of Medicine. Stowell's account prompted **Michael Harrison** to propose another alleged patient of Gull's: **J. K. Stephen**.

But the major claim that Gull was Jack the Ripper was made by **Joseph Gorman Sickert** in the final episode of the 1973 BBC Drama Documentary series *Jack the Ripper* and picked up and elaborated by **Stephen Knight** in *Jack the Ripper: The Final Solution*. The basic theory was that Gull, as a fraternal act of **Freemasonry**, prompted by **Lord Salisbury**, used his surgical skill to murder Mary Jane Kelly and her cronies (who were trying to blackmail the Government with their knowledge of the secret and illegal marriage of Prince Albert Victor to **Annie Elizabeth Crook**), leaving mutilations as Masonic penalties for betraying secrets.

The case for believing Gull to have been the Ripper rests on: the alleged visit by a policeman and a medium; accepting the amnesiac episodes and bloody shirt as incriminatory; and believing Joseph Sickert's story.

The case against rests on: the dubious provenance of the story woven around R. J. Lees; the likelihood that any blackout suffered by Gull and accompanied by a blood-stained shirt was caused by one of his epileptiform seizures; and the unreliability of Joseph Sickert's story.

H

H DIVISION, METROPOLITAN POLICE

From its inception the Metropolitan Police was divided into areas or divisions for administrative purposes, and each was identified by a letter of the alphabet. H Division covered Whitechapel. The area within its jurisdiction has varied over the years, but in 1888 it included the sites of three Ripper murders: Annie Chapman's, Elizabeth Stride's and Mary Jane Kelly's. (Today its boundary on the Spitalfields Market side of Commercial Street would exclude Annie Chapman's in Hanbury Street.) In 1965, H Division, Whitechapel, was renamed H Division, Tower Hamlets.

HALSE, DETECTIVE CONSTABLE DANIEL (b. 1839)

Witness at Catharine Eddowes' inquest. Joined City of London Police, 1863. Retired with rank of Detective Constable, 1891.

Patrolling the City on the night of 29–30 September he was at the bottom of Houndsditch at about 1.58 a.m. with Detectives **Outram** and **Marriott**. All three responded to **George Morris**'s whistle from Mitre Square. Halse directed an immediate search of the district, and himself went via Middlesex Street to Wentworth Street, returning to Mitre Square via Goulston Street, which he passed at about 2.20, at which time he did not notice the **Goulston Street grafitto** and the piece of Eddowes' apron.

From Mitre Square he went with **Detective Hunt** to Leman Street, and then back to the site of the Goulston Street graffito. Halse believed the chalk writing to be of recent origin, and urged that it be photographed so that Major Smith could have a print to examine. When Metropolitan Police objected that traders arriving for Petticoat Lane Market might see it and cause an anti-Semitic disturbance, Halse suggested that only the top line containing the word 'Juwes' be erased, but he was overruled.

HANBURY STREET

Annie Chapman's murder site.

A long road in Spitalfields and Mile End New Town, curving south-east from **Commercial Street** to Baker's Row (today's Vallance Road) in the Ripper's day; now terminating in a footpath leading out onto the Vallance Road end of Old Montague Street.

Originally Brown's Lane (for Jeffrey and/or William Browne, connections of the Wheler family who owned property in the area c. 1662) to the junction with Brick Lane; Montague Street (for family of the Earls of Halifax, who bought land in the area 1639) to the junction with Spital Street. Renamed after Quaker brewer Sampson Hanbury, who joined the board of Sir Benjamin Truman's brewery, 1803. Police poster seeking information following the murder named it as 'Old Brown's Lane'.

The murder site, no. 29 Hanbury Street, was at the northern end of the street on the left-hand side of the road, proceeding away from Commercial Street. For many years it was covered by part of the brewery premises of Messrs Truman, Hanbury, Buxton. A hotel is now being erected on the site.

In 1888, no. 29 was a four-storey building with **Mrs Hardyman**'s cats' meat shop in the ground-floor front room. A door to the left of the shop-front opened into a passage which ran the depth of the building, with the stairs up and cellar door leading from it. It terminated in the back door, from which two steps led into the small fenced yard containing the privy. The murder site was the backyard. The body was found lying against the fence to the left of the door, with the head toward the doorsteps. Buildings on the other side of the road, and further southeast on the other side of Brick Lane, retain the appearance of 1888.

This murder site has long been said to be haunted by the ghost/s of Annie Chapman/and her murderer. The brewery building also contains other alleged psychic presences.

HANDS, CHARLES
Journalist on *Pall Mall Gazette* in 1888. Alleged by **William Le Queux** to have devised theories for publication in competition with himself and **Lincoln Springfield**.

HANDS OF THE RIPPER (1971, Great Britain)
Film directed by Peter Sasdy. Stars Eric Porter, Angharad Rees. Ripper's daughter seeks psychiatric help on discovering that she's inherited father's knife-wielding interests; far-fetched, but with Angharad Rees on screen, who cares, and memorable finale in St Paul's.

HARDYMAN, MRS ANNIE or HARRIET or MARY
Surname also given as **HARDMAN**.
Witness at **Annie Chapman**'s inquest. A woman of medium height with 'a curiously rounded' chin. Kept cats' meat shop in ground-floor front room of 29 Hanbury Street, where she also slept with her 16-year-old son. They used the ground floor back as a kitchen to cook the meat.

On 8 September 1888 she was aroused at about 6.00 a.m. by the noise made by **John Davis, James Green** and **James Kent** in the passage. She sent her son to see what was going on, but saw and heard nothing of the murder until he returned and told her of it.

HARRIS, HARRY
Companion of **Joseph Lawende** and **Joseph Hyam Levy**, witnesses at Catharine Eddowes' inquest.

A Jewish furniture dealer of Castle Street, Whitechapel. He left the Imperial Club (16–17 Duke Street) with Mr Lawende and Mr Levy at approximately 1.34 a.m., 30 September 1888. Where Church Passage ran off Duke Street they saw a man and a woman (Eddowes) talking. Harris paid little attention, and later declared he would not be able to identify either. He was not called as a witness at the inquest. He did, however, tell an *Evening News* reporter (9 October) that in his opinion, 'neither Mr Levander [*sic*] nor Mr Levy saw anything more than he did, and that was only the back of the man'. Lawende clearly maintained that he had seen the man's face.

HARRIS, MELVIN
Theorist. Author, broadcaster. Publications include *Sorry, You've Been Duped* (1986), *Jack the Ripper: The Bloody Truth* (1987), *The Ripper File* (1990). A teacher and lecturer, Melvin Harris became a full-time broadcaster on BBC Radio, where he had his own programme 'Strange to Relate'. A noted and respected investigator of mysteries of all types, and a distinguished debunker, he did research for Yorkshire Television's *Arthur C. Clarke's World of Strange Powers* series, and has exposed a great many false mysteries and claims to paranormal experience.

As a hobby, he makes baroque oboes to professional standard, and the Melvin Harris Collection at the University of Seattle is the world's largest assemblage of recordings of wind instrument performances.

HARRISON, MICHAEL (1907–)
Author and theorist. Publications include *The Life of the Duke of Clarence and Avondale 1864–1892* (1972; US title: *Clarence: Was He Jack the Ripper?*) Former editor, market research executive, and creative director of an advertising agency, he is a prolific author of novels and biographies, and a distinguished Sherlockian.

His life of Clarence proved to the entire satisfaction of the overwhelming majority of researchers that the Prince could not have been the Ripper, by establishing his whereabouts (see under **Prince Albert Victor**) on the nights of 29–30 September and 8–9 November 1888.

He did, however, conclude that **Sir William Gull**'s papers, as described by **Dr Stowell**, suggested that the murderer might well have been some other patient of Gull's, whose name possibly began with 'S'. He also speculated that this patient might have had some association with Clarence, and so put forward the **J. K. Stephen** theory.

HARRISON, PAUL
Theorist. Author of *Jack the Ripper: The Mystery Solved*.

'HARRY THE HAWKER'
Acquaintance, possibly client, of Annie Chapman, mentioned at her inquest. Alleged by some witnesses (but not **Eliza Cooper**) to be the cause of the dispute and fight between Cooper and Chapman the week before the murder. Since some members of the inquest jury knew Harry and declared no interest in hearing testimony from him, he was not further identified or called as a witness.

HARSTEIN, EVA
Resident of 14 Berner Street. Told detectives **Grand** and **Batchelor** she had seen a blood-stained grapestalk and some white flower petals in the passage entry to Dutfield's Yard where **Elizabeth Stride**'s body was found. (See under **Matthew Packer** for importance.)

HART, LYDIA (fl. 1889)
Suspected Pinchin Street victim.

The New York *World*, 11 September 1889, reported, 'The name of Jack the Ripper's last victim is said to be Lydia Hart, a well-known character in the East End who has been missing from her normal haunts for nearly a week.'

Presumably a prostitute, Lydia Hart's identity with the Pinchin Street torso was never confirmed.

HART, POLICE CONSTABLE, 161H
Uniformed constable, first on the scene in response to **Police Constable Ernest Thompson**'s whistle on discovering **Frances Coles'** body. Hart then went to fetch a doctor. Cf. **Benjamin Leeson**.

HARVEY, POLICE CONSTABLE JAMES, 964 City
Witness at Catharine Eddowes' inquest. Joined City of London Police 1876; warrant no. 5045. Dismissed 1 July 1889 for reasons presently unknown. His beat on 30 September 1888 took him down Duke Street, along Church Passage and back, without actually entering Mitre Square. He entered Church Passage at 1.40 a.m. (estimated from his observation of Aldgate Post Office clock when he passed it) and saw and heard nothing suspicious.

HARVEY, MRS MARIA
Witness at Mary Jane Kelly's inquest.
According to **Joe Barnett**, Kelly's lover for the previous eighteen months, he had ceased cohabiting with her when she admitted prostitutes to stay in their room: first a German called **'Julia'**, then Mrs Harvey.
Maria Harvey deposed that she was a laundress and lived at 3 New Court, Dorset Street. She had slept with Kelly on the Monday and Tuesday before her death, and passed Thursday afternoon with her. She was in her room when Joe Barnett called (between 7.30 and 7.45, by his account), whereupon she left.
This testimony has caused some confusion, as it has always been assumed that Mrs Harvey was claiming to have been the 'young female' Barnett said was with Kelly when he visited her on the eve of the murder, and whom he did not know. Yet **Lizzie Albrook**'s press interviews make it evident that she was the person Barnett described, and he certainly knew Maria Harvey.
Mrs Harvey's first interview with *The Times* (10 November) clears the point up. She had spent the afternoon with Kelly, who came to visit her in New Court. They went out drinking, and separated at about 7.30 p.m. Mrs Harvey believed Kelly was going 'in the direction' of Leman Street which she 'was in the habit of frequenting' (i.e. soliciting in Aldgate). She did not in this interview mention Barnett at all.
Under oath at the inquest, however, she could not thus pass him over, but at the same time she was not asked questions relating to the precise time she had spent with Kelly or its whereabouts. She and Kelly had apparently returned to Miller's Court after their drinks, and no doubt intended to separate, allowing Kelly to proceed on her night's work. Barnett's arrival caused Mrs Harvey to make a speedy and unobtrusive departure, leaving Kelly and Barnett together, to be joined by Lizzie Albrook, who may well have arrived shortly before Barnett.
Mrs Harvey consistently stated that she had left two men's shirts, a boy's shirt, a black crape bonnet, a child's petticoat, a man's overcoat and a pawn ticket in Kelly's room, none of which except the overcoat was ever returned to her. It was assumed that the murderer had burned them in the grate, where he had lit a fire that certainly consumed a bonnet and some clothing. According to *The Times* the overcoat was a pilot coat, and according to

Walter Dew it was hanging over the broken window, serving as a curtain, which would explain why it was not burned.

HARVEY, DR S. J.

Harley Street consultant who was given the pseudonym 'Gilbart Smith' in Dr Robert Anderson's memoirs and treated both **Thomas Miller Beach** and Anderson, prescribing the latter three months sick leave for overwork exactly when he transferred from the Home Office to become Metropolitan Police Assistant Commissioner at the outset of the Ripper murders.

HATFIELD, JAMES

Witness at Mary Ann Nichols' inquest. Elderly pauper inmate of Whitechapel Workhouse, assisted **Robert Mann** in stripping the body for laying out. He denied having been told not to touch the body by **Sergeant Enright**, and was sharply defended by coroner **Wynne Baxter** when a juror pointed out that his memory was so unreliable that he had first shown the jurors Nichols' stays on the visit to the mortuary, and then denied that she had any. Baxter felt that it was enough that Hatfield had conceded his memory was bad.

HAWES, HARRY

Undertaker of 19 Hunt Street, Spitalfields, who arranged the very private interment of Annie Chapman at Manor Park.

HAWKES, MR

Undertaker who arranged and paid for the funeral and interment of Catharine Eddowes at Ilford. Probably Samuel Hawkes of Finsbury, but possibly George Hawkes of St Luke's.

HAYES, SUPERINTENDENT

Reported to Scotland Yard from Windsor that Annie Chapman had been arrested for drunkenness there, but never prosecuted.

HELSON, INSPECTOR JOSEPH HENRY, J Division (b. 1845)

Warrant no. 51389. Local Inspector, CID, J Division, Bethnal Green. Prominently engaged in the investigation, especially of Mary Ann Nichols' murder. Testified at her inquest, and made statements quoted by press. Received news of the murder at 6.45 a.m. and went to the mortuary where the body was being stripped. The full extent of the mutilation was shown to him. He was consulted by **Abberline** after Annie Chapman's murder, and concluded that she and Nichols were victims of the same hand.

Most importantly, his weekly report to Scotland Yard of 7 September described the search for 'a man named Jack **Pizer**, alias "**Leather Apron**" ', thus proving that Pizer's name was associated with 'Leather Apron' prior to Annie Chapman's murder, and at least three days prior to his arrest. Moreover the information came from someone who knew him intimately enough to call him 'Jack'. (All other written accounts call Pizer 'John'.)

HEMINGWAY, CHIEF CONSTABLE

Of Cardiff. Told a reporter he had no recollection of any woman fitting Mary Jane Kelly's description coming to the attention of the police.

HEWITT, –
See **Sickert's unnamed veterinary student**.

HEWITT, FRANCIS
Witness at inquest on Martha Tabram. Superintendent of George Yard buildings. Was sleeping twelve feet from the murder spot, but heard no sound. His wife said that early in the evening she heard a single cry of 'Murder!' which echoed through the building, but did not emanate from it. 'But the district round here is rather rough and cries of murder are of frequent, if not nightly occurrence in the district,' they explained. Hewitt told *The Times* he believed Tabram had been seen in a pub with two soldiers on the eve of her murder.

HEWITT, DR JOHN (1850–92)
Recent alleged suspect. Practised in Manchester prior to 1888. Confined to Coton Hill Asylum during that year, but was released from the asylum several times during the autumn. Subsequently married nurse from the asylum and moved to Bournemouth. Died in King's Norton of General Paralysis of the Insane.
   Discovered by **Steward Hicks**, c. 1985. Suggested as **Sickert's unnamed veterinary student**. Probably conclusively exonerated by Steward Hicks and **Colin Wilson** in 1988 when Coton Hill Asylum papers were placed in the Public Record Office, indicating that despite his occasional leave from the asylum, Hewitt had *not* been at large on the dates of the murders.

HICKEY, ELLEN
Produced by Police Constable 298H before Thames Magistrates, 7 December 1888, to answer charge of assault on **N. Cohen**, which was dropped because of Cohen's non-appearance. Since this was entered on the same minute of adjudication as the brothel-keeping charges brought against **Gertrude Smith** and **Mary Jones**, the likelihood is that Hickey was a prostitute who started a fight in the course of the brothel closure. The importance of the incident is that the same minute of adjudication covers **Aaron Davis Cohen**, suggesting that his visibly demented conduct while police were raiding Smith and Jones's brothel led to his arrest.

HICKS, STEWARD (1924–)
Accountant of Norwich. Theorist. Discovered **Dr John Hewitt**, and, after considerable research to establish that he was a plausible historical candidate as Walter **Sickert's unnamed veterinary student**, contacted **Colin Wilson**, who helped him make the exciting discovery that Hewitt had been released from confinement from time to time in the autumn of 1888, and with whom he finally made the disappointing discovery that these times did not coincide with the Ripper murders.
   Hicks made one very interesting minor point: that Lady Anderson (wife of **Sir Robert Anderson**) once remarked that the Ripper was interned in an asylum near Stone. Hicks took this to refer to Coton (near Stone, Staffs). The authors believe it more likely to refer to the City of London Asylum, Stone. But Hicks' source is unknown to us and has been forgotten by him. There is an oral tradition concerning a house in Stone, Gloucestershire, where 'Jack the Ripper' is said to have lived.

HOLLAND, ELLEN or EMILY ('NELLY') (b. 1838)

Described in one press report as **Jane Oram**.

Witness at **Mary Ann Nichols'** inquest. A friend of Nichols, who lived with her in a room shared with four other women at 18 Thrawl Street. After **Mary Ann Monk** had suggested that Nichols' body might be that of the woman she had known in Lambeth Workhouse, Ellen Holland positively identified her.

She was also the last person except her murderer known to see Nichols alive. She had been to see the second **Fire on the Docks** at Shadwell Dry Dock, and on her return (some time after 2.00 a.m.) met Nichols at the corner of Osborn Street and Brick Lane. Nichols told her she had earned her doss money twice over that night, but had drunk it away in **The Frying Pan**. She was off to earn it again and refused to accompany Holland back to Thrawl Street, saying she wanted to go somewhere where she could share a bed with a man (i.e. Flower and Dean Street).

In October 1888 Holland received two convictions at Thames Magistrates Court for drunk and disorderly behaviour.

HOLLAND, HENRY JOHN

Complainant about police conduct after Annie Chapman's murder.

A thin, sickly-looking youth with straw-coloured hair, living at 4 Aden Road, Mile End, he passed along Hanbury Street en route to work at Chiswell Street, when **John Davis** told him about the body. He went and looked at it, and then went to fetch a policeman from Spitalfields Market. The officer was on fixed point duty and told him he could not leave it under any circumstances. Holland reported his conduct at Commercial Street Police Station that afternoon.

HOLLAND, POLICE CONSTABLE, 814 City

Summoned by **George Morris** from the south side of Aldgate to go to the assistance of **Police Constable Edward Watkins** on the discovery of Catharine Eddowes' body in Mitre Square.

HOLLOWAY, ANDREW

Theorist. Author of 'Not Guilty?' in the *Cricketer*, December 1990, suggesting that **William Druitt** murdered **Montague John Druitt** to gain control of the family estates, and gave police bogus story that Montague was the Ripper to divert suspicion. No evidence is adduced in support of the motive, nor any to support the claim that police suspicions of Druitt were aroused by the family, nor even that police suspected Druitt at the time of his death. (But see under **G. R. Sims**.)

Mr Holloway further argues that Druitt was drugged or poisoned, his body dumped in the Thames or dislodged from its hiding place when the river flooded. Mr Holloway is in error in imagining police surgeons could not reliably differentiate between poisoned and drowned corpses in 1888.

HOLT, DR WILLIAM (born c. 1864)

MRCS, 1881. Intern., St George's Hospital, 1888–9. Amateur sleuth – **'The White-eyed Man'**.

Frightened a woman called Humphreys on 11 November 1888 when he emerged from fog in George Yard wearing spectacles, and with his face blackened. She asked what he wanted: he merely laughed and hurried away. Humphreys shouted, 'Murder', and a crowd, including a boxer called Bendoff, gathered and attacked Holt, which cries of 'Lynch him!' He resisted savagely, and was rescued by the police, whom he may have continued to resist. Taken to the police station, he established his identity and the facts that he came from Willesden and was attached to St George's Hospital. He had been going around Whitechapel in various disguises, hoping to discover the murderer. He was released the following day.

Press reports transformed his spectacles into white rings around his eyes. Cf. **E. Woodhall**.

HOME OFFICE

As the equivalent of other nations' Ministries of Justice, and the government department to which the Metropolitan Police was and is directly responsible, the Home Office was deeply involved in the Ripper investigation. It fell to the Home Secretary, **Henry Matthews**, to answer questions in Parliament arising from the press brouhaha, and it fell to Home Office officials to brief him.

Relations between the Home Office and the Metropolitan Police Commissioner's Office were poor, yet Home Office civil servants had control over important decisions – like the refusal to offer a reward for information – for which the police took responsibility in the eyes of press and public.

Their deep involvement and permanent need to be informed about the progress of the investigations means that many of the most important historical documents concerning the case are on the **Home Office files**, not the **Scotland Yard files**. For this reason we include a comprehensive listing with brief descriptions.

HOME OFFICE FILES

A descriptive listing of the Home Office files pertaining to the Whitechapel Murders held at the Public Record Office, Kew.

NB: Throughout, MEPO cross-refers to **Scotland Yard file** numbers. Our final item numbers do not correspond with revised folio numbers since the collection was microfilmed in 1988.

HO/144.220.A49301.A ('SUSPECTS' FILE')

1. 12 Oct. 88. Correspondence via Foreign Office from E. W. Bonham, Consul in Boulogne, concerning John Langan, against whom Bonham entertained suspicions. Langan's story later verified by police and he was released.
2. 10 Oct. 88. Letter from **Robert Anderson** re Donkin (see A49301,C,7) stating that the real name of the cabman's suspect was John Davidson and that his movements at the time of the murders had been accounted for. Also a copy of enquiry into Davidson signed by **Inspector Abberline** and **Supt. Arnold**.
3. 16 Oct. 88. Verification of Langan's innocence and release. (See 1 above.)
4. 23 July 89. Copy of letter in *The Times* by Revd Samuel Barnett re vice in Whitechapel.
5. 5 Aug. 89. Report by James Monro on above. (Copy of letter in MEPO 3/141, item 21, folios 139–44. Also see MEPO 3/141, folios 145–8.)
6. 27 Sept. 89. Another on the same.
7. 10 Sept. 89. }
8. 14 Oct. 89. } Two letters from J. H. Hazelwood alleging murders

committed by **Sergeant Thick**, with marginal minute, 'I think it is plainly rubbish – perhaps prompted by spite.'
9. 1 Oct. 89. Anonymous letter re doctor who took furnished rooms at 51 Abingdon Road, Kensington. He had a portmanteau containing surgical instruments. Described as strong, well-built, 45–50, 5ft 9ins, dark complexion, beard, moustache. Also supposedly similar to doctor in enclosed barely relevant cartoon about frightening a visitor.
10. 9 Oct. 89. Letter from **Chief Inspector Donald Swanson** to effect that above correspondent's suspicions are based on weak 'evidence'; that enquiries seem unjustified, and the theory the 'product of an excited imagination'.
11. Oct. 92. HO memo re request by Dr Arthur MacDonald of Washington to see all HO and Police medical reports on Ripper victims. HO declined to grant request.

HO/144/220/A49301.B
A large file, wholly concerning the question of a **reward** to be offered for information leading to the murderer's capture and conviction.
1. 31 Aug. 88. Letter from L. P. Walter and Son, 11–13 Church Street, Spitalfields, recommending that reward be offered. Reply from E. Leigh Pemberton that practice of offering rewards was discontinued.
2. 10 Sept. 88. Letter from **Sir Charles Warren** enclosing letter from Whitechapel MP **Samuel Montagu** offering £100 reward. Warren wrote: 'Will be glad to receive instructions by Secretary of State.' Reply from E. Leigh Pemberton. (See also MEPO 3/141, folios 170–6.)
3. 16 Sept. 88. Letter from B. Harris, Hon. Sec., Whitechapel Vigilance Committee, requesting Home Secretary to augment reward fund or state reason for declining. Reply from E. Leigh Pemberton.
4. 1 Oct. 88. Cheque for £300 from *Financial News* to be offered as reward in Government's name. Also letter from E. Leigh Pemberton to **Henry Matthews** saying that in view of recent murders he did not want to refuse as usual without giving Matthews time to reconsider earlier decision. Pemberton's letter contains two points of interest: (i) that Warren reported that everything was being done but he was sanguine about finding the killer, and (ii) that at 3.30 p.m. the Queen had telephoned to say how shocked she was and ask for information.
5. 2 Oct. 88. Letter from Balmoral to HO enclosing petition received from **George Lusk** requesting offer of reward. Press cutting from *The Times* quoting HO reply to Lusk and from the *Daily Telegraph* about a threatening man who sought out Lusk in a pub.
6. 1 Oct. 88. Telegram from one Bulling (unidentified) informing **Chief Constable Williamson** of Lord Mayor's £500 reward offer.
7. 7 Oct. 88. Letter from George Lusk requesting that pardon be offered to anyone not the real assassin. A minute by **Godfrey Lushington**: 'There is no reason to suspect an accomplice, quite the reverse. I therefore see no good in offering a pardon . . .' (cf., however, **Pardons**). A minute by Matthews: 'Before answering further – send copy to Commr. and request him to inform S[ecretary] of S[tate] whether any useful result could be achieved in his opinion by the offer of a pardon to accomplices.' Also draft of reply to Lusk.
8. 9 Oct. 88. Warren's reply to above request: 'during the last three or four days I have been coming to the conclusion that useful results

would be produced by the offer of a pardon to accomplices . . . [the murderer's] relatives or neighbours may have gradually unwittingly slid into the position of accomplices, and may be hopeless of escape without a free pardon.' Also letter from Godfrey Lushington to Matthews giving implications of a pardon offer and advising against. Also draft of Matthews' letter declining pardon offer.

10. 13 Oct. 88. Warren to HO, giving result of consultation with Anderson, Williamson and Divisional Superintendents, repeating earlier opinion that whilst no good would come from the offer of a reward, no harm would result, and that the 'hope of gain by giving information and help to the police is a powerful motive with ordinary people'.
11. 16 Oct. 88. Letter from William Bencraft, late of Melbourne Fire Brigade, giving case of reward inciting crime it should have prevented, and near conviction of innocent man.
12. 17 Oct. 88. Warren's reply to specific questions from Matthews re police investigation: (i) police had not yet exhausted every avenue of enquiry; (ii) anonymous letters still coming in, and 'one of the logical solutions as to the murders is that there may be several persons who are more or less assisting the murderer' (cf. **Accomplices of the Ripper**; (iii) 'I look upon this series of murders as unique in the history of our country.' (Cf. **Douglas Browne**, who quotes this otherwise unpublished phrase verbatim, thus demonstrating his own access to files before they were opened to public.)
13. 25 Oct. 88. Warren produces past evidence favourable to the offer of rewards, plus Divisional Superintendents' statements.
14. 1 Nov. 88. Warren draws attention to 1860 case when reward offer induced murderer to manufacture evidence against an innocent person, which led to his detection. HO minutes that if the murderer had been more skilful in concocting false accusations, an innocent man would have been hanged.
15. 10 Nov. 88. Memo stating cabinet decided to offer pardon to anyone not the actual murderer of **Mary Jane Kelly**. Also copy of pardon and document used as example of style.
16. Nov. 88. Report from *The Times* (not included) of Matthews' answers to questions in Parliament on rewards.
17. 29 Nov. 88. History of HO practice re rewards. Three handwritten documents: two memos and a list of rewards offered, 1878–84.
18. Missing.
19. Printed version of 17 entitled 'Memoranda on the Question of the Offer of Rewards by Government in Criminal Cases'.
19a. Copies of rewards and pardons for style.
20. 19 July 89. Copy of *Daily Chronicle* re question put to Matthews on reward or pardon in case of McKenzie murder. Matthews' reply, with copy of 19. Plus written answer: 'The circumstances of the present murder are, so far as known, almost identical with those of last year . . . a total augmentation of 1 inspector, 5 sergeants, and 50 constables was yesterday sanctioned.' Also includes a valuable memo from Monro, summarising the increase and decrease of plain-clothes men patrolling H Division over the period: 'Sept. 88, 27; Oct. 88, 89; Nov. 88, 143; Jan. 89, 102; Feb. 89, 47.'
(Other documents indicate that the dramatic reduction in numbers was prompted by financial constraints and, probably, the cessation of crimes

since Kelly's death; not any police conviction that the murderer was dead or incarcerated. See **Bachert, Cohen, Druitt, Macnaghten** for significance.)

HO/144/220/A49301.C
Probably the most important of the files, as it includes reports from Scotland Yard summarising the investigations into each of the murders.
1. 24 Sept. 88. Letter from B. Harris, Hon. Sec., Whitechapel Vigilance Committee, advising Home Secretary that his refusal to offer a reward would be made public at General Meeting and inviting his attendance. Matthews replied he was 'regrettably' unable to attend.
2. 29 Sept. 88. Letter from R. J. Neave, Hon. Sec., General Liberal Association of New Forest Division of Hampshire (Fordingbridge Branch), charging Government with callousness, neglect of duty and utter indifference to murders. Minuted: 'They are trying to make party capital out of the Whitechapel murders. Merely acknowledge.'
3. 30 Sept. 88. Letter (missing) from Vigilance Committee suggesting issue of reward. Minuted 'No reason to alter previous decision'.
4. 1 Oct. 88. Letter from Lieutenant Colonel Sewell, of Tower Hamlets Militia Division, informing HO that Sir Alfred Kirby, Commanding Officer, had offered £100 reward and 50 men to assist in apprehending murderer. Offer respectfully declined.
5. 2 Oct. 88. Clerk, Whitechapel Board of Works, requests police be strengthened. E. Leigh Pemberton replied Home Secretary satisfied police exercising every power they possess.
5a. 4 Oct. 88. Thomas Metcalf, Clerk, Whitechapel Vestry, urging Government to do all it can to apprehend murderer. Matthews wrote a long minute explaining his feelings re murders, then, perhaps deciding not to give such a stupid letter the time, noted 'or simply acknowledge'.
6. 1 Oct. 88. Letter, signature indecipherable, offering theory that murderer escaped through sewers, a method given in the writer's novel *In the Coroner's Ward*. Letter shown to Monro and read to Warren, and 'neither of them think it improbable'.
7. 5 Oct. 88. Gov. of Newcastle Prison enclosed description of George Donkin (see A49301,A,2).
8. 4 Oct. 88. Letter from Sir J. W. Ellis (former Lord Mayor of London) suggesting that cordon be thrown round suspicious area and all houses forcibly searched.
   Response from Warren to Ruggles-Brise: 'I am quite prepared to take the responsibility of adopting the most drastic or arbitrary measures that the Sec of State can name which would further the securing of the murderer, however illegal they may be, provided HM Govt will support me.'
   Response dated 5 Oct. from Matthews suggesting that searches be conducted of suspicious houses with owners' permission; that search warrants be applied for where permission refused; surveillance be maintained if warrant application rejected. He further requests report of all measures taken to date for detection of murderer, and asks, 'Have any of the doctors examined the eyes of the murdered women?' Also inquires if 'Mr Anderson's health has permitted him to return to duties'.

The following letters in this sub-section are out of sequence:

Commercial Street, Spitalfields, with (left) the **Britannia** public house, c. 1898

Women outside the doss house at 56 **Flower and Dean Street,** known as the White House, where **Mary Ann Nichols** stayed

Princess Alice public house, where major suspect **Leather Apron** was said to drink

Poor Jews Temporary Shelter, where suspect **David Cohen** may have stayed

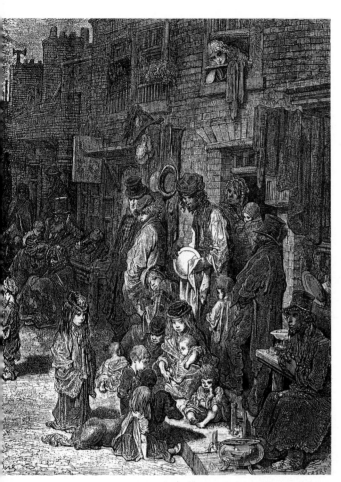

Gustav Doré's engraving of the Jewish street market in Wentworth Street, the heart of **Whitechapel** and **Spitalfields**

Great Scotland Yard (left), Metropolitan Police headquarters until two years after the Ripper murders (*Courtesy of the Metropolitan Police Museum*)

Henry Matthews, Home Secretary throughout the Ripper affair

Sir Charles Warren, Metropolitan Police Commissioner who resigned on the day of the last murder

James Monro, seen here in retirement, replaced Warren as Metropolitan Police Commissioner

Sir Henry Smith, Assistant Commissioner, City of London Police

Dr Robert Anderson, head of the Metropolitan CID

Chief Inspector Donald Swanson, desk officer on the Ripper case

Melville Macnaghten, Chief Constable, Metropolitan CID from 1891

Inspector Frederick Abberline, head of the detectives on the ground in the Ripper case, and **Superintendent Thomas Arnold,** head of 'H' Division, Whitechapel, taken from Abberline's own scrap book

Walter Dew

Sergeant George Godley

'H' Division, Whitechapel CID in 1889. Front row, second, third and fourth from left: **Sergeant Thick, Inspector Reid** and **Sergeant Caunter** (*Courtesy of the Metropolitan Police Museum*)

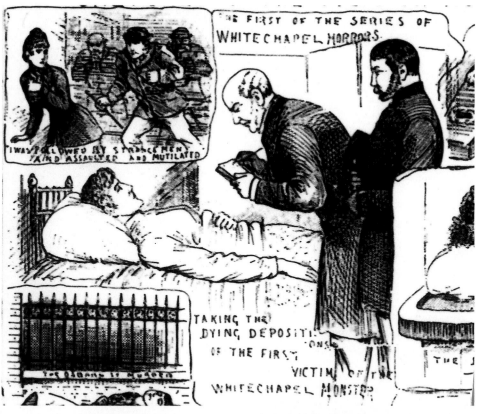

Emma Smith, first alleged victim of Jack the Ripper

Mortuary photograph of **Martha Tabran,** second alleged victim

George Yard Buildings, site of Martha Tabran's murder

Mortuary photograph of **Mary Ann Nichols,** first canonical victim

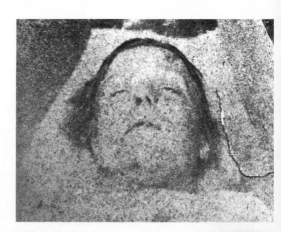

Buck's Row, Whitechapel, in the 1960s. The murder site was in the doorway of the garage to the left.

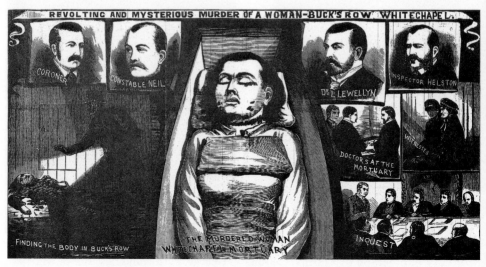

Illustrated press treatment of the Buck's Row murder

Mortuary photograph of
Annie Chapman, the
second canonical victim

The murder site, 29
Hanbury Street

Artist's impression of Annie Chapman

Mortuary photograph of **Elizabeth Stride,** the third canonical victim

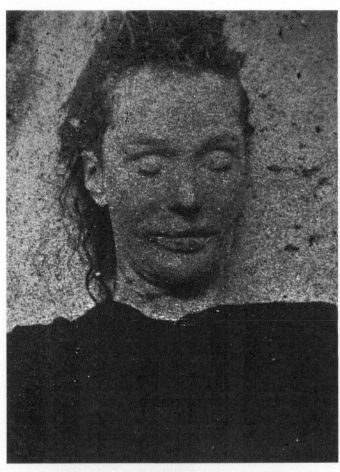

Artist's gratuitously unflattering impression of Elizabeth Stride

THE FIFTH VICTIM OF THE WHITECHAPEL FIEND.

Artist's impression of **Diemschutz** discovering Stride's body

Berner Street, 1909. The corner shop was a beer house in 1888. **Matthew Packer's** house was next door. **Dutfield's Yard** entry (marked by cartwheel) has lost its gates and the **International Working Men's Educational Club** has been extended upwards since the murder. Photograph identified by **Melvyn Fairclough**. (*Greater London Photograph Library*)

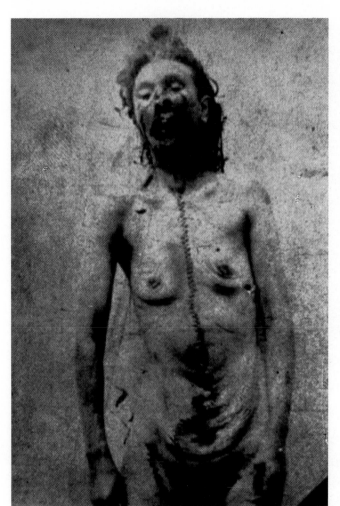

Mortuary photographs
of **Catherine Eddowes,**
the fourth canonical
victim

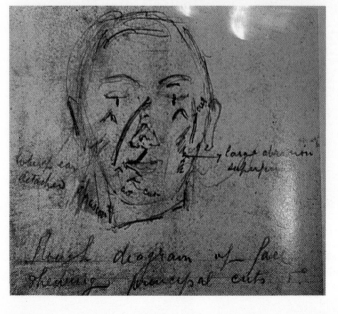

Police surgeon's diagram
of mutilations to
Catherine Eddowes' face

Police sketch of
Catherine Eddowes'
body in Mitre
Square

N⁰ˢ 108 ᵀᴼ 119

Doorway in
Goulston Street
where the Ripper
dropped part of
Catherine Eddowes'
apron in his flight

The Whitehall Mystery: a torso speculatively ascribed by some contemporary journalists to Jack the Ripper

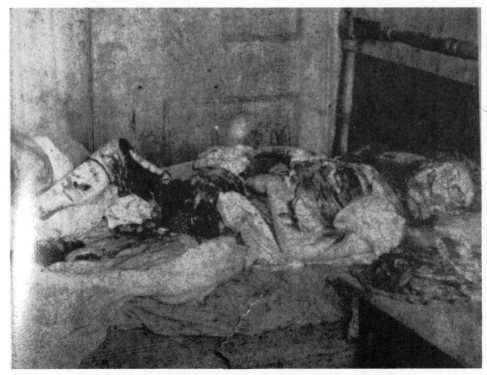

The mutilated body of **Mary Jane Kelly,** the last canonical Ripper victim

Annie Farmer, self-alleged victim
of assault by the Ripper

Alice McKenzie,
alleged Ripper victim

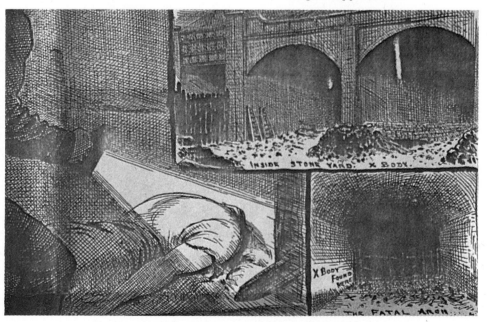

The **Pinchin Street Murder,** an alleged Ripper atrocity

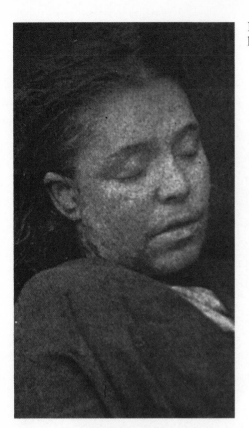

Mortuary photograph of **Frances Coles,**
last alleged Ripper victim

FRANCES
COLES

Frances Coles and **Thomas Sadler,** the man charged with her murder

19 Sept. 88. Letter from Warren to **Ruggles-Brise** complaining of hindrance to police and describing lines of investigation currently being followed. These were: (i) waiting to identify the lunatic **Issenschmidt** as man seen by **Mrs Fiddymont**; (ii) 'A man called **Puckridge** was released from an asylum on 4 August. He was educated as a surgeon – has threatened to rip people up with a long knife. He is being looked for but cannot be found yet.' (iii) 'A brothel keeper who will not give her address or name writes to say that a man living in her house was seen with blood on him on morning of murder. She described his appearance and said where he might be seen – when detectives came near him he bolted, got away and there is no clue to the writer of the letter.'

19 Sept. 88 Letter from J. S. Sandars, assistant to Ruggles-Brise, reporting to Matthews on the above. Plus two internal memoranda of no importance.

8a. 24 Oct. 88. Warren's reply to Matthews' letter of 13 Oct. requesting details of investigation. 'Very numerous and searching enquiries have been made in all directions and with regard to all kinds of suggestions which have been made: they have had no tangible result . . .' Enclosed was a minute from Robert Anderson: 'That a crime of this kind should have been committed without any clue being supplied by the criminal is unusual, but that five successive murders should have been committed without our having the slightest clue is extraordinary, if not unique in the annals of crime.' He went on to say that every hint, except the obviously absurd, was being investigated, and that the public, especially the inhabitants of the East End, had 'shown a marked desire to assist in every way, even at some sacrifice to themselves'. (See under **Anderson** for relevance of his reference to five murders, and no clue.)

Also enclosed was a set of reports by Chief Inspector Swanson, described by Anderson on 23 Oct. 88 as having 'special charge of the matter in this office': These reports are:

Sept. 88. Report on Martha Tabram (9pp.; also in MEPO 3/140, fol. 37–43).

19 Oct. 88. Report on Mary Ann Nichols (6pp.).

19 Oct. 88. Report on Annie Chapman (11pp.).

19 Oct. 88. Report on Elizabeth Stride (12pp.). Document contains several lengthy minutes discussing aspects of the reports' contents, the most important of which runs: 'Mr Murdoch, Please see Mr Wortley's pencil memo on Sir Charles Warren's letter. Shall police be asked at the same time for report on 2nd insane medical student from the London Hosp about whom (under the name of Dr–) there is a good deal of gossip in circulation. W. T. B.'

We do not know who was the author of this minute, addressed to Charles S. Murdoch, Principal Clerk. The pencilled memo to which he refers was by C. B. Stuart-Wortley, and read '?ask when the insane student, mentioned on page 6 of Annie Chapman papers, went abroad'. See under **John Sanders** for importance.

There is also the draft of a letter to Warren, dated 29 Oct. 88, listing questions noted on the above minute, including question about the insane student. (See also MEPO 3/140, 1 Nov. 88.)

8b. 29 Oct. 88. Letter from Sir James Fraser, Commissioner, City of London Police, enclosing report dated 27 Oct. from Inspector **James McWilliam** on Catharine Eddowes' murder.

8c. 6 Nov. 88. Report by Swanson on Eddowes' murder (11pp.)
Report by **Police Constable Alfred Long** re finding apron and **Goulston Street graffito** (2pp.).
Report by **Superintendent Arnold** re his decision to erase graffito (2pp.).
Report by Warren of his actions re **Goulston Street graffito**, including copy of the writing (8pp.).

8d. 6 Nov. 88. Reply to HO letter full of questions minuted on reports sent in 24 Oct. (see 8a above). Warren says that **'Lipski!'** was addressed by the man assaulting Stride to **Schwartz** (cf. MEPO 3/140, items 26–28) and the insane medical student is believed to have gone abroad.

8e. Newspaper reports from *The Times* of inquests into deaths of Ripper victims.

8f. Extract from *Daily Telegraph* containing Warren's letter of 3 Oct. 88 to Whitechapel Board of Works. Plus facsimile from same source of 'Jack the Ripper' letter.

8g. 29 Nov. 88. HO analysis of evidence. A chart of victims from Tabram to Eddowes, tabulating date, time and place of death, plus a description of injuries. Two observations are interesting:
(i) re Tabram the murder weapon is given as 'a knife or dagger', and a note states that although a bayonet is suspected, 'bayonet wounds are quite unmistakable'.
(ii) re Chapman, states that killer displayed 'some anatomical knowledge; knife must have been a small amputating knife or a well-ground slaughterman's knife'. Says of Time of Death: 'doubtful evidence points to something between 5.30 and 6; – but medical evidence says about 4 o'cl.'

9. Secret papers, transferred to A49301D (q.v., 1–5). These concerned the question of allowing an informer £100 to come to England to discover the murderer.

10. 15 Oct. 88. Letter from Samuel Montagu MP and petition from local residents praying for augmentation of police in Whitechapel. (See also MEPO 3/141 fol. 136–7 which includes petition.)

11. Tricycles for police. (No papers.)

11a. As above.

12. 15 Oct. 88. Letter from Godfrey Lushington to Henry Matthews and documents relating to contents. Concerns an imperfectly addressed letter to Jane Bromley opened by Post Office and found to contain an erroneously inserted letter from an unnamed gentleman of Eaton Place, to his son, expressing the view that General Brown was the murderer. The letter was sent to Warren, who responded on 17 October that General Brown had been questioned and cleared.

13. Tricycles for police. (No papers.)

14. As above.

15. 10 Nov. 88. Press cuttings from *Standard* re question in Parliament about Warren and, 13 Nov., his resignation.

16. 11 Nov. 88. Letter from Mr Thomas Blair of Dumfries suggesting that policemen 'of short stature, and as far as possible of effeminate appearance' should dress as women and act as decoys.

17. 10 Nov. 88. Letter from J. Smith of Burnham, Essex, recommending daily dose of cat-o'-nine-tails for murderer for 12 months prior to execution.

18. 12 Nov. 88. Letter (not included) from H. Walker requesting envelope

from HO in which he would reply with suggestion for capturing murderer. Minuted: 'police informed'.

19. 11 Nov. 88. Letter from James Young of Merton. Critical of police – says father was a superintendent, 'and was reckoned about as crafty as any man who ever misapplied his talents in a bad service', and refers to detectives as 'drink-sodden, bull-headed'. Offers own plan for catching Ripper.

20. 13 Nov. 88. Note from Warren: 'Mr H. Hales says that **Packer** believes the murderer to be his own cousin.'

21. 13 Nov. 88. Covering letter from Robert Anderson and full medical report (given verbatim under **Bond**), plus extracts from Anderson's letter to Bond stating reason for seeking assistance, to wit, the absence of reliable knowledge of the murderer's surgical skill and anatomical knowledge. (See also MEPO 3/140, item 30.)

22. 14 Nov. 88. Letter (not included) from **Dr Forbes Winslow** expressing view that murderer a homicidal lunatic, and placing his services at Govt disposal.

23. 15 Nov. 88. Letter (not included) from Woking Prison suggesting that Louis Solomon the murderer. Minutes state that this was an ordinary criminal case.

24. 16 Nov. 88. Letter from James Frederick Brooks suggesting that Govt offer free pardon to murderer, then renege on offer when he gives himself up. The minute uses rare notation which is the sign of the utmost contempt – 'not acknowledge'.

25. 23 Nov. 88. Letter from Oswald Crawford, Consul in Oporto, re inquiries into **E. K. Larkins**' cattle-boat theory. The minute is important, stating that the theory had been looked into and found untenable, with the comment, 'I fear this man is a troublesome "faddist".'

25a. Larkins memorandum and minute cited above.

25b. Larkins memo. See 25.

26. Tricycles for Police. Document endorsed 'See PRO HO 45/100002/A49594'.

27. Missing.

28. 9 Mar. 89. Letter from Larkins and copy of his memo sent to police. (See 25.)

29. 12 Mar. 89. Letter from A. H. Skirving, Ontario Police, giving details of a prisoner in Chatham, Ontario, whom he suspects to be murderer. The man, named Jack Irwin, was not in Britain during the crimes, however.

30. Missing.

31. 10 Feb. 92. E. K. Larkins' printed version of his theory.

31. 6 May 92. Letter from Charles Barber stating his belief (based on a dream) that **Deeming** was the murderer. Also account in *Spy*, 16 Apr 92, concerning Barber's efforts to convince the police.

33. 26 Jan. 93. Letter from E. K. Larkins enclosing papers on his theory and accusing head of CID of conniving at his suspects' escape.

34. 6 Feb. 93. Letter from Robert Anderson returning Larkins' papers. 'Mr Larkins is a troublesome busybody whose vagaries on the subject of the Whitechapel murders have cost this department, the Public Prosecutor and the Foreign Office a great deal of trouble. His theories have been tested and they have been proved untenable and worthless, and it is a mere waste of time attempting to deal with him on this subject.'

35. Missing.
36. 8 Nov. 94. Letter from Dr Gustave Olive of Nantes requesting a copy of Dr Bond's report, having been directed by the *Juge d'Instruction* to investigate a similar case there.
37. 22 Nov. 94. Re above. Report sent.
38. 3 Dec. 94. Concerns a letter from E. H. Pickersgill MP in *The Times* (23 Nov. 94) criticising police over a technical matter concerning a murder in Whitechapel the previous Saturday. The reply to the HO enquiry was that Pickersgill had confused the CID with the Public Prosecutor's Office and misunderstood the relevant regulation.

HO/144/220/A49301.D
Documents via Foreign Office.
1–5. Despatches and documents from and concerning Sir Augustus Paget, British Ambassador in Vienna, dated 12 Oct., 5 Nov., 7 Nov., 88, 2 Jan. and 26 Feb. 89, forwarded to HO by Sir Julian Pauncefote, Permanent Under Secretary of State, Foreign Office. All concern a man named Jonas who claimed to manage the Austrian affairs of an international political secret society. He believed the Ripper to be a former member who had been dismissed after denouncing society members to authorities in New York. The man was now in Britain under close observation by society members.

Jonas essentially wanted £165 to finance his journey to London to identify the man. HO thought the story a fabrication, as did Vienna authorities to whom he had revealed an alleged assassination plot in 1883 which never took place. But Paget was convinced and advanced £165 from his own pocket, after which Jonas requested a further £100. Monro advised firmly against further payments, and no action was taken when Jonas warned Paget of a forthcoming bombing campaign in London (which incidentally, never materialised).

Of considerable interest, however, is a minute from Warren and a response by Lushington.

On 12 Oct. 88, Warren wrote: 'As Mr Matthews is aware I have for some time past been inclined to the idea that the [murders] having been done by a secret society is the only logical solution to the question, but I could not understand them being done because the last murders were done by some one desiring to bring discredit on the Jews and the Socialists or the Jewish Socialists.'

Lushington replied, 13 Oct. 88: 'I cannot agree with the Commissioner that the only logical solution of the question is that the murders may probably have been done by a secret society. He also says that he cannot understand this having been done by a Socialist, because the last murders were evidently done by some one desiring to bring discredit on the Jews and Socialists or Jewish Socialists. It seems to me on the contrary that the last murder was done by a Jew who boasted of it.'

(Lushington must be referring to either the cry of '**Lipski**' or the **Goulston Street graffito**: possibly both, assuming both murders to be by the same hand.)

6. Dec. 88. Letter from Tomas Romero dated 26 Nov 88 giving description of man he believes to be the Ripper. (Letter misnumbered 5 in the files.)
7. 14 Dec. 88. Letter from George Strachey in Dresden concerning the

information supplied by American medical student Julius J. Löwenheim that a Polish Jew named Wirtkofsky whom he had met near Finsbury Square had threatened to kill a certain woman and the rest of her class. (Letter misnumbered 6 in file.)

8. 12 Nov. 88. Letter from George Hugh Wyndham, Minister Plenipotentiary to Brazil, enclosing original and translation of letter from P. J. Vanzetti, Italian residing in Saõ Paulo, concerning an incident in Oct. 87.

9. 10 Jan. 89. Communication from Mr Darling MP saying a constituent complained that information sent to Home Office had not been acknowledged. The constituent was **Larkins**!

HO 144/221/A49301.E
Small file on **Bloodhounds**.

1. 2 Oct. 88. Letter in *The Times* from Percy Lindley regarding use of bloodhounds.
2. 5 Oct. 88. Letter from Warren saying dogs impracticable in towns unless specially trained, and seeking annual expenditure for dogs. Draft letter of authorisation.
3. 23 Oct. 88. Letter from Warren noting miscalculation of expense and seeking sanction for excess.
4. 16 October. 88. Letter from J. H. Ashforth of Nottingham suggesting use of dogs, with minuted reply saying the experiment had been tried.

HO/144/221/A49301.F

1. 9 Nov. 88. Report from Warren to Lushington informing him of Kelly murder and saying the matter was in Anderson's hands.

HO/144/221/A49301.G
This file consists wholly of requests and sanctions for extra payments to officers drafted in from other divisions. They are mostly standard forms or letters. We list below only those subsections which for one reason or other deviate from the standard or contain possibly relevant information. (Also see MEPO 3/146 items 1–18.)

2. 21 Dec. 88. Receiver sanctions expenditure of £300 and requests that additional expenditure be subject to review.
4. 26 Jan. 89. Monro reports expenditure reached £306.13s. and requests additional expenditure of £200, saying, 'I am gradually reducing the number of men employed on this duty as quickly as it is safe to do so, but such reduction cannot be effected all at once.'
7. 15 Mar. 89. Monro reports cessation of all special patrols, expenditure having reached £351, and requests sanction of excess.

   Futher requests for men drafted into Whitechapel in consequence of renewed murders were made in July, Sept. 89 (McKenzie), Nov. 89, Feb., Mar. 90 (Pinchin Street), and Mar. 91 (Coles: a special refreshment allowance, this being the last request on file).

HO/144/221/A49301.H

1. 23 Dec. 88. Monro provides details of Rose Mylett's murder. Subsection also contains two internal memoranda of no interest.

HO/144/221/A49301.I
1. 17 Jul. 89. Monro forwards report on murder of McKenzie, and observes: 'I need not say that every effort will be made by the police to discover the murderer, who, I am inclined to believe, is identical with the notorious Jack the Ripper of last year.' Subsection also includes report by **Supt. Arnold**.
2. 5 Dec. 89. Unitemised expenses claim from Inspector Moore for £27.7s.5d and £49.3s.7d re murders in Whitechapel.
   (This claim is remarkably large. Note, e.g. that £300 covered all expenses of extra patrols drafted into Whitechapel for periods of a month or more. It would be very interesting to know what duties, late in 1889, justified such a claim from Moore.)

NB: There is no file 'J'.

HO/144/221/A49301.K
1. 11 Sept. 89. Monro reports to J. S. Sandars (Assistant Private Secretary to Matthews) about Pinchin Street murder, and states that it could have been the work of Jack the Ripper, but he is not inclined to believe it was. (See also MEPO 3/140, 11 Sept. 89.)

HORN OF PLENTY, THE
Former public house at corner of Crispin Street and Dorset Street (north side) where a nun of **Providence Row Night Refuge** said Mary Jane Kelly used to drink, and **Maurice Lewis** said he saw her with **'Danny'** and **'Julia'** the night she was murdered. Mistaken (from maps) by some authors for **The Britannia**.

HOUCHIN, DR EDMUND KING
H Division Police Surgeon in 1888, but is not known to have been consulted by the police or played any part in the Ripper enquiry. Subsequently certified **Aaron Kosminski**.

HOWARD, CHIEF CONSTABLE ANDREW CHARLES
Unwittingly precipitated **Monro**'s resignation as Metropolitan Commissioner.
   In 1890, Assistant Commissioner Pearson died unexpectedly and Monro wanted to promote Howard (like himself, a former Indian Police official) in his place. But **Henry Matthews** proposed **Evelyn Ruggles-Brise**, who would have brought bureaucratic Home Office habits into Scotland Yard. This was the last straw for Monro, who was already disputing with Matthews over the pension conditions in a new Police Bill. When Matthews proved intransigent, Monro resigned. When Matthews was criticised for forcing the resignation of a second Commissioner in two years (cf. **Warren**), he yielded on the issues, and Howard became Assistant Commissioner after all.

HOWARD, DR BENJAMIN (1836–1900)
MD, New York, 1858; MRCS, Eng., 1877; FRCS, Edin., 1879; Corresponding member, NY Academy of Medicine; late Resident Physician Mt Sinai Hospital, NY; late Att. Surgeon and Professor of Medicine, Long Island College Hospital, Brooklyn; Lecturer in Medicine, U of NY; Pro-

fessor of Medicine, U of Vermont; Surgeon Major and Acting Medical Director, US Army. Author of many distinguished papers and originator of movement to start an accident ambulance service in Britain. Died in New Jersey, USA.

In 1895 the Chicago *Sunday Times-Herald* published an article attributing the capture of Jack the Ripper to **Robert James Lees** (q.v. for full story). The newspaper explained that the truth had 'recently been told by Dr Howard, a well-known London physician, to William Greer Harrison, of the Bohemian Club in San Francisco'. Howard had been sworn to secrecy, but 'A London clubman, now in Chicago, who is acquainted with Dr Howard, is of the opinion that, being in a foreign country and perhaps under the influence of too much wine, Dr Howard has permitted his tongue to wag too freely.' The informant went on that, although Howard had not revealed the name of the distinguished physician (supposedly secretly certified and incarcerated by a committee of shocked colleagues who had learned he was the Ripper), Howard 'will doubtless be reprimanded by the Royal College of Physicians and Surgeons . . .'.

The newspaper's story, however, was not received from Dr Howard, but from an unnamed 'gentleman of this city' who felt free to talk now Howard had broken silence. The *Times-Herald* did not give Howard's Christian name, but the *People*, which picked up the story, described him as an Anglo-American. This fitted Dr Benjamin Howard, who wrote privately and furiously to the editor of the *People* on 26 January 1896, saying he had been absent from London and only just seen the article. Nothing in it had 'the slightest foundation in fact', he said. He insinuated a threat of legal action and said he knew nothing about Jack the Ripper except what he had read in the newspapers.

Possibly Benjamin Howard was not the doctor intended; possibly he was, without his knowledge or assent; possibly the name Howard was coincidentally devised by a hoaxer. But we should be interested if William Greer Harrison and the Bohemian Club of San Francisco could be identified.

HOWELLS, MARTIN (b. 1947)
Theorist. Co-author (with Keith Skinner) of *The Ripper Legacy* (1987). Actor/writer, born South Wales; educ. Pinner Grammar School, Guildhall School of Music and Drama. Conducted rock'n'roll band competing with schoolfellow Elton John. At Guildhall School won comedy prize for performance as Charley's Aunt. Appeared in over sixty television productions, and worked with both Royal Shakespeare and National Theatre Companies. 1983, wrote successful television series in New Zealand, where he now lives with his family.

HUNT, DETECTIVE BAXTER, City Police
Warrant No. 4088. Joined City Police, 1867, transferring from Metropolitan Police. Retired, 1895, with rank of Detective Inspector. Probably the Hunt who accompanied **Halse** from Mitre Square to Leman Street Police Station. Subsequently discovered a man called Conway who was Quartermaster-Sergeant with 18th Royal Irish Regiment, and confronted him with two of Catharine Eddowes' sisters. They did not identify him as her husband (who had enlisted as Quinn and was pensioned before he met Eddowes – see **Thomas Conway**).

HUSLING, BELLA

Registered **Inspector Abberline**'s death in 1929, giving his address as hers.
We do not know whether she was a housekeeper, cook-general, temporarily
employed resident nurse, or family friend or relative helping at the sickbed.
We do know that Abberline's wife Emma died at the same address the
following year.

HUTCHINSON, GEORGE

Informant. Told police he saw Mary Jane Kelly pick up a client at 2.00
a.m. before she died. Hutchinson was a resident of Victoria Home, **Commercial Street** (sometimes described as a Peabody Building), and by 9
November 1888 had been unemployed for some weeks.

At 6.00 p.m., 12 November, after Kelly's inquest had been concluded,
Hutchinson went to Commercial Street Police Station and made the following statement:

About 2 a.m. 9th I was coming by Thrawl Street, Commercial Street,
and just before I got to **Flower and Dean Street**, I met the murdered
woman Kelly, and she said to me Hutchinson will you lend me sixpence.
I said I can't I have spent all my money going down to Romford, she said
good morning I must go and find some money. She went away toward
Thrawl Street. A man coming in the opposite direction to Kelly, tapped
her on the shoulder and said something to her they both burst out
laughing. I heard her say alright to him, and the man said you will be
alright, for what I have told you: he then placed his right hand around
her shoulders. He also had a kind of small parcel in his left hand, with a
kind of a strap round it. I stood against the lamp of the **Queen's Head**
Public House, and watched him. They both then came past me and the
man hung down his head, with, his hat over his eyes. I stooped down and
looked him in the face. He looked at me stern. They both went into
Dorset Street. I followed them. They both stood at the corner of the
court for about 3 minutes. He said something to her. She said alright my
dear come along you will be comfortable. He then placed his arm on her
shoulder and [she] gave him a kiss. She said she had lost her handkerchief. He then pulled his handkerchief a red one and gave it to her. They
both then went up the Court together. I then went to the court to see if I
could see them but I could not. I stood there for about three quarters of
an hour to see if they came out. They did not so I went away.

For the description of this man furnished to the police, and elaborated to
newspapers, see under **Jack the Ripper: Descriptions of**.

NB: It was in newspaper interviews that Hutchinson described the red-
stoned seal on the man's watch-chain, and specified that the bag he carried
was American cloth. The press reports also altered Hutchinson's words
'Jewish-looking' to 'foreign-looking' – possibly a police-inspired prevent-
ative against **anti-Semitism**.

Hutchinson also told the press that he occasionally gave Kelly a shilling,
and he had looked out for the man unsuccessfully on 13 November. Also,
without being certain, he thought he had seen him in Petticoat Lane on 11
November.

Conspiracy theorists have alleged that Hutchinson was deliberately
excluded from **Dr MacDonald**'s very abrupt inquest. It has been speculated that Hutchinson's very detailed description is too elaborate to be
accurate; also that it is so theatrical as to suggest someone (possibly,

Stephen Knight suggests, **Walter Sickert**) in disguise. It has been speculated that Hutchinson may have been a former client of Kelly's. And
most researchers suggest that he was the man seen under the archway of
Crossingham's Lodging-House by **Sarah Lewis**.

HUTCHINSON, GEORGE, OF ELGIN, ILLINOIS
Alleged suspect.
Described thus in *Pall Mall Gazette*, 12 January 1888:
IS HE THE WHITECHAPEL MURDERER?
The Panama 'Star and Herald' asks this startling question while record-
ing a telegram from Elgin, Illinois, U.S.A., which runs:- 'Seven or eight
years ago George Hutchinson, an inmate of Elgin lunatic asylum, was
very handy with his knife. He delighted to visit the hospital slaughter-
house, and made many peculiar toys from bones. After escaping from
Elgin he was captured at Kankakee. He escaped from that place, and
murdered a disreputable woman in Chicago, mutilating her body in a
way similar to the Whitechapel cases. He was returned to Kankakee, but
afterwards again escaped, and has been at large for three or four years.'

HUTT, POLICE CONSTABLE GEORGE, 968 City
Warrant no. 5274. Joined City Police, 1879; retired, 1889. Came on duty to
oversee cells at Bishopsgate Police Station, 9.45 p.m., 29 September 1888,
and so took charge of **Catharine Eddowes** (q.v. for light conversation and
banter between them) until she was discharged at 12.55 a.m. Hutt saw her
turn left on leaving the police station and estimated it would have taken her
about eight minutes to reach Mitre Square.

HUXLEY, THE MISSES
According to one report, the name of the cigar makers living in the second
floor back room of 29 Hanbury Street (Annie Chapman's murder site).
Either misheard as or was misheard for **Mr and Mrs Copsey**.

HVEM VAR JACK THE RIPPER?
Book by Carl Muusmann (1908). The title asks 'Who was Jack the Ripper?'
The book concludes he was **Alios Szemeredy**. The first book to offer a
solution.

I

IDENTITY OF JACK THE RIPPER, THE
Book by David McCormick (1959; amended pbk 1962; revised ed., 1970).
Development of theory advanced in *Things I Know* by **William Le Queux**,
who based on highly questionable source/s the theory that the Whitechapel
Murders were committed at the behest of Czarist Secret Police by **Dr
Alexander Pedachenko**.

McCormick draws upon additional sources: chiefly **Dr Dutton's *Chron-
icles of Crime***, an edition of the ***Ochrana Gazette***, and a letter by **Sir Basil
Thomson** to support claims that Pedachenko was an alias of **Vassily
Konovalov**. He further claims (in the paperback edition of 1962, as in his
History of the Russian Secret Service, written under the pseudonym Richard
Deacon) that Konovalov also used the alias **Michael Ostrog**.

Ostrog's name was first published in connection with Jack the Ripper in
the 1962 paperback edition of *The Identity of Jack the Ripper*, where
McCormick quotes a letter which he says Basil Thomson wrote at the end
of his life (c.1939), and which reads in part:

> When I was in Paris recently I learned in talks with the French that they
> had always thought that the 'Ripper' was a Russian named Konovalov,
> who used the alias 'Mikhail Ostrog', under which name Scotland Yard
> knew him as an ex-convict and medical student. They did not, however,
> describe him as a surgeon, but rather as a barber's assistant.

The first edition of *The Identity of Jack the Ripper* appeared in 1959,
almost simultaneously with **Daniel Farson**'s television programmes identifying **M. J. Druitt** (by initials only) from the **Macnaghten memoranda**. At
this time, **Lady Aberconway**, owner of the memoranda, insisted that
suspects named therein should not be identifiably described. McCormick
appeared on Farson's programme and learned from him of the named
suspects. He used the information in his amended paperback edition,
noting that a young barrister from Dorset (i.e., M. J. Druitt) had been
found drowned in the Thames on the last day of 1888. It is noteworthy that
when he revised the book in 1970, with direct assistance from Lady
Aberconway, he did not draw attention to the fact that Ostrog, the suspect
named by Macnaghten whom he (McCormick) thought most likely to be
the Ripper, had been independently named by Sir Basil Thomson in a letter
which he had seen. Far from stressing this point, McCormick actually
quoted the letter differently, now representing that it made no reference to
Ostrog at all:

> When I was in Paris recently I learned in talks with the French that they
> had always thought that the Ripper was a Russian named Konovalov, or
> some name like that. They did not, however, describe him as a surgeon,
> but rather as a barber's assistant.

We know of no evidence outside McCormick's book for the existence of the Basil Thomson letter. We note that the facts now known about Ostrog are quite different from those alleged about **Konovalov**.

With the exception of Le Queux, none of Mr McCormick's sources has been traced. In the light of Mr McCormick's demonstrable tampering with the Thomson quotation, his book should be used with extreme caution by researchers.

ILLUSTRATED POLICE NEWS
Popular journal reporting exclusively on crime and boxing. Most of the well-known, but occasionally imaginative and inaccurate, line-drawings reproduced in books on Jack the Ripper are taken from its front covers, which routinely comprised collages illustrating the week's most sensational crimes (or, occasionally, boxing matches).

INQUESTS
A coroner is obliged to hold an enquiry into a sudden or inexplicable death, or a death where foul play is suspected. It must be held in a public place and be open to the press. Many (like **Montague John Druitt**'s) were held in public houses in the nineteenth century. The purpose is to determine the identity of the deceased, and establish the cause of death. The coroner must question all witnesses he believes to have material information, and they may also be examined by his jury and others with a legitimate interest in the case, such as the police.

Inquest papers have only survived for two of the Ripper victims: Catharine Eddowes (held in Corporation of London Archives) and Mary Jane Kelly (held in Greater London Record Office).

For the inquests on the Ripper victims, see under **Wynne Baxter, Mr Langham** and **Roderick MacDonald**.

INQUESTS: JURISDICTIONAL DISPUTES OVER
At Mary Jane Kelly's inquest a juror protested that the officiating coroner should have been **Wynne Baxter**, and was firmly quashed by **Dr Roderick MacDonald**, who further asserted that he, and not Wynne Baxter, might have conducted the inquest on Annie Chapman. He stated that Chapman had died in his area, but had been taken to a mortuary in Mr Baxter's; therefore it was right that Baxter should have sat on her case. Kelly now lay in a mortuary under his jurisdiction, and therefore he was the coroner hearing the case.

It has been suggested that this contretemps covered some official attempt to avoid revealing unpalatable facts; that Baxter's very thorough enquiries were unwelcome to authorities who had something to hide, and therefore the inquest was passed to MacDonald, who hurried it through with a deliberate evasion of embarrassing questions; or that the dispute was the aftermath of the very tense election the two men had fought the previous year.

The dispute arose from an administrative anomaly. Spitalfields, where both Chapman and Kelly died, was administered by Whitechapel for all purposes except coroner's inquests, the newly created coroner's division of Northeastern Middlesex (under MacDonald) having acquired it. MacDonald was right to say that both murders took place under his jurisdiction.

He was also correct to say that a coroner had to hold an inquest on a body lying within his division, and so Baxter had been correct to inquire into

Chapman's death once her body had been taken to Whitechapel mortuary, and he himself was right to inquire into Kelly's once her body had been taken to Shoreditch.

The real problem would have arisen if Shoreditch vestry had (justifiably) refused to meet the mortuary and burial expenses on a woman who had died outside their jurisdiction. In that case, Kelly would have had to be returned to Whitechapel mortuary and Baxter would have had to hold a second inquest on her. This happened in the case of Louisa Ellesdon the following year.

And in December 1889 the body of a man who died in a common lodging-house in Heneage Street, Spitalfields, had to lie on the kitchen table for three days and nights while the lodgers cooked and ate around him, because MacDonald would not allow it to be removed into the Whitechapel mortuary and Baxter's jurisdiction!

INTERNATIONAL WORKINGMEN'S EDUCATIONAL CLUB
A two-storey wooden building at 40 Berner Street which ran alongside the north side of Dutfield's Yard. At the rear were the printing offices from which the Yiddish journal *Der Arbeter Fraint* ('The Worker's Friend') was published. Acquired in 1885 by Jewish Socialists, it became one of the favoured centres for immigrant anarchists and intellectuals, especially following its acquisition in 1886 of the influential *Arbeter Fraint*. It was not, however, popular with orthodox Jews, who regarded the members as godless, disreputable, and tending to lower the reputation of Jews. Yet today it is best remembered as abutting on the murder of Elizabeth Stride, whose body was discovered by the club steward, **Louis Diemschütz**.

ISAACS, JOSEPH
Briefly suspected. A Polish Jewish cigar-maker, he resided at **Mary Cusins'** lodging house in Little Paternoster Row prior to Mary Jane Kelly's murder, and attracted attention by pacing his room at nights and departing the day after the murder, leaving a violin bow in his room.

On police advice, Mary Cusins followed him when he came to collect the violin bow on 5 December, and saw him take it to Mr Levenson's pawnshop. Isaacs asked Levenson to repair the bow, and while he was examining it, grabbed a watch and ran away. The following day he was arrested in Drury Lane and taken to Bow Street Police Station. **Inspector Abberline** was summoned, and removed him to Leman Street Police Station in a closed carriage under strong escort. The press believed he had been arrested as Jack the Ripper. Subsequently, however, he was only charged with stealing the watch.

ISSENSCHMIDT, JOSEPH (b. circa 1850)
Early suspect. Butcher of 59 Elthorne Road, Holloway, he suffered a breakdown when his business failed, and spent ten weeks in Colney Hatch Asylum during 1887.

On 11 September 1888, Drs Cowan and Crabb of Holloway informed police that they believed Issenschmidt to be the Whitechapel murderer. Police learned that he had been lodging with a Mr Tyler at 60 Milford Road since 5 September, that he was frequently out of the house, and was missing on the night of Annie Chapman's murder.

By 17 September he was confined to Fairfield Road Asylum, Bow, where

Sergeant Thick learned that he had told a number of women in Holloway that he was **'Leather Apron'**. He had been living by collecting sheep's heads, feet and kidneys from the market, which he dressed and sold in the West End; this casual work explained his absences from his lodgings. He had left his wife (of 97 Duncombe Road, Upper Holloway) following an argument.

Two days later **Abberline** reported that Issenschmidt was believed to be the man with a bloodstained hand seen by **Mrs Fiddymont**, and this would be confirmed as soon as the doctors thought he was fit to appear for identification. If Mrs Fiddymont did confirm this identification, it would be the only known evidence that Issenschmidt ever made an appearance in Whitechapel or Spitalfields at the time of the earlier murders, and it is just possible that this has some bearing on **Police Constable Sagar**'s recollection of a suspect in the vicinity of Butchers' Row, Aldgate. But in any case, Issenschmidt was not the Ripper, being safely incarcerated at the times of the later murders. He subsequently returned to Colney Hatch Asylum.

IZZARD, INSPECTOR, City Police
With Sergeants Dudman and Phelps, directed the maintenance of public order around Mitre Square following Catharine Eddowes' murder.

J

J DIVISION, METROPOLITAN POLICE
(See **H Division.**)
Established 1886 to cover Bethnal Green and parts of Mile End New Town, with Bethnal Green Road Police Station as its headquarters. Involved in the Ripper enquiry since Mary Ann Nichols' murder fell under the divisional jurisdiction.

JACK EL DESTRIPADOR DE LONDRES (1972, Spain/Italy)
Film directed by Jose Luis Madrid. Stars Paul Naschy, Patricia Loran.

JACK L'EVENTREUR
Book by **Jean Dorsenne** (1935). Floridly recounts every known (and some otherwise unknown) legendary incident and suspect, often in ways which reveal authorial imagination and French ignorance of English police methods. Purports to be based on recollections of 'Chief Constable G. W. H.', the last surviving officer engaged on the case, visited in his retirement in a Yorkshire village by Dorsenne. G. W. H., allegedly resident in Windsor at the time of the crimes, has not been identified. Since Dorsenne is interestingly free with the names of genuine police officers involved in the case, on rare occasions describing plausible and otherwise unknown actions of theirs, it might be useful to trace this supposed source.

JACK THE RIPPER (BBC TV)
Drama documentary, 1973. Produced by Leonard Lewis and Paul Bonner. Directed by David Wickes. See also **Jack the Ripper (Thames-Lorimar TV).**
See under *The Ripper File* (Lloyd and Jones).
This programme first introduced **Joseph Sickert** to the public, though neither the BBC nor the Scotland Yard information officer said to have introduced him wishes to be held responsible for purveying his theory.

JACK THE RIPPER
Book by Daniel Farson (1972). A straightforward account of the murders, with a few minor inaccuracies that do not affect its central thesis. A general description of previous theories, and then a full exposition of the case for **Montague John Druitt** as the Ripper. The book gives a full and scrupulous account of Farson's own research and its delays and setbacks.
Apart from the original discovery of Druitt in the **Macnaghten memoranda**, Farson's new work advancing on Tom Cullen's *Autumn of Terror* included the Australian evidence discussed under *The East End Murderer – I Knew Him*. Farson also suggested that **Lionel Druitt**'s brief practice in The Minories might have introduced Montague to the district, noting that

other hearsay evidence tended to link a man called Druitt with that street.

This book was the first to print the mortuary photographs of victims discovered by **Francis Camps** in the London Hospital.

JACK THE RIPPER (1958, Great Britain)
Film directed by Robert S. Baker and Monty Berman. Stars Lee Patterson, Eddie Byrnes, Ewen Solon. American detective solves case and Ripper (Solon) is flattened beneath descending lift. A good start but the pace flags; hype turned this medium melodrama into a box office success. (Video available.)

JACK THE RIPPER (Thames Lorimar TV) (1988, Great Britain/USA)
Film directed by David Wickes. Cf. **Jack the Ripper** (BBC TV). Stars Michael Caine, Lewis Collins. Much hyped whodunnit, which tails off into Sickert story of Masonic conspiracy, being investigated by **Abberline** (Caine) and **Godley** (Collins). Marred by false publicity claiming historical authenticity, but otherwise enjoyable centenary tv movie offering. (Video available.)

'JACK THE RIPPER' (nickname)
See under **'Jack the Ripper' letters**.

JACK THE RIPPER
Book by William Stewart (1939). Delightfully unpretentious book-length development of Arthur Conan Doyle's suggestion that a midwife could have escaped detection as the Ripper, since she would be expected to pass through the streets in a blood-stained apron.

Stewart added the suggestion that she might have been an illegal abortionist (basing it reasonably on the observation made in several contemporary newspapers that Mary Jane Kelly was three months pregnant). Unfortunately the entire theory has fallen with the discovery of **Dr Thomas Bond**'s full medical report on Kelly, which shows that she was not pregnant.

The charm of Stewart's research is well indicated by his practical experiment in tearing a piece of calico at dead of night in Mitre Square, in order to find out whether the murderer could have escaped being overheard. He found that the ear-splitting rending noise resounding through the enclosed square of those days would inevitably have disturbed watchman **George Morris**. (The authors' conclusion is that the Ripper used his extremely sharp knife to cut **Catharine Eddowes**' apron in half silently.)

JACK THE RIPPER: A BIBLIOGRAPHY AND REVIEW OF THE LITERATURE
Book by **'Alexander Garfield Kelly'** (1973, with Introduction by **Colin Wilson**; revised 1984). 60 entries of references in contemporary press; 214 entries of information on facts and theories; 38 entries of relevant biographical material; 112 entries of related fiction and drama; 46 entries of films, music etc. A tour de force.

JACK THE RIPPER, DESCRIPTIONS OF
Several witnesses describing men seen with victims before their deaths have been thought to have described the murderer. They were as follows:

Mrs Elizabeth Darrell saw a man of shabby genteel appearance, wearing a deerstalker hat and a dark coat. Estimated age, around forty. He had a dark complexion and foreign appearance (usually a euphemism for Jewish). He was a little taller than Annie Chapman to whom he was talking (and she was a little over 5ft tall). Mrs Long only saw the man from behind.

An unnamed witness – probably **Emily Walters** (i.e., the prostitute herself) – gave police a description which they issued to the public of a man seen entering 29 **Hanbury Street** with a prostitute at about 2.00 a.m., 8 September 1888. He wore a short dark jacket, dark vest and trousers, black scarf and black felt hat. Estimated age, about thirty-seven. Dark beard and moustache. Spoke with a foreign accent.

Police Constable William Smith described a clean-shaven man of respectable appearance wearing dark clothes and a hard felt deerstalker hat of dark colour. Age, about twenty-eight, Height 5ft 7ins. He carried a newspaper parcel 18ins long and 6–8ins wide.

Israel Schwartz was recorded by police as seeing a broad-shouldered man in a dark jacket and trousers, and with a black cap with a peak. His age was about thirty; his height about 5ft 5ins. His hair was brown, his complexion fair, and he had a small brown moustache. According to the *Star*, Schwartz said the man was respectably dressed, stoutly built, and wore a felt hat. The differences are almost certainly translation errors from Schwartz's Hungarian or Yiddish, and the police version is more likely to be accurate.

James Brown saw a stoutish man, about 5ft 7ins tall, wearing a long coat which almost reached his heels.

According to Home Office records, **Joseph Lawende** described a man of medium build and sailorly appearance wearing a pepper-and-salt coloured loose jacket; a grey cloth cap with a peak of the same colour, and a reddish neckerchief. His age was about thirty; his height 5ft 7–8ins. He had a fair complexion and moustache. According to *The Times* Lawende put his height at 5ft 9ins and said his appearance was shabby.

George Hutchinson saw a man of respectable Jewish appearance, wearing a long dark coat with astrakhan collar and cuffs, a dark jacket and trousers, light waistcoat, dark felt hat 'turned down in the middle' (i.e., the shape which evolved variously into Homburgs, Stetsons, Panamas and Trilbies), button boots; gaiters (i.e., spats) with white buttons, a linen collar, black tie with a horseshoe pin, and a thick gold chain. His age was thirty-four or thirty-five, his height 5ft 6ins. He had a pale complexion, dark hair and eyelashes, and a slight moustache curled up at the ends. He carried a small parcel wrapped in American cloth (oilcloth).

In the authors' opinion, only Mrs Darrell, Israel Schwartz and Joseph Lawende are likely to be describing the murderer. We have omitted **Matthew Packer**'s description/s of the man he saw with Elizabeth Stride, since we agree with the police conclusion that he varied his story so pliably as to be unreliable.

JACK THE RIPPER IN FACT AND FICTION

Book by **Robin Odell** (1965). A good and responsible account of the murders and the principal theories at the time of writing.

Odell does not name a suspect, but suggests that a *shochet* or ritual Jewish slaughterman would have possessed a sufficiently respectable appearance to approach prostitutes without alarming them, and the technical skill to cut throats rapidly while pushing bodies away so that he was not bloodstained. But see under **M.O**. for lack of bloodstaining. Nor was Odell aware that **Major Smith** had sent shochets' knives to pathologists, who reported that they could not have been used in the murders, being curved whereas the Ripper's blade was straight.

The psychoanalyst Lindsay Neustatter contributed an introduction to the book, concluding that the Ripper was 'a psychopath' without giving much meaning to that dubious term.

'JACK THE RIPPER' LETTERS

The name derives from a letter and a postcard posted to the Central News Agency on 27 September from London EC and 1 October from London E respectively.

The 'Dear Boss' letter was sent on to Scotland Yard on 29 September. It was written with red ink in a good educated hand. It ran:

25 Sept. 1888.

Dear Boss,
I keep on hearing the police have caught me but they wont fix me just yet. I have laughed when they look so clever and talk about being on the *right* track. That joke about Leather Apron gave me real fits. I am down on whores and I shant quit ripping them till I do get buckled. Grand work the last job was. I gave the lady no time to squeal. How can they catch me now. I love my work and want to start again. You will soon hear of me with my funny little games. I saved some of the proper *red* stuff in a ginger beer bottle over the last job to write with but it went thick like glue and I cant use it. Red ink is fit enough I hope *ha. ha*. The next job I do I shall clip the ladys ears off and send to the police officers just for jolly wouldnt you. Keep this letter back till I do a bit more work, then give it out straight. My knife's so nice and sharp I want to get to work right away if I get a chance. Good luck.

Yours truly
Jack the Ripper

Dont mind me giving the trade name
A second postscript in red crayon read:
  wasnt good enough to post this before I got all the red ink off my hands curse it No luck yet. They say I'm a doctor now *ha ha*
The 'saucy Jacky' postcard, also probably in crayon, read:
  I was not codding dear old Boss when I gave you the tip, youll hear about saucy Jacky s work tomorrow double event this time number one squealed a bit couldnt finish straight off. had not time to get ears for police thanks for keeping last letter back till I got to work again.

Jack the Ripper

The repeated nickname and references to cutting off ears suggested that these came from the same source, and when the Metropolitan police published facsimiles of them, it was immediately assumed that they were the work of the murderer. The Americanism 'Boss' was taken to be a clue to his nationality, and 'graphologists' have attempted to describe the murderer's character from examinations of these letters.

But since the 'Dear Boss' letter was published in the morning papers on 1 October, when the 'saucy Jacky' card was posted, the latter might easily have been an imitative hoax by another hand. There was an immediate flood of other imitative hoaxes, one posted to the *Daily News* on 1 October being signed 'Ripper' with an inserted 'Boss', though the City Police, who ultimately received it, never made it public.

After 1910 **Anderson** and **Swanson** both wrote that the 'Dear Boss' letter was the work of a journalist whom they could identify, and most researchers today conclude that they were probably correct. (See **Best** – for a suggested author.)

Among the more interesting of the other 'Jack the Ripper' letters was one which apparently intimated awareness that the police had heard from **R. J. Lees**. **Forbes Winslow** claimed to have received one at the height of the scare in November 1888, but as **Melvin Harris** showed by printing a facsimile, the date had been altered from 1889 to make it look more impressive.

But perhaps the most interesting problem set by the letters is one that cannot presently be solved. **Donald McCormick** describes a letter sent from Liverpool on 29 September that read:

Beware, I shall be at work on 1st and 2nd Inst., in Minories at twelve midnight, and I give the authorities a good chance, but there is never a policeman near when I am at work.

Yours,
JACK THE RIPPER

The letter is now missing from the files, so it is impossible to check. But if McCormick quotes and dates it accurately, it was posted before the name 'Jack the Ripper' had been released to the public. It is, of course, surprising that any writer in the habit of using the form 'inst' (for 'of the present month') should thus *predict* something to happen twenty-seven days *previously*.

See **Maria Coroner** for the only positively detected author of a 'Jack the Ripper' letter. See **Lusk letter** for the only other letter of any importance purporting to come from the murderer.

JACK THE RIPPER: 100 YEARS OF INVESTIGATION

Book by **Terence Sharkey** (1987). A sprightly commercial account of the murders and principal suspect theories as known up to early 1987, produced for the centenary of the murders. Marred by inaccuracies.

JACK THE RIPPER: ONE HUNDRED YEARS OF MYSTERY

Book by **Peter Underwood** (1987). An unambitious commercial account of the murders and the principal suspects as known early in 1987, padded out with contributions from well-known and unknown Ripperologists and aimed at meeting the anticipated centenary market. The book shows signs of haste in its many inaccuracies, and the frequent misidentification of places in the illustrations.

JACK THE RIPPER: OR WHEN LONDON WALKED IN TERROR

Book by **Edwin Thomas Woodhall** (1937). Pulp paperback proposing **Olga Tchkersoff** as the Ripper. It also muddles a sentence of **Melville Macnaghten**'s with **Dr Holt**'s misadventure (see **White-Eyed Man**). Woodhall misnames **Mary Jane Kelly** 'Marie J. Taylor', but places **Chief Inspector Swanson** prominently in the enquiry at the expence of **Abberline**.

JACK THE RIPPER, ORIGIN OF NAME

See under '**Jack the Ripper' letters**.

JACK THE RIPPER Public House
Name of **The Ten Bells**, Spitalfields, 1976–88.

JACK THE RIPPER, REASONS FOR CONTINUED INTEREST IN
The sudden commencement of the murders, their compression in time and geography, their brutality, the apotheosis of horror reached by the double event, their abrupt cessation, the overblown coverage by the press, and the mystery of the killer's identity – all contributed to making the murders the *cause célèbre* of their day, and subsequent bursts of speculation served to put them into the public consciousness. But there can be no doubt that what kept them there was the chillingly memorable soubriquet 'Jack the Ripper'.

'Jack the Ripper' passed into common English usage and symbolised the depths of utter depravity, its meaning understood even by those who knew nothing of the historical reality of the Ripper or even that there was a historical reality. Once one is aware of this adjectival usage it is surprising how often it is used in movies of the 30s, 40s and 50s, for example, long before the 'boom' in Ripper theories.

Another factor which had kept the Ripper alive in the public consciousness is the fascination of the theme for writers and film makers. Today this fascination is diluted by the growing number and our greater understanding of serial killers. But they are a comparatively late twentieth-century social phenomenon and earlier writers were drawn to explore the psychology of someone possessed by the compulsion to destroy without motive, or to examine the almost primal fear of the unknown which such a killer arouses.

That the Ripper can today still touch a nerve of a deep subconscious primal fear may also in part explain the near obsessive interest some people have in discovering the Ripper's identity, or attempting to put a face and personality to the killer and thereby perhaps exorcising the fear of the unknown. But interest in the Ripper's identity is quite recent, as demonstrated by the fact that of the twenty-seven non-fiction Ripper books, only five predate the discovery of the Macnaghten memoranda in 1959 and the resultant hopes that the Ripper had been or could be identified. International interest was further awakened in the 1970s, first by **Dr Stowell**'s theory that the Ripper was **Prince Albert Victor**, and then by the **Joseph Sickert/Stephen Knight** argument that the murders were Government-inspired.

The so-called game of 'Hunt the Ripper' may now have run its course, however, and it has admittedly become tedious to read of yet another 'final solution'. Hopefully in the future theories will be based on quality research and good evidence. This seems to be reflected by publishers, who appear wary of adding to the pile of Ripper books, and reviewers, who seem instinctively to be scathing (although recently their ignorance of the subject on which they are commenting is lamentable). But public interest shows no sign of abating, books continue to sell well, and tv ratings for documentaries about the Ripper are invariably high. Which all goes to show that the Ripper is more than just a mystery in search of a solution.

JACK THE RIPPER'S KNIFE
A broken surgical knife, now in the possession of **Donald Rumbelow**, has

often been exhibited or illustrated with the suggestion that it may have been the Ripper's weapon. The knife was given to Miss Dorothy Stroud in 1937 by Hugh Pollard, sporting editor of *Country Life*, who said it had belonged to Jack the Ripper. Since Pollard was the partner of gunsmith Robert Churchill, for many years Scotland Yard's ballistics expert, the provenance of the knife seemed excellent. It was then one of an unbroken pair, contained in a box lined with bloodstained velvet. Miss Stroud burned the box, gave one knife away, and used the other for carving and subsequently gardening, in the course of which she broke it.

Probably the same knife is described by **Douglas G. Browne**, who wrote in *The Rise of Scotland Yard*, 'A friend of the writer's possesses one of two surgical knives said to have been left by the Ripper beside his victims.' No such abandoned knives are known, though a canard in the *Pall Mall Gazette* asserted that the murder weapon was abandoned beside Annie Chapman's body. (And cf. **Thomas Coram**.)

According to **Dr Francis Camps**, the knife was a late nineteenth-century post-mortem knife with a special thumb-grip designed for 'ripping' upwards. **Bagster Phillips** had said that a mortician's dissecting-knife was the only type of surgical instrument that could have carried out the mutilations.

Today it is known that Rumbelow's knife is a surgeon's amputating knife of continental manufacture in the 1870s. A note on the **Home Office Files** states that Annie Chapman's injuries might have been made by a short amputating knife. Nevertheless, it is noted that Rumbelow's knife has a bevelled end and does not comply with the statement in post mortems that the victims were mutilated with a knife sharpened to a point. The authors suggest that if this knife has any connection with the Ripper, it may have belonged to **Michael Ostrog**.

JACK THE RIPPER: SUMMING UP AND VERDICT
Book by **Colin Wilson** and **Robin Odell** (1987). Survey of the known serious data timed for the centenary of the murders. A responsible and workmanlike job, but unfortunately it appeared contemporaneously with a flood of new information (e.g., the **Swanson marginalia**) which could not be included.

The unwary are warned that more trivial error has crept in than one would expect from two leading authorities in the field, with the editorial assistance of the late distinguished crime historian J. R. R. Gaute.

JACK THE RIPPER'S VICTIMS
See under **Mary Ann Nichols, Annie Chapman, Elizabeth Stride, Catharine Eddowes, Mary Jane Kelly**.

For alleged victims, see under **Frances Coles, Alice McKenzie, Rose Mylett, Emma Elizabeth Smith, Martha Tabram**.

JACK THE RIPPER: THE BLOODY TRUTH
Book by **Melvin Harris** (1987). Following his research into the **R. J. Lees** and **Dr D'Onston** stories for *Sorry, You've Been Duped!*, Harris determined to write a full exposé of the major hoaxes and fantasies surrounding the Ripper case. This occupies the bulk of the book, and contains valuable material on Lees and the **Prince Albert Victor** and **Sir William Gull** theories.

But in examining the D'Onston story in more detail, Harris discovered that many of the man's claims about himself were not, as was believed, fraudulent. (See under **Robert Donston Stephenson**.) Harris then came to the conclusion that Stephenson had more of the Ripper's essential qualities than any other known suspect, and so he was the Ripper. The argument has not persuaded other researchers.

Harris's book is lavishly illustrated in coffee-table format.

JACK THE RIPPER: THE FINAL SOLUTION

Book by **Stephen Knight** (1976). Probably the best-known book on the subject, worldwide, it presents and researches **Joseph Sickert**'s story that the Ripper was **Sir William Gull**, acting as a loyal (if demented) **Freemason** at the behest of **Lord Salisbury** to eliminate Mary Jane Kelly and her cronies, who were attempting to blackmail the Government with their knowledge of the secret and illegal marriage between **Prince Albert Victor** and Mr Sickert's grandmother, **Annie Elizabeth Crook**.

Justifiably admired for its detail, readability and important contributions to knowledge of the Ripper case (e.g., the discovery of **Israel Schwartz**'s testimony), the book's thesis has nevertheless failed to convince any researchers except those who start out with information deriving from Joseph Sickert's immediate circle. (See **Melvyn Fairclough, Jean Overton Fuller**.) Others note that Knight's sketchy account of the murders contains important omissions and inaccuracies that are used to support his case: e.g., the non-existent pile of coins and rings at Annie Chapman's feet (see under **Annie Chapman**); or the omission of direct medical evidence that all victims were killed where they were found.

It is also noted: that Knight offers no genuine evidence for the Masonic quality of the victims' mutilations; that none of his examination of outside records has substatiated Mr Sickert's story in the ways he imagined, and subsequent research has shown that parts are definitely undermined by those records (see, e.g., **Annie Elizabeth Crook** – especially the address in Cleveland Street; **John Netley; Thomas Mason**).

In the end, there is not a single piece of solid historical evidence adduced to support the sensational and controversial elements of Mr Sickert's story. Nonetheless, Stephen Knight holds an honoured place in the annals of Ripper research.

JACK THE RIPPER: THE FINAL SOLUTION (RWB TV)

TV documentary by RWB Productions, Australia, 1980; produced by Jeremiah Downing; directed by Gary Rhodes. Video available. A review of **Stephen Knight**'s theories. Interviews with Knight and location shooting in East End and at **Sir William Gull**'s grave. Offers nothing reliably new or different, although the map of the East End bears no resemblance whatever to the actual topography.

JACK THE RIPPER: THE MYSTERY SOLVED

Book by Paul Harrison (1991). The central thesis, that **Joseph Barnett** was the Ripper and committed the crimes to force Mary Jane Kelly to abandon prostitution, is a reworking of the argument more cautiously advanced by **Bruce Paley** in 1982, and is subject to the same objections: notably, the proposed motive lacks conviction. No new information is provided about victims or theories, some of the more historically important of the latter being dismissed subjectively. Harrison describes a different man from the one identified as Barnett by Paley (see under **Joseph Barnett**). If Harrison's identification is correct he adds interesting information about Barnett's subsequent career. But apart from a meeting with an alleged descendant in the East End who also believed Barnett to be the murderer, Harrison offers no proof of his claims. The descendant's 'evidence' was limited to an envelope of press cuttings.

Certain interesting original details are put forward concerning Barnett in the 1880s: that some newspapers said he was known as 'John' or 'Jack'; that he favoured Mac's common lodging-house off the Minories; that he first lived with Kelly at Whittlowe's in George Street. Unfortunately, no references are given, so that future researchers wishing to develop this line of enquiry will have to approach the author for sources.

The book skirts over problems presented by known historical documents and relies rather heavily on intuitive detective impressions rather than accepted historical methods. Nevertheless it offers an uncomplicated and workmanlike general survey.

JACK THE RIPPER: THE UNCENSORED FACTS
Book by Paul Begg (1988). The fullest and most responsible account in print of the five Ripper murders. Ten lengthy chapters give the history and background of events from 30 September to 7 December 1888. The victims' histories are explored in detail. Four brief chapters examine only the most serious historical suspect theories. Throughout there are detailed arguments examining the work of other researchers, and historical problems are firmly indicated. Begg does not commit himself to any theory, but does comment that **Sir Melville Macnaghten** was unlikely to have committed himself to a theory on a flimsy basis, and that the opinion of **Anderson** and **Swanson** must weigh heavily in the balance.

The book's unique feature is the full use of footnoting. Not only does it flesh out the earlier histories of the victims, and give many more facts about witnesses than any other on the subject, but the reader can trace them back to primary sources. This means that, while it may seem too drily informative for the casual reader, it is an imperative tool for the researcher (who is nonetheless advised to re-check primary sources, since occasional literals and misdatings have passed the proof-reading).

JACK'S BACK (1988, USA)
Film directed by Rowdy Harrington. Stars James Spader, Cynthia Gibb. Hunt for modern murderer who kills in exact imitation of Ripper. Adequate suspenser which could have made far better use of plot which was a reality genuinely feared in East End in centenary year.

JACKSON, ELIZABETH (d. 1889)
Described by New York *World* as the Ripper's tenth victim. Prostitute, living in Sloane Square. Parts of her body, identified by scars, were found in the Thames between 31 May and 25 June 1889. There is no reason to suppose that she was in any way connected with the Ripper.

JACOBS
Butcher. Belatedly and briefly suspected. **Benjamin Leeson** writes in *Lost London* that after Frances Coles' murder (1891):

a story circulated that the Ripper was a butcher, who wore blue overalls and a leather apron, and an English Jew named Jacobs, a perfectly harmless man, somehow attracted suspicion to himself. Possibly because, working in a slaughter-house, he always wore a leather apron.

People would point Jacobs out in the street as a suspected man, and more than once he had to run for it. I myself was often obliged to take him to the police station for protection. The thing so preyed on the poor fellow's mind that it finally caused him to lose his reason.

If Leeson can be relied upon here, he gives remarkable evidence of a belated revival of something very like the early '**Leather Apron**' scare.

JACOBS –
Socialist. Member of **International Workingmen's Educational Club**. Seen outside by **Morris Eagle** accompanying another man (possibly **Diemschütz**) down Berner Street toward Fairclough Street in search of police after the discovery of Elizabeth Stride's body. Nothing more is known about him.

JAMES, HENRY
Bethnal Green lunatic arousing short-lived suspicion. James was seen near the Foresters' Arms, Cambridge Heath Road, on 8 September 1888 by **Thomas Ede**. This was the height of the '**Leather Apron**' scare, and James was wearing a two-peaked cap and, Mr Ede thought, had four inches of knife blade protruding from his pocket. He also moved oddly, and seemed to have a wooden arm. Mr Ede was permitted to testify at Mary Ann Nichols' inquest on 17 September that he had seen this suspicious character, but returned a week later to say that he had now been shown James, a well-known harmless local lunatic, and confirmed that this was the man he had seen.

JAY, MASON
Theorist. Author of 'The Ripper – A Layman's Theory' in *The Criminologist*, Spring 1990. Deduces exclusively from secondary sources that the Ripper was 'a clean shaven female impersonator in drag' who escaped police cordons because they were looking for bearded Jewish immigrants. Mr Jay's most persistent position is an intuitive feeling that the skills and habits of a theatrical career would all serve a man trying to lure victims and make an unrecognised escape in dark and crowded streets.

'JENNY'
Prostitute interviewed at St George's-in-the-East Infirmary by the press on 1 October 1888, who said, 'she was absolutely sure of the identity of the murderer. She described him as a foreigner who habitually went about blackmailing unfortunate women [i.e., demanding from them with menaces] and threatening occasionally to rip them up.' She was also reported as saying he was about forty, stout and fair-complexioned. This appears to be a revival of the earlier '**Leather Apron**' stories.

'JILL THE RIPPER'
Generic term for stories suggesting the murderer was a woman. First proposed by the Reverend Lord Sydney Godolphin Osborne in a letter to

The Times during the terror, stating (without specifying) that the mutilations were self-evidently carrying out the sort of threats streetwalkers made to one another. ('I'll have your guts for garters', e.g., might fit.) Taken up by Sir Arthur Conan Doyle on the assumption that the murderer must have been heavily bloodstained when escaping through crowded streets (but see **M.O.**). He proposed that a midwife in a bloodstained apron would pass unquestioned, suggesting that a male murderer might have disguised himself thus as a woman.

Edwin Woodhall suggested **Olga Tchkersoff**.

William Stewart expanded Conan Doyle's suggestion to book-length, with the additional suggestion that 'Jill' was an abortionist. This theory is expanded with a lot of very dubious ornamentation by Ex-Detective Superintendent **Arthur Butler**. It falls on the evidence of **Dr Bond**'s medical report showing that Mary Jane Kelly was not pregnant.

An unusual and romantic variant is 'Convict SY5 45's Story', advanced by Richard Herd and allegedly revealed by a prisoner in Maidstone. This proposed that the Ripper was a devout nurse who was appalled when she discovered her husband had gone with a prostitute. So borrowing his clothes and knife she went out to avenge herself on the woman who had ruined her marriage, using **'Dr Stanley'**'s technique to prevent anyone remembering her asking questions in Whitechapel.

JIMMY KELLY'S YEAR OF THE RIPPER MURDERS

Booklet by **John Morrison** (London, n.d.). A photocopied collage of typescript, newspaper cuttings, handwritten comments, pages from books, and an extraordinary assemblage of photographs. The cover, for example, has cut-outs of helmeted policemen from the early twentieth century, a nondescript young man, and a decisively mid-twentieth-century floozy over the words 'Marie: Slain by Killer'.

A picture of two well-known actors is labelled

1927/1930 The Attorney General explaining that the letter's from Liverpool were in every detail consistent with the handwriting of recent samples taken of James Kelly's. This episode became known as: the day of the cover-up. [*sic*]

Along the side is written, 'I've got Kelly's handwriting. It matches L/Pool Letters.'

On LBC Radio in June 1986, Morrison declared that he has 'all the evidence in the world' to prove his theory that **James Kelly** was Jack the Ripper.

JOHANNES –

Landlord of **Charles Ludwig**. German tailor, resident in Church Street, Minories. Found Ludwig's habits objectionable.

JOHNSON, POLICE CONSTABLE JOHN, 866 City

Rescuer of **Elizabeth Burns**. On duty in The Minories during the early hours of 18 September 1888, Johnson heard a cry of 'Murder!' from Three Kings Court. There he found **Charles Ludwig** with a one-armed prostitute who gave her name as Elizabeth Burns. She said, 'Oh, policeman, do take me out of this.' Johnson cleared Ludwig away, and escorted Burns to the end of his beat where she said, 'He frightened me very much when he pulled a big knife out.' She said she had been too frightened to say so while

Ludwig was present. Johnson alerted other policemen and unsuccessfully searched for Ludwig himself.

JOHNSTON, EDWARD
Witness at **Elizabeth Stride**'s inquest. Assistant to Drs Kay and **Blackwell** at 100 Commercial Road. Informed of the murder by PC 436H, around 1.05 a.m. Notified Dr Blackwell, and went to Dutfield's Yard with the policeman, where he briefly examined the body prior to Dr Blackwell's arrival at precisely 1.16 a.m.

JONES, ELWYN
Author, Co-scripted BBC Television drama-documentary *Jack the Ripper* with **John Lloyd**, with whom he also co-authored spin-off book *The Ripper File*. Born in Wales, a former journalist, music critic and BBC administrator, he devised the highly popular television series *Z Cars* and its successors *Softly, Softly* and *Barlow*.

JONES, MARY (b. 1864)
Brothel-keeper. Charged, together with **Gertrude Smith**, before Thames Magistrates Court by **Inspector Ferrett** on 7 December 1888. The same court attendance minute included **Ellen Hickey** for assault, and **Aaron Davis Cohen** as a wandering lunatic, which suggests that the latter's irrational conduct led to his arrest during the course of the brothel-raid.

JONES, MR
Spitalfields pawnbroker. According to some sources, Mr Jones had issued the pawn tickets found in Catharine Eddowes' mustard tin. According to other sources, the pawnbroker's name was Smith.

JONES, SERGEANT, City
At Catharine Eddowes' murder-site, Jones found three boot-buttons, a thimble and a mustard tin containing two pawn tickets beside the body.

'JULIA'
Prostitute who lodged temporarily with Mary Jane Kelly. According to **Joseph Barnett** he ceased living with Kelly because she brought a prostitute called Julia to live with them. According to the *East London Advertiser*, Julia was German. She may have been **Julia Venturney** or **Van Teurney** who was living opposite Kelly in Miller's Court by the time of the murder.
   See also **Maurice Lewis**.

'JUWES' WRITING
See **Goulston Street graffito**.

K

KAMINSKY, NATHAN (b. 1865)
Recent alleged suspect. Jewish bootmaker of 15 Black Lion Yard with one
year's residence in Whitechapel parish. Diagnosed syphilitic, 24 March
1888, and treated in Ward BB, Whitechapel Workhouse Infirmary. Discharged, cured six weeks later. No known relatives. This is all that is
known of him.

Martin Fido surmises that he was '**Leather Apron**' (or one of the men so
described) on the grounds that his race, address and occupation fit
(especially) **Macnaghten**'s alleged description of that suspect. He further
notes that Kaminsky's address uniquely among suspects fits the topographical indications given by the piece of Catharine Eddowes' apron dropped
beneath the **Goulston Street graffito** and the **Metropolitan Police Area of
Search**. This leads him to suggest that Kaminsky was the Ripper.

There being no trace of Kaminsky under that name in the death registers
of England and Wales, Fido notes that his age, race and lack of known
relatives are identical with those given for **Aaron Davis Cohen**, and speculates that following the hunt for 'Leather Apron', Kaminsky had attempted
to change his occupation and identity prior to undergoing the attack of
raving mania which led to his arrest and incarceration under the incorrect
name of Aaron Davis or David Cohen. He postulates that some awareness
of the name 'Kaminsky' in the early search for 'Leather Apron' encouraged
the Metropolitan Police to believe that this was the same man as **Aaron
Kosminski** when they learned something about him from the City Police
who, he suggests, had watched Kosminski without informing the Met, as,
conversely, the Met had incarcerated 'Cohen' without informing the City
that their witness **Joseph Lawende** had thereafter identified him. Thus he
claims that the Swanson marginalia combine aspects of Kosminski and
aspects of Cohen under the impression that the two men were one.

This theory has proved totally unpersuasive to all other researchers, who
note that the circumstantial evidence against Kaminsky may be mere
coincidence, and that the remainder of the theory is entirely speculative
deduction. The general opinion would be that the 'Cohen' theory fell
as soon as the **Swanson Marginalia** unequivocally identified **Anderson's
suspect** as Kosminski.

KEATON, INSPECTOR LEWIS HENRY (1870–1970)
Informant and theorist. Joined Metropolitan Police, August 1891 (Warrant
no. 77010). Retired 1917.

In 1969 gave tape recorded interview recollecting that beat constables
during the Ripper scare had been encouraged to strap rubber to their
bootsoles, and that most policemen believed the murderer to have assaulted
his victims as they presented themselves for penetration from the rear (see

M.O.). He proposed the theory that the murderer was a doctor, collecting specimens of grossly venereally infected wombs for research purposes, with the hope of discovering an alleviation for genital burning sensations. Unfortunately obtrusive interviewing, drowning the inspector's words, makes it difficult to detect exactly what he says at a point when he appears to identify the suspected doctor as either a 'Dr Cohn' or 'Koch', or some one else, whose name he cannot recall, but who used strychnine (see **Neill Cream**).

'KELLY, ALEXANDER GARFIELD'

Pseudonym used (by common agreement) by no less than three authors: an academic when reviewing computer software; a Swedish short story writer; and a former librarian of New Scotland Yard, now employed in business (b. 1943). Author of *Jack the Ripper: A Bibliography and Review of the Literature*. Simply the world's best informed and most knowledgeable expert on secondary source material concerning the Ripper.

KELLY, JAMES (d. 1929)

Recent alleged suspect.

Murdered his wife Sarah Ann in 1883 at their lodgings with her parents in London. His behaviour had been changing over the previous six months, following an abscess in the neck and headaches. He had begun to object to Sarah's supposedly talking to 'people' on the street. Examining doctors found no evidence of insanity, but clearly Sarah's parents thought their son-in-law had been mentally afflicted. Kelly was sentenced to death, but reprieved and sent to Broadmoor Criminal Lunatic Asylum. In January 1888 he escaped and remained at large until 1927. In 1896 he asked the British consul in New Orleans to return him to England for recommittal to Broadmoor, but evaded Liverpool police when his ship docked. In February 1927 he presented himself at the main gate of Broadmoor and was readmitted, remaining there until his death.

John Morrison claims that Kelly's quarrel with his wife was over his having an affair with Mary Jane Kelly; that he escaped with the intention of rejoining Kelly in London. When he discovered that she had gone on the streets and abandoned or aborted the child she had been carrying for him, he proceeded to kill her, killing on the way all the women from whom he had made enquiries as to her whereabouts.

According to Morrison the authorities determined to cover up Kelly's alarming escape from the outset and were satisfied that there would be no further trouble once Mary Jane had been murdered. Only **Sir Charles Warren** persisted in wishing to notify the public and intensify the search. Therefore his resignation was enforced.

This theory is, we think, unique in the annals of the Ripper, inasmuch as it is presented with no supporting evidence; and no argument whatsoever is adduced or alleged in its favour. There is no recognition of the existence of contradictory historical evidence. We are merely given the author's unsubstantiated assertion that these things happened. The objection is clear: they didn't.

Mr Morrison claims to have documentary proof of all his statements. He has never produced it. Until such time as he does, the James Kelly theory cannot be given any credence.

See also **Inspector Chandler**.

KELLY, JOHN

Witness at Catharine Eddowes' inquest, and her lover. Worked several years as a jobbing market porter, frequently for a fruit salesman called Lander. Met Eddowes in a lodging house, possibly in **Flower and Dean Street** in 1881. As a Catholic he may have loosely 'converted' her, since she gave that as her religion when treated for a burned foot at Whitechapel Infirmary in 1887. He was described as 'quiet and inoffensive' with 'fine features' and 'sharp and intelligent eyes'. By the time of Catharine's murder he was a sick man, however, with a kidney complaint and a bad cough. For his movements on the day of the murder, see under **Catharine Eddowes**.

He presented himself to the police on reading in the newspapers of the pawn ticket in the name of Birrell found beside the body in Mitre Square. Prior to that he had not suspected that the Ripper's latest victim might be his common-law wife. He identified the body.

Altogether, Catharine Eddowes and John Kelly seem to have been an appealingly loyal and mutually supportive couple tossed around the economic abyss of the East End.

KELLY, MARY JANE or MARIE JEANETTE (c. 1863–88)

Supposedly aka 'Black Mary', 'Fair Emma', 'Ginger'.

Last Ripper victim.

Kelly's early history, as related to friends in London, was thus:

Born Limerick and moved to Wales in early childhood where her father, John Kelly, took a job at an ironworks in Carnarvonshire or Carmarthenshire. Had six or seven brothers and one sister. Her brother Henry nicknamed Johnto, joined Scots Guards. Married collier named **Davies** c. 1879, who died in a pit explosion two or three years later. Kelly went to stay with a cousin in Cardiff and became a prostitute. She was also ill, and spent the best part of a year in an infirmary there. Came to London, c. 1884, working first in a high-class West End brothel. At this period she frequently drove in a carriage. At least once she went to Paris with a gentleman, but returned in a few weeks, disliking living in France.

None of the above can be guaranteed as fact, since no supporting evidence has been traced in birth, marriage or death registers, or the records of Cardiff Infirmary, searched by the press in 1888, or the records of the Scots Guards. Nor did any of the friends relating it after her death claim firsthand knowledge of any part of it. Inferential support for the brother in the Scots Guards comes from the fact that **John McCarthy** observed letters from Ireland delivered for Kelly (though he thought they were from her mother), and Joe Barnett correctly believed the Scots Guards to be in Ireland at the end of 1888 (an unlikely fact for him to have known independently). There is inferential support, too, for the West End brothel from **Mrs Carthy** and the Press Association (below). According to **Jean Overton Fuller, Florence Pash** said that Kelly had cleaned floors at the Infirmary.

All her London acquaintances except Joe Barnett knew her as Mary Jane Kelly: he used the form 'Marie Jeanette', which was also engraved on her coffin and entered on her death certificate. Suspecting it to be an affectation, we have preferred the simpler version. One newspaper, however, reported that Kelly was her married name. If this was the case, all attempts to trace her past have been misdirected.

In 1988, BBC researchers for the *Timewatch* programme on the Ripper confirmed that the nuns of **Providence Row Convent** and Night Refuge, Crispin Street, Spitalfields, have a tradition that she stayed briefly with them and was sent out into domestic service from which she absconded to go on the streets. This was supported by the convent's solicitor, whose family had a tradition that they employed a maid sent from the convent who absconded and became a Ripper victim.

Kelly's East End acquaintances, talking to the press, believed her to have gone to the Ratcliff Highway district on her return from France, lodging at first in St George's Street (western end of today's Highway, between St George's Church and St Katharine's Dock) and, according to *The Star*, working for a **Mrs Buki**. Joe Barnett believed she lived with a man called **Morganstone** near Stepney gasworks. She resided with Mrs Carthy on Breezer's Hill prior to c. 1886, and Mrs Carthy said that Kelly's previous landlady, from St George's Street, had accompanied Kelly to Knightsbridge where they recovered a box of clothing from a French 'lady'. She left Mrs Carthy's to live with a man connected with the building trade, who, Mrs Carthy thought, wanted to marry Kelly. This was presumably Joseph Fleming, a mason or plasterer from the vicinity of Bethnal Green with whom she had been associating prior to meeting Barnett, who used to visit her while she was with Barnett, and of whom she was apparently very fond.

By April 1887 she was living at Cooley's Common Lodging House in Thrawl Street, Spitalfields, and on Good Friday, 8 April, she met Barnett. They lodged together thereafter, always in the neighbourhood of the 'wicked quarter mile' around **Dorset Street,** Thrawl Street and **Flower and Dean Street**. Their first home was in **George Street** (between Thrawl Street and 'Flowery Dean'). They moved to Little Paternoster Row, Dorset Street, until they were evicted for drunkenness and non-payment of rent. They went to **Brick Lane**, and finally, to 13 Miller's Court, Dorset Street, which was actually the partitioned-off ground-floor back room of 26 Dorset Street, reached through a doorway just inside the arched entry to Miller's Court. The rent was 4/6 [22½p] a week, and 30/- [£1.50p] arrears had accumulated by the time Kelly died.

Barnett and Kelly were remembered as a friendly and pleasant couple, giving little trouble except, occasionally, when drunk. She may well be the Mary Jane Kelley who was fined 2/6 [12½p] at Thames Magistrates Court for drunken disorderliness on 19 September 1888. Once she broke the window of 13 Miller's Court when drunk. This proved useful when she and Barnett lost the doorkey, as they were able to reach through the broken pane to pull back the spring-lock.

Julia Venturney, who lived opposite, believed Kelly was also seeing another man called Joe, possibly a costermonger, who visited her and gave her money. There was some suggestion that she may have been frightened of a man or men unknown to her East End associates. It has been suggested that these might have been *placeurs* who might have lost money by her return from France, if she had, in fact, accepted one of the contemporary contracts to work in a licensed French brothel. It was known to her friends that she was frightened by the Ripper murders and contemplated leaving London.

In the early evening of 30 October 1888 Barnett left Kelly. He variously described the reasons for their separation as being because she had resumed prostitution; because she had invited another woman called '**Julia**' to stay with them; because she had prostitutes to stay, '**Julia**' and **Mrs Harvey** being named. He continued friendly with her, however, visiting her and possibly giving her money.

On Wednesday 7 November, Kelly bought a halfpenny candle at McCarthy's shop (adjacent to the entry from Dorset Street to Miller's Court) and was subsequently seen in Miller's Court by **Thomas Bowyer** talking to a rather smart man of 27 or 28 with a dark moustache and 'very peculiar eyes'. (See **Unidentified Man Seen by Thomas Bowyer.**)

On Thursday 8 November, Kelly spent the afternoon with Maria Harvey, and the early evening with **Lizzie Albrook**. Joe Barnett visited her amicably between 7.30 and 8.00. Her subsequent movements are uncertain, though she may have been seen drinking with an Elizabeth Foster, and she may have been seen, intoxicated, in **The Britannia** at 11.00 p.m., accompanied by a young man with a moustache. She may even have been in **The Horn of Plenty** with Joe Barnett and '**Julia**'. (See **Maurice Lewis**.)

At 11.45 Mary Ann Cox saw her return home in the company of a stout, shabby, blotchy-faced man in his thirties with a carroty moustache and a billycock hat. He carried a quart pail of beer. Kelly was wearing a linsey frock and a red knitted crossover shawl. She was drunk and told Mrs Cox she was going to sing. Between midnight and 1.00 a.m. several witnesses heard her singing 'Only a violet I plucked from my mother's grave' in her room: Catherine Picket nearly went in to complain about the noise at 12.30.

At 2.00 a.m. **George Hutchinson** met Kelly in Commercial Street, where she addressed him by name and asked him for sixpence. Hutchinson watched her proceed toward Aldgate and pick up a client near Thrawl Street. He examined him closely under the light of the **Queen's Head** on the corner of Fashion Street as the two passed him, and followed them to Dorset Street, where he watched them go into Kelly's room. Then he waited outside for 45 minutes, sheltering under the arched entry beside Crossingham's Lodging House, before going home. Neither the client nor Kelly emerged during this time.

Sarah Lewis testified at Kelly's inquest that she had gone to Miller's Court at 2.30 in the morning. In Commercial Street she saw a man and a woman. She recognised the man as one who had frightened her and a friend in Bethnal Green Road the previous Wednesday, who had asked one of them – he did not mind which – to follow him. In Dorset Street she saw a short, stout man in a wide-awake hat standing in the entry to the lodging-house – presumably Hutchinson. She also saw a young couple walk down Dorset Street.

A woman described as **Mrs Kennedy** was reported in the press as saying she went to Miller's Court at 3.00 or 3.30 a.m. to stay with her parents. She saw a respectably dressed but intoxicated young man with a dark moustache talking to an intoxicated woman in Dorset Street. He said, 'Are you coming?' and the woman turned away. A poorly dressed woman without a hat was standing by. Mrs Kennedy said the man looked like a sinister man with a bag who had frightened her in Bethnal Green Road the previous Wednesday, in an encounter which seems very like that described subsequently by Sarah Lewis. The *Star* intimated doubts about the truth of Mrs Kennedy's Bethnal Green Road story, and there is a strong possibility that she was the same person as Sarah Lewis (cf. **Mrs Darrell/Mrs Long**), giving unreliable varied evidence.

Mrs Kennedy, Sarah Lewis, and **Elizabeth Prater** who lived in the room above Kelly's, all reported hearing a cry of 'Murder!' from the direction of

Kelly's room shortly before 4.00 a.m.

It has been suggested that Kelly's locked door, state of undress, and cut sheet indicate that she may have known her murderer and gone peacefully to sleep in his presence. All three points are capable of alternative explanation. But in any case it does not invalidate the general belief that the murderer introduced himself to his victims in the guise of a client.

Caroline Maxwell, Maurice Lewis and an unnamed woman mentioned in *The Times* all reported seeing Kelly out of doors at times between 8.00 and 10.00 a.m. (i.e. several hours after medical and other evidence indicated she was dead). (See under **Caroline Maxwell** for discussion.)

At 10.45 a.m. Thomas Bowyer saw the body through the window and he and **McCarthy** summoned the police. The spring-lock secured the door, and in the expectation that bloodhounds might be brought the room was not entered until 1.30 p.m. when **Superintendent Arnold** arrived with the information that the dogs would not be coming. On his orders, McCarthy broke open the door with a pick-handle.

For details of Kelly's extreme mutilation, see under **Dr Thomas Bond**. See under **Colin Kendell** for the suggestion that the body was not Kelly's.

Inside the small (12ft x 10ft) room there were remains of a fire in the grate which had burned clothing, including a woman's bonnet. It had apparently burned with sufficient heat to melt the solder at the spout and handle of a kettle in the grate. This seems surprising, given the slow and smelly conflagration usually created by used clothing, and **Arthur Douglas** asks pertinently how it was known that the damage to the kettle occurred on that particular night. **Inspector Abberline** surmised that the purpose was to illuminate the room. This, too, is surprising, given that half a candle was found on a table. Kelly's clothes were on a chair at the foot of the bed.

For discussion of the claim that her inquest was improperly manipulated by the authorities, see under **Inquests: jurisdictional disputes over**.

She was buried at Walthamstow Roman Catholic Cemetery on 19 November. Despite widespread publicity, no member of her family was traced to attend the funeral. A headstone was erected in 1986 by **John Morrison**.

As the last and most savagely mutilated victim, Kelly has featured largely in theories which propose that one particular woman was being sought by the murderer. See **Sir William Gull, James Kelly, 'Dr Stanley'**. **Jean Overton Fuller** claims that she was a personal acquaintance of **Florence Pash**, who reported that Kelly had worked as a nursemaid for **Walter Sickert**. None of these stories is supported by either probability or substantiating evidence.

Tom Cullen reports that she had a reputation for violence and a quick temper; also that she was nick-named 'Black Mary'. Other nicknames reported are 'Fair Emma' and 'Ginger'. All may be the consequence of confusion with other women (cf. **Lizzie Fisher**). Joseph Barnett told the *Star* (10 November 1898) that she had a little boy aged six or seven living with her, and that she occasionally visited a fellow-prostitute in the Elephant and Castle neighbourhood. Neither contemporary nor subsequent research has traced any positive information about this child or friend. (Cf '**Margaret**'.)

Walter Dew, who knew her well by sight, records that she was goodlooking and 'paraded' around the district, usually in the company of two or three friends. She never wore a hat, and she always wore a spotlessly clean white apron. The *Illustrated Police News*' drawing of her shows a woman whom **Colin Wilson** well describes as looking capable of 'felling a carthorse with an uppercut'. But since its drawing of Elizabeth Stride also shows a hatchet-faced harridan, utterly unlike the fine-boned good-looking woman in the mortuary photograph, we believe this to be a travesty. Mary Jane Kelly was almost certainly the best-looking as well as the youngest of the Ripper's victims.

KENDELL, COLIN

Theorist. In 'Did Mary Kelly Die' in the *Criminologist*, Autumn 1988, he puts forward the suggestion that Mary Jane Kelly's extreme facial muti-lation made her identification uncertain, so that **Caroline Maxwell** and other witnesses who believed they saw her alive later in the morning of 9 November 1888 might be correct.

Two later pieces in the *Criminologist* (Spring 1989 and Summer 1990) confirm the impression that Mr Kendell's well-presented and responsibly argued work is vitiated by a total dependence on secondary sources, and by argument from a predetermined conclusion. He has, in fact, been con-vinced by **Stephen Knight**'s *The Final Solution*, and is trying to work other data into supporting material for its case against **Sir William Gull**, without ever addressing himself to the basic problem of the lack of any contemporary source for Knight's story, which at present rests entirely on Mr **Joseph Sickert**'s unsubstantiated claims.

KENNEDY, MRS

Alleged witness to activities in Dorset Street and Miller's Court on the night of Mary Jane Kelly's murder.

The *Star* on 10 November 1888 reported Mrs Kennedy's claim to have gone to Dorset Street in the small hours of 9 November and seen a woman talking to a man, with another man or possibly a masculine-looking woman in the shadows. The *Star* thought her story seemed very doubtful, especially as it entailed comparison of the man she had seen with a man who had frightened her in Bethnal Green Road the previous Wednesday and whom she took to be the Ripper.

None the less, *The Times*, two days later, reported that **Inspector Abber-line** had interviewed her, eliciting the statement that she had gone to her parents' home in Miller's Court, and there saw a woman in the court talking to two men.

The *East London Advertiser* of 6 December printed the much fuller story given under **Mary Jane Kelly** above. The *Manchester Guardian* further reported that her companion in Bethnal Green Road was her sister, and that the encounter with the drunk man and woman took place in Commercial Street beside **The Britannia** or at the **Commercial Street** end of **Dorset Street**. G. R. Sims subsequently referred to the man seen by 'the Kennedy sisters'.

The similarities between her statements and the inquest testimony of **Sarah Lewis** create an obvious suspicion that they were one and the same. It is noteworthy, though, that the *East London Advertiser* was still referring to Mrs Kennedy by that name three weeks after Sarah Lewis had appeared before the press at the inquest. There are also consistent differences between their stories. Sarah Lewis said she saw a man (presumably **Hutch-inson**) standing in the doorway of the lodging house; Mrs Kennedy never mentioned him. Sarah Lewis said she was going to 'the Keylers'. Mrs

Kennedy said she went to her parents. Mrs Kennedy said she saw a woman in the presence of a man and one other person. Sarah Lewis never said anything like this in public (but see under **Sarah Lewis**).

There are differences and inconsistencies in the times given by the two. It is important, however, because *if* Mrs Kennedy was *not* Sarah Lewis, she may have seen a hatless woman (see under **Mary Jane Kelly**) on the street after Hutchinson had stopped watching the entry to Miller's Court.

KENT, JAMES
Witness at Annie Chapman's inquest. Labourer at **Bayleys'** packing-case works, summoned with **James Green** by **John Davis**. Kent went for a brandy before fetching canvas to cover the body.

The *East London Observer* found him an entertaining figure:
A youngish-looking man, with a bullet-head and closely-cropped hair, and a sandy, close-cut moustache. He wore a long overcoat that had once to be green, and into the pockets of which he persistently stuck his hands. He had a peculiar habit of lowering his neck into the blue and white spotted handkerchief which encased it when under examination and jerking it out suddenly whenever he was called upon to answer a question.

KENTORRICH, BARNETT
Resident of 38 Berner Street, adjoining Dutfield's Yard where Elizabeth Stride was murdered. Slept until 3.00 a.m. on 30 September 1888, not even disturbed by the noise accompanying the finding of the body. Expressed Orthodox Jewish hostility to the Socialist Jews of the **International Workingmen's Educational Club**.

KERBY, SERGEANT
Reinforced constables Thain and Mizen at Mary Ann Nichols' body. Kerby arrived on the spot while **Dr Llewellyn** was making his examination.

KEYLER, MR AND MRS
Residents of Miller's Court, Mary Jane Kelly's murder site. **Sarah Lewis** testified she went to stay the remainder of the night with them at about 2.30 a.m., 9 November 1888. If, however, Sarah Lewis was also the woman interviewed as **Mrs Kennedy**, then they may have been her parents, of 2 Miller's Court.

KIDNEY, MICHAEL (b. 1852)
Elizabeth Stride's lover and witness at her inquest. A waterside labourer, resident at 33 Dorset Street at the time of the inquest, Kidney had known Stride for three years and lived with her most of that time. He was seven years younger than her, and their relationship was relatively stormy. He said she was frequently absent when drinking, though he tried unsuccessfully to padlock her in. (She had a key, which **Dr Bagster Phillips** found on the body.) He thought her absences totalled about five months of the previous three years.

On 6 April 1887, Stride gave him in charge to PC 357H for assault, but failed to appear in court to proceed with the prosecution. Kidney was sent down for three days in July 1888 for being drunk and disorderly and using obscene language. At the time of the murder he had not seen her for about five days, but was not disturbed by her absence.

1 October 1888 he turned up drunk at Leman Street Police Station, saying he would have killed himself if he had been the policeman responsible for the beat where Stride was murdered, and asking to see a detective. At the inquest he claimed to have gone because he had heard something that led him to believe he could have trapped the murderer and caught him in the act if given command of a force of detectives with the power to position them. Pressed further, he admitted he had no information.

In June 1889 he was treated at Whitechapel Workhouse Infirmary for syphilis, and in September for lumbago and dyspepsia.

KILLEEN, DR TIMOTHY ROBERT

Examined Martha Tabram's body. LRCS (Ireland), 1885; Lic.K.Q.Coll.Phys. (Ireland), 1886. Frequently spelled Keeling or Keleene in the press. Medical Directories suggest he spent less than two years at the surgery in 68 Brick Lane from which he was called to examine the body at 5.30 a.m.

He estimated that death had occurred about two hours previously. There were 39 stab wounds, including 5 in the left lung, 2 in the right, 1 in the heart, 5 in the liver, 2 in the spleen and 6 in the stomach. The breasts, belly and private parts were the principal targets. At least 38 had been inflicted by a right-handed assailant. All but one could have been caused by an ordinary penknife. The exception was a wound on the sternum which had apparently been made with a dagger or sword-bayonet.

KLOSOWSKI, SEVERIN alias GEORGE CHAPMAN (1865–1903)

Alleged suspect. Born Nagornak, Poland. Son of Antonio Klosowski and Emile (née Ulatowski). Apprentice surgeon 1880–5. Student at Hospital of Praga, Warsaw, 1885–6. Assistant surgeon, 1886. Qualified Junior Surgeon, 1887. Came to England, June 1887. Worked for Abraham Radin, hairdresser of West India Dock Road: then, 1888–90, in basement barber shop below the White Hart (still standing) on the corner of Whitechapel High Street and **George Yard** (now Gunthorpe Street), first as assistant, then as proprietor. August or October 1889, married (possibly bigamously) Lucy Baderski or persuaded her they had gone through a form of marriage (they may have been previously cohabiting). A son was born, c. April 1890. The couple lived variously at Cable Street, Commercial Street and Greenfield Street. Whitsun 1890, they emigrated to New Jersey. Lucy returned alone, February 1891, and gave birth to a second child, 12 May.

Klosowski returned to England in the late spring or summer of 1891 and cohabited with a woman named Annie Chapman (no connection with the Ripper victim), adopting her surname and henceforth calling himself George Chapman. 1893–5 he was working at a hairdresser's in West Green Road, Tottenham. In 1895 he took his own premises on Tottenham High Road. He subsequently worked as barber in Hastings and publican in the City of London, Bishop's Stortford, Lambeth and Southwark. Between 1895 and 1901 he poisoned three successive women with whom he lived as husband, and was convicted and hanged in 1903.

For Abberline's stated reasons for suspecting Klosowski of being the Ripper, and manifest objections to them, see under **Abberline**. Since **H. L. Adam** records Abberline's alleged remark to Inspector **Godley**, 'You've got Jack the Ripper at last', and Adam also thanks Godley for his assistance in preparing *The Trial of George Chapman*, there is reason to suppose some such comment was made. It may even be true, as Adam asserts, that Abberline questioned Lucy Baderski closely about Klosowski's movements at the time of the murders, though there is as yet no evidence that Klosowski and Baderski had met by December 1888.

Dr Dutton's claims, as reported by **Donald McCormick** in *The Identity of Jack the Ripper*, are, however, demonstrably untrue. Dutton averred that Abberline overheard Klosowski addressed as 'Ludwig' in the barber's shop below the White Hart where he worked, and was startled as this suggested suspect hairdresser **Charles Ludwig**, arrested on 18 September 1888. Though told that Klosowski's name was so unpronounceable that his workmates called him 'Ludwig Schlosky', Abberline supposedly thought there was a striking likeness and made further checks on Ludwig at Scotland Yard. Returning to the Whitechapel barber's shop, Abberline found that Klosowski had flown, though some weeks later he traced him to the shop in West Green Road, Tottenham, and thence to Tottenham High Road.

As stated, this story is demonstrably untrue. Klosowski did not work in West Green Road until 1893, after Abberline had retired. He did not go there directly from the White Hart basement, and he did not move on to the High Road until 1895. Dutton as reported by McCormick is proved to be completely unreliable.

In the meantime, according to Dutton, Abberline had questioned commercial traveller **Wolf Levisohn**, who assured him Klosowski was not the Ripper, but expressed suspicion of a barber's assistant living in Walworth. This, according to Dutton, proved to be **Dr Pedachenko**, a man who looked so like Klosowski that the two exchanged identities for their nocturnal perambulations.

Despite the unreliability of the Dutton story, it may still be significant that Abberline, after rejecting other suspects known to him, finally concluded that the Ripper was a man who turns out to have been a Polish hairdresser, aged twenty-three at the time of the murders, who at one time resided in Greenfield Street, and whose name took the form K-something-ski. Cf. **Aaron Kosminski**.

KNIGHT, STEPHEN VICTOR (1952–85)
Researcher and theorist. Author of **Jack the Ripper: The Final Solution**. As a young journalist on the *East London Advertiser*, Knight was sent to interview **Joseph Sickert** when his story that the Ripper murders were carried out by **Sir William Gull** in order to protect the scandalous secret of **Prince Albert Victor**'s illegal marriage was publicised in the BBC drama-documentary *Jack the Ripper*. (See *The Ripper File* (**Jones and Lloyd**) for discussion of the programme.) Knight found Mr Sickert surprisingly persuasive, and embarked on research that convinced him his story was true.

Knight's book purveying the theory and the results of his research was a worldwide success, but one year after publication he suffered an epileptic fit, and a scan revealed a cerebral infarct. Though Knight continued writing, the epileptic attacks increased until, by 1980, they were striking every six weeks. Knight learned that he had a cerebral tumour, underwent a biopsy, and believed himself cured.

He joined the Bagwan Rajneesh's cult, adopting the name Swami Puja

Detal and completed his last book, *The Brotherhood* (1983), an attack on
Freemasonry. In 1985 it became apparent that the biopsy had not worked
and the tumour had returned. An operation was unsuccessful and Knight
died. Predictable and absurd rumours have since circulated to the effect
that he was assassinated by a Masonic conspiracy.

KOCH, DR
Recently alleged suspect. See **Dr. Cohn**.

KOLCHAK (1974, USA)
TV series (22 × 50 min) starring Darren McGavin; comedy-horror series,
spin-off from *The Night Stalker* about real vampire in Las Vegas; has crime
reporter encountering monsters etc; episode 'The Ripper'.

KONOVALOV, VASSILY (died c. 1908)
Recent alleged suspect. Born at Torshok, Tver (today's Kalinin). A junior
surgeon of medium height, slightly built, with broad shoulders, blue eyes,
heavy black eyebrows, and a curled and waxed black moustache. Suspected
of murdering a woman in Paris in 1887 (see **France, Murders in**), five
women in London, and a woman in Russia in 1891. He used the aliases
Alexei Pedachenko and **Andrey Luiskovo**. Occasionally transvestite, he
was wearing women's clothes when arrested in Petrograd [*sic*] and confined
to an asylum where he died.

The above details are taken from a lithograph copy of the ***Ochrana
Gazette*** (whereunder the entire piece is quoted and the anachronistic
reference to Petrograd discussed) cited by Donald McCormick in *The
Identity of Jack the Ripper*, and shown him by **Prince Belloselski**. McCormick quotes two other sources referring to Konovalov. The first is a letter
by **Sir Basil Thomson**, which allegedly says, 'in Paris recently I learned in
talks with the French that they had always thought that the "Ripper" was a
Russian named Konovalov, who used the alias "Mikhail Ostrog", under
which name Scotland Yard knew him as an ex-convict and medical student.' (See under **Michael Ostrog** for further discussion of this interesting
document cited thus only in McCormick's 1962 pbk edn.) The second is an
extract from Dr Thomas Dutton's *Chronicles of Crime:*

I have learned from a French doctor of a Russian junior surgeon, or
feldscher, who was known to him in Paris about 1885–88. He was suspected of having killed and mutilated a *grisette* in Montmartre, but he left
Paris before he could be arrested. This may account for Scotland Yard's
search for a Russian surgeon they believed to be in hiding. At last there
appears to be a hint as to motive. This surgeon, whose name was
Konovalov, was said to have a violent hatred of prostitutes due to a
relative of his having suffered cruelly from a woman of the streets. The
description of Konovalov exactly fits that of Pedachenko and the final
police assessment of what the 'Ripper' looked like.

The last two quotations offer interestingly suggestive parallels with information in the **Macnaghten memoranda** and elsewhere, but fall under the
caveat of unsourced material mentioned under **Donald McCormick**.

Searches undertaken by **N. P. Warren** and Paul Begg have failed to
uncover the requisite number of the *Ochrana Gazette*, but have found
reference to three men named Vassili Konovalov. Two were peasants
convicted of looting and related crimes in the 1905 civil war. The third,

Vasilii Vasilievitch Konovalov, from the village of Zhlobin in the Ukraine, was exiled, possibly in 1904, to the 'far North' for twenty-eight years. He was described as stocky, of medium height, with a round, clean-shaven face. There is nothing to connect this last man with the alleged Ripper suspect, or with the long-running Russian suspect **Nicolai Wassili**, although all three came from the Ukraine.

Dr Pedachenko is known to us from **William Le Queux's** *Things I Know* and other sources cited by McCormick, none of which directly links him with Konovalov. The probability is that they were not the same person. It is possible that Konavalov was known to the French police and suspected by some of them of being the Ripper.

KOSMINSKI, AARON (1864 or 1865–1919)
Suspect. A Polish Jewish hairdresser, who came to England 1882. In July 1890, he was sent from his residence at Sion Square for treatment at Mile End Old Town Workhouse Infirmary where the admission register noted that he had been insane for two years. He was discharged three days later into the care of his brother.

On 4 February 1891 he was readmitted to the Infirmary from 16 Greenfield Street, and on 7 February transferred to Colney Hatch Lunatic Asylum. Jacob Cohen of Carter Lane EC was the lay witness supporting his certification, and said of him 'that he goes about the streets and picks up bits of bread out of the gutter and eats them, he drinks water from the tap & he refuses food at the hands of others. He took up a knife and threatened the life of his sister. He is very dirty and will not be washed. He has not attempted any kind of work for years.'

Since Kosminski was not at this time a charge on the parish, and at his death his brother and sisters erected a sandstone headstone, this eccentric conduct was not the outcome of proud destitution. (The headstone bears the form 'Kosminski', for which reason we have preferred it over the many variant spellings to be found in the documents of his life.)

The Colney Hatch Admissions and Discharge Book remarked that the duration of his existing attack was six years and the cause was self-abuse. These two last details were also added in red ink to the preliminaries in the Male Patients' Day Book, which had originally noted that his existing attack had lasted six months, was not his first, and he had been aged 25 when he suffered his first attack. (Thus records variously ascribe the onset of his mental illness to 1885, 1888, and 1890.) The Day Book also noted his brother Wolf, of Sion Square, as his next of kin.

Dr Houchin, the medical witness recommending certification, described his delusions: 'He declares that he is guided and his movements altogether controlled by an instinct that informs his mind, he says that he knows the movements of all mankind, he refuses food from others because he is told to do so, and he eats out of the gutter for the same reason.'

The Colney Hatch doctors immediately recorded their observation that he was extremely deluded, and his 'Instincts' were probably aural hallucinations. He answered questions fairly, but was inclined to be reticent and morose. His delusions made communication difficult and he tended to refuse to be bathed.

Over the next three years, the doctors recorded their impressions in brief case-notes two or three times a year. The most persistent observation was that he was 'unoccupied' and 'incoherent'. His habits were clean and his

health fair. He alternated between periods of quiet apathy and noisy
excitement. In one of the latter, he became violent and attacked an attendant with a chair. By April 1894 he was noted as 'Demented and incoherent',
and on 13 April was transferred to Leavesden Asylum for Imbeciles.

Here it is clear that his condition had deteriorated markedly. He could
not answer even simple questions. He suffered aural and visual hallucinations, and could be noisy and troublesome. In 1919 he died of gangrene
of the left leg.

The first clear reference to this man as Jack the Ripper was made in the
Macnaghten memoranda of 1894. In the copy deposited in Scotland Yard,
Sir Melville described him thus:

Kosminski, a Polish Jew, & resident in Whitechapel. This man became
insane owing to many years indulgence in solitary vices. He had a
great hatred of women, specially of the prostitute class, and had strong
homicidal tendencies; he was removed to a lunatic asylum about March
1889. There were many circs connected with this man which made him a
strong 'suspect'.

In the rather fuller version left with his daughter, Macnaghten refined
the location 'Whitechapel' to 'the very heart of the district where the
murders took place', added his belief that he was still in an asylum, and
concluded, 'This man in appearance strongly resembled the individual seen
by the City P. C. near Mitre Square.'

Philip Loftus's recollections of the version of the document he had seen
twenty years previously apparently refer to this man when they mention 'a
Polish-Jew cobbler nicknamed Leather Apron'. Loftus's memory might, of
course, have been contaminated by the discussion of **'Leather Apron'** in
Tom Cullen's *Autumn of Terror*, which had been published at the time
when he wrote those words. But none of the other suspects named by
Macnaghten remotely matches Loftus's description.

A decisive mention of Aaron Kosminski is made in the **Swanson marginalia**, glossing **Anderson's Suspect** as sketchily described in Sir Robert
Anderson's memoirs. Anderson had said little more than that the suspect
was a low-class Polish Jew from Whitechapel whose people shielded him
from justice, and remarked, 'I will merely add that the only person who
ever had a good view of the murderer unhesitatingly identified the suspect
the instant he was confronted with him; but he refused to give evidence
against him.' Swanson continued:

because the suspect was *also a Jew* and also because his evidence would
convict the suspect, and witness would be the means of murderer being
hanged which he did not wish to be left on his mind.

And after this identification which suspect knew, no other murder of
this kind took place in London . . . after the suspect had been identified
at the **Seaside Home** where he had been sent by us with difficulty in
order to subject him to identification, and he knew he was identified. On
suspect's return to his brother's house in Whitechapel he was watched by
police (City CID) by day and night. In a very short time the suspect with
his hands tied behind his back, he was sent to Stepney Workhouse and
then to Colney Hatch and died shortly afterwards – Kosminski was the
suspect.

Since neither Swanson nor Macnaghten describes Kosminski accurately,
it is necessary to stress that he must be the man they mean. A thorough
search of contemporary London asylum records, Boards of Guardians'

pauper lunatic records, and death registers confirms that Aaron is the only man bearing any variant of the name Kosminski to have died in an asylum in England and Wales since 1888, and nobody named Kosminski or anything like it was in any asylum around London from 1888 until Aaron's incarceration. (The nearest contender is one Nathan Karnsky, committed in 1897.) Furthermore, Swanson's reference to 'his brother's house in Whitechapel' puts it beyond the bounds of possibility that any other Polish Jew will be found who better matches the main points Swanson lays down than Aaron who was discharged to Wolf's care in 1890.

That being said, it has to be conceded that both documents contain errors. Macnaghten rightly describes Kosminski as a Polish Jew from Whitechapel who went to an asylum and was still there in 1894. He believed his mania was caused by masturbation, as did the doctors at Colney Hatch. But he dates his incarceration wrongly, and if he described him as a 'cobbler nicknamed Leather Apron' would seem to have confused him with someone else.

Swanson, accepting without question Anderson's account of his poverty, Jewishness and residence in Whitechapel, rightly describes him as domiciled with his brother and transferred to Colney Hatch. He names the workhouse wrongly – an unimportant slip, in the authors' opinion, as so many Londoners regard almost anywhere between Aldgate and Bow as 'Stepney'. Far more damagingly, he believes the man died shortly after the transfer to Colney Hatch.

No researcher has even been willing to concede that Kosminski's guilt has been established. Two television programmes have done so (see *The Secret Identity of Jack the Ripper* and *Crime Monthly*).

The documentary case for Kosminski is very strong indeed. Nothing in Anderson's regrettably meagre section on 'the suspect' has been shown to be false. Swanson offers the only definite identification of this suspect by a man on the spot. Swanson and Anderson remained relatively close after they retired, and are not known to have disagreed. Neither suffered from senility. Both were men of probity. Nobody had such a good overview of the entire police information sent back from the investigation on the ground as they did. Nobody but Anderson ever claimed with certainty to know the identity of Jack the Ripper.

Kosminski uniquely fits all the points Anderson makes about his suspect. In addition to being a poor Polish Jew from Whitechapel, he had a home to go to where he could get rid of his bloodstains, and he had 'people' to shield him from justice. The medical assessment of his illness as caused by masturbation seems to correspond with an aside of Anderson's on the 'utterly unmentionable vices' which rendered him lower than a beast.

Macnaghten, by contrast, was not close to Anderson. He was not accurately informed about his own preferred suspect **M. J. Druitt**, so it is matter for little surprise that he should have been misinformed about Kosminski. By naming him at all he adds powerful confirmation that this man was a police suspect. It is persuasive, too, that this solution is unglamorous, unsensational and plausible: a poor, unknown, lunatic sex maniac, drawn from the majority population of the murder district.

More detailed argument in favour of Kosminski's guilt is hard to pursue without resting heavily on selected extracts from documents whose errors have yet to be satisfactorily explained, and so whose uncorroborated statements cannot be properly evaluated. Attempts to resolve the problem which do not propose Aaron Kosminski's guilt (like the 'David Cohen' theory) fall under the same ban. They employ selected data from suspect documents and interpret it without conclusive external support.

It is, therefore, the authors' considered opinion that the most important area of research in the field is the pursuit of data which may help us to understand why the major documents apparently pointing to Aaron Kosminski contain errors and contradictions.

The case against Kosminski is usually made with reference to this documentary uncertainty. If the police contradicted each other, it is suggested, they cannot really have known what they were talking about. A moment's reflection should show that this is the obverse of the error of taking the documents selectively as factual. Before we can dismiss the Scotland Yard chiefs as entirely wrong because some of them were confused, we need to know wherein their confusion lies.

The better case against Kosminski is that there is too long a gap between the cessation of the murders and his incarceration; that his family's skill in shielding him from the police enquiry and preventing him from murdering between 9 November 1888 and 3 February 1891 surpasses belief; that his form of delusionary schizophrenia seems incompatible with the skill to evade detection at times when Jacob Cohen might have seen him picking up bread from the gutters and drinking from taps.

Innocent or guilty, it is research centred on Aaron Kosminski, the authors believe, which will most likely lead to the identification of Jack the Ripper, if it has not done so already.

KOSMINSKI, MARTIN (b. 1845)

Jewish immigrant, known to **Joseph Hyam Levy**. Born Kalisch, Poland, son of a furrier. Married, 1872, at Duke's Place Synagogue. Took British naturalisation, 1877, and conducted furrier's business at various addresses until 1922, when the business continued under his son's name. His naturalisation application was supported by **Joseph Hyam Levy**, one of **Mr Joseph Lawende**'s companions when Catharine Eddowes was seen outside Mitre Square with a man whom City Police apparently believed to be her murderer. While Mr Levy denied having taken in the man's appearance, one newspaper believed he knew more than he was saying, and it has been suggested that he might have recognised that man with Eddowes as an associate or relative of Martin Kosminski.

Research has failed to establish any connection between Martin and **Aaron Kosminski**.

KOSMINSKI, WOLF

Brother of **Aaron Kosminski**; described in Colney Hatch Asylum records as his next of kin, residing at Sion Square, Whitechapel. On 15 July 1890, Aaron was discharged from Mile End Old Town Infirmary into the care of his (unnamed) brother, having been admitted there three days previously from Sion Square. The following year he was admitted to the infirmary from 16 Greenfield Street, which has led some researchers to deduce that this was his brother's residence. Three days later, however, Aaron was transferred to Colney Hatch where Wolf's address was noted as Sion Square.

Wolf may be the master tailor Woolfe Kosminski who died aged 86 at Baker Street, Stepney, in 1920, but this has not been proven.

KOZEBRODSKY, 'ISAACS' M.
Friend of **Louis Diemschütz**. Came down from **International Working-men's Educational Club** with Diemschütz and **Morris Eagle** to examine the woman lying in the passage when Diemschütz, after seeing his wife in the downstairs parlour, reported the presence of **Elizabeth Stride**'s body. Convicted with Diemschütz the following March when they fought with policemen whom they took to be reinforcements for a local mob attacking the clubhouse after an anti-rabbinical demonstration by members, in support of the unemployed.

KRANZ, PHILIP (1859–1922)
Original name Jacob Rombro.
Witness at Elizabeth Stride's inquest. Born in Podolia, Russia, fled the pogroms of 1881 and spent some time in Paris as a student. Came to London, and changed his name on advice from Morris Winchevsky (formerly Leopold Benedikt). He became editor of *Arbeter Fraint*, published from offices behind the **International Workingmen's Educational Club**. In 1889 Kranz moved to America and became editor of *Arbeter Zeitung*.

On 29–30 September 1888, he was in the offices of *Arbeter Fraint* from 9.00 p.m. until the discovery of the body at 1.00 a.m. His office door and window were closed, and he heard nothing above the singing from the club. On being told of the body, he looked at it and went to find a policeman.

L

LAMB, DAVID C.
Theorist. Salvation Army Commissioner whose memoirs, published in *Tit-Bits*, 23 September 1939, recalled that a visiting signwriter discussing the murders had remarked, 'I'll tell you who will be the next one to go: Carrotty Nell' (i.e. Frances Coles). Noting that 'Carrotty Nell' was indeed killed subsequently, and recalling the man's 'visions of blood' and 'strange demeanour', Lamb concluded that he was the Ripper. Lamb was subsequently misremembered by **Colin Wilson** for some years as General Booth suspecting his secretary.

LAMB, POLICE CONSTABLE HENRY, 252H
Witness at Elizabeth Stride's inquest. On duty in Commercial Road early morning, 30 September 1888, he was between Christian Street and Batty Street when two men appeared and said, 'Come on! There's been another murder!' He accompanied them, followed by **Police Constable Collins** 426H who, on arrival at the murder scene, was sent to fetch **Dr Blackwell**. Lamb sent one of the two men for assistance from the police station. Then shut the gates to make sure nobody left and searched the Club interior and yard. He remained at Berner Street until daybreak.

LANE, CATHERINE
Witness at Elizabeth Stride's inquest. Charwoman, married to dock labourer Patrick Lane. Resident at 32 Flower and Dean Street since 11 February 1888, but had known Stride six or seven years. Said Stride came to the lodging house following a quarrel with **Michael Kidney** (denied by Kidney). Lane last saw her between 7.00 and 8.00 p.m. on the night of her death.

LANGHAM, SAMUEL FREDERICK
Coroner, conducted Catharine Eddowes' inquest. Inquest held at the Golden Lane Mortuary, 4 and 11 October 1888. Langham conducted it reasonably expeditiously, without the fuss and bother that tended to surround **Wynne Baxter**'s proceedings; but equally, without the exaggerated despatch of **Dr Roderick MacDonald**.

Langham's notes are preserved in the Corporation of London Archives in the Guildhall.

LARKINS, EDWARD KNIGHT (fl. 1889)
Contemporary theorist. Clerk in HM Customs Statistical Department. On 13 November 1888 he drew police attention to Antoni Pricha who he believed resembled **George Hutchinson**'s man in an astrakhan coat. (See under **Scotland Yard files**: Missing Suspects File.)

Atrocities committed by Portuguese peasants in the Peninsular War persuaded Larkins that the Ripper must be a Portuguese cattleman sailing regularly on the vessels *City of London* and *City of Oporto*. He settled on **Manuel Cruz Xavier** as Nichols' murderer, and concluded that Chapman's was a copycat killing by **Jose Laurenco** (since Xavier did not return to England). When Laurenco deserted ship in Oporto in October 1888, Larkins suggested that he had worked in partnership with **Joao de Souza Machado**, who alone murdered Kelly. Machado at 41 was older than the others, and Larkins commented: 'being a man of mature age, the *sang froid* displayed upon the occasion of this murder is easily accounted for . . . This man's coolness seems to have stood him in good stead, as, in order to avoid suspicion, he continued to come over until the month of March 1889.' Since, however, he did not come over in July when Alice McKenzie was murdered, Larkins ascribed this killing to **Joachim de Rocha**, who had sailed with Xavier at the time of Nichols' murder.

Larkins' theories were investigated by the police and the British consul in Oporto, and found to be invalid. Larkins was not satisfied, feeling police had failed to recognise the overwhelming evidence that the criminal must be Portuguese. He had lists of shipping movements printed and distributed to various authorities, which apparently convinced the distinguished magistrate Montague Williams. By 1893 he was accusing **Dr Robert Anderson** of conniving at the escape of the murderer, and Anderson described him in a memo to the Home Office as 'a troublesome busybody'.

Larkins is the first of many obsessed Ripper theorists, setting a lamentable pattern of modifying his theories forcefully to meet new data; resolutely ignoring overwhelming evidence against his views; obstinately contradicting his critics. He is an object lesson to all who are certain they know the identity of the Ripper.

LAURENCO, JOSE (b. 1862)

Contemporaneously alleged suspect. Portuguese seaman sailing between London and Oporto on the *City of Cork*. Advanced by **E. K. Larkins** as accomplice of **Joao de Souza Machado** in killing Annie Chapman, Elizabeth Stride and Catharine Eddowes 'from a spirit of devilry', and possibly to emulate **Manuel Cruz Xavier**.

According to the shipping lists, he was not actually on board the vessel when it docked on 8 November 1888 opportunely for the Kelly murder. Initially, the ineffable Mr Larkins believed he was on board anyway, as a stowaway. Otherwise, as he sagely remarked, he could not have murdered Kelly. Subsequently he concluded that Kelly's murder was the single-handed work of Machado.

A further mark of Laurenco's guilt lay in the annotation 'Conduct – Good' beside his name. All other crew-members were given 'Conduct – very good'.

LAVE, JOSEPH

Witness at Elizabeth Stride's inquest. Passed through Dutfield's Yard shortly before her murder. A Russian-born recent immigrant from USA, Lave was living temporarily at the **International Workingmen's Educational Club**. He told the press that fifteen or twenty minutes before the discovery of the body he went out for fresh air and walked about for five minutes or so. The yard was so dark, he had to grope his way along the passage wall, and there was definitely no body there. 'Everything was very quiet at the time, and I noticed nothing wrong.'

According to **Donald McCormick** in *The Identity of Jack the Ripper*, Lave told the police that a stranger who pretended to be a Polish barber from George Yard (though he was obviously a Russian) was in the club 'earlier' that night. The description McCormick cites is similar to **George Hutchinson**'s suspect, with the soft hat replaced by a peaked cap.

The authors have found no trace of this alleged statement in police files or the press. See under *The Identity of Jack the Ripper* for a caveat against unsupported statements and quotations in that book.

LAWENDE, JOSEPH

Witness at Catharine Eddowes' inquest; possibly **Anderson's witness**. Commercial traveller in the cigarette trade, resident at 45 Norfolk Road, Dalston, with business premises in St Mary Axe.

In company with **Harry Harris** and **Joseph Hyam Levy**, he stayed late at the Imperial Club, 16–17 Duke's Place, on the night of 29–30 September 1888, because of rain. All three prepared to leave at 1.30 a.m. (as checked by Lawende's watch and the club clock) and left within about four minutes. Approximately fifteen yards from the club they saw a man and a woman standing at the entry of covered Church Passage which led to Mitre Square. Mr Lawende subsequently identified the woman by her clothes as Catharine Eddowes when shown her body in the mortuary.

Lawende, walking a little apart from the other two, was the only one to take in the man's appearance. See under **Jack the Ripper, Descriptions of** for his description. Lawende said the woman had her hand on her companion's chest; neither of them appeared to be angry; and there was nothing about them to draw his attention except that Mr Levy remarked that the court ought to be watched. Lawende did not think he would recognise the man if he saw him again. Despite this, the City police regarded him as a very important witness and sequestered him from the press prior to the inquest. At the inquest itself, City Solicitor **Crawford** said, 'Unless the jury wish it, I have special reason for not giving details as to the appearance of this man.' The coroner assented and Lawende described no more than the man's clothes.

Major Henry Smith's unreliable memoirs describe Lawende as 'a sort of hybrid German' and make it clear that Smith believed Lawende to have furnished a detailed description of the Ripper. He says that he regarded Lawende as the more reliable because he refused to follow leading questions, was plainly uninterested by the previous murders, and honestly stated that he doubted whether he would recognise the man again after his brief glance at him.

See under **Anderson's witness** for the importance of Mr Lawende.

'LEATHER APRON' (fl. 1888)

Suspect.

Police enquiries following the death of Mary Ann Nichols elicited from local prostitutes the information that they suspected a man who had been demanding money with menaces from them. (This practice, then called 'blackmailing', was very common in Whitechapel and Spitalfields.) Details about this man, nicknamed Leather Apron, appeared in the press from 4 September 1888, when it was remarked that he had not been seen much around the neighbourhood for the last few days.

The *Star* on 5 September 1888 gave the fullest account of him: he was a short, thickset man, 38–40 years old. He had black hair, a black moustache, and an exceptionally thick neck. He wore a close-fitting cap and a leather apron. He carried a sharp knife, and frequently threatened, 'I'll rip you up!' His movements were silent and sinister. His eyes glinted, and his smile was repulsive. A *Star* reporter claimed to have interviewed fifty women in three hours who all gave almost identical descriptions of him.

More interesting than the stagey description was the observation that he was most likely to be found hanging around the **Princess Alice** on **Commercial Street**, and that he had served a seven-day gaol sentence during the previous year for assaulting a woman. A search of the only local magistrates court records to survive has failed, as yet, to identify this conviction.

He was also said to be a specialist slipper-maker, though he did not work; to have threatened women in other parts of London; and to have a friend called 'Mickeldy Joe'. He was said to be Jewish, or at least of strongly Semitic appearance.

The last point became the dominant feature in the rising ferment of press reportage on Leather Apron. He was reported as sometimes carrying a pistol or a cudgel. He was said to have been seen in other parts of London. He was said to hang around common lodging houses. **Timothy Donovan** of **Crossingham**'s confirmed seeing him there some time before the murders began, wearing a deerstalker hat, and kicking him out for threatening a woman. He was also said to stay at an identified lodging house off **Brick Lane**. At the time when the *Star* reporter went there, however, Mickeldy Joe was in the house, and the reporter felt this encouraged the occupants to deny the allegation that Leather Apron patronised the place.

The police tried to dampen the scare by insisting that there was 'only suspicion' against him. But they did not suggest that there was suspicion against anyone else. On 6 September, the *Star* reported that Police Constables J43 and J173 had actually had the 'crazy Jew' in their hands the previous Sunday, without realising who he was.

On 7 September, a weekly report to Scotland Yard from **Inspector Helson** (J Division) said:

The inquiry has revealed the fact that a man named Jack Pizer, alias Leather Apron, has for some considerable period been in the habit of illusing [*sic*] prostitutes in this, and other parts of the Metropolis, and careful search has been and is continued to be made to find this man in order that his movements may be accounted for on the night in question, although at present there is no evidence whatever against him.

The following day, the finding of a leather apron in the yard (actually **John Richardson**'s) close to Annie Chapman's body produced a frenzy of anger against the unknown murderer, which took the form of active anti-Semitism. Jews were beaten up on the streets by men who asserted that 'No Englishman would commit such murders'.

On Sunday 9 September, a young woman called **Miss Lyons** believed she met Leather Apron.

The next day, the newspaper scare came to an end. **Sergeant Thick** arrested **John Pizer**, who appeared at the inquest on 12 September, was identified as Leather Apron, and conclusively cleared of the murder of Mary Ann Nichols. Henceforth, police reports referred to Pizer as 'Leather Apron, an early suspect'. There is, however, substantial evidence in the press that the public still believed an unknown man nicknamed Leather Apron was the murderer.

After the double murder, when the name 'Jack the Ripper' supplanted all fear of Leather Apron, a prostitute in St George's-in-the-East Infirmary told the press that she knew with certainty who the Ripper was: a man who went around blackmailing and assaulting women on the streets. Her account is highly reminiscent of the early Leather Apron reports.

On 20 September the *Echo* reported that police were looking for a man described by **Eliza Cooper** and **Elizabeth Allen**. Their description was suggestively reminiscent of aspects of Leather Apron. There are good reasons both for and against accepting the police case against Pizer. Given all the circumstances, there is still disagreement and confusion as to who Leather Apron really was. At this juncture his true identity remains speculative.

LEES, ROBERT JAMES (1849–1931)

Medium, alleged to have psychically identified the Ripper. Born in Birmingham; brought up in Hinckley, Leics. Supposedly evinced clairvoyant gifts aged 13. Married, 1871. For some time worked for the *Manchester Guardian*. By 1888 he lived in Peckham, and was noted as philanthropist, radical friend of Keir Hardie, and prominent Christian Spiritualist. Subsequently he resided in St Ives and Ilfracombe before retirement to Leicester. He wrote several books on spiritualism, and was distinguished as a medium giving private consultations. Allegedly he came to royal notice following a seance (variously described) at which the late Prince Consort spoke through Lees' mouth. For this reason he supposedly became known as Queen Victoria's medium. Biographers of Victoria have found no such connection.

Melvin Harris says that Lees' diaries preserved in Stansted Hall contain the following entries at the time of the double murder:

Tuesday 2nd October. Offered services to police to follow up East End murders – called a fool and a lunatic. Got trace of man from the spot in Berner Street. Wednesday 3rd October. Went to City police again – called a madman and fool. Thursday 4th October. Went to Scotland Yard – same result but promised to write to me.

Peter Underwood claims that it has long been suspected that these diaries have been tampered with. He does not say what difference the tampering might make to any interpretation of the section Harris quotes.

The first outside reference to Lees in connection with Jack the Ripper comes in a letter received by Scotland Yard on 25 July 1889. It reads, in full:

Dear Boss

You have not caught me yet you see, with all your cunning, with all your "Lees" with all your blue bottles.

I have made two narrow squeaks this week, but still though disturbed I got clear before I could get to work – I will give the foreigners a turn now I think – for a change – Germans especially if I can – I was conversing with two or three of your men last night – their eyes *of course were shut* and thus they did not see my bag.

Ask any of your men who were on duty last night in Piccadilly (Circus End) if they saw a gentleman put 2 dragoon guard sergeants into a hansom. I was close by & heard him talk about shedding blood in Egypt I will soon shed more in England.

I hope you read mark & learn all that you can if you do so you may and may not catch.

Jack the Ripper

No one has ever offered an explanation for the word 'Lees' in this letter other than the possibility that it refers to R. J. Lees.

On 28 April 1895 the Chicago *Sunday-Times Herald* published a sensational story to the effect that Lees had received a psychic impression of the murderer, and later recognised him on a bus. Seventeen murders later, the police asked for his assistance, and throughout the night Lees followed a psychic trail, ending at the house of an eminent physician. He was married with a son; had trained at Guy's; and had always been an ardent vivisectionist, taking pleasure in hurting animals. The police questioned the doctor and his wife, eliciting the admission that he suffered occasional losses of memory and had once come round to find his shirt bloodstained. But proofs of his guilt were found in the house, and after a medical court of inquiry he was committed to an asylum in Islington under the pseudonym 'Thomas Mason, 124'. He was still alive in 1895, though the public had been told he had died and been buried in Kensal Green cemetery. The entire story had allegedly been revealed to the paper by a Chicago gentleman who had learned that 'Dr Howard of London', a member of the informal commission of lunacy, had broken his vow of secrecy.

Melvin Harris argues persuasively that this story was a deliberate hoax, planted in the *Sunday-Times Herald* by the Chicago Whitechapel Club which met at the back of the newspaper offices.

When a version of the story was repeated in the *People*, **Dr Benjamin Howard** wrote a furious denial as soon as it came to his attention. Lees, however, never denied it; indeed, Cynthia Legh, who knew Lees from 1912, reported in *Light*, the Journal of the College of Psychic Studies (Autumn 1970), that she had heard him tell a variant half a dozen times. This confirmed his threefold rebuff at the hands of the police, though it spread it out between successive murders following discovery of 'the second' (unidentified) victim. Lees, however, went on to say that he thereafter obtained authority from Queen Victoria to assist the police after the next murder. This led him and an authoritative Scotland Yard official to follow the psychic trail to the home of a doctor whose wife held a position at court. The doctor was removed to a place of detention, and a beggar who died in Seven Dials that night was buried in his place. The Queen asked Lees to leave London for five years, lest rumours embarrassing the doctor's wife should emerge, and he was granted a pension for this period.

Lees' daughter Eva, both before and after his death, showed her father's clients and admirers 'documentary' evidence that he received a pension for his contribution to solving the Whitechapel murders. A gold cross, now in the possession of his great-granddaughter, is said to be the gift of grateful prostitutes.

In 1931 the *Daily Express* published an abridged version of the *Sunday Times-Herald* story with the claim that this was a 'document' left by Lees to be opened after his death. The editorial trailer the day before publication indicated that the paper harboured the gravest doubts about the document's validity, and **Melvin Harris** asserts that it was the deliberately fraudulent work of its crime correspondent, Cyril Morton.

Most subsequent accounts of Lees as connected with the Ripper investigation are embellishments or garblings of the *Express* story, though BBC researcher Ian Sharp's discovery of the *Sunday-Times Herald* original in the early 1970s made it available for those who wanted to use more of its fantastic detail in weaving their own fantasies.

Enquiries made by Mrs Brackenbury of the Society for Psychical Research in 1931 and D. J. West in 1948 failed to unearth anybody in Scotland Yard or the Home Office who had heard of Lees, or any relevant files. Mrs Brackenbury's informants included the keeper of the Criminal Record Office since 1901 and **F. P. Wensley**.

The suggestion that the sadistic West End physician might be **Sir William Gull** emanated from **Dr Thomas Stowell**, and gained support from **Stephen Knight**, whose researches suggested to him that Gull was the only medic with a house suitably close to the point where the eminent physician had escaped from Lees.

There is no reason to suppose that Lees' involvement in the case was greater than he recorded in his diary.

LEESON, SERGEANT BENJAMIN CHARLES (b. 1870)

Self-alleged police reinforcement at discovery of Frances Coles' body. Joined Metropolitan Police, 1891: Warrant No. 76483. Posted to H Division as PC 282. Subsequently CID, where he was closely associated with **F. P. Wensley**. Invalided out, 1911, following bullet wounds sustained in the Siege of Sidney Street, uttering the memorable words, 'They have shot me through the heart. Goodbye. Give my love to the children. Bury me in Putney.'

During his first month in the service, Frances Coles was killed. Leeson says in his autobiography that he heard a shrill whistle blast and made for Swallow Gardens where he found **Police Constable Ernest Thompson**, two night watchmen and a plain-clothes man gathered around her body.

This appears to be untrue. The inquest heard that Constables **Hart** and **Scott** came in response to Thompson's whistle with a plain-clothes man. No mention was made of Leeson or any watchmen. **Donald Rumbelow** remarks that working on the history of the Siege of Sidney Street he found Leeson's *Lost London* 'almost entirely untrustworthy'. Leeson describes the revived **'Leather Apron'** scare which focussed on **Jacobs**, and gives what may be an interesting account of the suspicions of ordinary police on the ground after the Ripper murders:

I am afraid I cannot throw any light on the problem of the Ripper's identity, but one thing I do know, and that is that amongst the police who were most concerned in the case there was a general feeling that a certain doctor, known to me, could have thrown quite a lot of light on the subject. This particular doctor was never very far away when the crimes were committed, and it is certain that the injuries inflicted on the victims could only have been done by one skilled in the use of the knife.

Melvin Harris speculatively ascribes the alleged document *The East End Murderer – I Knew Him* to conversations Leeson 'inevitably' held about the Ripper's identity when in Australia after being invalided out of the Police.

LE QUEUX, WILLIAM TUFNELL (1864–1927)

Writer and theorist. Educ. in London and Pagli, Genoa. Travelled widely. Journalist, appointed foreign editor of *The Globe*, 1891. Resigned, 1893, and devoted himself to freelance writing. His massive output includes ill-written novels and books of sensational gossip. An early and influential perpetrator of spy scares.

In 1888, he reported the Whitechapel Murders for the *Globe*, later recounting that he and **Charles Hands** and **Lincoln Springfield** 'practically lived as a trio in Whitechapel, and as each murder was committed we wrote up picturesque and lurid details while we stood on the very spot where the tragedy had occurred. One evening Springfield . . . would publish a theory of how the murders had been done . . . ; next night Charlie Hands would have a far better theory . . . and then I would weigh in with another theory in the *Globe*.'

After the October Revolution, Le Queux wrote several books on Russia. *The Rascal Monk* (1917) was a life of **Rasputin**. Subsequently, in *Minister of Evil* (1918), Le Queux claimed that it had been based on documents found among Rasputin's effects. Later still, in *Things I Know about Kings, Celebrities and Crooks* (1923), he claimed that the documents had included a manuscript on 'Great Russian Criminals', typed in French from Rasputin's dictation. This stated that **Dr Alexander Pedachenko** was Jack the Ripper. In elaborating the case against him, Le Queux included information from this document, allegedly gleaned from the Russians **Nideroest** and **Zverieff**.

In *Minister of Evil*, Le Queux mentions a man from Tver who escaped detection after murdering a young girl. This, too, could be a reference to Pedachenko.

It has been seriously doubted whether Le Queux received any such documents from Russia at all, and it is virtually certain that Rasputin never dictated the document on 'Great Russian Criminals' ascribed to him. Three other possibilities remain: that Le Queux invented the story entirely; that he extracted and embellished it from a Russian document; and/or that he received information from Nideroest (who was a journalist in London after 1906) and added to it an alleged documentary source to strengthen it. Le Queux himself claimed that he had not mentioned Pedachenko in earlier books, as it was only after 1918 that he acquired corroborative proof of his existence.

LETCHFORD, CHARLES
Resident of 39 Berner Street, interviewed by *Manchester Guardian* after Elizabeth Stride's murder. Said he walked up the road at 12.30 a.m., when everything 'seemed to be going on as usual'. Also stated that his sister stood outside her house in the street for ten minutes from 12.50 a.m. It has been surmised his sister was **Mrs Mortimer** (though cf. her maiden name, Skipp).

LEVISOHN, WOLF
Alleged informant on **Dr Pedachenko**. Jewish commercial traveller. In Whitechapel on business on 15 November 1888, he was abused by two prostitutes called De Grasse and Johnson when he refused their solicitations. They shouted, 'You are Jack the Ripper', and pleaded in defence that he looked like the Ripper because he carried a shiny black bag. An acquaintance of **Severin Klosowski**, he gave evidence at his trial.

According to **Dr Dutton**, as cited by **Donald McCormick**, he assured **Inspector Abberline** that Klosowski was not the Ripper, saying that a more likely suspect was a Walworth Road barber's Russian assistant whom he had seen in Commercial Street on 29/30 September 1888 (cf. **Dr Alexander Pedachenko**).

LEVITSKI, –
Alleged accomplice of **Dr Alexander Pedachenko**. In the story ascribed by **William Le Queux** to **Nicolai Zverieff**, Levitski was said to have accompanied Pedachenko to keep a look-out while he committed the Whitechapel murders. He was also alleged to have written the '**Jack the Ripper letters**', and to have been subsequently exiled to Yakutsk.

LEVY, JOSEPH HYAM (b. 1841)
Witness at Catharine Eddowes' inquest. Butcher, resident at 1 Hutchinson Street, Aldgate. Sponsored **Martin Kosminski's** successful application for naturalization, 1877. Possibly retired or died, 1892, whereafter he drops from trade directories.

Accompanied **Mr Joseph Lawende** and **Mr Harry Harris** from the Imperial Club, 16–17 Duke's Place, at 1.34 a.m., 30 September 1888. Levy, walking with Harris, was disconcerted by seeing a woman (later identified by Mr Lawende as Eddowes) talking to a man at the entry to Church Passage (leading to **Mitre Square**) and remarked, 'I don't like going home by myself when I see these sorts of characters about. I'm off.'

The *Evening News* of 9 October reported: 'Mr Joseph Levy is absolutely obstinate and refuses to give the slightest information. He leaves one to infer that he knows something, but that he is afraid to be called on the inquest.' At the inquest, Levy testified that he saw a woman outside Church Passage with a man about three inches taller than her, though he did not take any notice of them. Further, he thought 'that persons standing at that time in the morning in a dark passage were not up to much good'. Pressed by City Solicitor **Crawford**, he denied thinking their appearance was 'terrible', and stated that he was 'Not exactly' afraid for himself.

His hesitations and reservations, coupled with his definite acquaintance with Martin Kosminski, have led to the surmise that he might have recognised that man as a relative or connection of Kosminski's and chosen to withhold the evidence. (Cf. **Aaron Kosminski**.)

LEWIS, MAURICE
Informant. Acquaintance of Mary Jane Kelly. Tailor living in Dorset Street, who told the press he had known Kelly for about five years. He claimed to have seen her in **The Britannia**, about 10.00 a.m., 9 November 1888 (i.e. several hours after her death; see **Melvyn Fairclough, Colin Kendell** for significance).

He also said he saw her drinking with '**Danny**' and '**Julia**' in **The Horn of Plenty** on the night of the murder. Since 'Danny' was said to be **Joe Barnett's** nickname, and he had left Mary Kelly rather than have 'Julia' to live with them, the group poses the questions whether Lewis correctly identified Barnett and Kelly, or whether Danny was really Barnett's nickname.

LEWIS, SARAH
Witness at Mary Jane Kelly's inquest. Laundress of 29 Great Pearl Street. Deposed to **Inspector Abberline** that following 'words' with her husband she came to stay the rest of the night at Mrs Keyler's (first floor of no. 2

Miller's Court). She testified that she arrived around 2.30 a.m. as checked by Christ Church, Spitalfields, clock.

Abberline's notes of her deposition have her declaring that she saw 'a man standing over against the lodging house on the opposite side of Dorset Street', and there follow the crossed-out words 'talking to a female'. In her testimony she described this man as not tall but stout, and wearing a black wide-awake hat. She also said a young man passed along the street with a woman.

She gave an account of a man in a high round hat whom she had seen in Bethnal Green Road when out with a friend the previous Wednesday evening. This man had asked them to go down a passage with him, persuading them over their initial alarm by promising to treat them. In the passage he put down a black bag he was carrying and started to open his coat and feel for something, whereupon they ran away. Mrs Lewis now declared she had seen the same man accompanied by a woman, near **The Britannia** on her way to Dorset Street.

The obvious similarities between her story and that ascribed by the press to **Mrs Kennedy** strongly suggest that they were one and the same person.

LIPSKI, ISRAEL (1865–87)
Formerly Israel Lobulsk.

Murderer whose name was allegedly used in 1888 as an anti-Semitic insult. Born Warsaw. Emigrated to England, 1885, and worked as umbrella-maker. 1887, tried to establish his own business at lodgings in 16 Batty Street, adjacent to Berner Street. June that year, poisoned fellow-lodger Miriam Angel with nitric acid and tried to poison himself. His conviction was highly controversial, as some felt the prosecution was influenced by anti-Semitism, but he confessed the evening before his execution.

Israel Schwartz, who saw Elizabeth Stride assaulted in Berner Street approximately fifteen minutes before her body was discovered, told police the assailant shouted 'Lipski!' at him when he turned to watch. He was reported in the press as saying another man who stepped into the street shouted 'Lipski!' at the assailant. As Schwartz spoke almost no English, this pretty certainly represents a failure of interpretation, and it is probable that the police version is correct, since **Inspector Abberline** reported that he had questioned Schwartz particularly closely about the cry, but he was unable to say with certainty *to* (not *by*) whom it was addressed.

Surviving **Home Office Files** contain more questions about the cry of 'Lipski!' than any other aspect of Schwartz's story, because it suggested the assailant might have recognised the man stepping into the street and addressed him by name, in which case he could be traced to identify the assailant. Interested officials asked whether the word might, however, have been used as a sadistic verb: 'I am Lipski-ing this woman.' **Sir Robert Anderson** replied endorsing Abberline's opinion that 'Lipski!' was now a popular anti-Semitic insult, addressed to Schwartz on account of his strongly Semitic appearance.

LITTLECHILD, INSPECTOR JOHN
Head of Special Branch, 1883–93. In his reminiscences (1894) he remarked, 'Apart from dynamite conspiracies, and explosions, and the Whitechapel murders, perhaps no matter has been of such great importance at Scotland Yard as the discovery of the Great Turf Frauds of 1876.'

Since the last named was a massive national scandal entailing the complete reorganisation of the Detective Department into the CID following the corruption of very senior members, Littlechild's observation indicates the immense weight officially given to the Whitechapel murders.

LLEWELLYN, DR REES RALPH (1849–1921)

Witness at Mary Ann Nichols' inquest. Examined her body. Matric. U. of London, 1869. Hon. Certif. in Obst., 1873. LSA, 1873. MRCS, 1874. LRCP (Lond.), 1876. Medical Officer to E and EC Districts, and City Mission. Called from his surgery, 152 Whitechapel Road, at 4.00 a.m., 31 August 1888. After cursory examination of the body in Buck's Row, pronounced her dead. Noticed there was only a wine-glass and a half of blood in the gutter beside her, but had no doubt she had been killed on the spot.

Subsequently he made a full examination of the body in the Old Montague Street Workhouse Infirmary Mortuary. *The Times* reported his medical testimony thus:

Five of the teeth were missing, and there was a slight laceration of the tongue. There was a bruise running along the lower part of the jaw on the right side of the face. That might have been caused by a blow from a fist or pressure from a thumb. There was a circular bruise on the left side of the face, which also might have been inflicted by the pressure of the fingers. On the left side of the neck, about 1in. below the jaw, there was an incision about 4in. in length, and ran from a point immediately below the ear. On the same side, but an inch below, and commencing about 1in. in front of it, was a circular incision, which terminated at a point about 3 in. below the right jaw. That incision completely severed all the tissues down to the vertebrae. The large vessels of the neck on both sides were severed. The incision was about 8 in. in length. The cuts must have been caused by a long-bladed knife, moderately sharp, and used with great violence. No blood was found on the breast, either of the body or clothes. There were no injuries about the body until just about the lower part of the abdomen. Two or three inches from the left side was a wound running in a jagged manner. The wound was a very deep one, and the tissues were cut through. There were several incisions running across the abdomen. There were also three or four similar cuts running downwards, on the right side, all of which had been caused by a knife which had been used violently and downwards. The injuries were from left to right, and might have been done by a left-handed person. All the injuries had been caused by the same instrument.

See under **M.O.** for discussion of Dr Llewellyn's conclusion of left-handedness.

LLOYD, JOHN

Author. Co-scripted BBC TV drama-documentary *Jack the Ripper* with **Elwyn Jones**, with whom he also co-authored the spin-off book *The Ripper File*. Born in Wales, he worked as a television script-writer for many successful series, including *Braden's Week*, *Comedy Playhouse* and *That's Life*.

LODGER, THE (1944, USA)

Film directed by John Brahm. Stars Laird Cregar, Merle Oberon, George Sanders. Atmospheric chiller with enjoyably lurid performance by menacing Cregar; generally regarded as best version of Lowndes' story.

LODGER, THE: A STORY OF THE LONDON FOG (THE CASE OF JONATHAN DREW) (1926, Great Britain)

Film directed by Alfred Hitchcock. Stars Ivor Novello. Mysterious lodger suspected of being Ripper but (because he's British matinee idol Novello) turns out not to be; first movie version of Belloc Lowndes' story and has memorable finale. (Video available.)

LODGER, THE (THE PHANTOM FIEND) (1932, Great Britain)

Film directed by Maurice Elvey. Stars Ivor Novello, Elizabeth Allen, Jack Hawkins. Sound remake of 1926 silent version.

LOFTUS, PHILIP

Witness to existence of a possible third version of **Macnaghten memoranda**. A friend of **Melville Macnaghten**'s grandson **Gerald Melville Donner**, Loftus recalled seeing framed on the wall of Donner's home in the early 1950s what Donner maintained was 'the original' '**Dear Boss' letter**. At the same time, Donner showed him 'private notes, in Sir Melville's handwriting on official paper, rather untidy and in the nature of rough jottings. As I remember them, they gave three suspects: a Polish tanner or cobbler; a man who went around stabbing young girls in the bottom with nail scissors; and **M. J. Druitt**, a doctor of 41 years of age.'

In a letter to **Lady Aberconway**, dated 7 August 1972, Loftus further recalled that the Pole was 'nick-named **Leather Apron**'; that the bottom-stabber was 'probably **Thomas Cutbush**'; and that Druitt was named 'Michael'.

Since Loftus had read **Tom Cullen**'s *Autumn of Terror*, and remarked that the details of the Aberconway version of the **Macnaghten memoranda** seemed different from what he recollected seeing, it is possible that Cullen had contaminated his memory, introducing the nickname 'Leather Apron' and the name Cutbush. 'Michael' Druitt might have been a confusion with **Michael Ostrog**. Nail scissors, on the other hand, are mentioned nowhere else, and if they were described in more detailed notes on **Colicutt** than have survived elsewhere, may be an indication that Loftus actually saw a first draft of the memorandum, substantially different from the surviving documents.

LONG, POLICE CONSTABLE ALFRED, 254A

Discovered the piece of Catharine Eddowes' apron and the **Goulston Street graffito**. Joined Metropolitan Police, 1884; Warrant no. 69241; dismissed, July 1889, for being drunk on duty.

Drafted to Whitechapel from A Division (Westminster) among the extra patrols brought in during the Ripper scare, he discovered the bloodstained piece of apron and then noticed the graffito above it at 2.55 a.m. on 30 September 1888, his first night on duty in that street. He had previously passed through the street at 2.20 a.m., and believed that apron was not there at that time, but was not sure about the graffito. At the inquest he referred to his notebook entry for the wording, but had not observed the spelling J-U-W-E-S.

He was mildly criticised by a juror for not conducting a thorough search of the rooms in the building, but reasonably replied that he did not know of Eddowes' murder, and accepted **Mr Crawford**'s suggestion that on discovering the apron he thought the victim of a crime and not the criminal might be inside, and so made a complete tour of the open staircases and landings.

LONG, MRS ELIZABETH
Alternative name used by Mrs **Darrell** or **Durrell** and under which she testified at Annie Chapman's inquest.

LUDWIG, CHARLES (b. 1848)
alias **Charles Ludwig WETZEL.**
Briefly suspected. German hairdresser. Came to London from Hamburg, 1887 or 1888. Found employment with Mr C. A. Partridge in The Minories, and lodged with a German tailor named **Johannes** in Church Street, Minories, until his disorderly habits made him unwelcome, and he moved to a hotel in Finsbury.

In the small hours of Tuesday 18 September 1888, he accompanied prostitute **Elizabeth Burns** to Three Kings Court, Minories, which led to railway arches. There pulled a knife on her, and her cries of 'Murder!' attracted City **Police Constable John Johnson** from his beat. He dismissed Ludwig, and walked Miss Burns to the end of his beat, where she said, 'Dear me, he frightened me very much when he pulled a big knife out.' She explained that she was too afraid to make the complaint in Ludwig's presence. Johnson searched unsuccessfully for Ludwig and alerted other constables to the situation.

Ludwig appeared at a coffee stall in Whitechapel High Street at 3.00 a.m., and aggressively asked bystander **Alexander Freinberg** what he was looking at. When Freinberg apologised, Ludwig pulled his knife on him, whereupon Freinberg threw a dish from the stall at his head, and summoned **Police Constable Gallagher** 221H, who arrested him. Later in the day he appeared at Thames Magistrates Court, charged with being drunk and disorderly and threatening to stab.

The magistrates agreed to his being remanded in custody for a week. The police learned that Ludwig had brandished razors and alarmed fellow guests; also that he was believed to have had blood on his hands on the day of Annie Chapman's murder. His remands continued, as he was the most promising arrested suspect hitherto. The double murder, committed while he was under lock and key, conclusively proved that he was not the Ripper.

LULU (1978, France)
Film directed by Marcel Bluwal. Stars Danielle Lebrun, Michel Piccoli. Version of Fritz Wedekind's classic study of *femme fatale* finally killed by the Ripper.

LULU (1978, USA)
Film directed by Ronald Chase. Stars Elisa Lonelli, Paul Shenar.

LUSHINGTON, GODFREY (1832–1907)
Civil servant mainly responsible for Home Office attitudes to Metropolitan Police and the conduct of the Ripper case. Educ. Rugby and Balliol. Called to the Bar, 1858. Home Office counsel, 1869. Assistant Under-Secretary, 1876. Permanent Under Secretary, 1885–95, when he retired. KCB, 1892.

Served on several Royal Commissions.

In his early years at the Home Office he played lawn tennis with **Robert Anderson**, whom he regarded as a friend. Subsequently Anderson came to regard him as a dangerous individual libertarian, and blamed his irritant personality for worsening relations between Home Secretary **Henry Matthews** and Metropolitan Police Commissioner **Sir Charles Warren**, between whom it was Lushington's duty to mediate. 'A blister, not a plaister' was Anderson's preferred description of Lushington at this phase.

Lushington was also a personal friend of **Major Henry Smith**, and enjoyed annual dinner parties with him and the Reverend William Rodgers of St Botolph's, Aldgate, after the Police Ball. Lushington was persuaded by **Israel Schwartz**'s testimony to the cry of '**Lipski!**' in Berner Street that the murderer was Jewish.

LUSK, GEORGE AKIN (1839–1919)
Recipient of letter and human kidney allegedly from the Ripper. Started a building and decorating business with property inherited by his wife, Susannah, née Price. Specialised in restoration of music-halls. 1888, Susannah died, leaving him with seven children to care for. Lived at Globe Road, Mile End; subsequently moved to Caxton Street, Bow. A Freemason (Doric Lodge).

On 10 September 1888, he was elected president of the newly-formed Whitechapel **Vigilance Committee** in The Crown public house, Mile End Road. Under this aegis, he drew attention to himself by writing to *The Times*. In October he came to fear that his house was being watched by a sinister bearded man, and asked for police protection. On 16 October he received through the post the parcel containing the **Lusk kidney** and accompanying **Lusk letter**.

LUSK KIDNEY
Allegedly Catharine Eddowes' left kidney. Half a human kidney, preserved in spirits of wine, received in the post on 16 October 1888 by **George Lusk**. It was in a three-inch square cardboard box wrapped in brown paper, with a barely decipherable postmark: possibly London E. It was accompanied by a crudely-written letter. (See **Lusk Letter**.)

Lusk assumed it was a hoax and the organ probably a dog's, but friends persuaded him to hand it over for medical examination, and press reports stated that **Dr Openshaw**, Curator of the Pathology Museum at London Hospital, had declared it to be the 'ginny' kidney of a 45-year-old woman afflicted with Bright's disease, and removed from the body during the previous three weeks.

The following day Openshaw stated that he had only said the kidney was human and preserved in spirits of wine; everything else had been added by others (cf. **Mr F. S. Reed**). **Dr Sedgwick Saunders**, the City pathologist, pointed out to the press that the age and sex of a kidney could not be determined in the absence of the rest of the body, and that gin left no traces in the kidney. He maintained that the kidney which had stayed in the body was perfectly healthy, so he would expect the one removed to be equally healthy. He said that the preservation in spirits of wine indicated that it had come from a hospital or dissecting theatre and opined that it was a student hoax.

Major Henry Smith revived interest twenty-two years later in his memoirs, writing that he had shown the kidney to Mr Henry Sutton, senior surgeon at the London Hospital, and received from him the opinion that the kidney was not charged with fluid as would have been the case had it been in a body handed over to a hospital for dissection; that it showed symptoms of Bright's Disease; and that the length of renal artery attached was what would be expected from the length of renal artery reported as remaining in the body. Since Major Smith's memoirs are extremely inaccurate, and Saunders had denied the presence of disease, this seemed insubstantial until the discovery of **Dr Gordon Brown**'s report. This describes, very precisely, signs of Bright's Disease ('pale, bloodless, with a slight congestion at the base of the pyramid') in the kidney remaining in the body. It is further noted that Bright himself (fl. 1827) erroneously imagined the disease to be a consequence of alcoholism, which might explain the colloquialism 'ginny'. These considerations, coupled with the preservation of the kidney in spirits rather than formaldehyde, have led **N. P. Warren** to conclude that the kidney probably came from Eddowes' body.

Other researchers unhappily note that assessment of Lusk's kidney inevitably pits one bad source (Dr Saunders, now shown to be wrong about the Bright's Disease in the kidney left in the body) against another (Major Smith). We have no guarantee that all the Major's comments are as accurate as his recollection of Bright's Disease; no guarantee that Saunders was not as wrong about hospital preserving practices as he was about the health of the kidney in the body.

LUSK LETTER
Accompanied the piece of human kidney received in the post by **George Lusk** on 16 October 1888. It read:

From hell

Mr Lusk
  Sor
    I send you half the Kidne I took from one women prasarved it for you tother piece I fried and ate it was very nise I may send you the bloody knif that took it out if you only wate a whil longer
  signed   Catch me when
you can

Mishter Lusk.

Canadian 'graphologist' C. M. MacLeod suggested that the author was aged 20–45 with rudimentary education; possibly a heavy drinker; cockily self-confident. He also thought the writing showed a mind with vicious drive, great cunning, the capability of conceiving and carrying out any atrocity, and enough brains to hold down a steady job and mask his personality.

A more detailed analysis by **Thomas J. Mann** suggested that the letter was in its author's normal handwriting; that he was semi-literate with elementary copybook habits (not always understood), and had little familiarity with the act of writing. He thought the non-phonetic misspellings 'prasarved' and 'Mishter', the dialect 'tother' and the raised 'r' in 'Mr', indicated an English writer. The authors note that 'Sor' and 'Mishter' are two normal nineteenth-century transcriptions indicating a stage Irish accent.

LYONS, MISS
Believed she encountered **'Leather Apron'**. On Sunday 9 September, Miss Lyons encountered a strange man in **Flower and Dean Street**, Spitalfields, who persuaded her to meet him in the **Queen's Head** on the corner of Fashion Street and Commercial Street at 6.30 p.m. for a drink. While they were drinking he remarked, 'You are about the same style of woman as the one that's murdered.' On being asked what he knew about her, he replied, cryptically, 'You are beginning to smell a rat. Foxes hunt geese, but they don't always catch 'em.' Then he hurriedly left the bar. Miss Lyons followed him toward Spitalfields Church, until he realised she was behind him, at which point he rushed away and she lost sight of him.

Miss Lyons claimed that he looked exactly like the published descriptions of 'Leather Apron'. Excising the melodramatic details of 'glinting eyes' and a 'repulsive smile', this would mean that he was a stocky man of medium height with a very thick neck and a black moustache, probably wearing a tight-fitting cap and a leather apron. (But cf. **Edward McKenna**.) In any case, the entire incident suggests that during the 'Leather Apron' scare, men who approached prostitutes unconventionally were liable to be taken for the suspect.

Cf. **John Pizer**.

M

McCARTHY, JOHN (b. 1851)
Mary Jane Kelly's landlord. Born in France. Married, with four children.
Owned chandler's (i.e. grocer's) shop, 27 **Dorset Street**, on western side of
arched entry to Miller's Court. Let rooms in Miller's Court, known locally
as 'McCarthy's Rents'. Described as 'a gentlemanly-looking man'. He sent
Thomas Bowyer to collect Kelly's rent (30/- [£1.50p] in arrears) at 10.45
a.m., 9 November 1888. Then, after viewing the body through the window
himself, he sent him to Commercial Street Police Station. He broke open
the spring-locked door with a pick-handle on **Superintendent Arnold**'s
orders, 1.30 p.m. He gave press interviews evincing deep shock at the state
of the body. He was reported in the press as having lost a number of tenants
who left Miller's Court swiftly following the tragedy.

McCARTHY, POLICE CONSTABLE JOHN (b. 1863)
Mentioned in press as engaged on Ripper case, and in the **Macnaghten
memoranda** as being employed for that reason on **Cutbush** case in 1891.
Joined Metropolitan Police, 1881, serving with A and E divisions (the latter
in 1887) before transfer to Commissioner's Office. The date of this transfer
is unfortunately illegible in the records, but is likely to be 1887 or 1888.
Transferred back to E Division and promoted sergeant, 1894. Transferred
to CID, Commissioner's Office, 1896; Inspector, 1898; Chief Inspector,
1906; Superintendent, 1912. Retired, 1918. Appears to have been in
Special Branch from c. 1900.

McCORMACK, JOHN (b. 1839)
aka Bryant.
Lover of Alice McKenzie and witness at her inquest. Irish porter, working
casually for Jewish tailors in Hanbury Street. Lived with McKenzie as
common-law wife in lodging houses for six or seven years; on and off at
Gun Street, Spitalfields, 1888–9.

On 16 July 1889 he returned from work at 4.00 p.m.; he gave McKenzie
1/8d [8p] before she went out. They 'had words' as she was drunk.
McCormack left her to earn their rent while he went to bed, though he
claimed to be unaware that she was streetwalking. He identified her body in
the mortuary on 17 July.

McCORMICK, DONALD (1911–)
Theorist. Author of **The Identity of Jack the Ripper** (1959). Prolific author
of (especially) true crime, witchcraft and espionage history (often under
pseudonym Richard Deacon). 1946–73 with *Sunday Times* as N. African
Correspondent, Commonwealth Correspondent, Assistant Foreign Manager and Foreign Manager successively.

The conventions of his generation led McCormick to invent dialogue and eschew sources for many of his interesting discoveries and revelations, which means that some data traced back to him (e.g. the Liverpool **'Jack the Ripper' letters**; the 'doctor whose father knew **Druitt** at Oxford') rest on his unverifiable assertions.

In 1985, Mr McCormick responded to a request for a meeting to discuss the Ripper case with the regret that it would be pointless as some years earlier he had passed all his papers on the subject to another researcher who had not returned them. In 1986 he responded to a renewed request for a meeting with the regret that it was impossible because he was committed to a revised edition of *The Identity of Jack the Ripper*. The consequent impossibility of checking Mr McCormick's sources, and the variants between his original and revised editions in quotations from the same source (see under **Ostrog**), make *The Identity of Jack the Ripper* a book to be used with extreme caution.

MACDONALD, DR RODERICK (1841–94)

Coroner at Mary Jane Kelly's inquest. Born, Isle of Skye, son of a crofter. LRCS, LRCP (Edin.), 1867; FRCS, MD (Durh.), 1883. Practised medicine in East End. MO South District, Poplar Union. Surgeon to K Division, Metropolitan Police. MP for Ross-Shire. Appointed Coroner for North East Middlesex when the former East London and Tower division was partitioned into North- and South-East Middlesex, late 1887.

For his losing the coroner's election contest before his appointment, see under **Wynne Baxter**. For the dispute over the propriety of MacDonald's sitting on Kelly, see **Inquests, Jurisdictional Disputes**.

MacDonald was a Radical, known popularly as 'the crofter's MP'. It was unfortunate that he should be allocated to the conservative and prosperous East London coroner's division embracing Hackney, Shoreditch and Stoke Newington, rather than the Whitechapel, Spitalfields and dockland district which had supported him in the election.

He conducted Kelly's inquest (12 November 1888 at Shoreditch Town Hall) – the only Ripper victim's inquest to be completed in a single day's hearing. As soon as he perceived that a sufficient 'cause of death' had been established, he invited the jury to come to a finding and conclude proceedings if they chose, with the observation, 'There is other evidence which I do not propose to call, for if we at once make public every fact brought forward in connection with this terrible murder, the end of justice might be retarded.' The jury accepted the offer to conclude with alacrity.

MacDonald did not complete or sign the certificate of findings to which the jurors' signatures had been appended (now in Greater London Record Office).

It has been suggested by **Stephen Knight** and others that he was culpably assisting the police at the expense of a full and proper enquiry; possibly even aiding a cover-up. It is more likely that as a police surgeon he shared **Dr Phillips'** feeling that it was unnecessary and unhelpful to publicise injuries inflicted after death. It is also likely that he noted adverse criticisms of Wynne Baxter for conducting inordinately long inquests. But his despatch meant he closed proceedings without learning of **George Hutchinson's** pertinent evidence.

MACHADO, JOAO DE SOUZA (b.1847)

Alleged suspect. Portuguese cattleboat seaman advanced by **E. K. Larkins** as the accomplice of **Jose Laurenco** in murders of Chapman, Stride and Eddowes, and single-handed murderer of Kelly.

MCKENNA, EDWARD

Lodging house resident arrested on suspicion. For uncertain reasons – but one newspaper suggests that he threatened to stab people – McKenna aroused suspicions in Whitechapel throughout the day of 14 September and was eventually handed over to the Police. **Inspector Abberline** took charge of the questioning.

McKenna was 5ft 7in, slightly built, shabbily dressed, had a careworn appearance, sandyish hair, beard, and moustache, and wore a skull cap. His pockets contained an assortment of rags, handkerchiefs, two women's purses, several metal and cardboard boxes, a strip of leather, and a spring onion.

Particular interest was taken in McKenna because he resembled the description of the wanted man, particularly that of the man seen by **Miss Lyons** and by the potman of the **Ten Bells** at about 5.00 a.m. on the morning of Annie Chapman's murder. But McKenna said that he was sleeping at a common lodging house at 15 **Brick Lane** on the night of the murder and when investigation proved this to be true he was released.

MCKENZIE, ALICE 'CLAY PIPE' (c. 1849–89)

Aka Alice Bryant.

Alleged Ripper victim. Said to be a native of Peterborough. Her left thumb was distinctively injured in an industrial accident. From c. 1883 cohabited on and off with **John McCormack** in East End common lodging houses. From c. April 1889 the couple were usually resident at Mr Tenpenny's lodging house, 54 Gun Street, Spitalfields, which was managed by **Mrs Elizabeth Ryder**. McKenzie worked as a washerwoman and charwoman, principally for Jewish residents of the East End, but was also known to prostitute herself habitually.

She spent the day of Tuesday 16 July 1889 in the lodging house while McCormack was out at work. Around 4.00 p.m. he came home slightly the worse for drink and went to bed, giving McKenzie 1/8d [8p]: 8d to pay Mrs Ryder for the rent, and a shilling to spend as she pleased. McCormack testified that this was the last time he spoke to her, but since he did not dispute that there was some quarrel between them that afternoon or evening, and Mrs Ryder testified that McKenzie finally left the lodging house at about 8.00 p.m. after 'having words' with McCormack, it seems likely that they spoke again. Certainly McCormack went downstairs at about 11.00 p.m., and learned to his annoyance that McKenzie had failed to pay the rent.

According to a rumour reported in the *Pall Mall Gazette*, McKenzie spent the evening at the Cambridge Music Hall with a blind boy named George Discon, also resident at Tenpenny's. Discon believed that, after seeing him home to Gun Street, McKenzie went out again to a public house to meet an unknown man she had persuaded to treat her to drinks at the music-hall. (Five years later this was garbled in the *Sun* into the story that Mary Jane Kelly's murderer's voice had been heard by a blind boy in whom she took 'a passionate interest'.)

Between 11.30 and midnight, McKenzie passed along **Flower and Dean Street** going toward **Brick Lane**, and stopped to chat to three acquaintances called Margaret Franklin, Catherine Hughes and Sarah Marney, who were sitting on the steps of a lodging house at the Commercial Street end. All four may have gone on to a public house for a drink.

Very shortly after 12.50, **Police Constable Walter Andrews** found McKenzie's body close to a lamp-post on the western pavement of **Castle Alley**, her head toward the kerb, her feet toward the wall. Blood was flowing from two stabs in her throat, and her skirt was pulled up, revealing blood over her thigh and abdomen. Post mortem examination showed that this came from a long but not unduly deep wound running from below the left breast to the navel, seven or eight superficial scratches from this wound toward the genitals, and a shallow cut across the mons veneris.

Andrews heard footsteps approaching the alley, and encountered local resident Isaac Lewis Jacobs on his way to purchase supper. Jacobs remained with the body while Andrews summoned **Sergeant Badham** and further assistance. Both Jacobs and **Inspector Reid**, who arrived some time prior to 1.10 a.m., noticed that blood continued to flow from the throat to the gutter. But this had ceased and the blood was starting to clot when **Dr Bagster Phillips** arrived shortly after 1.10. Jacobs also noticed (as Mrs Ryder independently confirmed) that McKenzie was wearing odd stockings. Her clay pipe and an old farthing were found under the body, leading to the belief that the murderer might have repeated the deception it was suspected had been practised on Annie Chapman of offering a polished farthing as a sovereign, or an old farthing as a sixpence.

In the absence of **Dr Robert Anderson** on leave, **Colonel Monsell** assisted Commissioner **Monro** in directing the investigation. Following Dr Phillips' post mortem, **Dr Thomas Bond** was sent to make a further examination of the body, and his report shows that Phillips and he differed frequently in their interpretation of marks, Phillips strongly insisting that his prior observations made his conclusions preferable.

See under **Bond, Phillips** for their differing deductions concerning the murderer.

Wynne Baxter conducted the inquest (17 and 19 July; then adjourned to 14 August), which inevitably found murder against a person or persons unknown.

MACNAGHTEN, SIR MELVILLE LESLIE (1853–1921)

Author of essential **Macnaghten memoranda** naming three Scotland Yard suspects. Son of the last chairman of the East India Company. Educ. Eton.; 1873–87, overseer, family tea plantations. 1889–90, Assistant Chief Constable, CID, Scotland Yard. 1890–1903, Chief Constable. 1903–13, Asst Commissioner, CID. 1908, CB.

In 1881, he was attacked by Indian land rioters who, he said, 'assaulted me so badly that I was left senseless on the plain'. In consequence, he met **James Monro**, then Inspector-General of Bengal Police, who became a lifelong friend.

In 1887, he returned to England. Monro, by then Assistant Commissioner in charge of CID, Scotland Yard, offered him the post of Assistant Chief Constable. Before formalities were completed, Commissioner **Sir Charles Warren** learned that, in his words, Macnaghten was 'the only man in India who has been beaten by Hindoos', and objected to the appointment. The Home Office duly rejected Macnaghten, and Monro resigned.

Following Warren's resignation in 1888, Monro was appointed to succeed him, and in June 1889 Macnaghten took up his post at Scotland Yard. The press welcomed the appointment of Macnaghten in the prime of life. Macnaghten's memoirs explicitly refuse to rake over the 'old sore' of Monro's resignation; their persistent silence on **Anderson** and **Bradford**, and deprecatory mention of unnamed **Warren** (notably in connection with the **bloodhounds** incident), suggest lifelong resentment of his mentor's treatment, especially when contrasted with his warm reminiscences of all other close colleagues.

Most published reminiscences describe his charm and affability. **F. P. Wensley** called him 'a very great gentleman', saying his own career owed much to Macnaghten's encouragement. Major Arthur Griffiths (*Mysteries of Police and Crime*, 1898) said he was 'tall, well-built, with a military air'. H. L. Adam noted (in *Police Work From Within*, 1914), 'Sir Melville . . . is somewhat reserved in manner, shrewdly preferring to listen to what you have to say to talking himself . . . He is most adroit at leading you away from things he does not wish to discuss.'

Adam and Griffiths both described his delight in attending scenes of crime. *Vanity Fair* noted him as first Assistant Commissioner to make personal arrest of a burglar. Adam recalled (*CID: Behind the Scenes at Scotland Yard*) his 'extensive knowledge of crime and criminals, quite as extensive as that of his predecessor, Sir Robert Anderson', adding, 'He was a familiar figure at the scene of any murder case, which had special interest to the mind of a police official'. Griffiths said he was, 'essentially a man of action', and, 'It is Mr. Macnaghten's duty, no less than his earnest desire, to be first on the scene of any such sinister catastrophe. He is therefore more intimately acquainted, perhaps, with the details of the most recent celebrated crimes than anyone else at Scotland Yard.' Both men were struck by his collection of mug-shots, and remarked that he kept the Jack the Ripper victim photos under lock and key in his office.

In *Days of My Years*, Macnaghten himself confessed to taking a delight in many things criminous, revelling in the Chamber of Horrors at Madame Tussaud's. Despite H. L. Adam's comparison of his knowledgeability with Anderson's, it seems unlikely that Macnaghten's sensational tastes appealed to the austerely christian penologist Anderson. At any rate, Anderson recalls in his memoirs being vexed with a senior colleague who made a silly fuss about a threatening letter; Anderson's loyal underling, **Chief Inspector Swanson**, recorded privately that this colleague was 'Macnaghten: Ch. Const'.

In 1891 Macnaghten's relations with the CID seem to have come to a head, as it was reported that efforts were under way for him to transfer to the uniform branch. But somehow they were tided over. Macnaghten continued to serve under Anderson until the latter's retirement in 1901; then under his successor Major Edward Henry for two years; and finally stepped into the Assistant Commissioner's post himself. He certainly thought more highly of Henry than of Anderson, for he dedicates his book to him, as 'The best all round policeman of the twentieth century'.

On his retirement, the *Police Review* said: 'His tenure of office has been placid, and . . . it is in no sense belittling his services to remark that his rule did not enhance the proficiency or reputation of the C.I.Department. He carried on the work of his office with the assistance of an experienced staff, the leading members of which are debarred from filling positions for which they act as expert advisers.'

Macnaghten was further reported in the *Daily Mail* as saying that 'the greatest regret of his life was that he joined the force six months after "Jack the Ripper" committed suicide', and continuing: 'Of course he was a maniac, but I have a very clear idea who he was and how he committed suicide, but that, with other secrets, will never be revealed by me. I have destroyed all my documents and there is now no record of the secret information which came into my possession at one time or another.'

An early chapter of *Days of My Years* is devoted to 'Laying the Ghost of Jack the Ripper'. Macnaghten eliminated surplus murders (remarking that at one time or another fourteen victims had been ascribed to the Ripper). 'Suffice it at present to say that the Whitechapel murderer committed five murders, and – to give the devil his due – no more.' This establishes the canon followed by almost all subsequent writers, despite **Abberline**'s explicit and **Anderson**'s implicit attribution of a sixth. (**Martha Tabram**. Also cf. argument under **Elizabeth Stride**.)

Macnaghten gave from memory a very fair account of the scare, from Emma Smith to Pinchin Street (including the last because of personal recollections of investigating that case). His stated conclusions were:

Although . . . the Whitechapel murderer, in all probability, put an end to himself soon after the Dorset Street affair in November 1888, certain facts, pointing to this conclusion, were not in possession of the police till some years after I became a detective officer.

And:

I do not think that there was anything of religious mania about the real Simon Pure, nor do I believe that he had ever been detained in an asylum, nor lived in lodgings. [Cf. **G. Wentworth Bell Smith**.] I incline to the belief that the individual who held up London in terror resided with his own people; that he absented himself from home at certain times, and that he committed suicide on or about the 10th of November 1888 . . . [cf. **M. J. Druitt**].

The erroneous final date is a result of Macnaghten's reliance on memory.

For the possibility that Macnaghten believed, at some time, that the Ripper might have been a **Fenian**, see **Balfour**.

MACNAGHTEN MEMORANDA

Documents naming three Scotland Yard suspects. Two versions exist; a third has been described.

The **Lady Aberconway** version, discovered by **Daniel Farson** in 1959, comprises seven typed and numbered quarto sheets, with two handwritten inserts, the first numbered '6A'. These are described in pencil on typed sheet 6 as 'p 6A & 6B, written in ink and attached at end'. The very brief pencilled observations on the typed sheets (e.g., 'by my Father Sir M.M.' following the typed heading, 'Memorandum on articles which appeared in the Sun re JACK THE RIPPER on 13 Feb 1894 and subsequent dates') are in the hand of Lady Aberconway, as (according to her son) are the insert sheets, despite some obvious differences in character-formation and the solecism 'conjections'.

Pages 1–3, and part of 4, deal entirely with the case of **Thomas Cutbush**, who had been alleged in the *Sun* to be Jack the Ripper. Pages 4–5 give a brief, and not entirely accurate, summary of the murders of Nichols,

Chapman, Stride, Eddowes and Kelly. The last three words on page 5 and first three paragraphs on page 6 introduce Macnaghten's personal conclusions on the identity of the Ripper, including the confidential material naming three suspects which is on the handwritten sheets. This vital section (pages 5–6, 6A, 6B) runs thus:

A much more rational and *workable* theory, to my way of thinking, is that the 'rippers' [sic] brain gave way altogether after his awful glut in Millers Court and that he then committed suicide, or, as a *less* likely alternative, was found to be so helplessly insane by his relatives, that they, suspecting the worst, had him confined in some Lunatic Asylum.

No one ever saw the Whitechapel murderer (unless possibly it was the City P.C. who was a beat [sic] near Mitre Square) and no proof could in any way ever be brought against anyone, although very many homicidal maniacs were at one time, or another, *suspected*. I enumerate the cases of 3 men against whom Police held very [a pencilled addition in Lady Aberconway's hand reads '(here follows p 6A & 6B, written in ink and attached at end)'] reasonable suspicion. Personally, after much careful & deliberate consideration, I am inclined to exonerate the last 2, but I have always held strong opinions regarding *no 1*, and the more I think the matter over, the stronger do these opinions become. The *truth*, however, will never be known, and did indeed, at one time lie at the bottom of the Thames, if my conjections [sic] be correct.

No 1. Mr M.J. Druitt a doctor of about 41 years of age & of fairly good family, who disappeared at the time of the Miller's Court murder, and whose body was found floating in the Thames on 31st Dec: i.e. 7 weeks after the said murder. The body was said to have been in the water for a month, *or more* – on it was found a season ticket between Blackheath & London. From private information I have little doubt but that his own family suspected this man of being the Whitechapel murderer; it was alleged that he was sexually insane.

No 2. [Paper damaged, but no doubt should read 'Kos']minski, a Polish Jew, who lived in [paper damaged, but Farson, who saw it in an earlier state transcribes 'the very'] heart of the district where the murders were committed. He had become insane owing to many years indulgence in solitary vices. He had a great hatred of women, with strong homicidal tendencies. He was (and I believe still is) detained in a lunatic asylum about March 1889. This man in appearance strongly resembled the individual seen by the City P.C. near Mitre Square.

No 3. Michael Ostrog. a mad Russian doctor & a convict & unquestionably a homicidal maniac. This man was said to have been habitually cruel to women, & for a long time was known to have carried about with him surgical knives & other instruments; his antecedents were of the very worst & his whereabouts at the time of the Whitchapel [sic] murders could never be satisfactorily accounted for. He is still alive.

And now with regard to the 4 additional murders aserted [sic]? [added in pencil below, 'ascribed'] by the 'Sun' writer to the 'Ripper'. [Added in pencil in Lady Aberconway's hand, but certainly at a different time from the inked main text, '(here follows, on p 6.

1) The body of Martha etc:']

The remainder deals very briefly with Martha Tabram, Alice McKenzie, Frances Coles, and the Pinchin Street murder.

The Scotland Yard version, first described by **Donald Rumbelow** in

1975, comprises seven foolscap sheets in Macnaghten's own hand, headed 'Confidential'. They slightly reduce the passage quoted above from the Aberconway memorandum, but slightly increase the discussion of Cutbush, including some repetition, and transposing a substantial section of argument to follow the account of the five Ripper murders. We transcribe the whole:

Confidential

The case, referred to in the sensational story told in "The Sun" in its issue of 13th inst, & following dates, is that of Thomas Cutbush who was arraigned at the London County Sessions in April 1891, on a charge of maliciously wounding Florence Grace Johnson, and attempting to wound Isabelle Frazer Anderson in Kennington. He was found to be insane, and sentenced to be detained during Her Majesty's pleasure.

This Cutbush, who lived with his mother and aunt at 14 Albert St. Kennington, escaped from the Lambeth Infirmary, (after he had been detained there only a few hours, as a lunatic) at noon on 5th March 1891 – He was rearrested on 9th idem. A few weeks before this, several cases of stabbing, or 'jobbing' [sic] girls behind had recurred in the vicinity, and a man named Colicott was arrested, but subsequently discharged owing to faulty identification. The cuts in the girls dresses made by Colicott were quite different to the cut made by Cutbush (when he wounded Miss Johnson) who was no doubt influenced by a wild desire of morbid imitation. Cutbush's antecedents were enquired into by Ch. Inspr. (now Supt.) Chis[illegible], by Inspr. Race, and by P.S. McCarthy C.I.D. – (The last named officer had been specially employed in Whitechapel at the time of the murders there, –) and it was ascertained that he was born, & had lived, in Kennington all his life. His father died when he was quite young, and he was always a "spoilt" child. He had been employed as a clerk and traveller in the Tea trade at the Minories, & subsequently canvassed for a Directory in the East End, during which time he bore a good character. He apparently contracted syphilis about 1888, and, – since that time, – led an idle and useless life. His brain seems to have become affected, and he believed that people were trying to poison him. He wrote to Lord Grimthorpe, and others, – & also to the Treasury, – complaining of Dr Brooks, of Westminster Bridge Rd, whom he threatened to shoot for having supplied him with bad medicines. He is said to have studied medical books by day, & to have rambled about at night, returning frequently with his clothes covered with mud; but little reliance could be placed on the statements made by his mother or his aunt, who both appear to have been of a very excitable disposition. It was found impossible to ascertain his movements on the nights of the Whitechapel murders. The knife found on him was bought in Houndsditch about a week before he was detained in the Infirmary. Cutbush was a nephew of the late Supt. Executive.

Now the Whitechapel Murderer had 5 victims – & 5 victims only, – his murders were

(i) 31st Aug '88. Mary Ann Nichols, at Buck's Row, who was found with her throat cut, & with (slight) stomach mutilation.

(ii) 8th Sept '88. Annie Chapman – Hanbury Street: – throat cut – stomach & private parts badly mutilated & some of the entrails placed round the neck.

(iii) 30th Sept '88. Elizabeth Stride – Berner's Street. throat cut, but

nothing in shape of mutilation attempted, & *on same date*
Catherine Eddowes, Mitre Square, throat cut, & very bad mutilation, both of face and stomach.
9th November. Mary Jane Kelly – Miller's Court throat cut, and the whole of the body mutilated in the most ghastly manner.

The last murder is the only one that took place in a *room*, and the murderer must have been at least 2 hours engaged. A photo was taken of the woman, as she was found lying on the bed, without seeing which it is impossible to imagine the awful mutilation.

With regard to the *double* murder which took place on *30th* Sept., there is no doubt but that the man was disturbed by some Jews who drove up to a Club, (close to which the body of Elizabeth Stride was found) and that he then, 'nondum satiatus', went in search of a further victim whom he found at Mitre Square.

It will be noticed that the fury of the mutilations *increased* in each case, and, seemingly, the appetite only became sharpened by indulgence. It seems, then, highly improbable that the murderer would have suddenly stopped in November '88, and been content to recommence operations by merely prodding a girl behind some 2 years & 4 months afterwards. A much more rational theory is that the murderer's brain gave way altogether after his awful glut in Miller's Court, and that he immediately committed suicide, or, as a possible alternative, was found to be so hopelessly mad by his relations, that he was by them confined in some asylum.

No one ever saw the Whitechapel Murderer: many homicidal maniacs were suspected, but no shadow of proof could be thrown on any one. I may mention the cases of 3 men, any one of whom would have been more likely than Cutbush to have committed this series of murders:–
(1) A Mr M. J. Druitt, said to be a doctor & of good family, who disappeared at the time of the Miller's Court murder, whose body (which was said to have been upwards of a month in the water) was found in the Thames on 31st Dec. – or about 7 weeks after that murder. He was sexually insane and from private info I have little doubt but that his own family believed him to have been the murderer.
(2) Kosminski, a Polish Jew, & resident in Whitechapel. This man became insane owing to many years indulgence in solitary vices. He had a great hatred of women, specially of the prostitute class, & had strong homicidal tendencies; he was removed to a lunatic asylum about March 1889. There were many circs connected with this man which made him a strong 'suspect'.
(3) Michael Ostrog, a Russian doctor, and a convict, who was subsequently detained in a lunatic asylum as a homicidal maniac. This man's antecedents were of the worst possible type, and his whereabouts at the time of the murders could never be ascertained.

And now with regard to a few of the inaccuracies and misleading statements made by the "Sun". In its issue of 14th Feb, it is stated that the writer has in his possession a facsimile of the knife with which the murders were committed. This knife (which for some unexplained reason has, for the last 3 years, been kept by Insp. Race, instead of being sent to Prisoners' Property Store) was traced, & it was found to have been purchased in Houndsditch in Feb. '91, or 2 years & 3 months *after* the Whitechapel murders ceased!

The statement, too, that Cutbush "spent a portion of the day in making rough drawings of the bodies of women, & of their mutilations" is based solely on the fact that 2 *scribble* drawings of women in indecent postures were found torn up in Cutbush's room. The head & body of one of these had been cut from some fashion plate, & legs were added to show a woman's naked thighs & pink stockings.

In the issue of the 15th inst. it is said that a *light over*coat was among the things found in Cutbush's house, and that a man in a *light* overcoat was seen talking to a woman in Backchurch Lane whose body with arms attached was found in Pinchin St. This is hopelessly incorrect! On 10th Sept. '89 the naked body, with arms, of a woman was found wrapped in some sacking under a Railway arch in Pinchin St: the head & legs were never found nor was the woman ever identified. She had been killed at least 24 hours before the remains, (which had seemingly been brought from a distance,) were discovered. The stomach was split up by a cut, and the head and legs had been severed in a manner identical with that of the woman whose remains were discovered in the Thames, in Battersea Park, & on the Chelsea Embankment on 4th June of the same year; and these murders had no connection whatever with the Whitechapel horrors. The Rainham mystery in 1887, & the Whitehall mystery (when portions of a woman's body were found under what is now New Scotland Yard) in 1888 were of a similar type to the Thames & Pinchin St crimes.

It is perfectly untrue to say that Cutbush stabbed 6 girls behind – this is confounding his case with that of Colicott.

The theory that the Whitechapel murderer was left-handed, or, at any rate, 'ambi-dexter', had its origin in the remark made by a doctor who examined the corpse of one of the earliest victims; *other doctors did not agree with him*.

With regard to the 4 additional murders ascribed by the writer in the Sun to the Whitechapel fiend:–

(1) The body of Martha Tabram, a prostitute, was found on a common stair case in George Yard buildings on 7th August 1888; the body had been repeatedly *pierced*, probably with a *bayonet*. This woman had, with a fellow prostitute, been in company of 2 soldiers in the early part of the evening. These men were arrested, but the second prostitute failed, or refused to identify, and the soldiers were accordingly discharged.

(2) Alice McKenzie was found with her throat cut (or rather *stabbed*) in Castle Alley on 17th July 1889; no evidence was forthcoming, and no arrests were made in connection with this case. The *stab* in the throat was of the same nature as in the case of the murder of

(3) Frances Coles, in Swallow Gardens, on 13th February 1891 – for which Thomas Sadler, a fireman, was arrested, &, after several remands, discharged. It was ascertained at the time that Sadler had sailed for the Baltic on 19th July '89 & was in Whitechapel on the night of 17th idem. He was a man of ungovernable temper & entirely addicted to drink, & the company of the lowest prostitutes.

(4) The case of the unidentified woman whose trunk was found in Pinchin St: on 10th Sept. 1889 – which has already been dealt with.

M. L. Macnaghten
23rd Feb. 1894

Philip Loftus twice described the **Gerald Melville Donner** version of the memorandum, which he had seen in the early 1950s. The first description was in a letter to Lady Aberconway, 11 August 1972:

My recollections of the notes, which differ from those quoted in the American journalist Tom Cullen's book, 'Autumn of terror' in 1965, were that the three suspects were (1) MICHAEL JOHN DRUITT, a DOCTOR of FORTY ONE years of age.. (2) . . . A feeble-minded man (probably Thomas Cutbush), who followed young girls and stabbed them . . . with nail scissors. (3) a Polish Jew cobbler nick-named Leather Apron.

Unfortunately, I didn't take advantage of Gerald's offer to take a copy of the notes, although I believe that later he let someone else do so.

[Loftus' dots]

In the *Guardian* (7 October 1972) Loftus described them as

private notes, in Sir Melville's handwriting on official paper, rather untidy and in the nature of rough jottings.

As I remember them, they gave three suspects: a Polish tanner or cobbler; a man who went round stabbing young girls in the bottom with nail scissors; and M. J. Druitt, a doctor of 41 years of age.

Though [the notes quoted by Farson are] different in some respects from what I remember of Gerald's papers, they contain the same reference to Druitt.

The Donner version has never been seen since, and its status (draft, uncorrected version or misquoted version) is entirely a matter of speculation. It is not known how much omitted detail Loftus represents by his dots, nor whether he correctly recollected the errors of fact (e.g., Druitt's christian name). It would be valuable in the highest degree to recover it, to confirm wherein Macnaghten's errors lay; whether it was Colicutt who used nail scissors as a weapon; and whether the Polish Jew cobbler Leather Apron appears to be a description of **John Pizer** or some other supposed suspect.

The status of the Aberconway and Scotland Yard versions have been disputed, usually by researchers wishing to claim primacy for the version they have seen. Apart from Stephen Knight's wholly unpersuasive claim that the variants in the Aberconway version were introduced by Lady Aberconway herself, and represent her reflections and not her father's, such argument is unimportant. Whichever version was first drafted, there is no question that both versions represent Macnaghten's beliefs and expand his references in his memoirs and elsewhere to his knowledge of the Ripper's identity and suicide. We may note that he was not entirely certain of Druitt's guilt, and his alternative suggestion of a suspect confined to an asylum by his family fits the known facts about Aaron Kosminski.

It has been suggested (notably by **Donald Rumbelow, Colin Wilson** and **Robin Odell**) that the three named suspects may have been drawn at random from a much larger list of equal status, and need not have been the final three suspects alleged by **Major Griffiths** and **G. R. Sims** to have emerged from the enquiry. In view of the immense weight of evidence that many people (**Griffiths, Adam, Sims, Warren, Thomson**) knew of a belief emanating from Scotland Yard that the Ripper was found drowned in the Thames in December 1888, and the established fact that **Chief Inspector Swanson** believed **Anderson's suspect** to be Kosminski, Rumbelow's view must be doubted in two of the three cases.

These are the crucial documents from which all serious historical work attempting to identify Jack the Ripper has started.

MACPHERSON, EUEN
Researcher and theorist. Drew attention to **W. H. Bury** in 1986, and published an article on him in the *Scots Magazine* in 1988. His sensible and responsible choice of a suspect who had been identified by the *New York Times* in 1889, but thereafter virtually forgotten, makes us regret that McPherson has not produced the book-length study which Bury's case seems to merit.

MCWILLIAM, INSPECTOR JAMES
Head of City Police Detective Department. His involvement in the case was welcomed by the press when Catharine Eddowes' murder in Mitre Square brought in the City Police. In fact McWilliam's principal expertise was in untangling financial frauds (as was common with City detectives) and he appears to have contributed little. His long report to the Home Office on Eddowes was so uninformative (especially compared with **Donald Swanson**'s report covering the same material) that it carries a note by Home Secretary **Henry Matthews**: 'They evidently want to tell us nothing.'

McWilliam was required to liaise daily with Swanson on the case, but the conflicting claims in **Major Henry Smith**'s memoirs and the **Swanson marginalia** on **Sir Robert Anderson**'s memoirs indicate that the Metropolitan and City Police either did not share or did not agree upon the interpretation of information they had collected.

MADEWELL, LIZZIE (b.1879)
Traffic accident victim confused with **Alice Margaret Crook**. On 1 October 1888 Lizzie was run over by a hansom cab outside 1 New Bridge Street (opposite Anderton's Hotel in Fleet Street) and taken to St Bartholomew's Hospital where she remained until 20 October. The accident was reported without her name being given in *Illustrated Police News*, and **Stephen Knight** wrongly identified it with **John Netley**'s alleged attempt on the life of **Alice Margaret Crook**.

MADURO, ALONZO
Alleged suspect. An Argentinian and 'sort of international finance mystery man' who through business became known to Mr Griffith S. Salway of a City brokerage firm in Old Broad Street. Salway unexpectedly came across Maduro in Whitechapel on the night Emma Elizabeth Smith was murdered and later heard him say all prostitutes should be killed. Following Mary Jane Kelly's murder, Salway found surgical knives in Maduro's possession and became convinced he was the Ripper. He kept his knowledge secret until divulging it to his wife shortly before his death in 1952.

The story was told in an article by Alan Hynd in a 1956 issue of *True Magazine*, and quoted by Bill Doll in an afterword to the novelisation of the 1960 film *Jack the Ripper*. A version was reprinted in the New York *World Telegraph and Sun* in 1960, and attributed to Salway's daughter Mrs Elizabeth Ross. It was repeated by **Donald McCormick** in the revised 1970 edition of *The Identity of Jack the Ripper*.

MAHONEY, MRS ELIZABETH (born c. 1863)
Witness at Martha Tabram's inquest. Match-girl, working 9.00 a.m.–11.00 p.m. in Stratford factory. Accompanied her husband Joseph, a carman, to their residence in 47 George Yard Buildings at 1.40 a.m., 7 August 1888. Subsequently she went out to buy supper at a chandler's shop, returning within five minutes. She believed there was no body at that time on the landing where Tabram was subsequently found.

MALCOLM, MRS MARY
Witness at Elizabeth Stride's inquest. Wife of tailor Andrew Malcolm, of 50 Eagle Street, Red Lion Square.

She claimed to have been awakened at the time of the murder by an awareness of her sister Mrs. Elizabeth Watts' insubstantial presence, and feeling her kiss her. Subsequently she feared the murdered woman was Mrs Watts, and on a second visit to St George's-in-the-East mortuary she identified her from a mark on her leg caused by an adder's bite in childhood. Despite warnings from coroner **Wynne Baxter** to be sure her story was accurate, she persisted in identification, adding that subsequent to being rejected for drunkenness and immorality by her husband, Mr Watts of Bath, Elizabeth had married a Poplar coffee-shop owner who had died in a shipwreck on St Paul's Island; had thereafter lived an immoral life prostituting herself to (among others) a policeman; had received weekly small gifts of money from Mrs Malcolm; and had once handed over a newborn baby to Mrs Malcolm. Mrs Malcolm was sure she had never used the name Stride, but believed she had been nicknamed 'Long Liz'. She did not, of course, believe her to be Swedish.

The entire identification collapsed when the former Mrs Watts, now **Mrs Elizabeth Stokes**, appeared at a later hearing and denied it. Mrs Malcolm never explained herself.

MAN IN THE ATTIC (1953, USA)
Film directed by Hugo Fregonese. Stars Jack Palance, Constance Smith. Fourth remake of Lowndes' story, sharply directed using taut-faced Palance's repressed hysteria to good effect.

MANN, ROBERT
Pauper mortuary attendant. Helped James Hatfield wash and lay out Mary Ann Nichols' body in Old Montague Street Workhouse Infirmary mortuary (actually a shed, dangerously close to a ward). Mann claimed he had received no instructions to do this, but coroner **Wynne Baxter** instructed the jury to disregard his evidence as he had fits and was unreliable. (Cf. **Hatfield, Baxter**, for dispute at the inquest as to whether laying-out was authorised by the police.)

MANN, THOMAS J.
Author of 'The Ripper and the Poet: A comparison of Handwriting', *WADE Journal*, June 1975. Compares the **Lusk letter** with handwriting of **J. K. Stephen**, concluding the latter could not have written the former. Useful for its report on the Lusk letter by a member of the World Association of Document Examiners (WADE).

MANSFIELD, RICHARD (1854–1907)
American actor who suffered financial loss because of Ripper scare. Starring in a sensationally effective production of *Dr Jekyll and Mr Hyde* at the Lyceum Theatre when the murders began, Mansfield was promptly attacked by philistines who believed that histrionic representation of the transformation from a gentleman to a fiend encouraged serial murder. Despite offering a special benefit performance for the Suffragan Bishop of London's fund to open a laundry for the employment of reformed prostitutes, Mansfield suffered falling audiences and had to curtail his run.

Thames-Lorimar's allegedly historical drama documentary series **Jack the Ripper** claimed that Mansfield frequented East End prostitutes and was himself a suspect. The authors know of no historical evidence for either proposition.

'MARGARET'
Alleged friend of Mary Jane Kelly. A Press Association report named this woman as seeing Kelly on 8 November 1888, and hearing from her that she proposed to kill herself for want of money. A further report, no longer naming the source, added that Kelly had a young son living in her first floor flat. A third version in the *New York Times* called the victim **'Lizzie Fisher'**. As Kelly is not known to have a son (though Joe Barnett apparently believed she had, and her flat was on the ground floor, it is probable that the entire story describes Lizzie Fisher, mistakenly believed by 'Margaret' to be the Millers Court murder victim.

MARRIOTT, DETECTIVE CONSTABLE EDWARD
Police reinforcement at Catharine Eddowes' murder site. Joined City of London Police, 1885 (Warrant no. 5830); retired, 1909, after injuries sustained on duty.

At 2.20 a.m., 30 September 1888, he was at the corner of Houndsditch, near St Botolph's Church, with detectives **Halse** and **Outram**. On hearing of the murder, all three ran to Mitre Square. Only Halse testified at the inquest.

MARSHALL, WILLIAM
Witness at Elizabeth Stride's inquest. Gave his occupation as Labourer. *Either* (former) bootmaker of 64 Berner Street, b. 1841, *or* son of the above, b. 1865. He stood outside his house for about ten minutes around 11.45 p.m., 29 September 1888. He saw a woman he later identified as Stride on the pavement opposite with a man of clerkly appearance, 5ft 6in tall, stout, decently dressed in a small black coat, dark trousers and peaked sailorly cap. His voice was mild and accent apparently English. He said to Stride, 'You would say anything but your prayers.' The pair moved away up the road (in the direction of **Matthew Packer**'s shop and Dutfield's Yard).

Marshall's description of the coat and cap suggests this may also have been the man seen by **Police Constable Smith**; less probably by **Israel Schwartz** (who followed an intoxicated assailant approaching Stride from the other end of the road). Marshall's observation was imperfect, since he denied seeing the flower that all others recollected pinned to Stride's breast. His observation of clerkliness makes it probable that this was the man who left the Bricklayers' Arms with Stride at 11.00 p.m. as witnessed by **Best** and **Gardner**.

MASON, THOMAS (1817–1902)

Suggested by **Stephen Knight** to be identified as 'Thomas Mason 124' of the **R. J. Lees** story, and thus **Sir William Gull** pseudonymously incarcerated. Thomas Mason was a retired bookbinder whose address was given as Bookbinders' Alms Houses, Balls Pond, Islington, when he died of bronchitis senectus in Islington Infirmary.

Newspaper versions of the **R. J. Lees** story describe the unnamed guilty doctor as being incarcerated in an asylum under the pseudonym 'Thomas Mason, no. 124'. Knight, therefore, first identifies Gull with the legendary doctor, and then identifies Mason with Gull, misdating Mason's death as 1896.

There is nothing to indicate that the real Thomas Mason was in the lunacy ward. He was not on the pauper lunatic returns of the relevant years 1888–96. He appears to have nothing to do with either Gull or the Jack the Ripper case.

MATTERS, LEONARD (1881–1951)

Theorist and researcher. Author of *The Mystery of Jack the Ripper* (1929). Born Adelaide, S. Australia. Messenger boy on Perth *Daily News*, aged 13; chief Parliamentary correspondent, aged 20. Subsequently editor. Volunteered for Boer War. Thereafter managing editor of Buenos Aires *Herald*, and travelled widely as journalist in USA, Canada, West Indies and Japan. Labour MP for Kennington, 1921–31. London representative of *Hindu*, South India's largest circulation daily paper. JP, 1934–50.

A journalist of talent and brilliance, and a minor public figure commanding respect in widely varied areas of the world, Matters is a surprising man to become noted as the first 'Ripperologist'; more extraordinary still to be accused (cautiously by, e.g., **Donald Rumbelow**; flatly by **Melvin Harris**) of deliberately purveying fiction to provide a solution.

Neither his character nor his book warrants this condemnation. While his theory ('**Dr Stanley**') has persuaded no researcher known to the authors, failure to trace his main source does not justify concluding that he invented it.

MATTHEWS, RIGHT HONOURABLE HENRY, MP, PC (1826–1913)

Home Secretary 1886–92. First Roman Catholic minister of cabinet rank since the reign of Elizabeth. Moved to Lords as Viscount Llandaff, 1895. Witty, charming, generous, and a fine legal brain, Matthews was nevertheless seen by contemporaries as a poor cross-examiner and a bad 'House of Commons man', lacking the weight required of Victorian statesmen; he was often described as 'spry' or 'a French dancing master'.

He was unpopular with all political parties, according to hostile press commentators, and his resignation was eagerly canvassed in 1888. **Lord Salisbury**, however, feared the Government might fall if his Catholic cabinet minister resigned under criticism. By 1891, when Matthews wished to accept a peerage as a law lord, Salisbury still refused to accept his resignation, fearing loss of the resulting by-election, although he now saw Matthews as a liability in the House of Commons.

Matthews was much attacked for provoking the resignation of two Metropolitan Police Commissioners (**Warren** and **Monro**) in two years at the time of the Ripper crisis. **Sir Robert Anderson** believed that the tripartite friction between all three was entirely unnecessary, and would never have arisen had there been a more emollient Permanent Secretary in the Home Office than **Godfrey Lushington. Evelyn Ruggles-Brise**, on the other hand, blamed Matthews, saying he was 'quite incapable of dealing with men; he was a regular Gallio in his attitude to Warren's complaints. Later on he quarrelled with **Bradford**, and if you couldn't get on with Bradford you could get on with nobody.' (Gallio, governor of Achaea, refused to mediate between St Paul and the Jews of Corinth, for 'Gallio cared for none of these things'.)

When Monro and Warren quarrelled over which of them was finally responsible for the CID, and each offered resignation, Matthews accepted Monro's resignation, but retained him as head of the **Secret Department** with an office in Whitehall and the ungazetted and (at Monro's request) unremunerated title 'Head of the Detective Service'. When Warren protested improperly against being required to submit publications for Home Office approval, Matthews responded reprovingly, provoking Warren's resignation. When Monro resigned over provisions Matthews demanded in the Police Bill of 1891, and Matthews was criticised in Parliament, he claimed that they had always remained open to negotiation, and accepted Monro's demands.

Matthews and the Metropolitan Police were severely criticized for refusing to offer a reward for information in the Ripper case. Actually both were restrained by Home Office mandarins who cited principles laid down by Sir William Harcourt. (See **Rewards**.)

Matthews reacted badly to criticism, and the resolution of the Ripper scare became a matter of prime political importance since Salisbury refused to let him resign under fire.

MAXWELL, CAROLINE

Witness at Mary Jane Kelly's inquest. Wife of lodging house deputy from **Dorset Street**. Had known Kelly about four months and only spoken to her twice prior to 9 November 1888. She testified to seeing her standing at the corner of Miller's Court between 8.00 a.m. and 8.30 that morning, wearing a green bodice, dark skirt, and maroon crossover shawl. She described a conversation in which Kelly said she had 'the horrors of drink' upon her, and on being urged by Mrs Maxwell to try another drink to steady herself, said she had already done so and vomited it up. Mrs Maxwell told her, 'I pity your condition.' About an hour later, Mrs Maxwell said she saw her again, talking to a stout man in dark clothes and a plaid coat outside **The Britannia**.

Pressed by the coroner to be sure of time and date (since medical evidence was that Kelly had been dead for several hours), Mrs Maxwell insisted that she could place the date because she had been returning china her husband had borrowed from a house opposite. This evidence is popular with those theorists who want Kelly to have been pregnant, and suggest that Mrs Maxwell was referring to this as her 'condition'. Also with those who want the murderer to have escaped in Kelly's clothes, or somebody else to have been killed in Kelly's place. (Cf. **James Kelly, Konovalov, Colin Kendell**.)

All other researchers agree that Mrs Maxwell was in some way mistaken: most probably about the date, despite her returned china. We may note that she did not know Kelly especially well, and that the maroon crossover shawl (which **Mary Ann Cox** definitely saw her wearing the night before) was an important point of identification.

MEDICINE AND MEDICAL EVIDENCE
See under **Forensic science**.

'MERCHANT, DR' (1851–88)
Pseudonym devised by **B. E. Reilly** to conceal identity of alleged suspect **F. W. Chapman**. Identified by Reilly in *City* (the magazine of the City of London Police), February 1972, as a Brixton doctor whose decease shortly after the murders made him the only candidate in medical directories for **Police Constable Robert Spicer**'s suspect.

METROPOLITAN POLICE
Founded 1829 and responsible for all of London except the City. All Ripper murders except that of Catharine Eddowes fell within the Met's jurisdiction. As a force directly responsible to the Home Secretary, the Met was and is peculiarly vulnerable to political pressure.

In 1888, the Met was unpopular with the Radical press; partly because of the brutality with which it was felt the police and troops had put down the 'Bloody Sunday' demonstration by the unemployed in November 1887; partly because massed Metropolitan Police ranks turned out to control weekly demonstrations by the unemployed throughout the period; partly because in combating **Fenian** terrorism, senior officers in particular were inclined to tar all Irish Nationalists with the subversive brush.

The press, therefore, attacked the Met throughout the case, and frequently compared their work unfavourably with the City of London Police. There seems little justification for this judgment from today's vantage point, though research is handicapped by the destruction of City Police records.

METROPOLITAN POLICE AREA OF SEARCH
According to a report filed on 19 October 1888 by **Chief Inspector Swanson**, the district targeted for house-to-house interviews in the Ripper enquiry was 'bounded by the City Police boundary on the one hand, Lamb St., Commercial St., Great Eastern Railway and Buxton St., then by Albert St. [north end of today's Deal St.], Dunk St. [between today's Deal St. and Davenant St.], Chicksand St. and Great Garden St. [today's Greatorex St.] to Whitechapel Road and then to the City Boundary'.

The area includes the Thrawl Street vicinity of common lodging houses, but excludes the immediate vicinity of two of the murder sites: Buck's Row and Berner Street. (A third, Mitre Square, fell under the jurisdiction of the City police.) It also excludes: Mulberry Street, where **John Pizer** was arrested; Plumber's Row, in whose vicinity the suspect described by **Elizabeth Allen** and others allegedly lived; the Minories, where **M. J. Druitt** allegedly and **Charles Ludwig** certainly roomed; Sion Square and Greenfield Street, where **Aaron Kosminski** lived. (Cf. however, **Nathan Kaminsky**.)

It is not known why so much of the 'Ripper territory' was apparently eliminated from the enquiry.

METROPOLITAN POLICE FILES
See **Scotland Yard Files**.

'MICKELDY JOE'
Friend of **'Leather Apron'**. So described in some press reports. The only reporter who apparently encountered him wrote for the *Star* of 5 September 1888 that Joe was present in the **Brick Lane** lodging house 'Leather Apron' was alleged to use, and thereby encouraging its hostile denizens to deny the allegation. Unfortunately the reporter did not record any conversation with Mickeldy Joe, who seems to be the only known person who might have identified 'Leather Apron' with certainty.

MILES, FRANK (1852–91)
Recently alleged suspect. Colour-blind painter specialising in flattering portraits of society ladies. Friend of Oscar Wilde, with whom he lived in Salisbury Street, the Strand, 1879–81. Won Royal Academy's Turner Prize, 1880. Associated with some fashionable homosexuals, but believed to have preferred girls below the age of consent (12, prior to Criminal Law Amendment Act, 1885), for which police once tried to arrest him. Mental health gave way, 1887; confined to asylum at Brislington, near Bristol, until his death.

   Thomas Toughill suggests Miles as the Ripper in correspondence with **Colin Wilson**. The date of Miles' incarceration makes this *prima facie* impossible. An accidental premature obituary in a local paper is not, as Milesians suggest, evidence of a hushed-up escape.

MILL, MRS ANN
Acquaintance of Elizabeth Stride. Bedmaker at lodging house, 32 **Flower and Dean Street**. Reported in the *Manchester Guardian* as saying of Stride, 'a better hearted, more good natured cleaning woman never existed'. This is more probably speaking well of the dead than the severe reflection on cleaning women it implies.

MITCHELL, DETECTIVE SERGEANT JOHN (City Police)
Searched for Catharine Eddowes' husband. With **Detective Baxter Hunt**, traced a Thomas Conway in 18th Royal Irish, who proved to be the wrong man.

MITRE SQUARE
Catharine Eddowes' murder site. Small enclosed square in Portsoken Ward toward the eastern edge of the City of London. Contained by Mitre Street, King Street (today's Creechurch Lane), Duke Street (today's Duke's Place) and Aldgate. Between King Street and Mitre Square lies St James's Place (then colloquially known as 'the Orange Market'). Between Duke Street and Mitre Square lay the Great Synagogue (destroyed by enemy action, 1941) and Kearley and Tonge's Warehouse. Another warehouse owned by Kearley and Tonge lay on the northwest (King Street) side of the square next to **Police Constable Pearse**'s house. This was the warehouse watched by **George Morris**. Between Aldgate and the Square stands the Sir John Cass School.

   Access to the Square was by a broad lighted opening from Mitre Street; a covered narrow entry (Church Passage, demolished, 1985) from Duke

Street, south of the Great Synagogue and the warehouse; or from a narrow covered entry leading into St James's Square. To the right of the broad entry from Mitre Street, coming into the square, three unoccupied cottages formed a blind corner with a high fence sealing off a yard which, in 1888, lay between the school and the Square. The body lay on the pavement in front of the empty cottages.

Catharine Eddowes was seen talking to a man at the Duke's Place entry by **Joseph Lawende** and his companions; probably also at the Mitre Square end of Church Passage by two **unidentified witnesses** from the Orange Market.

None of the original buildings in the Square or the Orange Market now remains.

See also **Unidentified police constable, Unidentified witnesses at Mitre Square**.

MIZEN, POLICE CONSTABLE JONAS, 56H (b. 1848)

Sent by **Charles Cross** and **Robert Paul** to Mary Ann Nichols' body. Joined Metropolitan Police, 1873; Warrant no. 56678; retired, 1898. Served in H Division throughout.

At 4.15 a.m. on beat duty in Hanbury Street when Cross, passing, said, 'You are wanted in Baker's Row.' After further explanation Mizen went to Buck's Row, where **Police Constable Neil**, who had discovered the body, sent him for the ambulance.

M.O. (Modus Operandi or Method of Operation)

It is universally agreed that the Ripper's M.O. entailed cutting his victims' throats prior to mutilating their abdomens. It is generally agreed today that he seized them by the throat prior to using the knife (as shown by bruising on throat and neck seen in all cases except Mary Jane Kelly's, where the extensive mangling of the neck and face made such observation impossible). Disagreement ensues over the position from which he did this, the effect of his first onslaught, the degree of his skill, and his handedness.

Dr Llewellyn interpreted the bruising on Mary Ann Nichols' right jaw as a thumbmark, from which he deduced that a left-handed man stood in front of her, steadied the jaw with his right hand, and cut the throat from left to right with the knife in his left hand. Although this is the origin of the belief that the Ripper was left-handed, it has not proved persuasive to subsequent researchers. The M.O. proposed is clumsy, would be almost impossible to carry out silently, and would probably rip the murderer's own sleeve.

The *Lancet* of 29 September 1888 summarised **Dr Phillips**' evidence on Annie Chapman with the conclusion, 'There can be little doubt that [the murderer] first strangled or suffocated his victim, for not only were no cries heard, but the face lips and hands were livid as in asphyxia, and not blanched as they would be from loss of blood.' Phillips had actually said, 'I am of the opinion that the breathing was interfered with before death, but that death arose from syncope consequent upon loss of blood following the severance of the throat.'

In 1966 **Dr Francis Camps** drew attention to this important contemporary evidence for strangulation of the Ripper's victims:

Viewed in the light of other sadistic serial murders, strangulation would usually be a very significant feature. It seems very possible that the

Ripper silenced all his victims by strangling them, for in at least two cases, obstruction to the mouth is mentioned and the absence of bleeding is also a matter for comment. In all cases there was no sign or sound of a struggle, which tends to confirm this.

In 1968, Camps again observed that the victims

shared in common wounds which had been inflicted with a sharp knife and yet were associated with far less spillage of blood than might have been expected. This is in direct contradiction with the fact that they were all stated to have died without crying out. The probable explanation may lie in a comment in a contemporary number of the *Lancet* that it was strange that their faces were congested under the circumstances, which suggests that the absence of a cry was due to strangulation being the real cause of death, a common practice of sexual murderers.

Given that Annie Chapman's tongue was purple and protruding, Catharine Eddowes' tongue was swollen, Annie Chapman's, Mary Jane Kelly's, and Elizabeth Stride's fists were clenched – all signs of strangulation – Camps's conclusion has seemed persuasive to subsequent researchers.

Donald Rumbelow has also felt **Professor Cameron**'s extension of the theory to have some merit, reporting it thus:

Professor Cameron thought that the most likely position that the Ripper and his victim would have taken up would have been with her bending forward and the Ripper standing behind her; again, remembering the heavy garments that she was wearing . . . she would have found it easier in this position to have flicked them over her back. Possibly she might have had anal intercourse – which used to be a common way of birth control with these women – rather than normal vaginal penetration. In this position, anyway, it would have been a very simple matter for the Ripper to have strangled her. As he was doing so, he could even have battered their faces against the wall, which could explain the facial bruising of three of them . . . If the Ripper then cut their throats while still holding them from behind, the risk of staining his clothes with blood would have been minimal.

The authors demur. This theory is not easily compatible with the carotid arterial bloodflow consistently reported as being directly beside or under the neck and shoulders, and in Annie Chapman's case, against the fence beside her neck, fourteen inches off the ground. It was observed, too, that the victims' backs rather than fronts were saturated with blood. (But cf. **Inspector Keaton**.) The authors suggest that the Ripper stood in front of his victims in the normal position for standing intercourse; that he seized them round the throat with both hands, thus instantly silencing them and rapidly inducing unconsciousness; that he pushed them to the ground with their heads to his left, and cut their throats, drawing the knife toward him. The initial arterial bloodflow would thus be away from him and he would avoid heavy bloodstaining. Also (like Cameron's theory) this suggests the probability that he was right-handed.

For his alleged medical skill, see under **Doctor theories**.

MONK, MARY ANN

Identified Mary Ann Nichols' body and testified at her inquest. A young woman 'with a haughty air and a flushed face', Monk identified the body in the mortuary after a Lambeth Workhouse laundry mark had been found on its petticoat. Monk had been a fellow-inmate with Nichols.

MONRO, JAMES (1838–1920)

Assistant Metropolitan Police Commissioner in charge of CID until the outbreak of Ripper murders; 'Head of Detective Service', officially unattached to Metropolitan Police between murders of Mary Ann Nichols and Mary Jane Kelly; thereafter Metropolitan Police Commissioner until 1890.

Educ. Edinburgh High School, and Edinb. and Berlin Universities. Entered ICS by examination, 1857. Successively Assistant Magistrate, Collector, District Judge and Inspector-General of Police, Bombay Presidency. Resigned, 1884. Assistant Commissioner Metropolitan Police, 1884–8; then, with two month interval as unofficial 'Head of Detective Service', Commissioner, 1888–90, when he resigned. Founded and ran Ranaghat Christian Medical Mission, 1890–1903. He intended retirement in Darjeeling, but returned first to Scotland, but thereafter to Cheltenham and other parts of England, following his son-in-law's peregrinations.

Like **Dr Robert Anderson**, a millenniarist, looking forward to the Second Coming of Christ. A firm and decisive disciplinarian, he was none the less loved by practically all who served under him. Robert Anderson and **Melville Macnaghten** left glowing accounts: **Superintendent Williamson** almost resigned from the force when Monro's resignation as Assistant Commissioner was accepted. Rank-and-file police long remembered his determined struggle to secure the pension conditions they demanded. Sir Basil Thomson and Sir John Moylan, in their respective histories of the Metropolitan Police, spoke well of him. All agreed on his excellence as a detective, especially in bringing the **Fenian** dynamite campaigns of the 1880s under control. The rapid fall in crime figures after his appointment as Commissioner was ascribed by Anderson to his influence, though others have wondered whether it might not have been Anderson's own achievement (since the trend continued throughout his decade as Assistant Commissioner), or merely coincidence.

Monro's equals and superiors, however, may have found him a more difficult man than published accounts and his benign features suggest. His unpublished manuscript memoirs evince an elephantine memory for a grievance and an implacable impulse to self-justification. His career is studded with resignations on principle: from the Assistant Commissionership because he could not wrest absolute sovereignty over the CID from the Commissioner; from the Commissionership because he could not have his way over the Police Bill and the appointment of a Chief Constable.

Briefly, the disputes involving Monro were as follows. On coming to Scotland Yard he found Edward Jenkinson at the Home Office running an intelligence service to infiltrate the Fenian movement. Jenkinson may have been personally difficult: he expressed contemptuous views of the CID, Monro, Williamson and Anderson in private, but did not apparently come in conflict with the two last. Monro objected that Jenkinson did not always inform him which Fenians were Jenkinson's agents. Jenkinson also seemed dishonest to a man of Monro's undisputably rigid integrity. Monro complained at length to four successive Home Secretaries about him, and in January 1887 Jenkinson resigned and his intelligence service was abolished. Monro was given personal charge of the entirely new Secret Department (Section D).

This gave Monro direct access to the Home Secretary. He wrongly believed the same should be true of the CID, and resented **Warren's** insistence on exercising his authority over it, which Monro (with the support of his subordinates) believed to be deleterious. He was further outraged when Warren vetoed his appointment of Macnaghten as Assistant Chief Constable. (See under **Melville Macnaghten**.) This led to his own resignation and appointment to the unauthorised post in which the CID was encouraged to liaise with him behind Warren's back.

As Commissioner, his own quarrels with the Home Secretary arose again over the appointment of a Chief Constable, Monro wanting to appoint fellow Indian Civil Service veteran Andrew Howard, and Matthews wanting civil servant **Evelyn Ruggles-Brise**. The breaking point was the revised pension conditions in the new Police Bill.

This was the background of police and Home Office in-fighting which led many observers at the time and researchers since to conclude that Scotland Yard was preoccupied with squabbles at the time of the Whitechapel Murders, and there would have been a better chance of solving the mystery if Monro had been in charge with a free hand.

In practice, he was consulted by the officers on the case throughout, with Home Office encouragement. *The Times* reported that the superintendents on the case were visiting his office and not reporting to Warren. Additionally, on 22 September 1888, Matthews sent a memo to his Private Secretary, Evelyn Ruggles-Brise: 'Stimulate the police about the Whitechapel murders. Monro might be willing to give a hint to the CID people if necessary.'

In 1890 Monro told *Cassells Magazine* that he had 'decidedly' formed a theory on the case, adding, 'when I do theorise it is from a practical standpoint, and not upon any visionary foundation'. He also said, however, that the police had 'Nothing positive' by way of clues, with the rider that such crimes were difficult to solve since the victims as well as the murderer sought secret sites.

He resigned two years before the file was closed, but must be assumed to have known what (especially) Anderson and **Swanson** believed up to 1890.

After his retirement, he said in the presence of one grandson, 'the Ripper was never caught, but he should have been'. He left some papers on the subject with his eldest son Charles, who subsequently told a younger brother, Douglas, that the theory was 'a very hot potato', without revealing what it was. Douglas (who subsequently felt guilty about his advice) said, 'Burn the stuff, Charlie, burn it and forget about it.' It is feared that Charles Monro did so.

Monro's handwritten memoirs make no mention of the case, and are, apparently, the entirety of what he wrote or intended to write. They mention printed papers in England with reference to another case, and it is possible that these included whatever he held on the Ripper. Colin Wilson and Robin Odell, in *Jack the Ripper: Summing Up and Verdict*, mention a correspondent who has devised a theory proposing Monro as a suspect.

See under **Sir Robert Anderson** for Monro's later dispute over Anderson's permission to publish secret information in *The Times*; under **Arthur Balfour** for an alleged theory which may be connected with either or both of two cases Monro does describe in his memoirs, and which were, arguably, 'hot potatoes'.

MONRO'S SECRET DEPARTMENT

A police department separate from CID and uniformed branch which may also have been operating in Whitechapel, 1888.

In 1884, when James Monro was appointed Assistant Commissioner at Scotland Yard, he found that Edward Jenkinson controlled 'a kind of Central Bureau of intelligence . . . at the Home Office'. As described under **James Monro**, on Jenkinson's resignation in January 1887 and the closure of his organisation, it was replaced with a special section in Scotland Yard, under Monro's direct control, headed by **Chief Inspector Littlechild** with three second-class inspectors, one of whom was John Sweeney. They were not to be distinguished from other policemen; were to act with extreme confidentiality; and to be financed from Imperial rather than Metropolitan Police Funds. Administratively they were 'Section D'. They were also referred to by other names, including 'Home Office Crime Department', 'Special Irish Branch' and 'Special Branch'. Their duties entailed observation of anarchists and other subversives, including immigrants who might use asylum in London to plot terrorism on the continent.

This post gave Monro direct access to the Home Secretary, which **Sir Charles Warren** resented. It also led Monro to complain that he was overworked as head of both CID and Secret Department. He did not, however, accept Warren's recommendation that he relinquish the Secret Department post. Monro continued to control the Secret Department after his resignation as Assistant Commissioner, and retained control after becoming Commissioner. It is not known who commanded it after 1890.

In 1904, John Sweeney remarked in his memoirs that around 1887 the anarchists

> began to grow restless, they held frequent meetings; there was quite a small boom in the circulation of their revolutionary publications . . .

> One could never be sure of what those fellows would be up to at any moment, so that Scotland Yard had an anxious time keeping every movement of theirs under surveillance . . . It may be imagined how much extra work was put on the shoulders of the Special Department.

As the heirs of Jenkinson's 'Bureau', this department could work outside Metropolitan Police territory, and would certainly have places like the **International Workingmen's Educational Club** in Berner Street within their ken.

MONSELL, COLONEL BOLTON

Chief Constable, Metropolitan Police, 1886–1910. Visited Buck's Row and Hanbury Street murder sites. Then, in July 1891, shared with Commissioner **Monro** responsibility for directing the investigation of Alice McKenzie's murder.

MONTAGU, SAMUEL (1832–1911)

Subsequently Lord Swaythling. MP for the Whitechapel Division of Tower Hamlets, 1885–1900. Foreign-exchange banker and philanthropist. Montagu was a pillar of orthodox Judaism and a staunch Liberal. Supported many charities for the poor in general and immigrant Jews in particular in and around the East End. Bt, 1894. Baron Swaythling, 1901.

During the Ripper scare he supported the local Vigilance Committees, forwarding several of their requests and petitions to the Home Office. He strongly favoured the offer of a **reward** for information leading to the killer's arrest, and put up £100 personally for this purpose, trying in the first instance to offer it through the police.

MOORE, CHIEF INSPECTOR HENRY (b. 1848)
Described by **Walterr Dew** as in charge of the Whitechapel Murders case. Probably liaison officer between **Chief Inspector Swanson** (desk officer in overall charge of the case in Scotland Yard) and **Inspector Abberline** (heading the team of detectives on the ground).

Son of a former Metropolitan policeman. Worked as clerk on South Eastern and London, Chatham and Dover Railway, and subsequently in a silk warehouse. Joined Metropolitan Police, 1869 (Warrant no. 68911), serving in W Division (Clapham). 1878, promoted Sergeant, transferred to Y Division (Holloway). 1878, promoted Inspector and transferred to P Division (Peckham). 1881, transferred to CID (P Division); 1888, transferred to Commissioner's office (Scotland Yard). Retired, 1899. Appointed Superintendent of Great Eastern Railway Police, from which he retired, 1913.

Moore's exact role in the Ripper investigation is unknown. He outranked Abberline and was described both by Dew and in the *Pall Mall Gazette* in November 1889 as being in charge of the case. Yet in one document on the Scotland Yard files he expresses the hope that it is not out of order that he has done something that would normally fall within Abberline's province.

His fullest known remarks on the case occur in the *Pall Mall Gazette* of 4 November 1889 which reproduces an interview with R. Harding Davis that had appeared in the Philadelphia press. The status of the interview is uncertain: either Moore was at times exaggerating, or Davis was compensating for the prosaicism of truth by replacing it with data from the more lurid Agency reports of 1888, as when Moore reportedly said he had seen in Mary Jane Kelly's room where the murderer 'hung different parts of the body on nails and over the backs of chairs' (cf. medical report under **Dr Thomas Bond** for the fact that all body parts were on the bed or table). This means even his apparently useful observations in this article must be treated with caution.

MORGANSTONE – (or possibly MORGAN STONE)
Alleged former lover of Mary Jane Kelly. According to **Joe Barnett**, she lived with Morganstone in the neighbourhood of the Stepney gas works when she left the West End. This would correlate her association with him to the time when **Mrs Carthy** said she was living in St George's Street (the western end of the old Ratcliff Highway).

MORLAND, NIGEL (1905–86)
Founder-editor of the *Criminologist*, which first published **Dr Thomas Stowell**'s theory pointing to **Prince Albert Victor** as Jack the Ripper.

In the *Evening News* of 28 June 1976, Morland recalled a meeting with **Inspector Abberline**, saying he 'remembered distinctly [Abberline's] exact words', which were: 'you'd have to look for him [the Ripper] not at the bottom of London society but a long way up'.

Morland also wrote an introduction for Frank Spiering's *Prince Jack* in which he recalled being told by Sir Arthur Conan Doyle that the Ripper was 'somewhere in the upper stratum'; remembered learning from Edgar Wallace who the Ripper really was (Albert Victor, we infer from the context); and again described Abberline's words to him, this time saying, 'and I quote exactly: "I cannot reveal anything except this – *of course* we knew who [the Ripper] was, one of the highest in the land." '

In 1979 Morland published an article of his own in the *Criminologist*: 'Jack the Ripper: the Final Word'. This argued on the basis of handwriting that there was 'no justification whatever' for the identification of Prince Albert Victor with the Ripper.

Mr Morland, who had an extraordinarily large fund of anecdotes to tell about meetings with almost everyone criminous, was a charming man, fondly remembered by his many friends for his rather romantic disposition and excellent imaginative writing.

MORRIS, ANN
Martha Tabram's sister-in-law, and witness at her inquest. A widow described as a very respectable woman, living in 23 Fisher Street, Mile End. Testified to seeing Martha in a pub, possibly The White Swan, Whitechapel Road, at about 11.00 p.m. on the night of her death. Police revealed that Martha had been charged three times with annoying Mrs Morris and getting money from her, being sentenced to seven days hard labour on the last occasion.

MORRIS, ANNIE
Alleged alias of Elizabeth Stride. The *Yorkshire Post* (1 October 1888) reported: 'A woman known as **One-Armed Liz** living in a common lodging house in **Flower and Dean Street** told a reporter that she had accompanied **Sgt Thick** to the mortuary and had identified the body as that of Annie Morris, a prostitute now living in Flower and Dean Street.' (Cf. **Wally Warden, Annie Fitzgerald, Elizabeth Burns**.)

MORRIS, GEORGE JAMES
Witness at Catharine Eddowes' inquest. Watchman at Kearley and Tonge's warehouse in Mitre Square on the night of 29–30 September 1888.

Reported that the warehouse door was ajar and he had not heard a sound in the square. As a rule he heard the beat policeman's footsteps every fifteen minutes, but he heard nothing until **Police Constable Watkins** came to the warehouse for help at about 1.45 a.m. Watkins called, 'For God's sake, mate, come to assist me.' Morris picked up a lamp, asking, 'What's the matter?'

'Oh dear, here's another woman cut up to pieces,' was Watkins' reply. Morris saw the body and then ran to Aldgate where he found **Police Constable James Harvey**.

MORRISON, JOHN
Author of *Jimmy Kelly's Year of the Ripper Murders 1888*. Morrison calls his typed and photostated forty-page pamphlet 'the most authentic account ever of the Whitechapel murders'. In 1986 he erected a headstone over Mary Jane Kelly's unmarked grave, for which he gained a good deal of publicity.

MORTIMER, MRS FANNY (b. 1840)
Resident of **Berner Street**; told of empty street prior to Elizabeth Stride's murder. Née Skipp. Wife of William Mortimer, carman of 36 Berner

Street, and mother of his five children. Described as 'a clean and respectable looking woman . . . a strong contrast to many of those around her'.

She did not give evidence at Stride's inquest, but made important statements to the press which were followed up by police. She said she had been standing outside her door (three houses away from **Dutfield's Yard**) between 12.30 and 1.00 a.m., 30 September 1888. Her earliest reported statements suggested that she had been outside for about ten minutes; later reports placed her outside for practically the entire half hour, which seems improbable as she did not see other people known to be in the street at the time. (Cf. **Police Constable John Smith, Matthew Packer, Israel Schwartz**.) She said she went outside shortly after hearing the measured tread of a policeman. While outside, she saw nobody, except a man with a black bag who passed down the street, glancing up at the **International Workingmen's Educational Club** as he went (later identified as **Leon Goldstein**). She returned indoors shortly before hearing **Louis Diemschütz**'s horse and cart pass by, and five minutes later heard the commotion caused by the discovery of the body.

Robin Odell, in *Jack the Ripper: In Fact and Fiction*, gives an unsourced reference to Mrs Mortimer's stating that whilst in her doorway, prior to Goldstein's passing down the street, she heard a row going on somewhere; a bump, and a stifled cry. The authors have not traced this press report, though Mrs Mortimer certainly did say she thought the commotion on the finding of the body was 'a row at the Socialists' Club', and asserted that since Stride's face was still warm, 'the deed must have been done while I was standing at the door of my house'.

If the report cited by Odell is correct, it strongly suggests that Mrs Mortimer overheard the scuffle described by Israel Schwartz, leaving two puzzling facts: she did not look down the road to see the incident (which took place on the pavement of Berner Street, and not in Dutfield's Yard); and Leon Goldstein, passing by very shortly afterwards, saw no trace of Schwartz, Stride, her assailant or the man Schwartz saw come out of a pub across the road.

MOULSON, POLICE CONSTABLE GEORGE (1862–1905)

Reported the discovery of **Montague John Druitt**'s body. Joined Metropolitan Police, 1883. Warrant no. 67735. Retired, October 1905; died three months later. Summoned by waterman **Winslade** who pulled the body out of the Thames, 31 December 1888. It would appear to be Moulson's report, including pocket contents and wrongly estimated age, which was in part followed in Melville **Macnaghten's memoranda**.

MULSHAW, PATRICK

Witness at Mary Ann Nichols' inquest. Resident at 3 Rupert Street, Whitechapel. A night porter employed by Whitechapel Board of Works. On duty watching sewage works in Winthrop Street (parallel with and converging on **Buck's Row**) through the night of 30–31 August 1888. Dozed during the night, but assured the inquest he was awake from 3.00 to 4.00 a.m., when he saw and heard no one. He was reported as saying, 'Another man then passed by, and said, "Watchman, old man, I believe somebody is murdered down the street." ' Mulshaw went to see the body, joining police and **Harry Tomkins**. It is not known who the man addressing Mulshaw was, nor how he could have been 'another man', since no report has survived of Mulshaw's reporting any previous passer-by.

MUMFORD, JAMES
Saw Mary Ann Nichols' body. A horse slaughterman working at Barber's knacker's yard, Winthrop Street, Mumford accompanied **Henry Tomkins** at 4.20 a.m., 31 August 1888, around the corner to Buck's Row on learning from **Police Constable Thain** of the body. He and Mumford remained at the site until **Police Constable Neil** left for the mortuary.

MURDER BY DECREE (1979, Canada/Great Britain)
Film directed by Bob Clark. Stars Christopher Plummer, James Mason. Based on **Joseph Sickert**'s story of Masonic conspiracy, but fiction firmly established by name changes (**Gull** becomes Spivey, for example) and conspiracy being uncovered by Holmes and Watson, superbly interpreted by Plummer and Mason (though Holmes purists might disagree). (Video available.)

MUUSMANN, CARL
Author of *Hvem var Jack the Ripper?* (1908). Dutch author of first known full-length book attempting to identify the Ripper. Follows Austro-Hungarian press in suggesting **Alios Szemeredy**. Muusmann's claim to primacy noted by **Melvin Harris**.

MYLETT, ROSE (1862–88)
aka Catherine Millett, 'Drunken Lizzie' Davis, 'Fair Alice' Downey.
Alleged strangled Ripper victim. By her mother's account, formerly married to an upholsterer named Davis. Bore one son, c. 1881, who attended a school in Sutton at the time of Rose's death. Lived variously at her mother's in Pelham Street, Baker's Row, Spitalfields; at 18 George Street, Spitalfields; and in the Limehouse/Poplar district.
  She was seen by infirmary night-attendant Charles Ptolomay talking to two sailors at 7.55 p.m., 19 December 1888, in Poplar High Street, near Clarke's Yard. She was sober at the time, and saying, 'No, no, no!' to one sailor, whose manner was suspicious enough to draw Ptolomay's attention. At 2.30 a.m. a young woman, Alice Graves, saw her with two men outside The George in **Commercial Road**, apparently drunk.
  She was found dead in Clarke's Yard at 4.15 a.m. by **Police Constable Robert Goulding**. The body, still warm, was lying on its left side. The clothes were not disarranged. There was no obvious sign of injury. There was 1/2d [6p] in her possession. Death was certified by divisional surgeon **Brownfield**'s assistant, Mr Harris.
  Brownfield's post mortem was reported as saying
  Blood was oozing from the nostrils, and there was a slight abrasion on the right side of the face . . . On the neck there was a mark which had evidently been caused by cord drawn tightly round the neck, from the spine to the left ear. Such a mark would be made by a four thread cord. There were also impressions of the thumbs and middle and index fingers of some person plainly visible on each side of the neck. There were no injuries to the arms or legs. The brain was gorged with an almost black fluid blood. The stomach was full of meat and potatoes, which had only recently been eaten. Death was due to strangulation. Deceased could not

have done it herself. The marks on her neck were probably caused by her trying to pull the cord off. He thought the murderer must have stood at the left rear of the woman, and, having the ends of the cord round his hands, thrown it round her throat, crossed his hands, and thus strangled her. If it had been done in this way, it would account for the mark not going completely round the neck.

Positive though this seems, Brownfield presented it at the inquest (under **Wynne Baxter** at Poplar Coroner's Court, 2 and 9 January 1889) in the full knowledge that it was to be challenged. The police had not been convinced by the immediate medical conclusion of homicide. No discarded ligature had been discovered. The mark on the neck had been very hard to detect, and only circumvented one quarter of it. The congealed blood under the skin had done more to convince the doctors. **Dr Robert Anderson** personally observed that there was no trace of any struggle or of any other person's footmarks in the soft ground of the yard, and the body lay naturally. Furthermore, the evidence that there was no alcohol in the stomach conflicted with Alice Graves' report of seeing Mylett drunk. The original medical report declared that Mylett had never given birth, which was contradicted by her mother.

Anderson asked for **Dr Thomas Bond** to be sent to the mortuary to make a report. This resulted in first Bond's assistant, then General Police Surgeon Alexander McKellar examining the body, before Bond himself went to Poplar. His first report tentatively supported Brownfield's. Sent to reconsider, he came finally to the conclusion that the death was natural, Rose Mylett had choked to death while drunk, and the barely detectable mark on her neck had been caused by her stiff velvet collar.

Wynne Baxter protested in his summing-up against the interference with his powers represented by the medical invasion. He dismissed Bond's evidence on the ground that he had seen the body later than all the other doctors, and the jury returned a verdict of 'Murder by person or persons unknown'. Anderson had to file a report explaining his actions. He remarked positively in *The Lighter Side of My Official Life* (1910), 'the Poplar case of December, 1888, was death from natural causes, and but for the "Jack the Ripper" scare, no one would have thought of suggesting that it was a homicide'.

None the less, she was included as an 'alleged' victim in a list of the Whitechapel Murders made out in very elaborate calligraphy and preserved both on the Scotland Yard files and among the papers of Chief Inspector Swanson.

MYSTERIES OF POLICE AND CRIME

Book by Major Arthur Griffiths (3 volumes illustrated: 1898, 1901, 1902; 2 volumes unillustrated: 1899). A valuable true-crime anthology, by a man who was in close touch with Scotland Yard. In addition to the important descriptions of senior policemen on the case quoted under **Dr Anderson, Melville Macnaghten**, volume 1 gives Griffiths' account of the Ripper case as a whole, evidently derived from Sir Melville Macnaghten, since it closely follows the line of the **Macnaghten memoranda**.

The outside public may think that the identity of that later miscreant, 'Jack the Ripper' was never revealed. So far as absolute knowledge goes, this is undoubtedly true. But the police, after the last murder, had brought their investigations to the point of strongly suspecting several persons, all of them homicidal lunatics, and against three of these they held very plausible and reasonable grounds of suspicion. Concerning two of them the case was weak, although it was based on suggestive facts.

There follow the precise descriptions of the three suspects given under **M. J. Druitt, Kosminski** and **Ostrog**, and Griffiths concludes by saying, 'It is at least a strong presumption that "Jack the Ripper" died or was put under restraint after the Miller's Court affair, which ended this series of crimes.'

MYSTERY OF JACK THE RIPPER, THE

Book by Leonard Matters (1929; with new introduction, 1948). The first full-length English-language study of the murders, rightly praised for its pioneering survey of the facts in the case. The sometimes puzzling errors (e.g., the claim that Elizabeth Stride was remarkable among the victims in *not* having been seen with any man before her murder!) are of a kind that true-crime writers, accustomed to summarising conflicting detail from inaccurate newspapers, note with sympathetic awareness of similar faults in their own work. At this date it is regrettable that Matters decided not to interview elderly East Enders, on the grounds that their memories would be unreliable. Today, such 'unreliable' oral tradition would be invaluable.

Matters knew Major Griffiths' *Mysteries of Police and Crime* to contain the most authoritative previous account of the case, and dismissed his three suspects (unnamed, but clearly **Druitt, Kosminski** and **Ostrog**) along with **Dr Anderson**'s on the grounds that all were professed lunatics, and no lunatic could have escaped the police patrols, or would have restricted his victims to women of one kind. More specifically, he dismissed Druitt on the grounds that his family would have turned him over to the police. He dismissed Kosminski in the erroneous belief that Griffiths was referring to **Pizer**. He asserted that Ostrog's ability to escape discovery was implausible.

Matters has been severely criticised, however, for the conclusion of the book, wherein on deductive grounds he concluded that the '**Dr Stanley**' theory offered the most plausible solution. He rested his presentation of the Dr Stanley theory on two quoted (but unreferenced) sources: the lengthy statement of a former pupil of Stanley's, which Matters said he came across in a Spanish-language journal in Argentina and which included the brief deathbed confession of 'Dr Stanley'; and a statement made to Matters by a former West End demi-mondaine (**Mrs North**) about a gentleman who regularly entertained her in Monico's in the autumn of 1888, and whom she concluded to have been Dr Stanley after reading a piece on the subject Matters placed in the *People*, 26 December 1926. There is no reason to suppose Matters is any more fraudulent in quoting his florid Latin-American first source than his second.

Matters devised the (admittedly) fictitious name 'Stanley' for this best-known 'doctor' suspect.

N

NEARN, JAMES WILLIAM (b. 1857)
Recipient of Whitechapel Murder case souvenir. Joined Metropolitan Police, 1877; Warrant no. 61557; retired, 1902, as Inspector 1st class, CID. **Donald Swanson** signed his discharge certificate, describing his conduct as 'very good'. His nephew presented the Metropolitan Police History Museum with a pipe inscribed 'Souvenir to James Nearn, Whitechapel Murders, 1888, from six brother officers'. It appears that Nearn worked on the case with **Abberline** and **Moore**.

NEIL, POLICE CONSTABLE JOHN, 97J (b. 1850)
Witness at Mary Ann Nichols' inquest; discovered her body. Born in County Cork. Joined Metropolitan Police, 1875; Warrant no. 59168. Posted to J Division (Bethnal Green) where he remained until he resigned, 1897, after an injury received on duty.

Neil's beat was never further away from the murder site than Baker's Row (today's Vallance Road). He discovered Nichols' body in the gutter in Buck's Row at approximately 3.45 a.m. He was walking on his beat eastward along the Row toward Brady Street. He summoned **Police Constable Thain** to his assistance quietly, by signalling with his lamp down to Brady Street where Thain was passing. He was also joined by **Police Constable Mizen**, who had been directed to the woman lying in the gutter by the carters **Cross** and **Paul**. Neil sent Thain to fetch **Dr Llewellyn** and Mizen to fetch the ambulance (virtually a wheeled stretcher). He remained with the body.

The slaughtermen **Henry Tomkins** and **James Mumford** from Barber's knacker's yard in Winthrop Street were the first to join him. They stayed until Neil left for the mortuary at dawn. In the meantime, Llewellyn arrived and pronounced Nichols dead; and Sergeant Kerby arrived with another officer from H Division. Kerby had taken the body to the mortuary by the time **Inspector Spratling** arrived, and **Mrs Green**'s son James was sluicing the blood from the cobblestones. At 5.00 a.m. Neil went with Spratling to the mortuary.

In consequence of press criticism of police handling of the Whitechapel Murders in general and this one in particular, Standing Orders on the discovery of an apparently murdered body were tightened up. The policeman finding the body was to stay with it (as Neil did). The first assisting officer/s to arrive were to go for the doctor and for police reinforcements from the nearest station. An inspector was required to proceed from the station to the murder site as soon as possible. The body and the site should not be touched or interfered with except as ordered by the doctor and the inspector. (Cf. **Frances Coles, Police Constable Ernest Thompson** for these regulations in practice.)

NETLEY, JOHN CHARLES (1860–1903)

Identified by BBC researchers with a man of the same name alleged by **Joseph Gorman Sickert** to have driven the carriage for **Sir William Gull** and his co-conspirators to commit the Whitechapel Murders.

Born in northwest Paddington, a twin, the son of an omnibus conductor, Netley still lived in the Paddington district in 1903. He was, at his death, a bachelor carman, employed by Messrs Thompson, McKay and Co., who described him as very steady. He died in a traffic accident when the wheel of his van struck the obelisk on a pedestrian refuge in Park Road, where it joins Baker Street, near to the Clarence Gate of Regent's Park. Netley was flung out under the horses' hooves and his head was crushed by a wheel. The inquest jury returned a verdict of accidental death with a recommendation that van-drivers should be offered safety straps. The above are the only proven facts of Netley's life.

Joseph Sickert, as reported by Stephen Knight, alleges that Netley was an ambitious bisexual opportunist, who prostituted himself to socially prominent homosexuals in the 1880s, as well as being a heartless womaniser. He claims that Netley drove his own cab at the time of the Ripper murders, and had been in the habit of supplying it as clandestine transport for **Prince Albert Victor**'s visits to **Annie Elizabeth Crook** in Cleveland Street. He further claims that Netley drove Gull and his fellow-murderer/s on their forays to the East End, and that the murders took place inside the carriage, which then transported the bodies to the points where they were dumped. Sickert further claimed that Netley made two unsuccessful attempts to kill **Alice Margaret Crook** by running her down: one in the Strand or Fleet Street at the height of the Ripper scare, after which she underwent lengthy treatment in St Bartholomew's Hospital; the other in Drury Lane in 1892, after which Netley fled from an enraged crowd and drowned himself off Westminster Pier.

BBC researchers working on the drama-documentary series *Jack the Ripper* (see under **The Ripper File**, Lloyd and Jones) established the facts about Netley given above. They also established that there was a cab accident involving a little girl in Fleet Street in October 1888 (see **Lizzie Madewell**); and that a man whose name was misreported as 'Nickley' (a non-existent English surname) threw himself into the Thames off Westminster Pier in February 1892. Stephen Knight deduced that Netley must have been the man seen by **Israel Schwartz** assaulting Elizabeth Stride.

Stephen Knight found the proven existence of Netley one of the most persuasive elements in Joseph Sickert's fantastic story. Unlike all the other personae, he was neither a prominent public figure nor a demonstrable direct relative of Joseph Sickert's. Subsequent researchers note that Mr Sickert's account of Netley has varied to meet proven discoveries (e.g., his original story referred only to a single coach accident involving Alice Margaret Crook: the unsubstantiated one of 1892, though cf. *Sickert and the Ripper Crimes*), and that nothing whatever has been corroborated about Netley's sexual proclivities, his acquaintance with the famous, or even his one-time possession of his own coach.

None the less, it is not known how Joseph Sickert could have obtained any knowledge of this obscure man who died twenty years before his (Sickert's) birth, unless (as he claims) from the mouth of Walter Sickert. It is possible that the John Charles Netley identified by BBC researchers was not the John Netley described by Mr Sickert. Netley is named in torn pages from the diary of 1896 shown by Mr Sickert to **Melvyn Fairclough** and purporting to be **Inspector Abberline**'s cryptic solution of the mystery.

NEVE, POLICE CONSTABLE GEORGE, 101 H
Witness at Alice McKenzie's inquest. Ordered by **Sergeant Badham** to proceed from Commercial Street to Castle Alley at approximately 12.55 a.m., 17 July 1889, on account of the murder. Saw the body; searched alley, costermongers' barrows and space behind hoarding. Found nothing.

NEWSPAPER COVERAGE OF THE WHITECHAPEL MURDERS
Much of the lasting interest in this comparatively unimportant series of killings stems from the very full and sensational treatment it was given in the contemporary press. The Radical press – particularly the evening papers the *Star* under T. P. O'Connor and the *Pall Mall Gazette* under **W. T. Stead** – were quick to spot political advantage in a series of unsolved atrocious crimes in the East End, and featured the murders prominently with such advantage to their circulation that the rest of the press inevitably followed suit.

All Radical journalists recognised the advantage in highlighting depressed social conditions at a time when the first London County Council elections were being fought, and the Radicals had great hopes of taking the East End. Their candidate, the reformer, anti-imperialist and secularist Mrs Annie Besant, had gained a great victory by working for the successful match-girls' strike at Bryant and May's factory earlier in the year. Agency features of background and local colour for the Ripper murders, and ironic letters to the *Star* from Bernard Shaw, probably contributed to her winning the seat.

Stead, a prurient Puritan evangelical, also found in the murders exactly the sort of sensational material to boost circulation while he expressed editorial disapproval of prostitution and the social conditions under which it throve.

O'Connor, an Irish Nationalist MP, welcomed the opportunity to attack the Metropolitan Police chiefs for their clandestine attempts to link the legitimate parliamentary Irish party with **Fenian** terrorism. He relied on **Ernest Parke** to promote the circulation-building sensational aspects of the case.

The Radical press further welcomed the opportunity to hound **Sir Charles Warren** and the Metropolitan Police for their overheavy policing of demonstrations by the unemployed, which had led to one death in Trafalgar Square on 'Bloody Sunday' in November 1887. By heightening the Ripper scare, the Radicals could effectively accuse the police of neglecting their duty to protect citizens against criminals because they were too occupied with improper political actions.

Incautious modern authors and researchers have sometimes concluded that the editorial observations of the Radical extremists were balanced comments on the policing of the murders. It is wise to bear in mind that the *Star* claimed, in all seriousness, that the murders were caused by 'such economic systems as that of unrestricted competition, backed by the devil's gospel of *laissez-faire*'.

Since the Metropolitan Police were directly controlled by the Home Office, the Liberals saw an opportunity to join Radical extremists in a campaign which might bring down the unpopular Conservative Home Secretary **Henry Matthews** and so damage the Government. After Gladstone had espoused the cause of Irish Home Rule, the official Liberal Party was unusually sympathetic to Radicals and Irish Nationalists, at least while it was in opposition. Thus the responsible journals the *Morning Chronicle* and the *Morning* and *Evening News* joined the campaign, the latter scoring effectively with the early publication of the **'Dear Boss' letter** and 'Saucy Jacky' postcard which gave the Ripper his popular name, and by joining with the Whitechapel **Vigilance Committee** to employ the detectives **Grand** and **Batchelor** who appeared to expose the negligence of the police in failing to find Elizabeth Stride's abandoned grapestalk and establish that **Matthew Packer** had sold grapes to her companion. The *Daily Telegraph*, a popular newspaper, held in some contempt for the florid 'journalese' it pioneered under the influence of its leading correspondent G. A. Sala, had no political axe to grind, but joined in the criticism of Scotland Yard.

The Times had a reputation for social campaigning (it was nicknamed 'The Thunderer') and also normally featured rather full coverage of sensational murders, especially if they could be described as 'The Mystery' of a given locality. It inevitably took up 'The Whitechapel Mystery'. And so the most staid of the Conservative papers, the *Morning Post*, had little option but to feature the sensation which sold so many copies for its rivals.

With such massive coverage across the spectrum of the press, a range of papers, including the Socialist *Reynolds Newspaper*, the Liberal *Referee*, and the cheap rag the *Illustrated Police News*, milked the topic as often as they could for years after the sequence of murders had obviously finished.

At any point in the spectrum of opinion and respectability, editors might be at the mercy of unscrupulous hacks with phoney stories. *The Times* embroiled itself distastefully with a fraudulent anti-Semitic Viennese claim that the murders were of a kind enjoined on devout Jews by the Talmud if they had slept with Gentile women. And **William Le Queux** left a brief but graphic description of the way he and **Charles Hands** and **Lincoln Springfield** vied with each other to produce new 'theories', with precious little regard for the truth.

NICHOLS, MARY ANN 'POLLY' (1845–88)
First Ripper victim to be deliberately mutilated.

Daughter of locksmith, later blacksmith **Edward Walker** of Dean Street, Fetter Lane. 1864, married **William Nichols**, printer of Bouverie Street, and lived with him briefly at that address; subsequently at her father's at 131 Trafalgar Street, Walworth, and from c. 1874–80 at 6D Peabody Buildings, Stamford Street, Lambeth. During this time, bore children: Edward John, 1866; Percy George 1868; Alice Esther, 1870; Eliza Sarah, 1877; Henry Alfred, 1879. Considerable domestic disharmony from, at latest, 1877, at which time, apparently, William Nichols briefly eloped with a woman who had assisted at Mary Ann's accouchement with Eliza. Then or shortly thereafter Edward John took residence with Edward Walker and did not speak to his father again until after his mother's death. Mary Ann, however, either from 1877 or earlier, began drinking heavily and absconded from home five or six times. In 1880, the pair separated. Nichols retained the children (except Edward John) and paid Mary Ann 5/- [25p] per week allowance until 1882, when he learned she was living by prostitution. She then summonsed him for maintenance, but lost the case when he proved her immoral lifestyle.

Her movements after marital breakdown are surprisingly well documented:

6 Sept. 1880 – 31 May 1881	Lambeth Workhouse
31 May 1881 – 24 Apr. 1882	Not known
24 Apr. 1882 – 18 Jan. 1883	Lambeth Workhouse
18 Jan. 1883 – 20 Jan. 1883	Lambeth Infirmary
20 Jan. 1883 – 24 Mar. 1883	Lambeth Workhouse
24 Mar. 1883 – 21 May 1883	Lived with her father until her drinking caused friction, whereupon she left after a quarrel
21 May 1883 – 2 Jun. 1883	Lambeth Workhouse
2 Jun. 1883 – 25 Oct. 1887	Lived with **Thomas Stuart Drew** at 15 York Street, Walworth. In June 1886, respectably dressed, she attended her brother's funeral
25 Oct. 1887	One day in St Giles's Workhouse, Endell Street
26 Oct. 1887 – 2 Dec. 1887	Strand Workhouse, Edmonton
2 Dec. 1887 – 19 Dec. 1887	Probably mostly sleeping rough in Trafalgar Square. When the area was cleared and she was found destitute, she was readmitted to Lambeth Workhouse
19 Dec. 1887 – 29 Dec. 1887	Lambeth Workhouse
29 Dec. 1887 – 4 Jan. 1888	No record
4 Jan. 1888 – 16 Apr. 1888	Mitcham Workhouse (Holborn) and Holborn Infirmary (Archway Hospital)
16 Apr. 1888 – 12 Jul. 1888	Employed by **Mr and Mrs Cowdry** in Wandsworth until she absconded, stealing clothes. From the Cowdrys' she wrote to her father:

I just write to say you will be glad to know that I am settled in my new place, and going all right up to now. My people went out yesterday, and have not returned, so I am left in charge. It is a grand place inside, with trees and gardens back and front. All has been newly done up. They are teetotallers, and very religious, so I ought to get on. They are very nice people, and I have not much to do. I hope you are all right and the boy has work. So goodbye now for the present. Yours truly, 'Polly' Answer soon please, and let me know how you are.

12 Jul. 1888 – 1 Aug. 1888	No record
1 Aug. 1888 – 2 Aug. 1888	Gray's Inn Temporary Workhouse
2 Aug. 1888 – 24 Aug. 1888	18 Thrawl Street, where for 4d (2p) she shared a 'surprisingly' clean room with three other women and a bed with **Ellen Holland**
24 Aug. 1888 – 30 Aug. 1888	The 'White House', 56 **Flower and Dean Street**: a doss-house which allowed men and women to sleep together.

On Thursday 30 August she was seen walking alone in Whitechapel Road at 11.30 p.m. At 12.30 a.m. she was seen leaving The Frying Pan in **Brick Lane**. At 1.20 she went to 18 Thrawl Street, slightly tipsy. The deputy turned her away as she had not 4d, but she laughed as she went, saying, 'I'll soon get my doss money; see what a jolly bonnet I've got now.' She was wearing a bonnet the deputy had not seen before. At 2.30 a.m. Ellen Holland met her, drunk and staggering, at the corner of Brick Lane and Whitechapel High Street. Mary Ann told her she had earned her doss money three times over that day, and spent it. She refused to accompany Holland back to Thrawl Street.

At approximately 3.40, **Charles Cross** and **Robert Paul** saw her body lying in **Buck's Row** with the skirt pulled up. Within five minutes, Police Constables **Neil, Thain** and **Mizen** were on the scene, Neil having seen by the light of his lantern that the throat had been cut. They were joined by slaughtermen **Tomkins, Mumford** and **Brittain. Dr Llewellyn** was fetched and pronounced Nichols dead, ordering the body to be removed to the mortuary shed at Old Montague Street Workhouse Infirmary. While he was examining the body, an unknown man passed along Buck's Row: possibly the same who told **Patrick Mulshaw** there had been a murder.

Sergeant Kerby and Police Constable Thain took the body to the mortuary on an ambulance; it had left by the time **Inspector Spratling** arrived, and James Green (son of **Emma Green**) was already washing away blood from the cobblestones. Spratling went to the mortuary and was taking down a description of the body when the skirt was lifted and the abdominal mutilations discovered. Dr Llewellyn was summoned to make a further examination. By the time he arrived the body had been stripped and washed by **Robert Mann** and **James Hatfield**, although police insisted they had been instructed not to interfere with it before the medical examination. See under **Llewellyn** for her injuries.

Ellen Holland and other occupants of the White House and 18 Thrawl Street only knew her as 'Polly'. A Lambeth Workhouse laundrymark on her petticoat led to enquiries there, and the suggestion that the whereabouts of former inmates Mrs Scorer and Polly Nichols were uncertain. James Scorer, assistant salesman of Smithfield Market, had been separated from his wife for eleven years, but knew her friend Polly Nichols by sight. He was, however, unable to identify the body in the mortuary. **Mary Ann Monk** from Lambeth Workhouse eventually identified the body.

She was buried at Ilford Cemetery on 6 September.

Mary Ann Nichols was 5ft 2ins tall with greying hair, small delicate features, high cheekbones and grey eyes. Her front teeth were missing, and there was a scar on her forehead from a childhood accident. Her father and an *East London Observer* journalist both remarked that she looked a good ten years younger than her age. Ellen Holland stated that she was 'a very clean woman', and Dr Llewellyn commented on the surprising cleanliness of her thighs.

The natural tendency of the press was to blame the drunkenness and immorality of the deceased prostitutes for their marital shipwrecks. So it is worth noting that Polly Nichols' father, though himself unable to live comfortably with her drinking, clearly sympathised with her over her treatment at William Nichols' hands; that Nichols did not explicitly deny having temporarily deserted her for another woman; that her eldest son decisively took her side, and her youngest was living with her father at the time of her death, despite having been left in William Nichols' care at the time of the marital breakdown.

NICHOLS, WILLIAM (b. prior to 1844)
Estranged husband of Mary Ann Nichols. A printer of Bouverie Street at time of marriage (1864) in St Bride's Church, Fleet Street (the printers' church). Lived with her in Bouverie Street; at her father's home in Walworth; and in Peabody Buildings, Stamford Street, Lambeth, prior to marital breakdown, c. 1880. They had five children, born between 1866 and 1879.

In 1880, the eldest boy, Edward John, took his mother's side, and went to live with her father, **Edward Walker**. This household also had custody of the youngest boy by 1888. They insisted that the cause of the marital breakdown was William's desertion of Mary Ann for a woman who had assisted her through one labour. William only challenged this obliquely, saying, 'I have a certificate of my boy's birth two years after that', which suggests that he did indeed temporarily elope with the accoucheuse attending the birth of Eliza Sarah Nichols in 1877, two years prior to the birth of Henry Alfred. He blamed the marital breakdown on Mary Ann's persistent drinking and absconding on five or six occasions.

He paid her an allowance of 5/- [25p] a week until 1882, when he heard that she was living by prostitution (or, possibly, under the protection of **Thomas Drew**) and Lambeth magistrates accepted his case when the parish summonsed him for restoration of this maintenance. He last saw her in 1885.

At the time of the murder he was living at 12 Cobourg Road, Old Kent Road, and working for Perkins, Bacon and Co., printers of Whitefriars Road. He arrived at the mortuary on the evening of 1 September 1888, respectably dressed and carrying an umbrella, to inspect the body. Outside he met Mary Ann's father, Edward Walker, accompanied by Edward John Nichols, now twenty-one years old and an engineer. Walker said, 'Well, here is your son, you see. I have taken care of him and made a man of him.' Nichols responded, 'Well, I really did not know him; he has so grown and altered.' Inside the mortuary he made the lugubrious observation to the corpse, 'Seeing you as you are now, I forgive you for what you have done to me.' He emerged, visibly pale, to say, 'Well, there is no mistake about it. It has come to a sad end at last.'

He appears to have been a good example of the self-consciously respectable Victorian upper working class, aping lower middle class values.

NIDEROEST, JOHANN (born c. 1885)
Alleged link in transmission of information incriminating **Dr Alexander Pedachenko**.

German-Swiss who peddled information to journalists. Resident in London, probably 1905–15. In 1905 he tried to sell a bogus story of anarchists manufacturing bombs in Whitechapel. In 1909 he was charged with feloniously entering Prince of Wales Hospital, Tottenham, under false pretence of being anarchist murderer Paul Hefeld's brother. The case was dismissed because Nideroest's admitted intent – to procure the story of Hefeld for newspapers – seemed plausible and non-felonious. In 1910 he was alleged by A. T. Vassil'ev (*Ochrana*, 1930) to have helped Latvian anarchist Peter Straume escape from Whitechapel to Australia; inferential support for this claim is that according to Sir Basil Thomson, one-time head of Special Branch, Straume was 'Peter the Painter' of 'Siege of Sidney Street' fame; and according to recent research on Sidney Street, Straume was indeed one of 'Peter the Painter' (Gederts Eliass's) assumed names, and he did escape from Britain before the siege, although not actually involved in the Houndsditch murders for which the Sidney Street anarchists were wanted. In 1915 Nideroest was charged *in camera* at Bow Street under the Defence of the Realm Act. He was sentenced to three months imprisonment, then deported. In 1916, in Switzerland, he claimed that with other passengers on the destroyed vessel *Sussex* he had been coerced by allied authorities to swear she had been torpedoed, whereas she actually struck a mine. The *Star* claimed he had been proven 'an unscrupulous liar' on this occasion. The authors note that he was in a neutral country in wartime, denying a German atrocity, and either the *Star* or the allied authorities might equally have been lying unscrupulously.

William le Queux claimed that Nideroest learned from **Nicholas Zverieff** that Pedachenko was the real Jack the Ripper, and passed the information to the Ochrana (Czarist Secret Police). Le Queux alleged that this was documented in **Rasputin**'s manuscript *Great Russian Criminals* which he possessed, and that Rasputin commented, 'The report of Nideroest's discovery amused our Secret Police greatly, for, as a matter of fact, they knew the whole details at the time . . .'

Donald McCormick deduces that Nideroest was actually a Czarist counter-espionage agent. Other researchers note the very doubtful provenance of the alleged Rasputin manuscript which supplies the only known connection between Nideroest and the Ripper case.

NO ORCHIDS FOR LULU (1967, Austria)
Film. Mario Adorf as Ripper in version of much-remade story.

NORTH, MRS (b. 1871)
Informant. In 1888 lived in Chelsea, but frequently visited friends in Rupert Street (a notorious centre of prostitution). Played dominoes at Cafe Monico in Shaftesbury Avenue, where, July 1888, she met a striking and well-dressed professional man in his mid-forties who beat her at dominoes. She frequently saw him subsequently in the cafe, and noted that his attitude to women, and to the cafe demi-mondaines, was hard and cynical. Also he appeared to be listening to conversations around. He never stayed later than 10.30 p.m. During September he spoke casually about the murders while walking her part-way home, and made an appointment to meet her on Saturday, which he broke to visit the graves of his wife and son. When he met her again and apologised, he also teasingly claimed to be Jack the Ripper, and told her there would be one more murder.

In the 1920s Mrs North contacted **Leonard Matters**. He and she concluded that Mrs North's mysterious professional acquaintance was probably '**Dr Stanley**'. It is not known whether Matters shielded Mrs North's identity under a pseudonym as he did 'Stanley's'.

O

OCHRANA GAZETTE

Bulletin issued by the Ochrana (Czarist Secret Police) for circulation among its European sections, one number of which allegedly identified the Ripper.

Donald McCormick says he was shown a lithograph copy of the *Gazette* for January 1909 by **Prince Sergei Belloselski**, a Russian exile in London. One entry read:

KONOVALOV, Vassily, alias **PEDACHENKO**, Alexey, alias LUIS-KOVO, Andrey, formerly of Tver, is now officially declared to be dead. Any files or information concerning him from district sections should be sent to the Moscow Central District of Ochrana. Such information, photographs or identification details as may still exist might refer to KONOVALOV, PEDACHENKO or LUISKOVO either individually or collectively. If documents held by you do not contain these names, they should also be examined for any information concerning a man, answering the description of the above, who was wanted for the murder of a woman in Paris in 1886, *of the murder of five women in the East Quarter of London in 1888* and again of the murder of a woman in Petrograd in 1891.

KONOVALOV's description is as follows:

Born 1857 at Torshok, Tver. Height, medium. Eyes, dark blue. Profession, junior surgeon. General description: usually wore black moustache, curled and waxed at ends. Heavy, black eyebrows. Broad-shouldered, but slight build. Known to disguise himself as a woman on occasion and was arrested when in women's clothes in Petrograd before his detention in the asylum where he died.

[Our italics]

Donald Rumbelow has argued that this request for information reveals some uncertainty on the part of the Ochrana concerning the identity of the man known to have died in an asylum, and his crimes.

All subsequent efforts to trace this copy of *Ochrana Gazette* have failed. The anachronistic name 'Petrograd' for the city that was St Petersburg in 1909 and subsequently Leningrad has encouraged researchers to look through the files for 1914–17 in addition to the date specified by McCormick.

See under **France, murders in** for the possible Paris victim; under **Konovalov** and **Pedachenko** for further details about them and the improbability of their being one and the same person; under *The Identity of Jack the Ripper* for a caveat concerning uncorroborated material therein.

ODELL, ROBIN IAN (b. 1935)

Crime historian. Author of *Jack the Ripper: In Fact and Fiction* (1965).

Co-author with **Colin Wilson** of *Jack the Ripper: Summing Up and Verdict* (1987). Head of publications for an industrial research organisation; began scientific career in university zoology and physiology laboratories; worked in military hospitals with the RAMC during national service. F. C. Watts Memorial Prize, 1957. International Humanist and Ethical Union Prize, 1960.

Jack the Ripper: In Fact and Fiction was his first book in the field of true-crime. Since then he has also written on Major Armstrong, on Craig and Bentley, and co-authored with J. H. H. Gaute *Murder Whereabouts* (1986), *Murder Whatdunnit* (1988), and the classic true-crime reference works *The Murderers' Who's Who* (1979) and *The New Murderers' Who's Who* (1990).

Mr Odell's work is always marked by care, detail, and freedom from sensationalism or absurd claims to have overturned past beliefs.

OGAN, JON
Researcher and theorist. Author of 'Martha Tabram – the Forgotten Ripper Victim' in *Journal of the Police Historical Society*, no. 5, 1990. Ogan argues that Tabram could have been a Ripper victim, and suggests **Puckridge** as the murderer. The authors were intrigued to learn that Mr Ogan had anticipated us in tracing **John Sanders**.

OLSSON, SVEN
Witness at Elizabeth Stride's inquest. As clerk to the Swedish Church at 36 Prince's Square, he had known Stride for 17 years, and corrected important biographical details.

See under **Elizabeth Stride**.

'ONE-ARMED LIZ'
Informant. Well-known East End character and friend of Elizabeth Stride, whom at first she identified as 'Wally Warden' or 'Annie Morris'. Talked freely to the press after the double murder.

Possibly **Elizabeth Burns**.

OPENSHAW, DR THOMAS HORROCKS (1856–1929)
Identified **Lusk kidney** as human. Student at London Hospital and University of London; thereafter consulting surgeon, specialising in orthopaedic surgery. Taught anatomy at London Hospital, and from 1887, Curator of its anatomical museum. A short, sturdy Lancashireman, known to all his friends as 'Tommy'.

When the Lusk kidney was sent to him for identification, he was reported in the press as saying it was a woman's 'ginny' kidney preserved in spirits of wine. Dr Openshaw immediately wrote to *The Times* that he had said it was human and preserved in spirits of wine; the other details were journalistic embellishments. (Cf. **F. S. Reed**.)

ORAM, JANE
Witness at Mary Ann Nichols' inquest as reported in *The Times*. Her evidence is identical with that ascribed in coroner **Wynne Baxter**'s summation to **Ellen Holland**, who is not described as appearing. It is the authors' belief that 'Oram' is merely reportorial mishearing of Mrs Holland's name.

Police surgeons **Dr Bagster Phillips** and **Dr Thomas Bond**

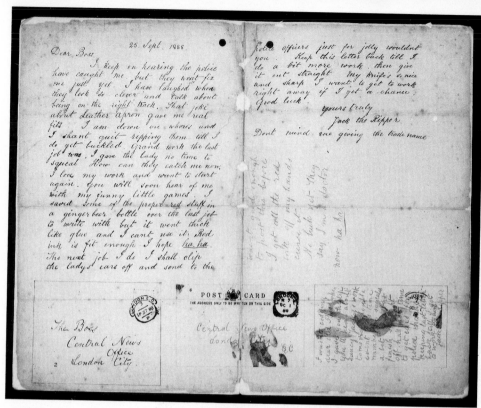

The **'Dear Boss' Letter** and the
'Saucy Jacky' Postcard which
gave the Ripper his nickname

George Lusk

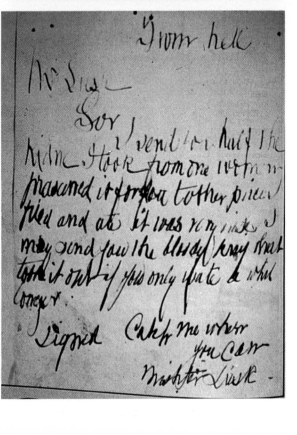

The Lusk Letter

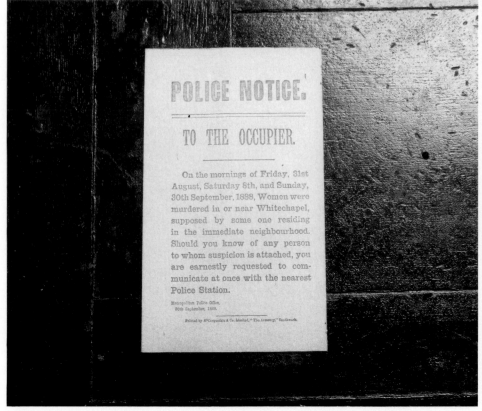

Prince Albert Victor, Duke of Clarence and Avondale

Sir William Gull

R. D. Stephenson (Dr D'Onston)

J. K. Stephen

Walter Sickert

Joe Barnett

Severin Klosowski

John Pizer: a newspaper picture Pizer said was
no more like himself than the Man in the Moon

Montague John Druitt

Artist's impression of an unknown suspect, used on American television for **Kosminski**

Aaron Kosminski's grave (small grave, centre right)

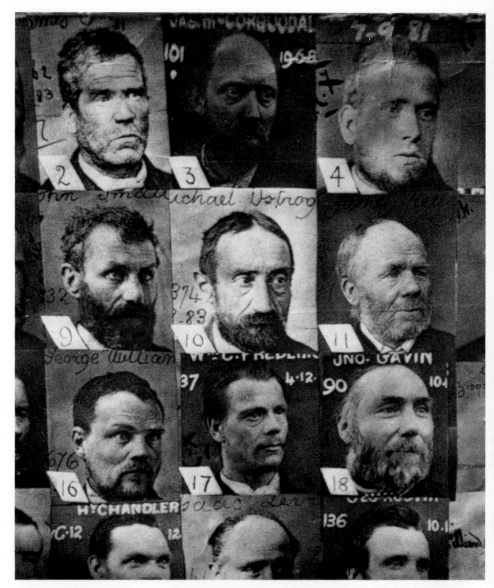

Michael Ostrog, centre

Michael Kidney, Elizabeth Stride's boyfriend, and **Elizabeth Tanner,** her landlady

Inspector Abberline interviews **Matthew Packer**

L. Forbes Winslow, alienist who believed he had identified the Ripper

Robert James Lees, spiritualist who believed he had identified the Ripper

Wynne Baxter, Middlesex Coroner

City Coroner's Court sitting on Catherine Eddowes

William Le Queux, unreliable journalist who reported the case and later accused **Dr Pedachenko**

G. R. Sims, journalist and confidant of Scotland Yard who believed he was a Ripper lookalike

READY FOR THE WHITECHAPEL FIEND. WOMEN SECRETLY ARMED.

Press impression of Whitechapel women preparing to face the Ripper

Illustrated press coverage of the last canonical murder

Christabel Aberconway's faithful reproduction of her father's (**Sir Melville Macnaghten**) private notes (copied in the early 1930s), which identify **Montague John Druitt** as the drowned suspect

...sible suspicion. Personally, & after much careful & deliberate consideration, I am inclined to exonerate the last 2, but I have always held strong opinions regarding no 1., and the more I think the matter over, the stronger do these opinions become. The truth, however, will never be known, and did indeed, at one time, lie at the bottom of the Thames, if my conjectures be correct. No 1. Mr M. J. Druitt a doctor of about 41 years of age & of fairly good family, who disappeared at the time of the Miller's Court murder, and whose body was found floating in the Thames on 3rd Dec: i.e. 7 weeks after the said murder. He (?) was said to have been in the water for a month or more — on it was found a season ticket between Blackheath & London. From private information I have little doubt but that his own family suspected this man of being the Whitechapel murderer; it was alleged that he was sexually insane

The old police files on the case

OSBORN STREET
See **Brick Lane/Osborn Street**. Named after the family of Sir Danvers Osborn of Chicksands Priory, Bedford, which inherited former property of the Montague-Dunk family in the district in 1771.

OSTROG, MICHAEL (born c. 1833)
aka Bertrand Ashley, Claude Clayton or Cayton, Dr Grant, Max Grief, Ashley Nabokoff, Orloff, Count Sobieski, Max Sobieski, and some twenty other aliases.
Suspect.

Confidence trickster and sneak thief, whom police records variously describe as a Russian, a Russian Pole and a Polish Jew. 5ft 11in tall with dark brown hair and grey eyes, normally dressed 'in a semi-clerical suit'. He had a scar on his right thumb and another on his right shin; two large moles on his right shoulder and one on the back of his neck; and by 1888 bore marks of flogging on his back.

He represented himself variously as a former surgeon in the Russian Navy and in the Imperial Russian Guard, sometimes claiming that he was compelled to leave the Russian Empire and evade the police after killing a man in a duel. The earliest account of him so far traced is in 1863, when under the name Max Grief he swindled hoteliers and others in Oxford where was sentenced to ten months imprisonment. In 1864 he was convicted at Cambridge as a rogue and a vagabond, and sentenced to three months. In July 1864 he appeared in Tunbridge Wells, where he represented himself as Count Sobieski, exiled son of the King of Poland. He ingratiated himself with respectable people from whom he obtained money and property. On leaving Tunbridge he went to Exeter where he was sentenced in December to eight months for fraud and felony.

In January 1866 he was acquitted of a fraud charge at Gloucester Quarter Sessions. He went to Kent, where on 19 March he stole a gold watch and other articles from Esther Carpenter in Maidstone. In Chatham he became friendly with Thomas White, from whom he stole a gold cross on 13 April, and gave it to Esther Brenchley – apparently a barmaid at the Bull Hotel, Rochester. On 26 April he stole two books from James Burch in Chatham. Under the name of Bertrand Ashley alias Ashley Nabokoff, and described as 'the great Russian swindler', his age given as twenty-two, he was tried before Mr Justice Channell at the Assizes that August. To Ostrog's manifest astonishment, Channell observed that light sentences had proved ineffective, and sentenced him to seven years penal servitude.

In May 1873 he was released on ticket-of-leave. Later in the month he stole valuable silver from Captain Milner at Woolwich Barracks. He then went to Windsor, staying from July to December at the South Western Railway Hotel. During this time he introduced himself to the probably homosexual assistant master of Eton Oscar Browning (subsequently dismissed for taking 'too personal an interest in the boys') and having been given the run of his library, stole two valuable books. He was traced to a house in the West End of London by Superintendent Dunham, but escaped over the roof with a loaded eight-chambered revolver. Then he returned to Eton with an accomplice and stole some valuable cups. (By a curious coincidence, **Melville Macnaghten** was captaining a cricket team playing against his old school at the time.) Ostrog now wrote to a one-time friend that he was returning to Russia and could be contacted via a Mr Carl Swedenburg, Poste Restante, Berlin.

In fact he went to Burton-on-Trent where he was arrested by Superintendent Oswell, despite his vehement protest that he was a Swedish doctor visiting the breweries. At the police station he produced his revolver, and was only prevented from firing it by Superintendent Oswell's seizing his wrist and turning the muzzle back on its owner. He was taken to Slough and confronted by Superintendent Dunham.

In January 1874 he conducted his own defence at Bucks Quarter Sessions, and seemed chagrined to receive a ten-year sentence on his conviction. He appears to have been released on licence without completing the full term, for in 1883 the *Police Gazette* issued a description of him as wanted for failure to report.

In July 1887 he stole a metal tankard from George Bigge at Woolwich Barracks, and was arrested after being chased across Woolwich Common by cadets. Described as well-educated and gentlemanly, he evidently looked younger than his age, which was now estimated as late thirties or early forties. He was wearing cricketing clothes and dropped a black Gladstone bag in his flight. He declared himself to be a visiting Belgian named Dr Bonge, and swallowed nux vomica on the way to the police station. He made a further attempt to starve himself to death while in custody.

At Woolwich Police Court he claimed to have been on his way to play cricket when a fit of sunstroke gave him an irresistible impulse to run a race, which he thought he was doing when the cadets chased him. At one point he took his overcoat from the rail, told the court he was going to France, and had to be prevented from leaving. He claimed to be a medical man who would be ruined if his friends in France heard of the affair; he also claimed to be the last of four brothers who had all committed suicide, and that his wife had been unfaithful to him. Held on remand until August, he was then confronted by Superintendent Dunham, who described him as 'one of the most desperate criminals who ever lived'. It emerged that he had attempted to throw himself under a train when en route to Holloway Prison.

In September 1887 he was tried at the Old Bailey and pleaded insanity, but Dr Herbert Hillier declared, 'He is only shamming', and Ostrog was sentenced to six months hard labour. On 30 September he was transferred from Wandsworth Prison to the Surrey Pauper Lunatic Asylum, suffering from mania; cause unknown. He was discharged on 10 March 1888 on expiry of sentence, described as recovered.

In October 1888, at the height of the Ripper scare, he was again described in the *Police Gazette* as wanted for failure to report, and it was observed that 'Special attention is called to this dangerous man'. His subsequent, and crucially important, career is as yet unknown.

He was first publicly named in connection with Jack the Ripper by **Donald McCormick** in the paperback edition of *The Identity of Jack the Ripper* (1962), where McCormick quotes a letter which he says **Basil Thomson** wrote at the end of his life (c. 1939), and which reads in part: 'When I was in Paris recently I learned in talks with the French that they had always thought that the "Ripper" was a Russian named Konovalov, who used the alias "Mikhail Ostrog", under which name Scotland Yard knew him as an ex-convict and medical student. They did not, however, describe him as a surgeon, but rather as a barber's assistant.'

Ostrog also has a curious half-life in footnotes to different editions of McCormick's *History of the Russian Secret Service* (published under his nom-de-plume, 'Richard Deacon'). Ostrog is variously described as a possible or definite alias used by Konovalov/Pedachenko. See under **The Identity of Jack the Ripper** for a caveat against McCormick's use of the Thomson letter. We note that the facts now known about Ostrog are quite different from those alleged about **Konovalov**.

Sir Melville Macnaghten, however, decisively named Ostrog as one of the three suspects, each far more likely than **Thomas Cutbush** to be Jack the Ripper. He described him thus in 1894:

MICHAEL OSTROG, a mad Russian doctor and a convict and unquestionably a homicidal maniac. This man was said to have been habitually cruel to women, and for a long time was known to have carried about with him surgical knives and other instruments; his antecedents were of the very worst and his whereabouts at the time of the Whitechapel murders could never be satisfactorily accounted for. He is still alive.

Thus the Aberconway version of Macnaghten's memorandum. The Scotland Yard version includes the observation that he was 'subsequently detained in a lunatic asylum as a homicidal maniac'. It should be noted that 'antecedents' is police parlance for 'criminal record'.

In *Mysteries of Police and Crime*, **Major Arthur Griffiths** follows Macnaghten very closely, without naming the three suspects, and gives a little extra detail in his account of Ostrog:

The second possible criminal was a Russian doctor, also insane, who had been a convict both in England and in Siberia. This man was in the habit of carrying about surgical knives and instruments in his pockets; his antecedents were of the very worst, and at the time of the Whitechapel murders he was in hiding, or, at least his whereabouts were never exactly known.

Outside the alleged letter quoted variously by McCormick, Sir Basil Thomson did in fact make one oblique published reference to Ostrog, saying in *The Story of Scotland Yard* that 'the belief of C.I.D. officers at the time was that [the murders] were the work of an insane Russian doctor and that the man escaped arrest by committing suicide at the end of 1888'. This appears to combine Ostrog with Druitt.

No public reference to Ostrog or any qualified Russian doctor has been found in the press prior to the publication of Major Griffiths' book. One press observation is very speculatively linked to him. **N. P. Warren** found an account in the *Daily Telegraph* for 20 October 1888 of a man who asked Emily Marsh at her father's shop in Jubilee Street for **George Lusk**'s address. She gave it him without the house number, and it was in that form that the parcel containing the **Lusk kidney** was addressed. The man fitted the general description of Ostrog, except for having an Irish accent and 'clerical costume' rather than a 'semi-clerical suit'.

The demonstrable facts support Macnaghten's suspicion of Ostrog to the extent that we know the police were indeed looking for him in October 1888 (though not necessarily in connection with the Whitechapel murders). Until his movements that October and November are known, or some other suspect is conclusively shown to have been the Ripper, Ostrog remains a plausible historical suspect.

OUTRAM, DETECTIVE SERGEANT ROBERT

Went to scene of Catharine Eddowes' murder.

Joined City Police 1865. 1867, allocated to plain-clothes patrol. March 1876, Divisional detective; May, same year, Detective Sergeant. 1890, Detective-Inspector. Retired 1895. Most of his work (as was common for a City detective) involved financial fraud.

Talking with Detectives **Halse** and **Marriott** at southern corner of Houndsditch when they received news of the murder, and immediately went to Mitre Square.

P

PACKER, MATTHEW

Berner Street fruiterer whose statement about Elizabeth Stride was taken personally by **Sir Charles Warren**, yet who was not called as an inquest witness.

An elderly man residing at 44 Berner Street, two doors down from Dutfield's Yard, Packer and his wife and their lodgers Sarah Harris and Harry Douglas were all questioned by **Sergeant Stephen White** on 30 September 1888 in house-to-house enquiries following the murder. All said they had seen and heard nothing suspicious, and Packer said he saw nobody standing in the street or going up toward the Yard when he closed the shutters of his front window, from which he sold fruit, at 12.30 a.m.

The police were correspondingly disconcerted when the *Evening News* of 4 October reported that private detectives **Grand** and **Batchelor** had elicited from Packer that a woman with a white flower pinned to her dark jacket had come to his shop at 11.45 p.m., 29 September, in the company of a stout, clerkly man about 5ft 7in in height, with a wide-awake hat, dark clothes, and a sharply commanding manner. This man bought half a pound of black grapes which he and the woman ate as they stood opposite the shop in the rain for about half an hour, before passing over the road to glance at the **International Workingmen's Educational Club**, from which community singing could be heard. Knowing that **Diemschütz** and others had described a grapestalk in Elizabeth Stride's left hand, and **Mrs Eva Harstein** had seen a grapestalk and some white flower petals in the passage after the body had been removed from Dutfield's Yard, the detectives and the newspaper were satisfied that Packer was describing Stride, although other witnesses had thought she wore a red flower.

On 2 October, Grand and Batchelor recovered a grapestalk from the rubbish in the drain where the police had washed the Yard down. They took Packer to the City Mortuary in Golden Lane to test his veracity by showing him the body without revealing it was the Mitre Square victim and not the Berner Street victim. Packer unhesitatingly said he had never seen Catharine Eddowes before, and on 4 October the *News* went to press with the major story that Packer had seen and spoken to 'the murderer'. The *News* reporter asked if any detective or policeman had inquired whether he had sold grapes to anyone that night, urging him to be careful in answering, 'for this may prove a serious business for the London police'. The paper capitalised his answer: 'Except a gentleman who is a private detective. NO DETECTIVE OR POLICEMAN HAS EVER ASKED ME A SINGLE QUESTION NOR COME NEAR MY SHOP TO FIND OUT IF I KNEW ANYTHING ABOUT THE GRAPES THE MURDERED WOMAN HAD BEEN EATING BEFORE HER THROAT WAS CUT!!!'

On the afternoon of 4 October, Grand and Batchelor took Packer to St George's-in-the-East mortuary where he identified Stride as the woman he had seen. On their return they met Sergeant White, despached to Berner Street by **Chief Inspector Moore** to re-interview Packer and take him to identify Stride. Packer told White, 'I believe she bought some grapes at my shop about 12 o'clock on Saturday.'

At 4.00 p.m. Grand and Batchelor took Packer in a hansom cab to Scotland Yard to see Sir Charles Warren. Warren took down the following statement in his own hand:

Matthew Packer

Keeps a small shop in Berner Str has a few grapes in window. Black & white. On Sat night about 11 p.m. a young man from 25–30 – about 5.7. with long black coat buttoned up – soft felt hat, kind of hunter hat

rather broad shoulders – rather quick in speaking. rough voice. I sold him ½ pound black grapes 3d. A woman came up with him from Back Church end (the lower end of street) she was dressed in black frock and jacket, fur round bottom of jacket a black crape bonnet, she was playing with a flower like a geranium white outside and red inside. I identify the woman at the St George's mortuary as the one I saw that night. – They passed by as though they were going up Com[mercial] Road, but instead of going up they crossed to the other side of the road to the Board School, & were there for about ½ an hour till I shd. say 11.30. talking to one another. I then shut up my shutters. After they passed over opposite to my shop, they went near to the Club for a few minutes apparently listening to the music. I saw no more of them after I shut up my shutters. I put the man down as a young clerk.

He had a frock coat on – no gloves.

He was about 1½ inch or 2 or 3 inch – a little bit higher than she was.

The statement is initialled CW. and dated 4.10.88. It is the only statement to police or press in which Packer places all these events between 11.00 and 11.30. But where he places them an hour later in his statement reported by White, Warren has queried this in the margins and reverted to the times given to him personally.

Despite the clear importance of Packer's testimony, he was not called as a witness at the inquest. (Cf. **Mrs Fanny Mortimer, Israel Schwartz**.) The police responded to the *Evening News* attack with an immediate statement that the greengrocer was unreliable and contradicted himself. They said there was no evidence that there were any grapes in Elizabeth Stride's hand.

Packer certainly tended to seek publicity. He returned to the press at the end of October, saying that on the 27th he had again seen Stride's male companion, who had leaped on a tram in Commercial Road when Packer called a shoeblack's attention to him. He now claimed that he had also seen him several times prior to the murder. In the second week of November he claimed that a man buying rabbits had told him that the Ripper was his cousin in America. The *Illustrated Police News* believed that the police took this story seriously enough to have **Inspector Abberline** take the details from Packer.

PALEY, BRUCE
Theorist. Author of 'A New Theory on the Jack the Ripper Murders' in *True Crime*, April 1982.

A south Londoner, Paley is relatively historically responsible. He does not select remote or highly specious data on which to construct a sensational imaginative edifice, but boldly takes the solution of **Joseph Barnett** as the most probable murderer. This compels him to deduce that the motive for the previous murders was to frighten Mary Jane Kelly off the streets. But his work on Barnett's background is impressive, and his conclusions are presented cautiously.

PALMER, AMELIA (often described as FARMER)

Witness at Annie Chapman's inquest. The fullest press account of her, describing her husband, so names her, for which reason we have preferred Palmer to Farmer. Pale-faced, dark-haired wife of ex-soldier and dock labourer Henry Palmer, she washed and cleaned for East End Jewish residents following an accident which limited her husband's ability to work. She lived at 30 **Dorset Street** for four years and was a friend of Annie Chapman, concerning whom she gave police some biographical evidence. She wrongly described Annie's former husband as Frederick Chapman, veterinary surgeon. (Cf. **John Chapman**.)

She saw Chapman several times in the week before the murder. Early in the week, in Dorset Street, Annie complained of feeling unwell. The following day, beside Spitalfields Church, she again complained of illness, and said she had eaten and drunk nothing all day. Palmer gave her twopence, warning her not to spend it on rum. At the end of the week the two again met in Dorset Street. Chapman said she felt too ill to do anything, but added, 'It's no good my giving way. I must pull myself together and go out and get some money or I shall have no lodgings.'

PANCHENKO, DR DIMITRI

In his book *The Medical Murderer* (1957) Rupert Furneaux writes of a St Petersburg doctor named Panchenko who was a supplier of poisons and also suspected of being involved in several murders.

In 1911 Patrick O'Brien de Lacy, apparently a descendant of the Irish Kings and a member of the hereditary nobility of the Province of Grodno, married the daughter of General and Madame Buturlin. They were extremely wealthy, but had bequeathed the bulk of their fortune to their son. De Lacy decided to murder his brother-in-law and then his in-laws by feeding them cholera and diphtheria germs, an epidemic of both diseases at that time raging in St Petersburg, and he offered Dr Panchenko 620,000 roubles to procure the germs and help in their administration. Unfortunately for de Lacy, his excited explanation of his plans to his mistress, Madame Muraviora, was overheard and reported to General Buturlin following the death of his son. Panchenko was arrested and confessed, receiving a fifteen-year prison sentence. De Lacy was imprisoned for life.

More needs to be known about Dr Panchenko, but his name, his residence in St Petersburg, and his involvement in several murders, suggest that he could be the original of Dr Pedachenko.

PARDONS

Extraordinarily, a pardon was offered on 10 November 1888 'to any accomplice, not being a person who contrived or actually committed the murder' who gave information leading to the murderer's apprehension and conviction. This was expressly confined to the murder of Mary Jane Kelly alone, Home Secretary **Henry Matthews** explaining to the Commons on 23 November that 'In the case of Kelly there were certain circumstances which were wanting in earlier cases, and which made it more probable that there were other persons, who, at any rate after the crime, had assisted the murderer.'

Matthews himself had laid down the general rule on pardons: that they should only be granted 'where more than one person appears to have been concerned in a crime with varying degrees of guilt and where all reasonable efforts have been made without success to discover the criminals'.

Home Office Permanent Secretary **Godfrey Lushington** offered cogent reasons in October for not offering any pardon with respect to the Whitechapel murders: that it would make the public fear an accomplice as well as a murderer; and that it would be interpreted as an admission of police failure.

It is not known what circumstances persuaded Matthews that the Kelly murder, unlike its predecessors, invited the offer of a pardon; nor what evidence for any accomplice existed, beyond the possibility that unusually bloodstained clothing would have to be disposed of after the Miller's Court atrocity; or, indeed, whether it was merely a palliative to public opinion. See under **Dr Phillips**.

Cf. **Rewards**.

PARKE, ERNEST (1860–1944)

Journalist. Educ. Stratford-on-Avon Grammar School. Worked on the *Star*, and in 1889 as editor of the *North London Press* made the first public allusion to the possibility that **Prince Albert Victor** might be implicated in the **Cleveland Street Scandal**. For this *lèse majesté* he was tried and imprisoned on fabricated charges. Subsequently he became a director of the Northern Newspaper Co., Darlington, and JP for Warwickshire.

T. P. O'Connor, the Irish Nationalist who founded and edited the *Star*, wrote of Parke in his autobiography: 'He might be trusted to work up any sensational news of the day, and he helped with "Jack the Ripper", to make gigantic circulations hitherto unparalleled in evening journalism.'

PASH, FLORENCE (1862–1951)

Alleged friend of Mary Jane Kelly. Artist. Daughter of shoemaker Daniel John Pash. Married (1) Albert Alexander Humphrey; (2) Major C. T. Holland. One son, Cecil. All predeceased her. Friend and close associate of **Walter Sickert**.

According to **Jean Overton Fuller**, she told elements of the **Joseph Sickert/Stephen Knight** story in 1948; especially hinting that a seagull in a painting by Walter Sickert was a clue to the Ripper crimes (cf. **Sir William Gull**) and giving information, allegedly from Walter Sickert, that Joseph Sickert was Walter's illegitimate son.

Ms Fuller says that Mary Jane Kelly was a friend of Florence Pash, who usually described her as a Welsh or Irish woman who fell to prostitution and once lived close to a house of ill repute. She also said that Kelly had once washed floors in Cardiff Infirmary. Ms Fuller also says that Florence Pash was accompanying **Alice Margaret Crook** in 1892 when the alleged attempt to run her down was made, and that Florence Pash believed Walter Sickert was being blackmailed by Mary Kelly over his supposed

involvement in the alleged liaison between **Prince Albert Victor** and **Annie Crook**.
See **Sickert and the Ripper Crimes**.

PATRICK, POLICE CONSTABLE JOHN, 91H (b. 1860)
Arresting officer in **Aaron Davis Cohen**'s case. Joined Metropolitan Police, 1880; warrant no. 65077. Served in H Division (Whitechapel) until 1891, when transferred to V Division and promoted sergeant. Retired, 1906, with rank of Sergeant and R (Reserve) standing, denoting high competence and reliability.
On 7 December 1888, Patrick appeared as the complainant (i.e., arresting officer) charging Cohen before Thames Magistrates with being a wandering lunatic (i.e., a person whose mental condition made him unable to look after himself, and who had no apparent family or friends able or willing to care for him). When the magistrates ordered him to be sent for observation to Whitechapel Workhouse Infirmary, Patrick delivered him there at 5.00 p.m.

PAUL, ROBERT
Witness at Mary Ann Nichols' inquest.
A carter, employed at Corbett's Court on the corner of **Hanbury Street** and **Commercial Street**, he was on his way to work from his home, 30 Foster Street, Whitechapel, at about 3.45 a.m. when **Charles Cross** drew his attention to Nichols' body lying in **Buck's Row**. Paul felt her hands and face, and said, 'I think she's breathing, but it's very little if she is.' The two went on together in search of a policeman, finding **Police Constable Mizen** at the corner of Hanbury Street and Baker's Row (Vallance Road). Cross was subsequently puzzled by Paul's sudden disappearance when he slipped into Corbett's Court, while Cross was proceeding toward the City.
Despite Paul's instant availability for press interviews, it seems to have taken the police some time to identify and find him, and he did not appear at a hearing until the inquest had reopened after a fortnight's adjournment. Walter Dew incorrectly recalled that 'The police made repeated appeals for him to come forward, but he never did so.' It is possible that Dew was confusing Paul with the **unidentified man in Buck's Row** whom **Inspector Abberline** seems to have been seeking at the time of the inquest.

PAUMIER, MRS
Believed she saw the Ripper. Young chestnut vendor working on corner of Widegate Street and Sandys Row (about two minutes walk from **Dorset Street**) on the morning of 9 November 1888. A man about 5ft 6ins tall, dressed in black coat, speckled trousers and black silk hat, approached from Artillery Row (Dorset Street direction). He had a black moustache and a black shiny bag, and said to her, 'I suppose you have heard about the murder in Dorset Street?' Mrs Paumier had. The man grinned, and said, 'I know more about it than you do', walking away down Sandys Row. Mrs Paumier believed him to be the man who had accosted **Sarah Roney** and her friend.

'PEARLY POLL' (b. 1838)
See under **Mary Ann Connolly**.

PEARSE, POLICE CONSTABLE RICHARD, 922 City

Resident of **Mitre Square**. Lived at no. 3 (northwest side of Square, adjacent to Kearley and Tonge's warehouse) with wife and family. He went to bed around 12.20 a.m., 30 September 1888, and slept through all the disturbance until called by a policeman at 2.20 a.m. following the discovery of Eddowes' body and arrival of doctors and police reinforcements. He could plainly see the spot where the murder was committed from his bedroom window.

PEDACHENKO, DR ALEXANDER (1857?–1908?)

alias **Count Luiskovo**.

Non-contemporaneous alleged suspect. Native of Tver where he joined the staff of the Maternity Hospital. At some time, according to a subsequently untraced Glasgow evening newspaper article by Hector Cairns, cited by **Donald McCormick**, he was a surgeon in Glasgow; also a member of Russian Secret Service. In 1888, when known to Ochrana (Secret Police) as 'the greatest and boldest of all Russian criminal lunatics', he was living with his sister in Westmoreland Road, Walworth. With Ochrana approval, he committed the Ripper murders, assisted by a friend named **Levitski** and a tailoress named **Winberg**. The Ochrana's aim was allegedly to discredit the Metropolitan Police, who were perceived by Czarists as irresponsibly tolerant of emigrant dissidents and anarchists living in (especially) the East End. When the plot succeeded and **Sir Charles Warren** resigned in disgrace, Ochrana smuggled Pedachenko to Moscow, destined for exile to Yakutsk. In fact, five months later he was caught red-handed trying to murder a woman called Vogak, and sent to a lunatic asylum where he died.

All the above, with the exception of the Cairns article, is, according to **William Le Queux** in *Things I Know* (1928), allegedly drawing on a manuscript document dictated by **Rasputin**, which itself purportedly uses information from the Ochrana, **Nideroest** and **Zverieff**.

Donald McCormick, citing Dr Dutton's *Chronicles of Crime*, adds that Pedachenko was the double of **Severin Klosowski**; that he worked in Westmoreland Road, Walworth, as a barber-surgeon in the employ of a hairdresser named William Delhaye; that he also assisted a Walworth doctor at St Saviour's Infirmary, which was attended by victims Tabram, Chapman, Nichols and Kelly. Also that **Wolf Levisohn** advised **Inspector Abberline** to investigate a barber in Walworth in connection with the Ripper murders. McCormick identified the doctor at St Saviour's as John Frederick Williams.

According to a lithographed copy of the **Ochrana Gazette** for January 1909, shown to Mr McCormick by **Prince Belloselski**, but as yet untraced by subsequent researchers, the Ochrana knew Pedachenko to be an alias of **Vassily Konovalov**, the murderer of a woman in Paris in 1886 as well as the five Ripper victims of 1888.

None of the above sources and lines of transmission, with the exception of McCormick's discovery of the existence of Delhaye and Dr Williams, and the possible exception of Hector Cairns, can be regarded as historically reliable. Although a Russian poisoner named **Dr Panchenko** has been traced by **N. P. Warren**, there is no solid evidence for the existence of Dr Pedachenko. Apart from both being described as natives of Tver, there is no similarity between Pedachenko and the alleged Ochrana description of

Vassily Konovalov; nor does the latter resemble the three Russian criminals of that name traced by N. P. Warren.

PENNETT, POLICE CONSTABLE WILLIAM, 239H
Discovered the **Pinchin Street** torso. On beat duty at 5.15 a.m., 10 September 1889, he discovered the torso of a woman, lacking head and legs, under a railway arch in Pinchin Street. He summoned assistance, and then assisted in arrests of two sailors and a bootblack found sleeping under adjacent arches.

PHELPS, SERGEANT (City Police)
Assisted **Inspector Izzard** and **Sergeant Dudman** with crowd control at **Mitre Square** after Catharine Eddowes' murder.

PHILLIPS, ANNIE (b. 1865)
Catharine Eddowes' daughter and witness at her inquest. Wife of a lamp-black packer, resident at Dilston Road, Southwark Park Road, at time of murders. Last saw her mother twenty-five months previously, at which time Annie was confined and paid her mother to attend her. She had not seen her father (**Thomas Conway**) and brothers since they ceased living with the Phillipses at Acre Street, Southwark Park Road, eighteen months previously. The entire family withheld addresses from Catharine, fearing that she would try to obtain money from them.

Mrs Phillips said her parents had parted on bad terms seven or eight years previously because of Catharine's drinking. Thomas Conway was a teetotaller. He knew that Catharine subsequently lived with **John Kelly**. He had been on fairly bad terms with the Phillipses when he parted from them. According to **John Kelly**, Catharine went to Bermondsey on the last day of her life to try to find Annie and borrow money from her. If she made the attempt, she failed to find her. (See under **Catharine Eddowes** for Mrs Phillips's changes of address in Bermondsey district.)

PHILLIPS, DR GEORGE BAGSTER (1834–97)
H Division Police Surgeon; conducted or attended post-mortems on four of the five Ripper victims, and was called to the murder sites of three. MRCS, Lic. Midwif., Lic. Soc. Apoth., 1861. Police surgeon from 1865. Residence and surgery, 2 Spital Square, Spitalfields.

Called to examine Annie Chapman's body at 6.20 a.m., 8 September 1888, he arrived at 29 Hanbury Street c. 6.30. In addition to the body itself, he noted a piece of muslin and a comb in a paper case (presumed to be the contents of Chapman's torn pocket) placed in order at her feet. He attended the inquest on 14 September 1888, and was reported as describing the body *in situ* thus:

The left arm was placed across the left breast. The legs were drawn up, the feet resting on the ground, and the knees turned outwards. The face was swollen and turned on the right side. The tongue protruded between the front teeth, but not beyond the lips. The tongue was evidently much swollen. The front teeth were perfect as far as the first molar, top and bottom, and very fine teeth they were. The body was terribly mutilated . . . The stiffness of the limbs was not marked, but was evidently commencing. He noticed that the throat was dissevered deeply; that the incisions through the skin were jagged, and reached right round the neck . . . On the wooden paling between the yard in question and the next, smears of blood, corresponding to where the head of the deceased lay, were to be seen. These were about 14in. from the ground, and immediately above the part where the blood lay that had flowed from the neck . . .

[Answering questions from the coroner]: He should say that the instrument used at the throat and abdomen was the same. It must have been a very sharp knife with a thin narrow blade, and must have been at least 6in. to 8in. in length, probably longer. He should say that the injuries could not have been inflicted by a bayonet or sword-bayonet. They could have been done by such an instrument as a medical man used for *post-mortem* purposes, but the ordinary surgical cases might not contain such an instrument. Those used by slaughtermen, well ground down, might have caused them. He thought the knives used by those in the leather trade would not be long enough in the blade. There were indications of anatomical knowledge which were only less indicated in consequence of haste. The whole of the body was not present, the absent portions being from the abdomen. The mode in which these portions were extracted showed some anatomical knowledge . . . He should say that the deceased had been dead at least two hours, and probably more, when he first saw her; but it was right to mention that it was a fairly cool morning, and that the body would be more apt to cool rapidly from its having lost a great quantity of blood. There was no evidence . . . of a struggle having taken place. He was positive that the deceased entered the yard alive . . .

A handkerchief was round the throat of the deceased when he saw it early in the morning. He should say it was not tied on after the throat was cut.

On Saturday afternoon he made his post mortem examination at Whitechapel Workhouse Infirmary Mortuary: an inadequate and insanitary shed about which he protested, with the full support of coroner **Wynne Baxter**. His autopsy observations were reported thus:

He noticed the same protrusion of the tongue. There was a bruise over the right temple. On the upper eyelid there was a bruise, and there were two distinct bruises, each the size of a man's thumb, on the forepart of the top of the chest. The stiffness of the limbs was now well marked. There was a bruise over the middle part of the bone of the right hand. There was an old scar on the left of the frontal bone. The stiffness was more noticeable on the left side, especially in the fingers, which were partly closed. There was an abrasion over the ring finger, with distinct markings of a ring or rings. The throat had been severed as before described. The incisions into the skin indicated that they had been made from the left side of the neck. There were two distinct clean cuts on the left side of the spine. They were parallel with each other and separated by about half an inch. The muscular structures appeared as though an attempt had been made to separate the bones of the neck. There were various other mutilations of the body, but he was of opinion that they occurred subsequent to the death of the woman, and to the large escape of blood from the division of the neck. At this point Dr. Phillips said that, as from these injuries he was satisfied as to the cause of death, he thought that he had better not go into further details of the mutilations which could only be painful to the feelings of the jury and the public

The Coroner decided to allow that course to be adopted. Witness, continuing, said, – The cause of death was apparent from the injuries he had described. From these appearances he was of opinion that the breathing was interfered with previous to death, and that death arose from syncope, or failure of the heart's action in consequence of loss of blood caused by severance of the throat . . .

[Answering questions from the Coroner]: The deceased was far advanced in disease of the lungs and membranes of the brain, but they had nothing to do with the cause of death. The stomach contained a little food, but there was not any sign of fluid. There was no appearance of the deceased having taken alcohol, but there were signs of great deprivation and he should say she had been badly fed. He was convinced she had not taken any strong alcohol for some hours before her death. The injuries were certainly not self-inflicted. The bruises on the face were evidently recent, especially about the chin and the sides of the jaw, but the bruises in front of the chest and temple were of longer standing – probably of days. He was of the opinion that the person who cut the deceased's throat took hold of her by the chin, and then commenced the incision from left to right. He thought it was highly probable that a person could call out, but with regard to an idea that she might have been gagged he could only point to the swollen face and protruding tongue, both of which were signs of suffocation.

The following important points in the report should be noted:
(1) The bruises from Chapman's fight with Eliza Cooper (see under **Annie Chapman**) were clearly distinguishable from the bruises caused by her murderer.
(2) The bloodstains on the fence (which included one described in the press as a very strong splash, as if from arterial bleeding) were beside her head and neck, suggesting her throat was cut as she lay on the ground.
(3) Signs of asphyxiation prior to throat-cutting. (Cf. under **Francis Camps.**)
(4) Time of death placed at least one hour before **Mrs Darrell** testified to seeing her alive. And – importantly – the police preferred Phillips' testimony (see under **Inspector Chandler; Home Office Files**), though today we note the imprecision of his estimate, based on impressions of rigor mortis and body cooling, unsupported by rectal or liver temperatures.
(5) No trace of spirits or large quantities of alcohol consumed. (Cf. **Timothy Donovan, Frederick Stevens.**)
(6) Murder committed on the spot. (Cf. **John Netley.**)
(7) Unsuccessful attempt to decapitate, but handkerchief round neck not, as some writers have suggested, placed to hold the head on.
(8) Evidence of anatomical knowledge.

Dr Phillips was recalled on 19 September to give the further evidence of posthumous mutilation omitted in his original testimony. He deferred to the coroner, though regretting his decision 'in the interests of justice'. Baxter insisted that the evidence must be given 'for various reasons which he need not then enumerate', and suggested that not all medical men might agree with Phillips that the mutilations occurred after death. Both agreed that the evidence was indecent, so the court was cleared of women and boys, and the daily press refrained from reporting parts of it. The following description is, therefore, a composite from *The Times* and a special report in the *Lancet*:

The abdomen had been entirely laid open: the intestines, severed from their mesenteric attachments, had been lifted out of the body and placed on the shoulder of the corpse; whilst from the pelvis, the uterus and its appendages with the upper portion of the vagina and the posterior two-thirds of the bladder, had been entirely removed. No trace of these parts could be found and the incisions were cleanly cut, avoiding the rectum, and dividing the vagina low enough to avoid injury to the *cervix uteri*. Obviously the work was that of an expert – of one, at least, who had such knowledge of anatomical or pathological examinations as to be enabled to secure the pelvic organs with one sweep of the knife, which must therefore have been at least five or six inches in length, probably more. The appearance of the cuts confirmed him in the opinion that the instrument, like the one which divided the neck, had been of a very sharp character. The mode in which the knife had been used seemed to indicate great anatomical knowledge.

[In answer to questions from the coroner]: He thought he himself could not have performed all the injuries he described, even without a struggle, under a quarter of an hour. If he had done it in a deliberate way such as would fall to the duties of a surgeon it probably would have taken him the best part of an hour.

This is the firmest statement made by any doctor ascribing surgical expertise to the Ripper. We note that the lower cut extracting the uterus was indeed exceptionally impressive, which makes the contrasting injury to the bladder the more surprising (cf. **Doctor theories**).

At 1.20 a.m., 30 September 1888, Dr Phillips was summoned to Leman Street Police Station, and directed from there to Berner Street, where he arrived around 2.00 a.m. At Elizabeth Stride's inquest on 3 October, he reported:

The body was lying on the near side, with the face turned toward the wall, the head up the yard and the feet toward the street. The left arm was extended and there was a packet of cachous in the left hand . . . The right arm was over the belly. The back of the hand and wrist had on it clotted blood. The legs were drawn up with the feet close to the wall. The body and face were warm and the hand cold. The legs were quite warm. Deceased had a silk handkerchief round her neck, and it appeared to be slightly torn. I have since ascertained it was cut. This corresponded with the right angle of the jaw. The throat was deeply gashed, and there was an abrasion of the skin about 1½in. in diameter, apparently stained with blood, under her right brow. At 3 p.m. on Monday at St George's Mortuary . . . Dr. Blackwell and I made a *post-mortem* examination . . . *Rigor mortis* was still thoroughly marked. There was mud on the left side of the face and it was matted in the head . . . The body was fairly nourished. Over both shoulders, especially the right, and under the collar-bone and in front of the chest there was a blueish discoloration, which I have watched and have seen on two occasions since. There was a clean-cut incision on the neck. It was 6in. in length and commenced 2½in. in a straight line below the angle of the jaw, ½in. over an undivided muscle, and then becoming deeper, dividing the sheath. The cut was very clean and deviated a little downwards. The artery and other vessels contained in the sheath were all cut through. The cut through the tissues on the right side was more superficial, and tailed off to about 2in. below the right angle of the jaw. The deep vessels on that side were uninjured. From this it was evident that the haemorrhage was caused through the partial severance of the left carotid artery. Decomposition had commenced in the skin. Dark brown spots were on the anterior surface of the left chin. There was a deformity in the bones of the right leg, which was not straight, but bowed forwards. There was no recent external injury save to the neck. The body being washed more thoroughly I could see some healing sores. The lobe of the left ear was torn as if from the removal or wearing through of an earring, but it was thoroughly healed. On removing the scalp there was no sign of bruising or extravasation of blood . . . The heart was small, the left ventricle firmly contracted, and the right slightly so. There was no clot in the pulmonary artery, but the right ventricle was full of dark clot. The left was firmly contracted so as to be absolutely empty. The stomach was large, and the mucous membrane only congested. It contained partly digested food, apparently consisting of cheese, potato and farinaceous powder. All the teeth on the left lower jaw were absent . . . Examining her jacket, I found that while there was a small amount on the right side, the left was well plastered with mud . . .

[In answer to the coroner's questions]: The cause of death is undoubtedly from the loss of blood from the left carotid artery and the division of the windpipe. The blood had run down the waterway to within a few inches of the side entrance of the club. Roughly estimating it I should say there was an unusual flow of blood considering the stature and nourishment of the body.

Dr Phillips was recalled to the resumed inquest on 5 October, and answered further questions thus:

he had made a re-examination with regard to the missing palate, and from very careful examination of the roof of the mouth he found that there was no injury to either the hard or the soft palate. He had also carefully examined the handkerchiefs, and had come to the conclusion that the stains on the larger handkerchief were those of fruit. He was convinced that the deceased had not swallowed the skin or inside of a grape within many hours of her death. The apparent abrasion which was found on washing the flesh was not an abrasion at all, as the skin was entire underneath . . . He found that the deceased was seized by the shoulders, pressed on the ground, and that the perpetrator of the deed was on the left side when he inflicted the wound. He was of the opinion that the cut was made from left to right of the deceased and from that, therefore, arose the unlikelihood of such a long knife having inflicted the wound described in the neck. The knife was not sharp pointed; but round and an inch across. There was nothing in the cut to show an incision of the point of any weapon . . .

[H]e could not form any account of how the deceased's right hand became covered with blood. It was a mystery. He was taking it as a fact that the hand always remained in the position he found it in resting across her body. Deceased must have been alive within an hour of his seeing her. The injuries would only take a few seconds to inflict; it might have been done in two seconds. He could not say with certainty whether the sweets being found in her hand indicated that the deed had been done suddenly . . . There was a great dissimilarity between this case and Chapman's. In the latter the neck was severed all round down to the vertebral column, the vertebral bone being enlarged with two sharp cuts, and there being an evident attempt to separate the bones . . . The murderer would not necessarily be bloodstained, for the commencement of the wound and the injury to the vessels would be away from him, and the stream of blood, for stream it would be, would be directed away from him, and towards the waterway already mentioned . . . He had reason to believe that the deceased was lying on the ground when the wound was inflicted.

See under **Elizabeth Stride** for comments on Phillips's observations re the knife, grapes, and Stride's teeth.

It is impossible to work out what kind of assault Phillips envisaged. He explicitly described Stride's extremely muddy left side and head; believed that the murderer *pushed* her to the ground *from* her left side, began his cut at the left side of her throat while himself on her left, yet would have been clear of the stream of blood from her left carotid artery which flowed entirely between her left side and the wall. This is all geometrically impossible, and there is either misreporting or muddled thinking involved. **Dr Blackwell** originally suggested that Stride had been pulled over backwards by her scarf, and might have had her throat cut before she fell. Later he seems to have concurred with Phillips that she had been pressed to the ground by the shoulders. Assuming she was between the wall and her assailant, the position of the head shows that he must have pressed her to his left, and as she landed on her left side, this would suggest that she was facing the wall at the time (cf. under **Francis Camps**). But it seems utterly impossible for the murderer thereafter to have been on her left.

The interesting comparison with Annie Chapman shows that Chapman's neck had been mutilated in exactly the same way as Mary Jane Kelly's.

Phillips attended Catharine Eddowes' post mortem, and although the press reports do not mention his denying the skill of the Mitre Square murderer, Coroner Wynne Baxter's summing-up gives an accurate précis of his evidence, so it is almost certainly from Phillips that Baxter took the point that there were 'unskilful injuries . . . in the case in Mitre Square – possibly the work of an imitator'.

On Friday 9 November, Dr Phillips was summoned at 11.00 a.m. and arrived at Mary Jane Kelly's room in Miller's Court at 11.15. He later testified, 'I looked through the lower of the broken [window-]panes and satisfied myself that the mutilated corpse lying on the bed was not in need of any immediate attention from me. I also came to the conclusion that there was nobody else upon the bed or within view to whom I could render any professional assistance.'

When the door was forced open at 1.30, Phillips noted that it struck the table at the left of the bed. It was reported that cursory medical examination concluded that the uterus had been taken away, but following the very thorough post mortem carried out by Phillips in the presence of his assistant and Drs **Bond** and **Brown**, all parts of the body were accounted for. (But cf. the report under **Dr Thomas Brown** describing the missing heart.) Phillips' report to the inquest was extremely brief and omitted the post mortem results:

The mutilated remains of a female were lying two-thirds over towards the edge of the bedstead nearest the door. She had only her chemise on, or some underlinen garment. I am sure the body had been removed subsequent to the injury which caused her death from that side of the bedstead which was nearest the wooden partition, because of the large quantity of blood under the bedstead and the saturated condition of the sheet and the palliasse at the corner nearest the partition. The blood was produced by the severance of the carotid artery, which was the immediate cause of death. This injury was inflicted while deceased was lying at the right of the bedstead.

On 22 July 1889, Phillips submitted a very long report on Alice McKenzie, concluding:

After careful & long deliberation I cannot satisfy myself, on purely Anatomical & professional grounds that the perpetrator of all the "Wh Ch. murders" is our man. I am on the contrary impelled to a contrary conclusion in this noting the mode of procedure & the character of the mutilations & judging of motive in connection with the latter.

I do not here enter into the comparison of the cases neither do I take into account what I admit may be almost conclusive evidence in favour of the one man theory if all the surrounding circumstances and other evidence are considered, holding it as my duty to report on the P.M. appearances and express an opinion only on Professional grounds, based upon my own observation.

(Cf. under **Dr Thomas Bond**.)

It was very much on Phillips' urging that a **Pardon** for non-murdering accessories was offered. It is not known what arguments he adduced.

PHOENIX, MRS ELIZABETH

Sister-in-law of **Mrs Carthy**. Lived at 157 Bow Common Lane, Burdett Road. On 11 November 1888 she went to Leman Street Police Station and stated that from published description of Mary Jane Kelly she believed her to be a person who lodged with Mrs Carthy several years previously. Police action, if any, is unknown, but the press traced Mrs Carthy and recorded interviews supporting **Joe Barnett**'s story that Mary Jane had worked in the West End.

PIGOTT, WILLIAM HENRY (1835–1901)

Briefly suspected. Son of a Gravesend insurance agent who prospered for a time as a publican in Hoxton, but had fallen on hard times by 1888, and was apparently mentally unstable.

Pigott arrived in Gravesend at about 4.00 p.m., Sunday 9 September 1888, telling various people he had walked from Whitechapel. In The Pope's Head public house he aroused the landlady's suspicion by expressing hostility to women, and she sent for the police. Superintendent Berry noticed an injury to his hand which Pigott explained by saying a woman had bitten it in a back yard behind a Whitechapel lodging-house. Later he changed the location of the incident to Brick Lane. A shirt in his bag had blood-spots on it, and the police surgeon believed his shoes showed signs of having been wiped clean of blood. **Inspector Abberline** took him back to Whitechapel, where he was put in an identity parade before **Mrs Fiddymont**, **Joseph Taylor** and **Mary Chappell**. The first two completely failed to identify him. Mary Chappell picked him out from the line, but then said she wasn't sure he was the man she had seen in the Prince Albert shortly after Chapman's murder.

After he had been cleared, it is uncertain whether Pigott was turned over to his friends for placement in an asylum, or sent direct to Whitechapel Workhouse Infirmary.

PINCHIN STREET

Eponymous site of the **'Pinchin Street murder'**, though the actual murder took place elsewhere. A short road in St George's-in-the-East parish, running east-west from Backchurch Lane to Christian Street, parallel with Cable Street and edged by Great Eastern Railway arches on the south side. The north side was fenced off by palings, behind which lay Pinchin and Johnson's oil and paint works. The street was uninhabited, regarded as unsalubrious, if not actually dangerous, and known locally as 'Dark Lane'. The torso was found at the western side of the arch, probably next to Backchurch Lane.

The existing railway runs on modern arches adjacent to Cable Street. But the old arches, now converted to garages and stores, can still be seen.

PINCHIN STREET MURDER

Unsolved crime, briefly attributed to the Ripper.

On 10 September 1889, **Police Constable Pennett**, on beat duty in Pinchin Street, found a woman's torso, lacking head and legs, covered by part of an old chemise, under a railway arch in Pinchin Street. His attention was in part attracted by the smell, as it was starting to decompose. The abdomen was mutilated, one reporter feeling that the injuries were reminiscent of the Ripper's handiwork and claiming that the womb was missing. The arms and hands were well formed and showed no signs of manual labour, despite which it was speculated that the woman might have been a factory worker.

One news agency speculated that it might be the body of **Lydia Hart**, an East End prostitute who had been missing for some days. **James Monro**'s report to the Home Office, dated 11 September, opens by noting that the estimated date of death, 8 September, is the anniversary of Annie Chapman's murder. None the less, he dismisses the likelihood of the killing being the Ripper's work after considering the **M.O.**

Melville Macnaghten makes several references to the case, probably because, with Frances Coles' murder, it was the only Ripper-related crime on which he personally worked. The general conclusion, then and since, has been that this torso murder was in some way connected with the **Whitehall Mystery**.

PINHORN, INSPECTOR CHARLES (b. 1849)

Warrant no. 51109. With Superintendent West, he took charge of the on-site investigation of Elizabeth Stride's murder, 30 September 1888. He was personally in charge of the on-site investigation at **Pinchin Street**, 10 September 1889.

PIZER, JOHN (1850–97)

Cleared suspect, named by police as **'Leather Apron'**. A Polish Jewish boot-finisher, probably born in England, Pizer lived at 22 Mulberry Street from 1854, where first his father (until his death) and then his stepmother headed the household. Pizer may have been of a roaming disposition, as he did not sleep there on the nights of the 1871 or 1881 censuses.

His age and occupation make it virtually certain that he was the man described in court and press reports as 'John Pozer' who attacked James Willis, another boot-finisher, at his work-place in Morgan Street, St George's, in July 1887. 'Pozer' poked his head through the open sweatshop window and said, 'No wonder I can't get any work when you have got it all.' Willis was told to send him away, but 'Pozer' stabbed him in the hand when he approached. For this, 'Pozer' was sentenced to six months hard labour.

On 4 August 1888, John Pizer appeared before Thames Magistrates, charged with indecent assault. The case was dismissed, and no further details are known at present.

On the night of 30–31 August 1888, Pizer was staying at Crossman's common lodging house in Holloway, and at 1.30 a.m. walked down to Seven Sisters Road and talked with a policeman about the glow in the sky visible from the **fire at London Docks**. The following day he went to Westminster where he stayed in a lodging house in Peter Street. He described a curious incident on Sunday 2 September, however, when he claimed that two unknown women in Church Street asked him if he was 'the man', which he took to mean Nichols' murderer. If Church Street was today's Fournier Street, Spitalfields, then, contrary to his assertion that he did not leave Westminster for a week, he must have made a return to the East End. (Cf. **Miss Lyons**' story of a similar incident the following Sunday.) On 4 September the stories that the Whitechapel murderer was an unknown local Jew nicknamed 'Leather Apron' broke in the press, with occasional suggestions that he had been temporarily arrested by J Division (Bethnal Green) constables following a woman's complaint on Sunday 2 September. (The police subsequently denied this.)

On Thursday 6 September, Pizer returned to 22 Mulberry Street, staying on and around the premises for the next four days as his brother warned him that there was 'a false suspicion' against him. On 7 September, Inspector Helson mentioned him in his weekly report to Scotland Yard: 'The inquiry has revealed the fact that a man named Jack Pizer, alias Leather Apron, has for some considerable period been illusing prostitutes in this, and other parts of the Metropolis, and careful search has been and is continued to be made to find this man in order that his movements may be accounted for on the night in question, although at present there is no evidence whatever against him.'

At this point we may note the following indications that Pizer might be 'Leather Apron': (i) Helson's report is the first time the nickname 'Leather Apron' was attached to any known person; (ii) Pizer's stabbing conviction and assault charge, coupled with his race and occupation, must have led any responsible police force to question him in connection with the accusations against 'Leather Apron'; (iii) some descriptions of Pizer suggest a physical resemblance to the descriptions of 'Leather Apron', with a dark moustache and a thick neck (a drawing of Pizer in the *Star* showing a bespectacled man with a beard was, according to Pizer, no more like him than the man in the moon); (iv) Pizer's habit of staying in lodging houses around London matched 'Leather Apron's' reputation for threatening women in other parts of the metropolis.

On the morning of Monday 10 September **Sergeant William Thick** and another officer went to 22 Mulberry Street where Pizer opened the door to them. When Thick said, 'You're just the man I want', Pizer turned pale and trembled. Thick arrested him and took away some of his leather-working knives and his hats ('Leather Apron' having been described as wearing a deerstalker). He was taken to Leman Street police station where he was shown in identification parades to **Mrs Fiddymont** and **Emmanuel**

Violenia. The former was unable to identify him; the latter positively identified him as a man he had seen talking angrily with a woman outside 29 Hanbury Street in the early morning of 8 September, and said that he knew Pizer as 'Leather Apron'. Pizer expressed outraged astonishment at this identification, but Violenia was in any case dropped from the case as unreliable. The following day, Sergeant Thick told the *Star* he was 'almost positive' Pizer was Leather Apron. No other evidence was found against him, and on Tuesday evening Pizer was released.

On Wednesday 11 October he was summoned to Annie Chapman's inquest to be cleared of suspicion of murder. Here, in answer to the opening questions, he said that he was Leather Apron. The undoubted fact of his presence in Holloway on the night of Mary Ann Nichols' murder was brought out, and Pizer was told he could go. He protested. 'Sergeant Thick who arrested me has known me for eighteen years – ' but was interrupted by Coroner **Wynne Baxter** with the remark, 'Well, well, I do not think it is necessary for you to say more.'

Sergeant Thick then gave the only testimony ever elicited that Pizer was known as 'Leather Apron': he said that 'He had known Pizer for many years, and when people in the neighbourhood spoke of "Leather Apron" they meant him.'

The press was totally unable to confirm this. Pizer, when interviewed, said he had not known he was referred to as Leather Apron until Thick arrested him, and observed that while he used to wear a leather apron home from work, he had not done so for some time, having been out of work. His neighbours, family and friends unanimously denied that he had ever been nicknamed Leather Apron.

We may note that: (i) Thick's identification only became positive at the inquest; (ii) Helson's identification uniquely refers to Pizer as 'Jack', suggesting that his information came from someone who knew Pizer intimately; (iii) a *Daily News* report, apparently using information supplied by Thick, wrongly identified Mulberry Street with the large parallel road, Plumber's Row; (iv) 'Leather Apron's' alleged habit of lodging at a doss-house or doss-houses in and around Brick Lane accords ill with Pizer, whose home was nearby; (v) no attempt was made by police or press to have Pizer identified as 'Leather Apron' by prostitutes who had described the latter, or by **Tim Donovan** who claimed to know him very well by sight. None the less, all subsequent police reports described Pizer as Leather Apron, an early suspect who had been cleared.

It was reported that Pizer was given handsome financial compensation by newspapers which had described him incautiously, and further reported that these sums had been exaggerated. It is possible that he received no more than £10 from **Harry Dam** for the *Star*'s over-enthusiastic vilification of Leather Apron. On 11 October 1888, Pizer summonsed Emily Patswold for calling him 'Leather Apron' and hitting him. She was fined 10/- [50p].

In July 1897, Pizer, whose health had always been poor (he suffered from a hernia), died of gastro-enteritis in the London Hospital, still resident at 22 Mulberry Street.

POCOCK, FREDERICK (b. 1892)

Informant. Told **Daniel Farson**, after publication of the first edition of Farson's *Jack the Ripper*, that his mother had known of a man called **Druitt** who lodged in the attic of a fried fish shop next to the railway arch in

The Minories in 1888 and who was reputed to burn rubbish in the cellar furnace after the murders. An alarming man who accosted Pocock's mother during the Ripper scare apparently resembled the mysterious lodger.

POLICE METHODS

The police were severely criticised in the contemporary press (and by subsequent authors) for their methods of investigating the Whitechapel Murders. It was alleged that their two basic methods were completely ineffective: swamping the district with uniformed patrols, who, the press claimed, were a serious nuisance, arresting passers-by at random; and house-to-house interviews gleaning any information concerning suspicious sounds or sights, rather than making positive deductions from the site of crime and following them through.

In fact, both methods are still probably efficient in such cases. The swamping may have contributed to the increasing intervals of time between each murder (one week between the first and the second; three weeks between the second and the double murders; six weeks between the double murders and the last) as it became harder for the assassin to be sure of accosting a woman unobserved. The blanket pursuit of evidence and stray observations is unquestionably the best way of identifying recurrent suspicious figures in serial murders, although the difficulty of retrieving matching factors from the mass of information made it hard to use properly until the advent of computers. Negative experience in, e.g., the Cannock Chase murders or the Yorkshire Ripper case has conclusively proved, however, that the approach is far more efficient than the pursuit of the single prominent clue.

Other more dramatic methods proved quite ineffective when tried: notably, the use of **bloodhounds**, and policemen in disguise, including decoys dressed as women.

Contrary to popular belief, however, the police investigation of the case was professional and competent.

POLLARD, MAJOR HUGH (1888–1966)

Important link in provenance of **Jack the Ripper's knife**. Sports editor of *Country Life*. An authority on ancient and modern firearms, and partner of gunsmith Robert Churchill, the well-known ballistics expert frequently consulted by Scotland Yard. Pollard gave expert evidence in more than one *cause célèbre*. In 1937 he gave his assistant editor, Miss Dorothy Stroud, a pair of late nineteenth-century surgical knives in a box lined with blood-stained velvet, telling her they were Jack the Ripper's knives. The surviving knife of the pair was given by Miss Stroud to **Donald Rumbelow**.

POPLAR HIGH STREET

Site of Rose Mylett's death. Residential and shopping thoroughfare running from King Street (today's Ming Street) to Naval Row and East India Dock Wall, north of the Isle of Dogs. The body was found in Clarke's Yard, a disused lot where builder George Clarke stored materials, on the south side of the street, opposite England's Row. Elizabeth Stride's husband John kept a coffee-house in Poplar High Street for some years after their marriage. Today the whole area is rebuilt, and Clarke's Yard has vanished beneath flats to the west of the Jerusalem public house.

POZER, JOHN (b. 1850)
See under **John Pizer**.

PRATER, MRS ELIZABETH
Witness at Mary Jane Kelly's inquest. Wife of boot machinist William Prater who had deserted her five years previously. Lived in the room immediately above Mary Jane Kelly, whom she had known well for some five months. Returned home approximately 1.00 a.m., Friday 9 November 1888, and stood at the archway from **Dorset Street** to Miller's Court, beside McCarthy's shop, waiting for a man who was living with her. He did not come, and she spoke to no one and saw nothing suspicious.

Having gone to bed, she was awakened by her kitten Diddles running over her neck. Heard and ignored a cry of 'Murder' from somewhere. Observed that the lodging house light was out, so assumed it was later than 4.00 a.m.

In 1892, when Canadian journalist **Kathleen Blake Watkins**, 'Kit' of the Toronto Mail, visited the district, she was still living in the same room.

PRESTON, CHARLES
Witness at Elizabeth Stride's inquest. A barber, resident at 32 **Flower and Dean Street** for eighteen months, he had seen Stride in the kitchen of the lodging house between 6.00 and 7.00 p.m., 29 September 1888. He gave some familiar erroneous biographical data about her – see under **Elizabeth Stride**, *Princess Alice* (vessel) – and mentioned a drunk and disorderly charge brought against her following an incident in the **Queen's Head**.

PRINCE ALBERT, THE
Public house in Brushfield Street, licensed to **Mrs Fiddymont**. Known locally as 'the clean house', it no longer exists.

PRINCE ALBERT VICTOR, DUKE OF CLARENCE
See **Albert Victor**.

PRINCE JACK: THE TRUE STORY OF JACK THE RIPPER
Book by **Frank Spiering** (1978). An elaboration of **Dr Thomas Stowell**'s suggestion that **Prince Albert Victor** was Jack the Ripper, drawing on **Michael Harrison**'s biography, *Clarence*, allegedly supported by notes of **Sir William Gull**'s that Spiering claims to have found in the New York Academy of Medicine. No trace of these notes has been found by staff of the Academy. Some of Spiering's other claims suggest a very cavalier attitude to historical authenticity.

Spiering's challenge to the Queen to release supposed suppressed information about Albert Victor's whereabouts during the murders has been effectively met by the Royal Archives, which produced very clear evidence of the Prince's movements.

The book has never been published in England, though there has never been any restriction on importing the US editions.

PRINCE OF WALES (subsequently Edward VII)
See **Albert Edward**.

PRINCESS ALICE (PUBLIC HOUSE) now The City Darts
Allegedly frequented by **'Leather Apron'**. On the corner of Wentworth Street and Commercial Street. Press reports claimed that, prior to the murders, 'Leather Apron' and **'Mickeldy Joe'** were often to be seen lurking on the road opposite the pub. **Thomas Sadler** picked up **Frances Coles** in the Princess Alice. In the 1980s the pub was completely refurbished, and its name changed.

PRINCESS ALICE (VESSEL)
Alleged by Elizabeth Stride to have played a part in her past. Large saloon steamer owned by the London Steamboat Company, sank in collision on the Thames with the collier *Bywell Castle* in September 1878, both captains culpably ignoring Thames navigation regulations. An estimated 600–700 people on board the *Princess Alice* were drowned, and several hundred bodies were laid out in Woolwich Town Hall.

Elizabeth Stride told many acquaintances that she had been employed on the vessel as a stewardess, and her husband as a seaman. She said that he and a varying number of their children were drowned in the disaster, and that a passenger escaping up a companion-way had accidentally broken her hard palate with the heel of his boot. On 8 October 1888, several newspapers reported that Woolwich newspapers for 1878 revealed that a woman named Stride had identified the bodies of her husband and children. Subsequent research has failed to find any trace of such reports at the time of the disaster, and evidence at the inquest indicated that the entire story was a fabrication. Stride did not apparently work for the London Steamboat Company; her husband did not die in the disaster; they had no children in England; Stride's hard palate had never been injured.

PROVIDENCE ROW NIGHT REFUGE AND CONVENT
Alleged one-time residence of Mary Jane Kelly. Located at 50 Crispin Street, opposite **Dorset Street**, and still extant; the apparently established and plausible tradition of an association with the last Ripper victim (see under **Mary Jane Kelly**) is elaborated in the story told by **Joseph Sickert** and **Stephen Knight**.

In 1860, the Revd (later Monsignor) Daniel Gilbert opened a night refuge for homeless women and children in former stables at Providence Row, Finsbury Square. Nuns of the Order of Sisters of Mercy ran it. When the accommodation proved too small, land once used for fairs off Crispin Street was purchased, and the present home built and opened in 1868.

According to the Sickert/Knight story, Mary Kelly was taken in by the nuns of Providence Row. A little later a shop-owner in Cleveland Street wanted an assistant and mentioned this to **Walter Sickert**, who in turn mentioned it to Edmund Bellord, a Cleveland Street estate agent, who was a member of the committee of the refuge. The nuns recommended Mary Jane Kelly, who thereupon went to Cleveland Street and became associated with **Annie Elizabeth Crook**.

In 1973, an elderly nun interviewed by BBC Television said that 'in 1915 she had been a novice in Providence Row, directly opposite the pub where Kelly and Chapman rubbed shoulders daily'. (Knight wrongly identified this as **The Britannia**, which was at the other end of Dorset Street. The reference is obviously to **The Horn of Plenty**.) The nun also remembered being told by an old sister who was in Crispin Street at the time of the murders, 'if it had not been for the Kelly woman, none of the murders would have happened'.

PUCKRIDGE –

Suspect. 19 September 1888, **Sir Charles Warren** wrote to the Home Office, 'A man called Puckridge was released from an asylum on 4 August. He was educated as a surgeon – he has threatened to rip people up with a long knife. He is being looked for but cannot be found yet.'

Nothing more is known about this promising suspect. (See also **Jon Ogan**.)

PURKISS, WALTER

Witness at Mary Ann Nichols' inquest. Lived with his wife, child and servant in Essex Wharf (demolished 1990) immediately opposite the murder site. He was the manager, and he and his wife occupied the second floor front bedroom. He went to bed about 11.00 p.m. or shortly after on 29 September 1888 and awoke at various times during the night, especially between 1.00 and 3.00 a.m. His wife had a very sleepless night, and believed she was pacing the bedroom at the time the murder must have taken place (c.3.30 a.m.). Neither heard anything, although the night was unusually quiet.

Q

QUEEN'S HEAD, THE
Site of **George Hutchinson**'s sighting of Mary Jane Kelly with astrakhan-collared man, and one of Elizabeth Stride's alleged drunken disturbances. Pub on the corner of **Commercial Street** and Fashion Street (site today occupied by Banco de Bilbao).

According to **Charles Preston**, Elizabeth Stride was in police custody some four or five months before her death, for being drunk and disorderly at the Queen's Head. She was released the following day on bail. Since Stride appeared at Thames Magistrates Court, drunk and disorderly (sometimes with obscene language) in February, July (twice), August and October before her death, we wonder what made the Queen's Head incident special.

At 2.00 a.m. on 9 November, **George Hutchinson** stood under the light outside the Queen's Head to wait for Mary Jane Kelly and the client he had watched her pick up in Commercial Street come past him on their way back to Dorset Street. As they did so, he peered into the man's face, and remarked that he looked 'very surly' (unsurprisingly, we feel, under the circumstances).

R

RACE, INSPECTOR WILLIAM NIXON (b. 1855)
Arrested **Thomas Cutbush**. Joined Metropolitan Police, 1880; Warrant no. 64541; invalided out, 1898. Race had an outstanding record of criminal arrests, starting with one of the Blind Beggar Gang (see under **gangs, East End**) taken on the steps of the Carlton Club picking a victorious candidate's pocket while he harangued electors on election night. The Cutbush case was seen as one of his personal triumphs, especially as he cleared an innocent suspect in the investigation. (The authors do not know who this was.) Colleagues felt he was shabbily treated by his superiors, who refused him promotion to superintendent for no good reason, and downgraded him to invalid him out with a reduced pension when this preyed on his mind and affected his health.

RASPUTIN, GRIGORI EFIMOVICH (1871–1916)
Alleged author of alleged unfinished manuscript, *Great Russian Criminals*, naming Ochrana (Czarist Secret Police) agent **Dr Alexander Pedachenko** as the Ripper. Russian monk, with increasing influence over the Tsarina from 1905 as his quasi-faith healing offered the only effective treatment for her son's haemophilia. His supposed interference in state affairs was resented by the nobility, until a group of aristocrats murdered him. His sensational death and the assassins' over-heated defence of their actions gave him a legendary and undeserved reputation as a sinister, depraved and almost supernatural *éminence grise*.
    William Le Queux claimed that the Kerensky government (July–November 1917) sent him two bundles of documents found among Rasputin's effects. At different times he claimed that one or the other comprised the unfinished manuscript in French, *Great Russian Criminals*. C. W. Shepherd, who ghosted three books for Le Queux, told **Donald Rumbelow** that he had once seen a large envelope 'plastered with seals and codes' which Le Queux told him contained the Russian material. That is the sole evidence for its physical existence.
    Serious doubts about the alleged Rasputin manuscript are raised by: its alleged reliance on information from the Ochrana – an institution with which, according to its head, A. T. Vassil'ev, Rasputin had no connection; its alleged composition in French, a language apparently unknown to Rasputin (as Le Queux himself noted); and its subject, 'Great Russian criminals', which Rasputin's daughter has assured **Colin Wilson** held no interest for her father.

REED, MR F. S.
Medical attendant, possibly responsible for exaggerated claims concerning the **Lusk kidney**. According to Joseph Aarons, members of the **Vigilance**

Committee originally took the kidney to Dr Frederick Wiles' surgery at 56 Mile End Road, where in Wiles' absence his assistant, Reed, examined it. Reed pronounced it human and preserved in spirits of wine, and took it on to **Dr Openshaw** at the London Hospital. On his return, according to Aarons, Reed declared that it was part of the left kidney of a woman accustomed to drinking who had died at the time of the Mitre Square murder. Openshaw subsequently denied these details.

REEVES, JOHN SAUNDERS (born c. 1865)
Witness at Martha Tabram's inquest; discovered her body. A waterside labourer with a slight dark beard and moustache, and wearing earrings, he left his residence at 37 George Yard Buildings at 4.45 a.m., 7 August 1888, and found the body on the first floor landing. He at once went to find a policeman and returned with **Police Constable Barrett**.

REID, INSPECTOR EDMUND JOHN JAMES (b. 1846)
Head of local CID during Whitechapel murders. Joined Metropolitan Police, 1872, after a varied career including experience as a pastry-cook and ship's steward. Warrant no. 56100. Entered CID, 1874; promoted Sergeant, 1878; Detective Inspector at Scotland Yard, 1884; sent to organise J Division (Bethnal Green) CID, 1886; appointed to succeed **Frederick Abberline** as Local Inspector (Head of CID) H Division (Whitechapel), 1888, where he remained until retirement as the longest-serving detective inspector in 1896.

He was described by the *Weekly Dispatch* as 'one of the most remarkable men of the century' and he reached professional standards in acting, singing and legerdemain. He made frequent balloon ascents in the early 1880s, receiving a medal for going to a record height in 1883. He made possibly the first parachute descent in England from 1000ft above Luton, c.1876. He was featured as 'Detective Dier' in ten novels by Charles Gibbon.

In 1896 he gave press interviews on his career, including references to the Ripper case; in 1903 he wrote two letters to the *Morning Advertiser* following correspondence based on Abberline's suggestion that **Severin Klosowski** (George Chapman) was the Ripper. Reid believed there were nine Ripper murders, that of Frances Coles being the last. He challenged the notion that the Ripper showed surgical expertise, declaring the mutilations were nothing but 'a number of slashes all over the body of the victim, even after the murderer knew his victim was dead'. He believed wrongly that 'at no time was any part of the body missing'. He believed there was evidence that the Ripper's knife was blunt. He believed the murderer had been dead for some years, because that would be the consequence of his particular kind of mania. But he did not appear to have heard of the three suspects listed by **Major Arthur Griffiths** who match the three in the **Macnaghten memoranda: M. J. Druitt, Kosminski** and **Michael Ostrog**.

Reid's confident and erroneous assertions indicate that conclusions and definite information familiar to (at least) **Robert Anderson** and **Donald Swanson** appear not to have been made known at the level of Detective Inspector.

REILLY, B. E.
Theorist. Author of a short article, 'Jack the Ripper – the Mystery Solved',

in *City*, the magazine of the City of London Police Force. A responsible piece of writing, this takes **Police Constable Spicer**'s story and identifies the only Brixton doctor to die shortly after the murders, pseudonymously naming him '**Dr Merchant**' (cf. **F. W. Chapman**) and suggesting that the theory is no less plausible than any other. The following month's issue contained an article from I. M. Bartlett suggesting that the dates of 'Merchant's' death and Spicer's subsequent sightings of his suspect meant that the two men were necessarily different.

REWARDS FOR INFORMATION

Several individuals and organisations, including **Samuel Montagu**, MP for Whitechapel, the Lord Mayor and Corporation of London, and the Officers of the Tower Hamlets Militia, offered cash rewards for information leading to the apprehension and conviction of the Whitechapel Murderer. By October 1888 the total on offer had reached about £1,200 (say £42,000 at today's values), and Angela Burdett Coutts had promised a pension of a pound a week for life to any successful informant who secured a conviction.

The Government, however, did not offer a reward and this resulted in much opprobrium being levelled at Home Secretary **Henry Matthews** and the Metropolitan Police Commissioner **Charles Warren**, although neither had any rigid objection to the principle of rewards. Matthews was, on Civil Service advice, following a precedent laid down by his Liberal predecessor Sir William Harcourt. Up to 1884 the Government had offered rewards for information in major criminal cases, usually of £100. This was discontinued following the commission of a crime and false denunciation of an individual, solely for the purpose of collecting the reward money. The Government did, however, have the option of offering a reward in special cases which were, as a rule, those in which the beneficiary was not the person upon whose evidence a conviction was gained. The Whitechapel Murders were not such a case.

A rather large item for 'incidental expenditure in the apprehension and conviction of criminals' in the annual Metropolitan Police Accounts indicates that payment of small sums to professional underworld informers was, as always, a clandestine component of efficient detective work.

Cf. **Pardons**.

RHIND, NEIL

Authority on **M. J. Druitt** as schoolmaster. A distinguished Blackheath local historian, Mr Rhind has discovered more than seemed possible about Mr Valentine's school in Eliot Place and Montague John Druitt's connection with it. The bulk of his material is privately circulated and has been delivered in lectures.

Essentially he has established that Mr Valentine's establishment occupied the same building, but was not the same institution, as the famous prep school attended by Benjamin Disraeli. Valentine was not a great deal older than Druitt, and the latter joined the staff sufficiently early (1880) and was sufficiently prominent in local sporting associations patronised by Valentine for Mr Rhind to believe he was a consequential resident assistant master. An utterly impenetrable silence in both written record and oral tradition on the reason for Druitt's sudden dismissal at the end of November 1888 leads Mr Rhind to join others in speculating that it may well have been sexual interference with a boy or boys.

RICHARDSON, MRS AMELIA

Witness at Annie Chapman's inquest. Mrs Richardson is listed in street directories as the occupant of 29 Hanbury Street. She rented the first two floors, living in the first-floor front room with her fourteen-year-old grandson Thomas Richardson, and using the cellar and yard for her business of making packing-cases in which she was assisted by her son **John Richardson** and a man named John Tyler. She sub-let the ground floor to **Mrs Hardyman**.

She knew nothing of the murder till she heard a disturbance at about 6.00 a.m., 8 September 1888, and sent her grandson to investigate. He returned, saying, 'Oh, grandmother, there is a woman murdered!' Mrs Richardson went to see the body in the yard, but not being properly dressed, hurried back to her room. The police then took possession of the house.

RICHARDSON, JOHN

Witness at Annie Chapman's inquest. Son of **Amelia Richardson**, he lived at 2 John Street, Spitalfields, and worked in his mother's packing-case business and as a porter at Spitalfields Market.

About 4.45 a.m., 8 September 1888, he called in at 29 Hanbury Street on his way to work to check the cellar door padlock. The street door and passage to the back yard were never locked, and some months earlier a saw and a hammer had been stolen from the cellar when someone broke the padlock. Richardson also occasionally checked the building to make sure prostitutes and their clients were not using it, having once found a man and a woman on the stairs. He saw nobody on the premises, or in the yard, where he sat on the step and tried to trim a piece of loose leather off his boot with an old table knife he used to cut up carrots for his rabbit. He was not more than three minutes in the house, and only learned of the murder when told of it at the market.

The inquest insisted on seeing his knife when it learned that he had carried one; it proved impossible that it should have been used for the murder. The discovery of his leather apron under the tap in the backyard caused a temporary sensation, as the **'Leather Apron'** scare was at its height. The police tried to reconcile Richardson's testimony with **Dr Phillips'** estimate that Annie Chapman must have been dead for at least two hours when he inspected the body (about 6.30 a.m.) by claiming that the back door opening to the left obscured the body from Richardson's view as he sat on the steps. Contemporary photographs and drawings of the yard make this deduction completely unconvincing. The virtual certainty is that Bagster Phillips' estimate was wrong.

RINGER, MR AND MRS WALTER

Landlord and landlady of **The Britannia** public house on the corner of Dorset Street and Commercial Street. In local parlance the pub was often called 'The Ringers" or 'Mrs Ringer's'.

RIPPER, THE (1985, USA)

Film directed by Christopher Lewis. Stars Tom Schreier, Wade Tower, Mona Van Pernis. Ripper's ring transfers evil of former owner to college professor; intelligently written, but very gory murders, more padding than a settee, and ultra cheap. Shot on video for home market. (Video available.)

RIPPER AND THE ROYALS, THE

Book by Melvin Fairclough (1991). Substance of the book is recapitulation of **Joseph Sickert**'s present allegations about his grandmother's supposed secret liaison with and clandestine marriage to **Prince Albert Victor**, and the consequent murders undertaken at the behest of highranking **Freemasons** to preserve the secret. (Cf. **Jack the Ripper: The Final Solution** and **Sickert and the Ripper Crimes**.) Sympathetically and painstakingly pieced together from Joseph Sickert's fragmentary recollections by Mr Fairclough, his personal friend.

Mr Sickert now says that the conspiracy was headed by **Lord Randolph Churchill**, who employed **John Netley** and **Frederico Albericci** to assist himself and **Sir William Gull** in their forays to the East End. The claim is supported by cryptic entries in a diary of 1896, said by Mr Sickert to have been the work of **Inspector Abberline**, which identify the leading conspirators and characterise them by reference to nursery rhymes.

Since the book has not appeared at the time of writing, the authors are unable to comment on the probable authenticity of the source material, and are grateful to Mr Fairclough for supplying outline information.

RIPPER FILE, THE

Book by Elwyn Jones and John Lloyd (1975). Based on BBC Television drama documentary *Jack the Ripper* in which fictional detectives Barlow and Watt investigated the crimes from the supposed standpoint of modern policemen. Interlinking speculations of Barlow and Watt present an uncritical dismissal of the police of 1888 as incompetent, and lean heavily toward a mysterious and unproven wish to suggest **Freemasons**' involvement in the crimes. But in general the BBC research behind the scenes (by Paul Bonner, Leonard Lewis, Karen de Groot, Ian Sharp and Wendy Sturgess) was outstanding, and the bulk of the book can be recommended as an excellent collection of abridged factual reports and statements pertaining to the case.

RIPPER FILE, THE

Book by Melvin Harris (1989). Not to be confused with the book of the same title by Elwyn Jones and John Lloyd, Melvin Harris's second contribution to the subject (his first being *Jack the Ripper: The Bloody Truth*) is largely a reconstruction of the Ripper crimes through extracts from the contemporary press, and is valuable for anyone wanting to capture the atmosphere of the period.

A short chapter addresses the new discoveries and theories which emerged contemporaneously with *The Bloody Truth*. He dismisses the **Swanson marginalia** because subjectively he cannot accept the extraordinary story it relates. He rejects **Anderson**'s claims by using contemporary criticisms of him out of context to suggest that he was 'flighty' with the truth. In his final chapter he develops his case for **Robert Donston Stephenson** as the Ripper, revealing, at times, what Stephenson did and thought, without giving any sources beyond his own intuitive assertions.

RIPPER LEGACY, THE

Book by **Martin Howells** and Keith Skinner (1987). Howells and Skinner postulate a complicated and largely speculative motive for the murders, resting on Druitt's assumed homosexuality and resentment over his mother's illness. They also speculate that he may have been assassinated by high-placed Oxbridge associates to protect the establishment against the discovery that the Ripper was one of their number.

Apart from its immense readability, the strength of the book lies in its very detailed research, establishing new facts, and notably advancing an explanation of the alleged Australian document *The East End Murderer – I Knew Him*.

RIPPEROLOGY AND RIPPEROLOGISTS
Terms coined by **Colin Wilson** for expertise and experts on Jack the Ripper. Not favoured by the authors, as it has increasingly become associated with cranks and charlatans.

ROBERTSON, TERENCE
Journalist, possibly researcher. Author of 'Madman Who Murdered Nine Women' in **Reynolds News**, 29 October 1950, which claims that '**Fairy Fay**' was the first victim. The article concludes: 'But handed down through the years at Scotland Yard is the unshakeable belief that the "Ripper" was a sailor, probably a Pole . . . Nothing in the years that have passed has come to light to alter the Yard's theory, which marked the closing of their files . . . He was a Polish sailor.'

The factual inaccuracy of earlier parts of the article, coupled with the absence of any surviving supportive document on the **Scotland Yard Files**, makes the conclusion questionable, but there might once have been some support for it. (Cf. **Anderson's suspect**, especially if 'sailor' was a misreading of 'tailor'.)

ROBINSON, POLICE CONSTABLE LOUIS FREDERICK, 31 City
Arrested Catharine Eddowes. First name sometimes given as 'Lewis'. Joined City of London Police, 1886. Warrant no. 5921. Retired (as PC303C Bishopsgate), 1912.

On duty in Aldgate High Street at 8.30 p.m., he saw a crowd gathered around a woman (Eddowes) drunk on the pavement outside no. 29. He stood her up and leaned her against the house shutters, but she slipped sideways. With the assistance of **Police Constable George Simmons**, he took her to Bishopsgate Police Station.

ROCHA, JOACHIM DE (b. 1865)
Alleged suspect. Portuguese cattleman, advanced by **E. K. Larkins**.

RONEY, SARAH
Believed she was accosted by the Ripper. Friend of **Mrs Paumier**. Walking with a friend through Brushfield Street (Spitalfields Market) on Wednesday 6 November, she was approached by a man who wanted either of them – he didn't mind which – to come with him alone. They refused, and asked him what he had in the bag he was carrying. 'Something the ladies don't like,' was his reply. They believed him to be the Ripper, and Mrs Paumier believed him to be the man she saw in Artillery Row on 8 November.

The similarity of this story to that told by **Sarah Lewis** and **Mrs Kennedy** marks the suspicion that fell on men who accosted young women incautiously during the Ripper scare.

ROOM TO LET (1950, Great Britain)
Film directed by Godfrey Grayson. Stars Jimmy Hanley, Valentine Dyall. Nosey reporter finds Ripper dispensing psychiatric care in asylum; based on radio play by Campion-creator Margery Allingham.

ROOTS, INSPECTOR J.
Author of report, dated 26 December 1888, addressed to **Inspector Abberline**, and giving details on **Robert Donston Stephenson**, whom he said he had known for twenty years.

ROSENWATER, IRVING
Researcher. Author of 'Jack the Ripper – Sort of Cricketing Person?' in *The Cricketer*, January 1973. Traces amateur cricketing career of **M. J. Druitt**, and establishes that he was playing cricket in Dorset the day after Mary Ann Nichols' murder, and at Blackheath within hours of Chapman's murder.

'ROSY' (fl. 1888)
Spitalfields prostitute. Found sitting on brick dustbin at the back of a yard off Heneage Street by **Police Constable Robert Spicer** on the night of 29–30 September 1888. She was accompanied by a 'Brixton Doctor' whom Spicer strongly suspected of being Jack the Ripper. (Cf. **'Dr Merchant.'**) Her receipt of a florin [10p] from the client suggests that she was unusually attractive by local meretricial standards. The usual fee was 4d–6d [2–2½p].

ROWE, PETER
Epistemologist and tentative theorist. Ex-Superintendent, City of London Police. Under pseudonym 'William Vincent' he contributed articles on the Ripper to the *Police Review* between December 1977 and April 1988. In a seven-page contribution to Peter Underwood's ***Jack the Ripper: One Hundred Years of Mystery***, he cautiously makes the case for **Thomas Sadler**'s having murdered Frances Coles, showing the strengths and weaknesses from the point of view of bringing the case to trial. He also notes that it would be impossible to bring a satisfactory case against him in relation to the earlier Ripper murders.

Like so many who test history by the standard of legal evidence, however, he disregards the *historical* evidence that the police at the time, with more information than has come down to us, continued to believe Sadler had killed Coles even after the courts had acquitted him; and, unlike the press, did not believe he had committed the earlier murders.

RUGGLES-BRISE, EVELYN JOHN (1857–1935)
Home Office civil servant. Private Secretary to four successive Home Secretaries, including **Henry Matthews**. (In TV series *Yes, Minister* terms, the 'Bernard' to Matthews' 'Hacker' and **Godfrey Lushington**'s 'Sir Humphrey'.) 1895–1921, Prisons Commission Chairman, introduced Borstal system. KCB, 1902.

As a civil servant and son of a civil servant, Ruggles-Brise was fully conversant with the mandarin view of tension between police and Home Office, which makes his sympathetic assessment of **Sir Charles Warren** the more valuable. He was well informed on the Ripper case, seeing and annotating many of the documents sent to the Home Office.

Matthews' proposal in 1891 that he should be transfered to Scotland Yard as Chief Constable precipitated **James Monro**'s resignation.

RUMBELOW, DONALD (b. 1940)

Crime historian and researcher. A professional policeman (sergeant in the City of London Police), Rumbelow has maintained a parallel authorial career, producing standard works on the history of the City Police and the 'anarchist' murders of 1910–11 (the Tottenham outrage, the Houndsditch Murders, and the Siege of Sidney Street). Since the publication of *The Complete Jack the Ripper* in 1976, he has been internationally recognised as the leading authority on the subject.

Beyond his published work, he has made vital scholarly contributions to the field by transferring material from dead City Police files and his private collection to the Corporation of London Archives, and cataloguing it for the use of researchers. He discovered and identified the best-known photograph of Mary Jane Kelly's remains when it was in danger of destruction. He has thrown considerable energy into preserving endangered historical material that was seen as cluttering up shelf space in police archives.

RYDER, ELIZABETH

Witness at Alice McKenzie's inquest who identified her body. Wife of cooper Richard John Ryder and deputy of the lodging house at Gun Street where McKenzie lived, she gave evidence on her movements on the night of her death.

S

SADLER, JAMES THOMAS

Possible murderer of Frances Coles. Briefly a Ripper suspect. Merchant seaman; a fireman on the *Fez*. Sadler had twenty-six sailing discharges on his person when he was arrested in February 1891. He was paid off from the *Fez*, at London Docks, on 11 February, and picked up Coles in the **Princess Alice** in **Commercial Street** that night. He bought half a bottle of Irish whisky and spent the night with her. The following afternoon they spent a couple of hours drinking at The Bell in Petticoat Lane, after which Sadler paid for Frances to buy herself a secondhand crape bonnet at a shop in Baker's Row. She kept her old bonnet, pinned under her dress. The two continued drinking in various pubs, until Sadler was mugged in Thrawl Street and Frances deserted him. He turned up at her lodging house, 8 White's Row, at 11.30 p.m. and quarrelled furiously with her. At 12.30 he left, and at 12.35 she too went out.

An hour later, Frances met another prostitute called Ellen Callagher in Commercial Street, and despite Ellen's warnings, went off in the direction of The Minories with a violent man in a cheesecutter hat who had given Ellen a black eye. Sadler, meanwhile, got into a fight with dock-workers when he attempted to return aboard the *Fez*; made two attempts to gain admission to a lodging house in East Smithfield; and at 2.00 a.m. was found by the police, drunk and battered on the pavement outside the Mint. He was not seen again until he presented himself to the London Hospital at 5.00 a.m., once again injured from fighting.

Railway carmen 'Jumbo' Friday and two brothers called Knapton walked past and through the railway arch footpath known as Swallow Gardens between 2.00 a.m. and 2.12, seeing nothing untoward, though they noticed a man and a woman at the Royal Mint Street edge of the dark and dismal railway arch. One of the Knaptons shouted 'Good night' to them. 'Jumbo' Friday thought the man looked like a ship's fireman, and noted the woman's distinctive round bonnet.

At 2.15 a.m., **Police Constable Ernest Thompson** found Frances Coles almost dead, with her throat cut, in the pitch-dark centre of Swallow Gardens. He heard a man's footsteps running away in the direction of Royal Mint Street.

Police interest quickly turned to the ship's fireman seen by Jumbo Friday, who identified Coles' bonnet as that he had seen on the woman at Swallow Gardens. Soon police had traced the specific fireman, Sadler, who had spent the previous day with Coles, bought the bonnet, quarrelled with her, and last been seen a few hundred yards away from the murder site before disappearing for several hours. Moreover, the following morning Sadler sold his knife for a shilling to a seaman called Duncan Campbell in a Sailors' Rest. Sadler was arrested on Sunday and charged with murder, making little objection.

He pulled himself together when he realised the police were investigating his movements over the previous three years, and he was in danger of being charged with all the Ripper murders. His union engaged Messrs Wilson and Wallace, solicitors, to act for him, and they instructed counsel, so that Sadler was properly represented when Treasury counsel and solicitors put the case against him at the inquest. Sadler's lawyers had seven witnesses ready to testify to his movements on the night of 12–13 February, and the fact that his repeated bloodstaining was the result of several fights. These witnesses were unnecessary. Treasury counsel effectively threw in the towel when Thomas Fowles and Kate McCarthy came forward to say they were the young couple 'Jumbo' Friday and the Knaptons had seen, and they had recognised them. Sadler left the inquest a free man.

Despite this, the police were quite certain he had killed Frances Coles, as the **Macnaghten memoranda** indicate and the writings of **Major Arthur Griffiths** and **H. L. Adam** hint.

SAGAR, DETECTIVE CONSTABLE ROBERT (1852–1924)

Reported as describing watch on a suspect in apparently unpublished memoirs. Abandoned medical training at St Bartholomew's Hospital to join City Police, 1880. Detective Constable, 1884. Sergeant, 1888. Detective Sergeant, 1889. Detective Inspector, 1890. Retired, 1905. **Major Henry Smith** wrote, 'a better or more intelligent officer than Robert Sagar I never had under my command'.

In *Reynolds News*, 15 September 1946, Justin Atholl wrote:

Inspector Robert Sagar, who died in 1924, played a leading part in the Ripper Investigations. In his memoirs he said: 'We had good reason to suspect a man who worked in Butchers' Row, Aldgate. We watched him carefully. There was no doubt that this man was insane, and after a time his friends thought it advisable to have him removed to a private asylum. After he was removed, there were no more Ripper atrocities.'

The authors have not succeeded in tracing these memoirs. The reference seems important, as apart from the mention of work, the account seems to match what the **Swanson marginalia** say of **Kosminski**.

ST GEORGE'S-IN-THE-EAST

Parish where Elizabeth Stride was murdered and the Pinchin Street torso was found. Nicholas Hawksmoor's St George's on The Highway is the parish church.

Lying between **Commercial Road** and the northern edge of the docks, the parish was most infamous for containing the Ratcliff Highway, an arterial road running from the Royal Mint to Limehouse which was full of cheap taverns, brothels, opium dens (at the Limehouse end), slopshops (selling seamen secondhand clothes) and exotic petshops (where seamen could sell animals collected in foreign lands). Mugging, pocket-picking and shanghaiing (kidnapping to provide crews for shorthanded merchantmen) were rife. The Ratcliff Highway Murders of 1811, in which two households were murdered in their beds by robbers, had created the greatest scare in London prior to the Ripper case. In an attempt to improve the image of the district, the Ratcliff Highway had been renamed St George's High Street by 1888.

Elizabeth Stride, alone among the Ripper victims, worked in this direction (though Mary Jane Kelly probably lived in the neighbourhood of the Ratcliff Highway when she first came to the East End). We may note that Stride would be familiar with docklands life from the years when her husband kept a coffee-shop in Poplar, and that she knew the Swedish Church off Ratcliff Highway where she was given charity as a Swedish national.

SALISBURY, MARQUESS OF, RIGHT HONOURABLE ROBERT CECIL (1830–1903)

Prime Minister, 1886–92. Not directly involved in Ripper investigation, though his determination to retain his only Catholic cabinet minister and avoid a risky by-election forced **Henry Matthews** to remain Home Secretary, and gave political urgency to the enquiry. Falsely accused by **Joseph Sickert** and **Stephen Knight** of promoting **Freemasons'** conspiracy to murder Mary Jane Kelly. Salisbury was not a Freemason.

Knight and **Jean Overton Fuller** both claim that Salisbury visited **Walter Sickert**'s studio and silently paid him £500 for an inferior painting. This, both say, was a bribe to enforce his silence over the conspiracy. However, in *Noble Essences*, Osbert Sitwell describes Sickert as relating the anecdote, but with reference to the painter A. Vallon, and not himself. The painting was a commissioned family portrait, and Salisbury's silent payment was evidence of his disgust at the quality of the finished work, not of any form of bribery. The painting is still in Hatfield House.

SANDERS, JOHN WILLIAM SMITH (1862–1901)

Suspect. Son of an Indian Army surgeon (d. 1867). Entered London Hospital as student, 1879. Out-patient dresser, 1880–1. At this time he was living with his mother, Laura Tucker Sanders, at 20 Abercorn Place, Maida Vale.

Early in 1881, hospital records note: 'Became ill and was placed in an Asylum. Away with Dr Swete [?].' The Hospital examination book records that Sanders 'Retired because of ill-health'. If the name 'Swete' is correctly transcribed, this would appear to be Dr Edward Horatio Walter Swete of Worcester: the only Dr Swete in the Medical Directories of the time. Medical certificates issued in February 1887 show that Sanders' condition had worsened to the point that he was subject to attacks of violence; made unprovoked assaults on friends; he tyrannised over his household, although he had previously been of a shy and retiring nature. He was apparently placed in an asylum at Virginia Water where he spent the next nine years, before transferring to West Malling for three years, and finally to Heavitree Asylum, Exeter, where he was admitted in 1899 and remained until his death. His death certificate inexplicably describes him as 'Medical Student of Barnsley'.

On 19 October 1888, **Chief Inspector Swanson** supplied reports on the murders for transmission to the Home Office. That on Annie Chapman included the remark, 'Enquiries were also made to trace three insane medical students who had attended London Hospital. Result, two traced, one gone abroad.' (Cf under **Major Henry Smith**.) An undated Home Office memo of about 27 October 1888 runs: 'Please see Mr Wortley's memo on Sir Charles Warren's letter. Shall the police be asked at the same time for report as to what has become of the 3rd insane Medical Student from the London Hospital about whom (under the name of Dr –) there is a good deal of gossip in circulation.' [Dash in original.]

Two days later the Home Office made the request, writing to **Warren**: 'Reference is made to three insane medical students, and it is stated that two have been traced and that one has gone abroad. Mr Matthews would be glad to be informed of the date when the third student went abroad and whether any further enquiry has been made about him.'

Warren's reply quoted a report sent in by **Inspector Abberline**: 'I have to state that searching enquiries were made by an officer in Aberdeen Place [*sic*], St John's Wood, the last known address of the insane medical student named "John Sanders", but the only information that could be obtained was that a lady named Sanders did reside with her son at no. 20, but left that address to go abroad some two years ago.'

Since Laura Tucker Sanders continued to be listed as the occupant of 20 Abercorn Place (evidently the address Abberline mistranscribed) and John was in an asylum in England, the neighbours were presumably underinformed about the family's misfortunes.

The 'good deal of gossip in circulation' about Sanders is not known to have percolated to the press: an interesting instance perhaps, of serious suspicions being kept secret at a high level in the Home Office and Scotland Yard. (Cf the suspects named in the **Macnaghten memoranda**.) Some garbling of Sanders may lie behind the frequent suggestions that Scotland Yard believed the Ripper to be a medical student (see under **Ostrog, Sergeant Stephen White**), sometimes apparently confusing him with **M. J. Druitt** in the suggestion that he drowned in the Thames.

SANDY'S ROW
Northern extension of Middlesex Street (Petticoat Lane) on the boundary of the City of London with Spitalfields.

Mrs Paumier was selling chestnuts on the corner of Sandy's Row and Widegate Street on the morning of Mary Jane Kelly's murder when she was accosted by a man she believed might have been the Ripper.

Although improved shop fronts and road surfaces detract to some extent from the period atmosphere, this little junction of narrow streets and old buildings is the most picturesque of all surviving Ripper-related sites.

SAUNDERS, DR WILLIAM SEDGWICK
Witness at Catharine Eddowes' inquest. MRCS (St Thomas's), 1846. MD, Castleton Med Coll (USA), 1849. Medical Officer of Health and Public Analyst, City of London.

At Eddowes' inquest, Saunders said he had found no trace of poison in his analysis of the contents of the stomach. He had attended the post mortem at Golden Lane Mortuary, and he agreed with **Dr Sequeira** and **Dr Gordon Brown** that the murderer did not possess any anatomical skill, nor, in his opinion, had he any design on any particular organ. His stated concurrence with Dr Brown is curious, since Brown, though declining to accept the coroner's invitation to ascribe 'skill' to the murderer, had consistently asserted that he thought the murderer displayed 'anatomical knowledge', and apparently thought that this had been employed to locate the missing kidney.

Following the publicity given to the **Lusk kidney**, with the misinformation that it was a woman's 'ginny' kidney, reported in the press as emanating from **Dr Openshaw** (cf. **F. Reed**), Saunders told the *Evening News*:

> It is a pity that some people have not the courage to say they don't know. You may take it that there is no difference between the male and female kidney . . . You may take it that the right kidney of the woman Eddowes was perfectly normal in its structure and healthy, and by parity of reasoning you would not get much disease in the left. The liver was healthy and gave no indication that the woman drank. Taking the discovery of half a kidney and supposing it to be human, my opinion is that it was a student's antic. It is quite possible for any student to obtain a kidney for this purpose.

(But see under **Dr Gordon Brown** for signs of Bright's Disease in the right kidney.)

In 1972 Mr A. L. Lee of Torquay wrote to Colin Wilson that his father had worked in the Golden Lane Mortuary under Saunders' direction. (He had misheard or misremembered his forename as 'Cedric'.) A Dr Stanley had been a close friend of Saunders, and frequently visited him at the mortuary, until one day he remarked in Mr Lee senior's hearing, 'The cows have got my son. I'll get even with them.' Shortly after this the murders started, and subsequently Saunders told Mr Lee senior, 'Yes, he was Jack the Ripper.'

Prima facie this is exciting confirmation of the existence of **'Dr Stanley'**, though it is puzzling that **Leonard Matters** should have indicated that he made up the name to conceal the identity of the suspect. Noting the possibility that Stanley was the doctor's forename, however, we must also observe that Mr A. L. Lee further recalled having read an article in the *People* in the 1920s naming Dr Stanley – probably the piece which Matters had written and which elicited his second witness to the doctor's existence (**Mrs North**). And it is therefore possible that unconscious recollection of the name in the article contaminated Mr Lee's memory.

SCHWARTZ, ISRAEL

Witness to assault on Elizabeth Stride. Possibly **Anderson's witness**. Immigrant of Hungarian, probably Jewish, extraction. Resident of 22 Ellen Street (which crosses Berner Street). In appearance, Semitic and thespian.

On 30 September 1888 he gave information to Metropolitan Police recorded on file by **Chief Inspector Swanson**:

> 12.45 a.m. 30th Israel Schwartz of 22 Helen Street [*sc*. Ellen St], Backchurch Lane, stated that at this hour, on turning into Berner Street from Commercial Street [*sc*. Road] and having got as far as the gateway where the murder was committed, he saw a man stop and speak to a woman, who was standing in the gateway. The man tried to pull the woman into the street, but he turned her round and threw her down on the footway and the woman screamed three times, but not very loudly. On crossing to the opposite side of the street, he saw a second man standing lighting his pipe. The man who threw the woman down called out, apparently to the man on the opposite side of the road, 'Lipski', and then Schwartz walked away, but finding that he was followed by the second man, he ran so far as the railway arch, but the man did not follow so far.

> Schwartz cannot say whether the two men were together or known to each other. Upon being taken to the Mortuary Schwartz identified the body as that of the woman he had seen. He thus describes the first man,

who threw the woman down:- age, about 30; ht, 5ft 5in[s]; comp., fair; hair, dark; small brown moustache, full face, broad shouldered; dress, dark jacket and trousers, black cap with peak, and nothing in his hands.

Second man: age, 35; ht., 5ft 11 in[s]; comp., fresh; hair, light brown; dress, dark overcoat, old black hard felt hat, wide brim; had a clay pipe in his hand.

Swanson's report goes on to observe:

If Schwartz is to be believed, and the police report of his statement casts no doubt on it, it follows if they [Schwartz and **Police Constable William Smith**] are describing different men that the man Schwartz saw and described is the more probable of the two to be the murderer.

He points out, however, that fifteen minutes separated the incident Schwartz witnessed and the finding of the body; ample time for Stride to have escaped and accosted or been accosted by her murderer.

Schwartz was barely noticed in the press, the *Manchester Guardian* of 2 October, for example, saying, 'During the day all sorts of stories were brought to the police . . . Another story was to the effect that a man of light complexion had been struggling with the woman Stride in Berner Street and that he threw her down, but it being thought that it was a man and wife quarrelling nobody interfered with them.'

On 10 October the *Star* published an interview with Schwartz – the only detailed account of his story known outside the Home Office Files:

Information which may be important was given to the Leman Street police yesterday by an Hungarian concerning this murder. The foreigner was well dressed, and had the appearance of being in the theatrical line. He could not speak a word of English, but came to the police station accompanied by a friend, who acted as interpreter. He gave his name and address, but the police have not disclosed them. A *Star* man, however, got wind of his call, and ran him to earth in Backchurch Lane. The reporter's Hungarian was quite as imperfect as the foreigner's English, but an interpreter was at hand, and the man's story was retold just as he had given it to the police. It is, in fact, to the effect that he saw the whole thing.

It seems that he had gone out for the day, and his wife had expected to move, during his absence, from their lodgings in Berner Street to others in Backchurch Lane. When he first came homewards about a quarter before one he first walked down Berner Street to see if his wife had moved. As he turned the corner from Commercial Road he noticed some distance in front of him a man walking as if partially intoxicated. He walked on behind him, and presently he noticed a woman standing in the entrance to the alleyway where the body was found. The half-tipsy man halted and spoke to her. The Hungarian saw him put his hand on her shoulder and push her back into the passage, but feeling rather timid of getting mixed up in quarrels, he crossed to the other side of the street. Before he had gone many yards, however, he heard the sound of a quarrel, and turned back to learn what was the matter, but just as he stepped from the kerb a second man came out of the doorway of a public house a few doors off, and shouting out some sort of warning to the man who was with the woman, rushed forward as if to attack the intruder. The Hungarian states positively that he saw a knife in the second man's hand, but he waited to see no more. He fled incontinently to his new lodgings.

He described the man with the woman as about 30 years of age, rather stoutly built, and wearing a brown moustache. He was dressed respectably in dark clothes and felt hat. The man who came at him with a knife he also describes, but not in details. He says he was taller than the other but not so stout, and that his moustaches were red. Both men seemed to belong to the same grade of society. The police have arrested one man answering the description the Hungarian furnishes. The prisoner has not been charged, but is held for inquiries to be made. The truth of the man's statement is not wholly accepted.

The *Star* was wrong in imagining Schwartz had only come to police attention the previous day, and there is every sign in the files that his story *was* 'wholly accepted' both on 30 September when it was taken, and in November when an exchange of memos discussed the cry of **'Lipski'** (q.v. for discussion of **Abberline**'s probable greater accuracy than the *Star* reporter's).

Other differences between the *Star* account and the police files are the suggestion that Stride was pulled into Dutfield's Yard and not thrown on the pavement of Berner Street; that the man leaving the pub carried a knife and not a pipe; and that he shouted the warning to the assailant and apparently chased Schwartz. The differences are probably owing to interpretation difficulties, and the immediacy of the police report makes it more probably accurate.

The most puzzling feature of the Schwartz incident is that there is no report in the press of his being called to testify at Stride's inquest, and no report of any closed session when he might have testified in camera. Two other important witnesses did not testify either.

Schwartz's evidence was in the highest degree material. It would be a serious offence for the police to withhold an important witness from the coroner, and **Wynne Baxter** was not a coroner who would let any such defalcation of duty pass by lightly.

So there remains the possibility that **Dr Robert Anderson**'s passing remark in the exchange of memos over the cry of 'Lipski' was accurate and not a slip of the pen: that he meant what he said when he wrote, '. . . the evidence given by Schwartz at the inquest in Elizabeth Stride's case . . .', and he was not misremembering.

SCIENCE AND SCIENTIFIC EVIDENCE
See under **Forensic Science**.

SCOTLAND YARD FILES
The files have been available to all researchers in the Public Record Office at Kew since 1976, and had been used by certain individuals (notably **Douglas Browne**, **Stephen Knight**, BBC researchers, and **Donald Rumbelow**; also, apparently, **Leonard Matters**) prior to being opened generally. They were originally closed until 1992. It is normal for serious crime files to be closed for seventy-five or a hundred years, to protect the innocent who may be mentioned in them. The interesting question is why they should have been closed as late as 1892.

The version of the **Macnaghten memoranda** deposited among them gives a clear and important pointer to Scotland Yard's principal suspects. (See under **Douglas Browne** for the suggestion of another clue the files may once have held.)

The purloining of papers as souvenirs goes back to at least the second decade of the century, when somebody took Ripper- and Crippen-related documents which were only returned to Scotland Yard in 1987. About a hundred papers from the 'Suspects' file went missing about ten years ago and we append some account of them to this descriptive listing of the surviving files.

The documents in these files are not in date order, but prior to micro-filming in 1988 were provided with an index which lists the contents in chronological order. We have followed this system. Cross-references HO are to **Home Office files**.

MEPO 3/140 Separate Murders
Emma Elizabeth Smith

| | 180–203 | These folios are no longer in the files. They were noted as missing in December 1983. |

Martha Tabram

1. 7 Aug. 88	33	Photograph of Martha Tabram.
2. 10 Aug. 88	34	Report by Inspector Ellisdon of discovery of the body.
3. 16 Aug. 88	44–48	Report by Inspector Reid of identification of body and of soldiers' parade before 'Pearly Poll'.
4. 24 Aug. 88	49–51	Report by Inspector Reid of conclusion of Tabram inquest.
5. Sept. 88	37–43	Report by Chief Inspector Swanson of inquiry into Tabram murder, prepared at Commissioner's request. Also in HO/144/220/A49301,C,8a.
6. 25 Sept. 88	52–59	Report by Inspector Reid of inspections at Tower and Wellington Barracks for man seen by **Police Constable Barrett**.
7.	33	Tabulated details of Tabram murder.
8. 19 Oct. 88	60	Index to report prepared by Swanson.

Mary Ann Nichols

| 9. 31 Aug. 88 | 239–241 | Report by Inspector Spratling on finding of body. |
| 10. 7 Sept. 88 | 235–238 | Report by Inspector Helson on identification of body. States (a) 'no doubt that the murder was committed where the body was found'; (b) 'in all probability there was only one murderer'; (c) 'a man named Jack Pizer, alias Leather Apron, has for some considerable period been illusing [*sic*] prostitutes in this and other parts of the Metropolis and careful search has been made and is continued to be made to find this man . . . though |

at present there is no evidence against
him.'

Annie Chapman

11. 8 Sept. 88	9–11	Report by Inspector Chandler on discovery of body. Appended note by Acting Superintendent West that Chandler is making investigation, with Sergeants Thick and Leach, Inspector Reid being on annual leave. A minute notes Abberline told that morning to combine Chapman and Nichols enquiries.
12. 11 Sept. 88	12–13	Report by Inspector Styles, Y Division, of visit by Drs Cowen and Crabb; their suggestion that Issenschmidt was the Ripper; and enquiries therein.
13. 13 Sept. 88	14–15	
14. 14 Sept. 88	16	Report by Inspector Chandler of enquiries at 1st Battalion, Sussex Regiment, concerning piece of envelope found near body.
15. 14 Sept. 88	17	Report by Inspector Abberline re (a) **Edward Stanley**; (b) enquiries at London Hospital with no useful outcome; (c) special report re a memo submitted by Commissioner; (d) arrest of **Edward McKenna**.
16. 15 Sept. 88	18–20	Report by Inspector Chandler on further enquiries at Sussex Regiment.
17. 17 Sept. 88	21–23	Report by Sergeant Thick on enquiries into Issenschmidt.
18. 18 Sept. 88	24–25	Report by Abberline giving opinion that Issenschmidt is man seen by **Mrs Fiddymont** and stating difficulty of gaining access to Issenschmidt for identification. A minute noted that **Williamson** had seen the doctor at the asylum.
19. 19 Sept. 88	26–28	Report by Thick of interview with Mrs Issenschmidt. Item 17 was originally appended.
20. 19 Sept. 88	29–31	Report by Inspector Helson summarising investigation of Issenschmidt.
21. 19 Sept. 88	242–247	Abberline's summary of Chapman and Nichols investigation. Comments on Pizer of special interest.

Elizabeth Stride

22. 4 Oct. 88	211	Report by Inspector Moore referring to **Packer**'s statement to *Evening News*

(not included) that he had not been
interviewed by police. Moore stated he
had sent Sergeant White to take Packer
to mortuary to identify Stride, and
White had returned and submitted
report. Telegrams between Scotland
Yard and H Division mentioned.

concerning theory of 'two brainy men'
in City Police, 'a far more intellectual
class of men than their brethren of
Scotland Yard'. This concluded
Eddowes went to Mitre Square by prior
appointment with her killer; that
Stride's killer would not have had time
to keep the appointment had he not been
interrupted; ergo Stride's murderer was
not Eddowes' murderer, but the two
killers worked in concert. George
Lewis, 'the great criminal lawyer of Ely
Place', concurred! An interesting and
mysterious observation, however, is: 'It
is an open secret . . . that certain
members of a quasi-religious
organisation whose eccentric methods
have again and again encountered
adverse criticism at the hands of the
press and the public have been closely
watched for some time past.'

Rose Mylett
(A separate file MEPO 3/143 includes papers on Wynne Baxter's complaints about the superfluity of doctors examining the body.)
34. 28 Dec. 88   1–2   Extract from *Daily Chronicle*.
35. "   "   Extract from *Daily Chronicle*.

Alice McKenzie
36.   259   Photograph of McKenzie.
37. 17 Jul. 89   272–273 Sergeant Badham's report of finding the
                            body, and his part in subsequent
                            events.
38. 17 Jul. 89   274   Police Constable Andrews' report on
                            finding the body.
39. 17 Jul. 89   294–297 Report by Inspector Moore.
40. 18 Jul. 89   259–262 Medical report by Dr Bond erroneously
                            dated 8 July: 'I see in this murder
                            evidence of similar design to the former
                            Whitechapel murders, viz. – sudden
                            onslaught on the prostrate woman, the
                            throat skilfully and resolutely cut with
                            subsequent mutilation . . . I am of the
                            opinion that the murder was performed
                            by the same person who committed the
                            former series of Whitechapel murders.'
                            [This directly contradicts **Dr Phillips**
                            (item 47 below) and apparently
                            contradicts Bond's own earlier general
                            report (item 30 above) which postulated
                            no skill at all on the murderer's part; not
                            even the skill of a butcher.]

41. 19 Jul. 89   284–287   Statement forwarded by Inspector Moore in which William Wallace Brodie confessed murdering McKenzie. Appended note by Inspector Arnold dismisses story as Brodie of unsound mind.

42. 19 Jul. 89   280–281   Report from Inspector Moore requesting instructions from Scotland Yard re Brodie. Minuted response, 'Let him be charged as a lunatic.'

43. 19 Jul. 89   279   Report from Inspector Haines, Convict Supervision Office, that Brodie had conviction for larceny.

44. 19 Jul. 89   282   Report from Sergeant Godley on enquiries about Brodie's brothers.

45. 19 Jul. 89   283   Report from Sergeant Bradshaw on enquiries at Brodie's lodgings.

46. 20 Jul. 89   288   Report from Inspector Moore on Brodie's committal proceedings at Thames Magistrates Court. (Verbatim report in *Evening Standard*, 20 Jul. 89.)

47 22 Jul. 89   264–271   Dr Phillips' medical report on McKenzie, concluding, 'I cannot satisfy myself . . . that the perpetrator of all the Whitechapel murders is one man. I am on the contrary inclined to the contrary conclusion.' (Cf. Dr Bond in item 40 above.)

48. 22 Jul. 89   275   Statement by Margaret Franklin who saw McKenzie in Brick Lane.

49. 22 Jul. 89   276   Statement by **Elizabeth Ryder**, deputy of McKenzie's lodging house.

50. 23 Jul. 89   278   Report by Sergeant Bradshaw confirming Brodie in South Africa between 6 Sept. 88 and 15 Jul. 89.

51. 24 Jul. 89   278   Report by Sergeant McCarthy, L Division, of interview with George Dixon who was in McKenzie's company the night of her murder.

52. 27 Jul. 89   277   Sergeant McCarthy reports failure to find corroboration of Dixon's story.

53. 27 Jul. 89   290–291   Inspector Moore reports Brodie liberated and rearrested for fraud.

54.   292–293   Extract from *Kimberley Advertiser*, 29 Jun. 89, reporting Brodie confessing to Whitechapel Murders there while drunk.

Pinchin Street Murder
55.   Plan of district.

56. 10 Sept. 89   136–140   Swanson reports discovery of remains: 'absence of attack on genitals as in

series of Whitechapel murders
beginning in Buck's Row and ending in
Miller's Court'. [First known limitation
of Ripper canon to the five murders
specified in **Macnaghten memoranda**.
But subsequent dismissal of Pinchin
Street torso as Ripper victim rested on
circumstantial evidence rather than
knowledge or belief that the Ripper was
dead or incarcerated.]

57. 10 Sept. 89   170–173   Percy J. Clark's detailed examination of
the remains.

58. 11 Sept. 89   125–134   Monro's report to J. S. Sandars: see
HO144/221/A49301, K, subs. 1.

59. 11 Sept. 89   148–150   Inspector Reid's report with appended
note from Inspector Moore, enclosing
reports [not included] from Sergeant
Thick and White describing
investigations conducted with Sergeant
Godley and referring to bloodstained
clothing in Batty Street.

60. 11 Sept. 89   141–145   Post mortem report by Dr C. A.
Hibbert.

61. 11 Sept. 89   146–147   Comments by Dr Hibbert [written 11
Sept. but re-dated 16 Sept.].

62. 11 Sept. 89   135   Extract from London edition of *New
York Herald*, stating John Cleary
informed night editor on 7 Sept. 89 of
murder in Backchurch Lane [off which
runs Pinchin Street; so did Cleary
anticipate body dumped there three
nights later?].

63. 11 Sept. 89   151   Inspector Pattenden suggests incident
following which woman was taken by
police to London Hospital may lie
behind Cleary's statement.

64. 12 Sept. 89   152   Missing.

65. 12 Sept. 89   153–157   Report by Swanson on man called
Leary.

66. 12 Sept. 89   158–159   Report by Inspector Moore on Mr Miller
of the *Star*'s suspicion that Cleary might
be former *Globe* compositor.

67. 12 Sept. 89   160–165   Report by Swanson and statement from
John Arnold, newsvendor of Charing
Cross, saying he was 'John Cleary'. On
leaving King Lud pub, had been told
by a soldier in Fleet Street, 'Hurry up
with your papers. Another horrible
murder in Backchurch Lane.' Had then
gone to *Herald*. Soldier 35/36; 5ft 6ins;
fair complexion and moustache; carried
parcel.

68. 12 Sept. 89   166–169   Notes on remains by Dr Phillips.
69. 24 Sept. 89   174–175   Inspector Moore reports no progress in enquiry; Acting Superintendent West seeks permission to bury remains; minutes debate burial or preservation.
70. 30 Sept. 89   176–177   Moore reports on burial and preservation.
71. 5 Oct. 89   178–179   Moore reports body preserved in spirits in sealed container and buried 4 Oct. 89.

Frances Coles
72. 13 Feb. 91   113–116   Inspector Arnold reports discovery of body and Dr Phillips' opinion that murder is unconnected with previous crimes.
73. 14 Feb. 91   97–108   Report by Swanson giving statement of **James Thomas Sadler** who met Coles in Princess Alice pub and was suspected of murdering her.
74. 15 Feb. 91   119–121   Report on identification of body by James William Coles, father, and Mary Ann Coles, sister.
75. 16 Feb. 91   117–118   Report of Sadler's arrest.
76. 18 Feb. 91   63–64   Moore submits photographs of Coles.
77. 21 Feb. 91   65–74   Swanson reports trying to interview Mrs Sadler.
78. 25 Feb. 91   81–82   Statement of Kate McCarthy.
79. 25 Feb. 91   83–85   Statement of Thomas Fowles.
80. 27 Feb. 91   88–89   Missing.
81. 2 Mar. 91   75–78   Moore's report on Sadler's movements over previous years.
82. 3 Mar. 91   79–80   Report on Sadler's whereabouts 16–20 Jul. 89.
83. 3 Mar. 91   86–87   Missing.
84. 11 Dec. 91   90–91   Swanson reports on complaint against Sadler by his wife.
85. 16 Dec. 91   92–93   Sergeant Buswell reports no further cause for complaint since Mrs Sadler saw Swanson.
86. 1 Jan. 92   94–95   Sergeant Buswell reports Sadler has shop doing 'good ready money trade' and a changed character.
87. 4 Mar. 92   96   Buswell reports renewed strife between Sadlers.
88. 10 Mar. 92   109   Buswell reports no developments chez Sadler.
89. 9 May 92   110   Buswell reports Mrs Sadler summonsing husband.
90. 16 May 92   111   Sadler bound over to keep the peace for six months.
91. 2 Jan. 93   112   Sadler reports intention of changing address.

MEPO 3/141

Folios 32–135 are missing. They were present when the files were deposited at the Public Record Office, and are believed to have 'gone missing' at the same time as folios 180–203 (*Emma Elizabeth Smith*) in MEPO 3.140, a loss noted in December 1983.

The documents were seen by Elwyn Jones and John Lloyd (or their researchers) during preparation of the 1973 BBC Television series *Jack and Ripper*, and the book *The Ripper File*, based on the series, makes reference to a file of suspects in MEPO 3/141. Clearly this file contained the missing folios 32–135, and is described by us as 'Missing Suspect File'.

The remaining documents are as follows:

1. 10 Sept. 88	175–176	Letter from **Samuel Montagu** MP offering £100 reward.
2. 13 Sept. 88	173–174	Letter from Home Office to Warren re Montagu's offer. (Cf. HO 144/220/A49301, B, subs. 2.)
3. 19 Sept. 88	170–172	Letter [not sent] from Warren to **Henry Matthews**.
4. 30 Sept. 88	184	Police handbill requesting information re Chapman and Nichols.
5. 13 Oct. 88	185	Extract from *Daily Chronicle* mentioning: suspicious man admitted to London Hospital; arrest of John Foster in Belfast; bloodhounds; and (perhaps most importantly) allegation that police believed 'Juwes' was Yiddish for 'Jews'.
6. 17 Oct. 88	136–137	Letter (not included) from Samuel Montagu enclosing Whitechapel traders' petition for increased police numbers.
7. 22 Oct. 88	164–166	Report from Superintendent Arnold on Whitechapel beats, detailing absences due to sickness, leave, etc., and suggesting augmentation by 25 constables.
8. 22 Oct. 88	167–169	Letter from **Godfrey Lushington** to Commissioner re petition of East End women [not included: see under **Henrietta Barnett**] and requesting information re prostitution, brothels, lodging houses, etc.
9. 25 Oct. 88	158–163	Reply to above: 62 brothels in H Division; 233 common lodging houses; 1,200 prostitutes.
10. 26 Oct. 88	138	Note of Commissioner's request for augmentation of 306 men.
11. 10 Nov. 88	150–157	Report from Dr Bond. (See MEPO 3.140, item 30; HO 144/220/A49301, C, subs. 21.)

12. 29 Nov. 88	149	Request from Lushington for map of H Division with number of inhabited houses and population estimate.
13–31		19 subsections concerning formal applications and sanctions of payment allowances to policemen drafted into Whitechapel. Dated Mar., Jul., Aug., Sept., Oct., Nov. 89; Jan., Feb. 90; Mar. 91.
32–135		The Missing Suspects' File (see below).

Add. ff. 32–35:

32. 27 Jul. 89	148	Letter from Lushington to Monro re letter in *Times* from **Samuel Barnett**.
33. 3 Aug. 89	145–147	Report from Superintendent Arnold re interview with Barnett.
34. 5 Aug. 89		Reply from Monro re Barnett letter. (Cf. HO 144/220/A49301, A, subs. 5.)
35. Feb. 94		The **Macnaghten memorandum**.

MEPO 3/142

This file contains many letters claiming to be from the murderer. Most are childish and repetitious; a few are chilling; none are believed to be genuine. They were sent to police, newspapers, businesses, etc. One was washed ashore in a bottle.

The most interesting item is a note by **Inspector Moore** showing that as late as 1896 he believed the **Goulston Street graffito** to be a useful example of the murderer's genuine handwriting, and thought some of the '**Jack the Ripper' letters** were genuine also. (**Abberline, Robert Anderson, Dew, Macnaghten** and **Swanson** are known to have believed the opposite.)

The Missing Suspects File
(MEPO 3/141 32–135)

Jones and Lloyd comment on the absence of any papers on **Druitt, Kosminski** and **Ostrog** on the file when they saw it.

The bulk of the file appears to have consisted of police reports on suspects indicated by members of the public. At least a hundred men were taken to police stations for carrying black bags, having foreign accents, accosting women, or talking about the Ripper in pubs. Such suspects were promptly released on proving their respectability – generally a matter of proving their identity (as **Police Constable Spicer** complained). There was also a batch of reports from the Divisions, apparently in response to a Scotland Yard request of 17 January 1889, listing all persons detained in connection with the Whitechapel Murders since 31 October 1888.

The file also contained documents on **Robert Donston Stephenson** and **Wentworth Bell Smith** which have been quoted by earlier researchers (e.g., **Stephen Knight, Donald Rumbelow, Melvin Harris, Colin Wilson** and **Robin Odell**).

The following are illustrative of the kind of material now missing:

18 Dec. 1888	Report from Kingston Police Station that John

	Hemmings and William Shuber had reported the strange behaviour of Arthur Henry Mason of Kingston to Police Constable Robert Large, 548T. Mason was questioned and released.
27 Sept. 88	Bremen police respond to enquiry from Scotland Yard (not included) saying, 'evidently the hairdresser Mary is the person referred to'. 7 August 1888, 'Mary' (a male) had completed a seven year sentence; been rearrested and sent to Oslebshausen from which he would be released, 7 August 1889.
19 Oct. 1888	Detective Baring of Bremen writes that 'Mary' had been arrested several times for assaulting women and girls in the breasts and private parts with a sharp instrument, and attempting to rape a young girl in his barbershop.
22 Oct. 1888	Abberline reports that 'Mary', undergoing 12 months imprisonment, 'could not be connected with the recent murders in Whitechapel'. Also notes: 'With regard to the man Wetzel [i.e., **Charles Ludwig**]. It has been clearly proved that he was in no way concerned in the matter. He also was under remand at the time the Berner Street and Mitre Square murders were committed. See reports herewith.' [Reports not included.]
5 Oct. 88	Chief Constable, Rotherham, reports discharged soldier James Oliver as believing 'Dick Austin' to be the Ripper: a 'perfect woman hater' who said that if he had his will he would 'kill every whore and rip her inside out'.
16 Oct. 88	Report from Abberline on unsuccessful appeal to Divisions for any information re Austin.
19 Oct. 88	Chief Constable, Rotherham, reports second interview with Oliver who added nothing material. Requests copies of 'Jack the Ripper' letters.
24 Oct. 88	Chief Constable, Rotherham, says Oliver thought 'Ripper' handwriting very like Austin's – 'especially that of the letter (written with steel pen) that of post-card (written with quill) he does not think so like'.
14 Jan. 89	Police Constable S. Richards reports on information laid by Richard Wingate Baker (or, possibly, baker) of 10 Church Street, Edgware Road, who suspected Pierce John Robinson, a man who had entered partnership with him five weeks previously. Wingate Baker's suspicions were aroused by Robinson's falling silent during conversation about the murders, and his sending his mistress, Miss Peters of High Street, Portslade, near Brighton, a letter expressing 'fear that he would be caught today'.

Subsequent investigations by Superintendents
Waghorn and Arnold and Sergeant Thick showed
that Robinson was a religio-maniac and quack
doctor; that he had formerly lived at Mile End
where he was convicted of bigamy. His bigamous
wife knew that he had been with Miss Peters in
Portslade on the night of 9 November 1888.

The above section of the file included the documents on Wentworth Bell
Smith, and appears to have dealt with suspects the Yard took seriously for
at least a time. The next section contained the reports from Divisions
following the Yard's general enquiry of 17 January 1889.

A DIVISION, King Street
13 Nov. 1888. **Edward Knight Larkins** pointed out artist's model Antoni
Pricha to Police Constable Thomas Maybank 61A, suggesting he fitted
description of the wanted man. Pricha proved an alibi for 8/9 November
and was released.
8 Dec. 1888. Edwin Burrows of Victoria Chambers (a common lodging
house) was brought in, wearing a peaked sailor cap, by Detectives Bradshaw of H Division and Godley of J Division. A Division police knew him
and confirmed his story that he was an occasional vagrant, struggling to
subsist on an allowance of £1 a week from his brother.

A DIVISION, Rochester Row
21 Dec. 1888. Mrs Fanny Drake of Clerkenwell Green turned in Mr
Douglas Cow of Cow & Co., India Rubber Merchants, because he fitted
murderer's description and grinned frighteningly at her. Cow proved his
identity and was released.

A DIVISION, Hyde Park
22 Nov. 1888. Martha Spencer lodged a complaint against James Cornell,
an Irishman who had walked with her in the park and frightened her
with conversation about the Ripper. He proved his respectability and was
released.

B DIVISION, Walton Street
17 Nov. 88. Richard Watson turned in Oliver Matthews because the latter
carried a black bag.

G DIVISION, King's Cross
12 Nov. 1888. John Avery of Willesden confessed to the murders and said
he would commit more had he not lost his bag. Sentenced to 14 days hard
labour as drunk and disorderly.
13 Nov. 1888. John Murphy, Massachusetts seaman of no fixed abode,
wearing cloth cap with peak, brought in from Holborn Casual Ward where
a knife had been found on his person. Abberline investigated, and Murphy
was released when his account of himself proved true.
25 Nov. 1888. W. Van Burst, a Dutchman resident at Bacon's Hotel,
Fitzroy Square, brought in for accosting women at King's Cross Station.
'Enquiries were made which proved satisfactory and he was allowed to go.'
25 Nov. 1888. Alfred Parent of Paris, also resident Bacon's Hotel, Fitzroy

Square, given in custody by prostitute Annie Cook as he offered her a sovereign to go with him, or five sovereigns to spend the night, which she thought a suspiciously large sum. Following enquiries, Parent was released. 28 Dec. 1888. Joseph Denny, wearing long astrakhan-trimmed coat, seen accosting women and brought in. Released after enquiries.

This file also contains reports on Robert Donston Stephenson.

SEASIDE HOME, THE
See **Convalescent Police Seaside Home**.

SECRET IDENTITY OF JACK THE RIPPER, THE
TV documentary by Cosgrove-Muerer Productions (Los Angeles) broadcast throughout the English-speaking world with the exception of Britain, November 1988.

Dramatised reconstructions of the murders were slotted into deliberations by a panel of experts from Scotland Yard, the FBI, the Milton Helpern International Institute of Forensic Sciences, and the British Bar, under the chairmanship of Peter Ustinov. The panel was invited to choose between **Prince Albert Victor, 'Dr D'Onston', M. J. Druitt, Sir William Gull** and **Kosminski** as the most likely Jack the Ripper. The panel unanimously voted for Kosminski, though it is known to the authors, who were associated with the programme, that this apparent unanimity included such varying private opinions as that the case had not been proved, or that the 'Kosminski' case incorporated information applicable to **David Cohen**.

The original feature of the programme was the **FBI psychological profile** of the Ripper.

British rights were bought up by Thames TV, and to date it has not been broadcast in the UK, but a video version has been released.

SEQUEIRA, DR GEORGE WILLIAM (1859–1926)
First doctor to examine Catharine Eddowes' body. LSA (London Hospital) 1886. With a surgery at 34 Jewry Street, Dr Sequeira was quickly called to the scene in Mitre Square, where he pronounced the body dead, but made no detailed examination while **Dr Gordon Brown**'s arrival was awaited. At the inquest he said that he agreed with Dr Brown's evidence, but in answer to questions from the coroner stated that he believed the murderer showed no skill and had not been seeking any particular organ in extracting the kidney and the uterus. (Brown had said that he showed anatomical knowledge, apparently because he thought the kidney had been specifically sought.)

SERIAL MURDER
Jack the Ripper would today be described as a sexual serial murderer. The condition is often described as 'Brittain's Syndrome', after Dr R. P. Brittain, whose essay 'The Sadistic Murderer' in *Medicine, Science and the Law* (1979) was one of the earliest sophisticated studies of the condition.

Unfortunately, Brittain's description is based on an unstated number of cases, some of whom, it transpires in the course of the text, were *not* murderers. He describes the sadistic murderer as a withdrawn, introspective personality, who might strike acquaintances as a loner, but would not seem dangerous. He may appear obsessive and moralistic, though privately he will practise varied sexual perversions. Brittain notes that the sadistic murderer may or may not rape his victim, or masturbate over or otherwise abuse the corpse.

Elliott Leyton's *Hunting Humans* (1986) is more intellectually adventurous. Leyton, an anthropologist, notes the increase in this form of crime in USA, Great Britain (but *not* Northern Ireland) and West Germany. By comparison of cases, including non-sexual, non-serial mass-murderers, Leyton concludes that the social gratification afforded by such crimes is more important than the sexual opportunism. He suggests that rather rigidly class-divided societies with a highly competitive ethos provide the best nurture for the disorder, and that the sexual serial murderer is really 'stealing' the most valued property (its attractive womenfolk) of a class he fears or to which he enviously aspires. He points persuasively to several serial murderers who appear to have derived more gratification from the publicity following their arrest than from the orgies which constituted their crimes.

Unfortunately he does not say how large a base he is working from, and probably has no firsthand acquaintance with such criminals. His secondary sources sometimes mislead him in crime history, and he is peculiarly inadequate in his treatment of the Ripper, wrongly believing him to have been proved to be a doctor, and questionably arguing that the late Victorian middle classes so 'feared' the people of the social abyss that the Whitechapel murders were self-protective class revenge.

Interestingly, however, **Colin Wilson** has long made similar observations about the misleading pattern of sexual assault in modern 'recreational' murder. Wilson argues that technological civilisation having granted the primal needs of most people (for food, shelter and security), humankind next turns to seek increased sexual gratification, and finally seeks ways of achieving social distinction and self-esteem. Like Leyton, Wilson suggests that vicarious publicity is a powerful unconscious goal of this type of murderer. Like Brittain he notes that the murderer will be conscienceless, though Brittain attributes probable inferiority feelings to such men, whereas Wilson thinks they are of the 'dominant five per cent' which he believes to be found in all groups of males. Potential murderers, however, lack the skills or position to achieve satisfying dominance in their own society. Thus, like Leyton, Wilson feels they are avenging themselves on powerful groups which have refused them equal positions of power.

A totally different view is presented by Joel Norris in *Serial Killers* (with William Birnes, 1988), whose physical examination of 12 serial murderers and study of written cases leads him to believe that the condition is almost entirely neurological; that its physical causes are lesion of the limbic area of the brain and excess doses or absorption of lead and cadmium. In Norris's view it is a diagnosable and treatable disease which is at present reaching epidemic proportions in USA. Norris, like Leyton and Wilson, has garnered some erroneous beliefs from secondary sources in crime history, but by its nature, his theory is less adversely affected by a few wrong facts about murderers.

SHARKEY, TERENCE
Author. Wrote entertaining *Jack the Ripper: 100 Years of Investigation* (1987). Also writes radio plays and stories, and, as a teacher of management skills to government, industry and commerce, writes industrial film scripts.

SHELDEN, NEAL
Researcher. Author of 'Victims of Jack the Ripper' in *True Detective*, January 1989. An exceptionally responsible and professional investigation of the background of the five canonical victims by a serious and gifted researcher.

SHUSTER, SEYMOUR
Druittite theorist. Author of 'Jack the Ripper and Doctor-Identification' in *International Journal of Psychiatry*, 1975. Suggests **M. J. Druitt** may have witnessed a surgical operation as a child and that the trauma manifested itself in frightening fantasies which he expressed by using a knife on East End prostitutes. Links together many themes in a diversionary piece.

SICKERT, JOSEPH GORMAN (1925–)
Informant. Artist and picture restorer. Claims to be illegitimate son of artist **Walter Sickert**, and that the illegal marriage between his grandmother, **Annie Crook**, and **Prince Albert Victor** was witnessed by Mary Jane Kelly, whose subsequent attempts at blackmail led to **Sir William Gull** and other Freemasons committing the Ripper murders at the behest of **Lord Salisbury**.

Joseph Sickert's story was first publicised in the BBC TV drama-documentary *Jack the Ripper* (1973) and subsequently investigated and enlarged by **Stephen Knight** in *Jack the Ripper: The Final Solution* (1976). In 1978, whilst continuing to claim descent from Walter Sickert and Prince Albert Victor, Joseph Sickert confessed to the *Sunday Times* that the story of the Masonic conspiracy was 'a hoax; I made it all up'.

Following the arrest of Peter Sutcliffe, 'The Yorkshire Ripper', Mr Sickert attracted press attention when he claimed to have been harassed and had his life threatened by Sutcliffe. Next, after the death of Stephen Knight, he claimed to have rediscovered a forgotten document which showed that he, Sickert, was entitled to part of the profits of *The Final Solution*. He also retracted his earlier confession, saying he only made it to save the reputation of Walter Sickert. He also revealed his possession of some diaries which he said **Inspector Abberline** had given to Walter Sickert in 1928 for transmission to **Alice Margaret Crook** (by then Mrs Gorman). These purport to contain 'the key to the whole ghastly affair', a claim examined by **Melvyn Fairclough** with sympathy and respect.

In 1990, **Jean Overton Fuller**'s *Sickert and the Ripper Crimes* provided hearsay corroboration of parts of Joseph Sickert's story. According to information given piecemeal to Ms Fuller's mother by **Florence Pash**, Joseph Sickert was Walter's illegitimate son, and the descendant of an heir to the throne, and Walter Sickert had at some time hired Mary Jane Kelly as a nursemaid.

Authorities on Walter Sickert and Prince Albert Victor have not accepted Joseph Sickert's claim to be the child of the former and grandchild of the latter, but Mr Sickert's familial claims are irrelevant to Ripper research, except for the alleged connection with Mary Jane Kelly. No evidence beyond the uncorroborated claims of Ms Fuller has emerged to support such a connection.

The Masonic conspiracy story has not impressed Ripper researchers, who cannot imagine the Government concerning itself with any attempt by East End prostitutes to bring the Royal family into disrepute. Those parts of Mr Sickert's story which can be tested have been shown by **Simon Wood** to be untrue.

It is to be regretted that overall extreme caution is recommended in examining any story emanating from or otherwise associated with Mr Sickert.

SICKERT, WALTER RICHARD (1860–1942)

Recently alleged suspect. Major British painter, of Danish extraction. RA, 1934; resigned, 1935. Founder member of informal New English Art Club; impressionist, responsible for schism which led the Newlyn Group of exterior painters to withdraw. Sickert and his followers in the 'Camden School' concentrated on depressed urban interiors which (with vaguely Degas-like paintings of music-halls) became Sickert's best known and most influential work.

According to friends and associates, Sickert was interested in several murders and criminal cases, and his not otherwise exceptional interest in the Ripper case may have gained a frisson from his having allegedly occupied a room once used by the Ripper himself. (See **Sickert's veterinary suspect.**)

Joseph Gorman Sickert has alleged that Walter knew of a Masonic conspiracy to murder prostitutes who were blackmailing the Government, and **Stephen Knight** came to the conclusion that Sickert was himself one of the murderers. In 1990, **Jean Overton Fuller** claimed that Sickert alone had committed the murders, a conclusion essentially based on the opinion of **Florence Pash** that he must have seen the bodies of all the Ripper victims since he described their injuries graphically.

Both Joseph Sickert and Ms Fuller maintain that Sickert incorporated clues to the Ripper's identity in some of his paintings or their titles. With regard to the latter, Dr Wendy Baron, the authority on Sickert, has pointed out that he customarily gave his work 'joke' titles after the manner of Victorian genre painters whose pictures 'told a story'.

Whilst Walter Sickert was interested in the Ripper crimes, and painted scenes which seem grotesque to some tastes, both Joseph Sickert's and Ms Fuller's stories remain entirely uncorroborated. Extreme caution is recommended.

SICKERT AND THE RIPPER CRIMES

Book by **Jean Overton Fuller** (1990). The book proposes the hypothesis that **Walter Sickert** was Jack the Ripper. The conclusion is based almost wholly on a claim, attributed to Sickert's friend **Florence Pash**, that he had seen the bodies of all the victims, and the *assumption* by Ms Fuller's mother that this must have been at the murder sites (and not, say, in the mortuary; in illustrated papers; or in his imagination).

Ms Fuller attributes to Florence Pash *prima facie* corroboration of **Joseph Sickert**'s claim that Walter was his father, and the catalyst of the Ripper crimes was the relationship between his maternal grandmother **Annie Elizabeth Crook** and **Prince Albert Victor**.

Florence Pash allegedly gave her story piecemeal in 1948 to Violet Overton Fuller, the author's mother. The main claims attributed to Miss Pash are: that Walter Sickert knew the identity of the murderer and painted clues into some of his pictures (notably a seagull in the painting *Ennui*); that the murders were connected with the illegitimate child of an (unnamed) member of the Royal Family; that a child entrusted to Miss Pash's care was in 1892 the victim of a road accident which Walter Sickert claimed to be a murder attempt and which Joseph Sickert later ascribed to **John Netley**; that Joseph Sickert is the illegitimate son of Walter Sickert, and Miss Pash knew his mother **Alice Margaret Crook** very well; and, most importantly, that Miss Pash not only named Mary Jane Kelly, but knew her personally.

Serious doubts are raised, however, by Ms Fuller's assertion that Florence Pash also related the story of a £500 bribe paid to Sickert by Lord Salisbury. This is completely untrue (see under **Lord Salisbury**). There is no evidence that Sickert ever represented himself as the artist concerned or the overpayment for a bad painting as any form of bribe. It seems, then, that Miss Pash received this fictional variant of an actual anecdote in Walter Sickert's repertoire from someone wishing to give verisimilitude to the whole story. This raises the question of how much more of Florence Pash's story came from the same source, and throws doubt on its validity as independent uncontaminated support for Joseph Sickert's story.

The most compelling material in Miss Pash's story is the claim that she knew Mary Jane Kelly personally and named her as a nanny hired by Walter Sickert. We note, however, that Miss Pash's story conflicts with Kelly's own account of her life in London as reported by **Joe Barnett** (and for which there is some inferential support; see **Mrs Carthy**).

In view of all the foregoing, it is recommended that the story be treated with extreme caution until valid corroborative evidence is provided.

SICKERT'S UNNAMED VETERINARY STUDENT
Alleged suspect.

Sir Osbert Sitwell, in *A Free House* (1947) and *Noble Essences* (1950), stated that Sickert's conversation persistently returned to the Tichborne claimant and Jack the Ripper; the latter because 'he thought he knew the identity of the murderer.'

Some years after the murders Sickert took a room in 'a London suburb' (believed by Sacheverell Sitwell to refer to his Camden lodgings in Mornington Crescent). The elderly couple owning the house told him that the previous occupant of his room was the Ripper. He was a veterinary student. Consumptive and delicate-looking, he would sometimes stay out all night and then rush to buy the first edition of the morning newspaper. He sometimes burnt the clothes he had been wearing. When his health began to fail, his widowed mother took him home with her to Bournemouth where he died three months later. Sickert noted the man's name in the margin of a copy of Casanova's *Memoirs* which he subsequently gave to Albert Rutherston, who did not decipher Sickert's marginal scrawls, and lost the book in the blitz.

Donald McCormick claims to have been told the story of the veterinary student by 'a London doctor who knew Sickert and whose father had been at Oxford with **Montague John Druitt**'. McCormick claims that his informant told him the student's name was something like Druitt, Drewett or Hewett. He also suggested to McCormick that Sickert had repeated this story to **Sir Melville Macnaghten** at the Garrick Club, the inference being that this was the 'private information' which convinced Macnaghten of Druitt's guilt.

N. P. Warren has established that the only appropriately named veterinary student at the Royal Veterinary College (itself the only veterinary college outside Scotland in 1888) was George Ailwyn Hewitt, aged 17–18 in 1888. He lived at Aldershot and died in 1908. Warren has also established that of 131 RVC students who failed to proceed with their studies beyond the end of 1888, only one came from Bournemouth: Joseph Ride, who was 27 in 1888.

Cf. also **Steward Hicks**.

SICKINGS, LAURA
Child who thought she found bloodstains left by Ripper. Reported in the press, 12 September 1888, as having found a stain or sprinkle of blood on the fence of no. 25 Hanbury Street, which, coupled with a piece of bloodstained paper found in the **Bayleys'** packing-case manufactory yard, suggested that the murderer had escaped after killing Annie Chapman by crossing two yard fences to the west and leaving through the house passage of no. 25. In the evening papers the same day, **Inspector Chandler** confirmed that the stain was actually urine.

SIMM, CLARENCE (d. 1951)
Recently alleged suspect. His widow, Betty Simm, was reported in *Weekly World News*, 20 June 1989, as saying that he had made a deathbed confession to having killed fourteen prostitutes as a teenager 'to free them from a life of sin'. She herself had met him in London in 1905. Polygraph operator Gerald Mevel, who tested Mrs Simm, said, 'There is less than one half of one percent chance she is lying.'

The authors have in their possession other correspondence suggesting that it is not unknown for unhappy widows to come to the erroneous conclusion that their late husbands were the Ripper.

SIMMONS, POLICE CONSTABLE GEORGE (City)
Assisted **Police Constable Louis Robinson** in taking Catharine Eddowes to Bishopsgate Police Station on 29 September 1888.

SIMONDS, MARY ELIZABETH
Witness at Annie Chapman's inquest. Nurse at Whitechapel Infirmary who, with Frances Wright, stripped and washed Chapman's body, on the orders of the Clerk to the Parish Guardians, and not the police.

SIMS, GEORGE ROBERT (1847–1922)
Journalist with good police contacts, frequently reporting Ripper stories. Also self-alleged casual contemporaneous suspect. Best remembered as the author of 'Christmas Day in the Workhouse', Sims was a prolific author and journalist, writing thirty plays and many books of reminiscences and of London low-life, upon which he was an expert. Originally employed in the City, he began his literary career on the staff of *Fun*. During 1874–7 he wrote for the *Daily Dispatch*, and from 1877 until his death, under the pseudonym 'Dagonet', he wrote the 'Mustard and Cress' feature of light-hearted snippets in the *Referee*.

From 1891 he made frequent reference to an incident of 1888 when a coffee-stallholder in Whitechapel believed that Sims' portrait, advertising his latest book, was the perfect likeness of a suspicious man with blood-stained cuffs who had come to his stall shortly after the double murders and announced that the stallholder would hear of two more murders the following day. (The incident was reported in some newspapers.) Sims, possibly sportively, affected to believe that the Ripper really did look exactly like himself.

At some point he apparently learned of **Melville Macnaghten**'s suspicion of **M. J. Druitt**, for he took to describing the Ripper as a man known to the police as having drowned in the Thames at the end of 1888, and also as a man who travelled to the East End from the West End or City. His insistence on this in 1903 provoked **Inspector Abberline** to publicise his suspicion of **Severin Klosowski**, and hence **Inspector Reid**'s announcement of his own beliefs on the case. **Inspector Cunningham** and **Benjamin Leeson** have both been named as policemen who guided Sims round London low-life districts.

See also under **Mrs Kennedy**.

SIXTH SENSE, THE (1972, USA)

TV series (25 × 50 min) starring Gary Collins, Patty Duke Astin, Robert Foxworth; college professor investigated cases of psychic phenomena; episode 'With Affection, Jack the Ripper'.

SMITH, EMMA ELIZABETH (1843–88)

Alleged Ripper victim. Widow, resident 18 George Street, Spitalfields. On 2 April 1888, Bank Holiday Monday, she spent the evening, probably soliciting, in and around Whitechapel High Street. Shortly after midnight she was returning home along Osborn Street, when three youths – the youngest no older than 18, by her account – who had followed her from Whitechapel church, assaulted her opposite Taylor Bros Mustard and Cocoa Mill on the corner of Brick Lane and Wentworth Street. She was robbed and raped, and a blunt instrument was forced into her vagina, tearing the perineum. She was taken to the London Hospital where she passed into a coma and died of peritonitis, 5 April. Police assumed she was a victim of an Old Nichol gang (see **gangs, East End**) but never arrested the perpetrators.

In September, the press started describing her as a Ripper victim. Her abdominal injuries, combined with the location of Martha Tabram's murder, are often assigned to the legendary 'first victim' of December 1887 (see **'Fairy Fay'**). It is possible that she was the Elizabeth Smith whose frequent appearances at Thames Magistrates Court on drunk and disorderly charges ceased abruptly after 14 December 1887. But the name is sufficiently common for this to be merely speculative.

SMITH, FOUNTAIN (b. 1861)

Annie Chapman's brother and witness at her inquest. A tall man with dark hair and a heavy brown moustache; said he had seen his sister shortly before the murder and given her 2/- [10p].

SMITH, G. WENTWORTH BELL

Alleged suspect. Agent of the Toronto Trust Society. (NB: The authors suspect mistranscription of Truss Society which had office in Finsbury Square and solicited donations.) About 5ft 10in tall. Dark hair and complexion; beard and moustache so close-cropped as to suggest need of a shave. Good, possibly false, teeth. Well dressed and well conducted. Foreign appearance. Multilingual. Peculiar splay-footed, weak-kneed gait.

Came on business to Britain for a period of months or a year, 1888–9. Established office in Godliman Street, St Paul's. August 1888, moved to rooms at 27 Sun Street, Finsbury Square, advertised as vacant in the *Daily Telegraph* by Mr and Mrs E. Callaghan.

Mr Callaghan noticed that he wrote fifty to sixty foolscap sheets of religious outpourings at a time. He had religious delusions about women and claimed to have performed 'some wonderful operations'. He seemed obsessed with prostitutes, saying many walked through St Paul's Cathedral during services, and they, and especially East End prostitutes, should be drowned. He wore a different suit every day; stayed out very late at nights, coming and going silently in rubber-soled felt-topped galoshes. On his return he often threw himself down on the sofa and 'foamed'. He kept three loaded revolvers hidden in his chest of drawers. He talked to himself, and once received a postcard reading 'We can't get through it. Can you give me any help? Dodger.'

On the night of Martha Tabram's murder he arrived home at 4.00 a.m. claiming falsely that his watch had been stolen in Bishopgate. Two or three days later he left the Callaghans' declaring that he had to return to Canada, but he was still in England the following month. The Callaghans believed him to be a lunatic, and Mr Callaghan concluded, 'Without doubt this man is the perpetrator of these crimes.' He then claimed to have gone to the police and advised them of Bell Smith's suspicious behaviour; also to have been visited independently by police inquiring for Smith following reports from a lady south of the Thames. (Subsequently **Abberline** and **Swanson** could find no record of these contacts.)

The following year, when the Callaghans had moved to Gainsborough Square, Victoria Park, a woman acquaintance told Mr Callaghan that she had been accosted by a foreign-looking man in Worship Street, and realised he was the same man she had seen washing himself at a standpipe at 4.00 a.m. in the morning after one of the Whitechapel Murders, and had then followed back to Sun Street. Mr Callaghan decided from her description that this was Wentworth Bell Smith. He informed **Dr L. Forbes Winslow**, and stories promptly started appearing in the press that Winslow knew who the Ripper was; that he was in possession of his boots; and with the help of six men would be arresting him very shortly. Chief Inspector Swanson interviewed Winslow, who maintained that the press had misinterpreted his claims. He showed Swanson Callaghan's written statements, and Swanson observed that somebody had changed the date of Smith's late homecoming at 4.00 a.m. from 9 August to 7 August, thus making possible the suggestion that it related to Martha Tabram's murder. Swanson also noted that the felt-topped boots were extremely old and moth-eaten.

Despite the police investigation and dismissal of Callaghan's story in 1889, which Forbes Winslow seems to have told Swanson he endorsed, Winslow fell increasingly under the delusion that he had identified the Ripper, and told variations on this story for the rest of his life, though he did not name Bell Smith to the public. He added details: that Smith came from a well-to-do family, had studied medicine at college, and became unhinged from overwork. He accepted the conclusion of a newspaper that a student arrested for attempted suicide and sent to Broadmoor early in 1890 was his suspect. In 1910 he apparently forgot having accepted this conclusion, and agreed that a lady who wrote to him from Australia had correctly identified a man who sailed to Melbourne in 1889, calling himself 'Jack', as his suspect and the Ripper.

Wentworth Bell Smith may have behaved oddly and disliked prostitutes, but apart from his living reasonably close to the vicinity of the crimes until August 1888, there is nothing known about him to connect him with them. Nor does it seem probable that Forbes Winslow's varied information about 'his suspect's' later career applied to Smith.

NB: A correspondent has drawn our attention to a passage in Colin Wilson and Robin Odell's *Jack the Ripper: Summing Up and Verdict* which can be read as meaning that the words 'Without doubt this man is the perpetrator of these crimes' were Swanson's conclusion about Wentworth Bell Smith. In fact, Swanson wrote them as a direct quotation from Mr Callaghan, and did not agree with the conclusion.

SMITH, GERTRUDE (b. 1831)
Procuress, with **Mary Jones** charged by Inspector Ferrett with brothel-keeping, 7 December 1888. Fined £10 with 5 guineas costs the following day. Entered on same minute of adjudication at Thames Magistrates Court as **Aaron Davis Cohen**, suggesting that his arrest was part and parcel of the activity surrounding the brothel raid.

'SMITH, DR GILBART'
See **Dr S. J. Harvey**.

SMITH, H.
Undertaker of Hanbury Street, who supplied hearse for Annie Chapman.

SMITH, MAJOR HENRY (1835–1921)
Subsequently Lieutenant Colonel Sir Henry, KCB. Acting Commissioner, City of London Police, September 1888. Educ. Edinburgh Academy and University. Worked as bookkeeper in Glasgow until death of his father. 1869, commissioned in Suffolk Artillery Militia, taking care of his mother, first as man-about-town in London; thereafter as sporting country gentleman in Northumberland, where he remained after her death. In 1879 he began casting about for employment, preferably in senior ranks of the police. He failed to gain appointments in Scotland, Newcastle and Liverpool. In 1875, six years after his original application, he was appointed Chief Superintendent, City of London Police. 1890–1901, Commissioner. KCB, 1910.

Popular and worldly, he was good at public relations and was given a favourable press (especially compared with Scotland Yard) at the time of the Whitechapel Murders. **Sir James Fraser**, the Commissioner, was on leave at the time of the Mitre Square murder within the City Police boundaries, so Major Smith took immediate charge of the investigation. The press felt that the City Police, under his direction, were frank and helpful whereas the Metropolitan Police were obstructive and secretive. But see under **James McWilliam** for the Home Office view that the City was more secretive than the Met.

In his memoirs *From Constable to Commissioner* (1910) he wrote, 'There is no man living who knows as much of those murders as I do', a claim that was accepted at face value until the discovery in 1988 of G. H.

Edwards' caveat concerning the major's veracity, written on the title-page of the Scotland Yard library copy, and the realisation that some of the major's anecdotes were demonstrably untrue. Thus, he claimed that he was 'within five minutes of the perpetrator one night, and with a very fair description of him besides' – apparently a reference to his story of finding a public sink where the Ripper had just washed his bloodstained hands shortly after the Mitre Square murder. Yet the major's documented movements that night make it impossible for him to have been five minutes behind the Ripper, and a few pages later he placed the same incident shortly after the Miller's Court murder.

Other important stories the major told include his tracing of an insane (but innocent) suspected medical student with a reputation for passing off polished farthings as half-sovereigns when the Metropolitan Police requested his help in searching for him (cf. under **John Sanders, Inspector Reid**); his giving orders to his constabulary to frequent pubs, smoke sociable pipes and collect gossip when on duty during the scare; and his receipt of an unsigned letter from Hoxton promising information if the major would keep an assignation with the writer – an assignation which produced no acknowledged recognition of him, but only a subsequent letter promising definite information (which never materialised) in the future. Smith accepted the **Lusk kidney** as unquestionably genuine, though his account of how it came into the hands of the City Police is most inaccurate. He expressed lasting indignation against **Sir Charles Warren** for erasing the **Goulston Street graffito** before it had been photographed, as Smith claimed he had ordered it should be.

Smith fiercely attacked **Sir Robert Anderson**'s claim to know the identity of the Ripper, accusing him of irresponsible anti-Semitism and designating his investigation 'fruitless'. The clear implication is that the Ripper's identity was completely unknown, but see below.

Without naming Smith, **Sir Melville Macnaghten** challenged his memory when he wrote:

Only two or three years ago I saw a book of police reminiscences (not by a Metropolitan officer) in which the author stated that he knew more of the 'Ripper murders' than any man living, and then went on to say that during the whole of August 1888 he was on the tiptoe of expectation. That writer had indeed a prophetic soul, looking to the fact that the first murder of the Whitechapel miscreant was on 31st August of that year of grace.

H. L. Adam, in the preface to *The Trial of George Chapman*, names Major Smith as one of the senior policeman who had confidentially told him that the Ripper's identity was definitely known. (It is quite clear that they were not referring to Chapman alias **Severin Klosowski**.) It is worth noting, therefore, that Smith's personal profession of ignorance is rather restrictively worded: 'I must admit that . . . [the Ripper] completely beat me and every police officer in London; and I have no more idea now *where he lived* than I had twenty years ago' [our italics]. There is no clue in the major's writing as to who his suspect might have been (cf. **Sagar**); nor do his generalised diatribes against Anderson indicate whether or not he knew who **Anderson's suspect** was. The curious wording above draws our attention to the fact that while the tone implies that Anderson's claim was completely false, the major's words are restricted to saying that Anderson's investigation was fruitless, and his comments were an outrageous affront to the law-abiding Jewish community since he asserted that the Ripper's 'people' shielded him from the law.

SMITH, POLICE CONSTABLE WILLIAM, 425 H (b. 1862)
Joined Metropolitan Police, 1883, transferring into H Division, 1886. Warrant no. 67565. Retired, 1910.

His beat on 29–30 September 1888 was around Commercial Road, Gower Street, Christian Street and Fairclough Street, including such interior streets as Berner Street. It took twenty-five to thirty minutes to walk. About 12.30 a.m., 30 September, he saw a woman whom he later identified as Elizabeth Stride standing in Berner Street with a man opposite Dutfield's Yard. The man was about 5ft 7in; clean-shaven; aged about 28; respectable-looking, wearing dark clothes and a dark-coloured hard felt deerstalker hat. Stride had a flower in her jacket. At about 1.00 a.m. when he returned to Berner Street he saw a crowd of people around Dutfield's Yard, and on investigating found Police Constables 12H and 232H present. He saw Stride's body and went to the police station for an ambulance, **Edward Johnston** arriving as he left.

NB: It has been suggested that the **Macnaghten memoranda**, which describe three Jews driving up to Dutfield's Yard (cf. **Louis Diemschütz**, **Joseph Lawende**) and an otherwise unknown policeman seeing a suspect near Mitre Square, may have confused the locations of the double murder, and the policeman may be Smith.

SPICER, POLICE CONSTABLE ROBERT, 101H (b. 1866)
Self-alleged captor of Jack the Ripper. Joined Metropolitan Police, 1887. Warrant no. 72541. Discharged, April 1889, for being drunk on duty, unnecessarily interfering with two private persons, and considered unfit for the Police Force. Thereafter school groundsman; resident in Saville Row, Woodford Green.

In March 1931 he wrote to the *Daily Express* that one night after the Ripper had committed two murders,

I had worked my beat backwards, and had come to Heneage Street, off **Brick Lane**. About fifty yards on the right down Heneage Street is Heneage Court. At the bottom of the court was a brick-built dustbin. Both Jack and a woman (**Rosy**) were sitting on this. She had 2s [10p] in her hand, and she followed me when I took Jack on suspicion. He turned out to be a highly respected doctor, and gave a Brixton address. His shirt cuffs still had blood on them. Jack had the proverbial bag with him (a brown one). This was not opened and he was allowed to go.

I saw him several times after this at Liverpool Street Station accosting women, and I would remark to him, 'Hello, Jack! Still after them?' He would immediately bolt.

He was always dressed the same – high hat, black suit with silk facings, and a gold watch and chain. He was about 5 feet 8 or 9 inches and about 12 stone, fair moustache, high forehead, and rosy cheeks.

Interviewed by an *Express* reporter, Spicer said that eight or nine inspectors all working on the case were at the station, and Spicer, to his amazement, got into trouble for arresting a respectable doctor. The CID allowed him no further part in investigating the man's story, and Spicer said he was so disappointed that his heart was no longer in police work. He did not, however, as some writers have assumed, make the specifically false claim to have resigned over the issue.

An oral tradition, deriving from Spicer's family, is that the suspect was not a qualified doctor, but a medical student at London Hospital.

See also **F. W. Chapman, Rosy, B. Reilly, 'Dr Merchant'**.

SPIERING, FRANK

Theorist and alleged researcher. Author of *Prince Jack* (USA, 1978). An American former private detective turned scriptwriter, he became interested in the Ripper Case following publication of **Dr Thomas Stowell**'s theory in 1970. By his own account, he then came to England and through the aid of an unnamed friend gained access to **Scotland Yard** and **Home Office files**. He also claimed to have seen 'a copy of Dr. William Gull's notes, bound in an ancient portfolio', kept in, of all places, the New York Academy of Medicine.

According to **Nigel Morland**'s Introduction to the book, Spiering is 'a dedicated writer, a man who puts authenticated research above everything else. He has probed into the Ripper case . . . with a mind unimpressed by baseless facts.' According to all other reviewers, Spiering deals more in fiction than in facts. The *Sunday Times* of 13 August 1978 disclosed that Spiering had dramatised a polite telephone call to himself from the Home Office in which an official granted him immediate access to documents he wanted to see, not trusting the mail to catch him before his scheduled flight home. The Home Office retains Spiering's written thanks for this courtesy. But for public consumption he described it as a 'mysterious' call to his London hotel which led him to suspect that the Home Secretary was on to his methods, was still trying to cover-up **Prince Albert Victor**'s guilt, and left Spiering with 'a slight trace of anxiety'.

SPITALFIELDS

Parish in which Annie Chapman and Mary Jane Kelly were murdered. Named after the 'New Hospital Without Bishopsgate' founded by Walter and Rose Brown in 1187, run by Austin canons and lay helpers, and subsequently known as St Mary's Hospital (or 'Spittal'). After the canons were reprimanded by the Archbishop of Canterbury in 1303 for financial mismanagement and neglect of patients, and for 'frequenting the houses of Alice la Faleyse and Matilda, wife of Thomas', the hospital was rarely free from financial troubles until its closure in 1538. East of the hospital ground was a large field, once called Lolesworth, which was broken up for clay for a brickworks and found to contain a Roman graveyard. Lolesworth Field was the original 'Spittal Field'.

Daniel Defoe recalled the district as full of 'deep, dirty and unfrequented lanes' in his childhood, but already by 1640 building was attracting such noteworthy residents as Nicholas Culpeper the herbalist. An influx of Huguenot refugees after the Revocation of the Edict of Nantes in 1685 led to extensive development, and in 1695 there were 1,300 houses in the narrow, densely populated streets. The Huguenot silk-weaving community was nevertheless generally prosperous, and some of the finest Georgian domestic architecture in London survives in the parish from their period. In 1682 John Balch opened a fruit and vegetable market which survives at the time of writing, but is listed for redevelopment.

The industrial revolution ruined the handloom weaving trade, and by

1807 the streets were full of undesirable common lodging houses and the area was regarded as a slum. The construction of **Commercial Street** in 1845 cleared some foul lanes, but in 1888 **Samuel Barnett** still designated the neighbourhood around **Dorset Street,** Thrawl Street and **Flower and Dean Street** 'the wicked quarter mile'. Those three streets and their offshoots were infested with prostitutes, attracted by the cheap common lodging houses within easy walking distance of St Botolph's Aldgate, where the police tacitly tolerated prostitutes using the surrounding pavement as a beat for soliciting.

The whole parish was increasingly undergoing Jewish settlement throughout the 1880s, being adjacent to **Whitechapel** and close to the Great Synagogue in Duke's Place and the neighbouring Bevis Marks Synagogue.

SPITAL SQUARE
Dr G. Bagster Phillips' surgery was at no. 2. The square, known originally as Spital Yard, was laid out on the site of St Mary Spital's precinct in the 1600s, though most of the buildings were not erected until the 1720s. It was a residential square for silk merchants and master weavers, preserving its privacy from through traffic by barriers. The original name, Spital Yard, is preserved in a cul-de-sac leading off the square which is believed to follow the line of an entrance to the old Priory of St Mary Spital. John Wesley's mother was born there in 1669.

SPOONER, EDWARD
Witness at Elizabeth Stride's inquest. A horse-keeper, resident at 26 Fairclough Street. Between 12.30 and 1.00 a.m. he stood outside the Bee Hive public-house with a young woman. At 1.00 a.m. he saw **Louis Diemschütz** and another man running towards him, shouting, 'Murder!' and 'Police!' He accompanied them back to Berner Street where he saw blood flowing from Stride's throat. He mentioned the flower on her jacket and cachous in her hand, but not the grapestalk.

SPRATLING, INSPECTOR JOHN (1840-c.1934)
Witness at Mary Ann Nichols' inquest. A clerk prior to joining Metropolitan Police in 1870. Warrant no. 53457. After fairly rapid series of promotions, became divisional Inspector, J. Division (possibly succeeding **Inspector Reid** in 1887). Retired, 1897. He is said to have boasted that he smoked blacker tobacco and drank blacker tea than anyone else in the Met, and that he lived so long that he drew more from the Met in pension than in pay.

He was called to Buck's Row at 4.30 a.m., 31 August 1888, as Nichols' blood was being washed away. He went to the mortuary to take a description of the body, and discovered the extent of the injuries when it was stripped, so recalled **Dr Llewellyn.** He and **Sergeant Godley** searched the murder area, especially the East London and District Railway embankments and lines, and the Great Eastern Railway Yard. They found nothing to excite interest.

SPRINGFIELD, LINCOLN
Journalist, responsible for early sensational stories and theories. (See under **William Le Queux.**) In *Some Piquant People* (1924) he claims that **Harry**

Dam was responsible for the potentially libellous suggestion that **John Pizer** was '**Leather Apron**'.

'SQUIBBY'
Criminal, pursued by mob during Ripper scare.

Walter Dew's memoirs describe the pursuit of a very violent local criminal known as 'Squibby' who had thrown a half-brick at a policeman while resisting arrest, shortly after the murder of Annie Chapman. A mob, perceiving policemen chasing a man, assumed that he was the Ripper, and joined in the hunt. When Squibby was arrested in a house in Flower and Dean Street, he gave himself up willingly for fear of the crowd. Normally it took four men to restrain him. The mob pursued the closed carriage in which Squibby was taken to Commercial Street Police Station, and besieged the station for a time, an incident mentioned in the press.

Benjamin Leeson also mentioned Squibby as a well-known East End criminal. It seems likely that he was either William Squibb (b. 1860) who was charged at Thames Magistrates' Court with theft of a watch in February 1888, or the identically aged Charles Squibb who threatened to blind a constable when arrested for trying to steal a watch and chain in August of the same year, or a relative of theirs if the two were in fact different men.

'STANLEY, DR' (died c. 1918)
Fictitious name devised by **Leonard Matters** for alleged suspect advanced by him in 1929.

A brilliant London doctor at 'X' Hospital (Charing Cross?) with a large and aristocratic practice. Resided in Portman Square. Devoted life to study of cancer. Once acted as anaesthetist for Joseph Lister at a Berkeley Street Sanatorium. Had a son named (possibly by Matters) 'Herbert' or 'Bertie' in whom he placed great hopes. Herbert contracted syphilis from Mary Jane Kelly on Boat Race night, 1886, and subsequently died. 'Stanley' set out to avenge his son by killing Kelly and her friends. With his mission complete he travelled the world, settling in Buenos Aires in 1908.

In *More Studies in Murder*, American true-crime writer Edmund Pearson said the 'Dr Stanley' theory bore 'about the same relation to the facts of criminology as the exploits of Peter Rabbit and Jerry Muskrat do to zoology'. Most subsequent writers have agreed. Matters' introduction may contain warnings to this effect, though they could equally be scrupulous warnings that he could not verify a theory deductively offered as history. Matters claimed to rest on two sources: a Spanish account published in a journal he found in Argentina, allegedly by a junior colleague who received the story from Stanley around the time of his death; and '**Mrs North**', who had known a man who seemed to be the doctor in 1888.

Daniel Farson's *Jack the Ripper* (1972) describes a letter from Mr Barca of Streatham, saying that between 1910 and 1920 there was a dive called 'Sally's Bar' in Buenos Aires, allegedly owned by Jack the Ripper.

Colin Wilson heard from Mr A. L. Lee of Torquay that his father had met Dr Stanley, by that name, as a friend of 'Cedric Saunders' who believed him to be the Ripper. (See under **Sedgwick Saunders** for possible contamination of Mr Lee's memory.) A version of this story may have been told to **Michael Harrison** (b. 1907) in childhood, who writes, 'the most slanderous identification, I remember, being that of the venereally infected son of a royal surgeon'.

The authors know of oral tradition suggesting that, without names attached, the story of the doctor avenging his son was current in London before 1910, and note interesting parallels between the 'Doctor Stanley' and the **William Gull** stories.

STANLEY, EDWARD 'THE PENSIONER'

Witness at Annie Chapman's inquest. A bricklayer, resident at 1 Osborn Place, Brick Lane, known to associates as an ex-soldier drawing a pension from the Essex Regiment. Sometimes paid for Chapman's bed at **Crossingham's Lodging-House** at weekends, as well as for **Eliza Cooper**'s. (See under **Annie Chapman** for allegation that the fight between the two women concerned soap borrowed for his use.) Members of the coroner's jury knew the other man in Chapman's life, **'Harry the Hawker'**, but wanted the less familiar Stanley summoned, in case the Sussex Regiment envelope found near her body was connected with him.

Stanley admitted that he had never been in or drawn a pension from any regiment. He had known Chapman for about two years, since she had lived at Windsor. He had been in Gosport between 6 August and 1 September 1888, and had last seen Chapman when he met her at the corner of Brushfield Street on 1 September.

STAR TREK (1967, USA)

TV series (79 × 50 min) starring William Shatner and Leonard Nimoy; cult sf series about adventures on and off starship USS Enterprise; episode 'Wolf in the Fold' by Robert Bloch.

STEAD, WILLIAM THOMAS (1849–1912)

Publicist of crimes and alleged informant. Journalist. Worked for *Northern Echo*, 1871–80. Assistant editor, *Pall Mall Gazette*, 1880–3; editor, 1883–90. Started *Review of Reviews*, 1890. Took up psychical research. Drowned on *Titanic*.

Stead was a founder of the 'new journalism', which improved layout; and pursued sensational crusades: e.g. for the rescue of General Gordon in 1884; for the Criminal Law Amendment Act in 1885 (restraining child prostitution by raising the age of consent). As editor of the radical and (by the standards of the times) sensational *Pall Mall Gazette*, Stead gave heavy coverage to the Whitechapel Murders, using them as part of the radical campaign (more vehemently conducted in the *Star*) attacking the **Metropolitan Police**.

He accepted articles on the case from **Robert Donston Stephenson**, according to whom he also supplied the information that the victims had been sodomised. The medical report on Catharine Eddowes has since proved that the information was wrong, and there is nothing to substantiate Stephenson's claim that it was supplied by Stead.

STEPHEN, JAMES KENNETH (1859–92)

Recently alleged suspect. Educ. King's College, Cambridge. BA, 1882; tutor to **Prince Albert Victor** during his formal residence at Cambridge, 1883; MA, 1885; Fellow, 1885. Suffered serious blow to the head, 1886, which ultimately caused brain damage and death. Published and edited the *Reflector*, 1888; contributed to *Pall Mall Gazette*. Clerk of Assize, South Wales circuit, 1888–90. Returned to residence in Cambridge, 1890, publishing pamphlet in defence of compulsory Greek. 1891, committed to St Andrews Hospital, Northampton, where he died.

Stephen was a scintillating political speaker, and President of the Cambridge Union, 1880. He contributed to *Granta* and other university journals; he published three volumes of undistinguished verse. Some friends felt that the *Reflector* showed marks of mental instability, and his shifting career – don, journalist, lawyer, and again don – is quite unlike the steady Victorian legal progress of his brothers. He furiously resisted the notion that his mind had given way at the end of his life, and his untimely death provoked a good deal of undistinguished obituary verse in Cambridge University journals.

Stephen was proposed as a suspect in Michael Harrison's *Clarence* (1972). Harrison's motive was unusual: in an interview on BBC Radio (reported in the *Listener*, 17 August 1972) he remarked that he had to deal with **Dr Thomas Stowell**'s suggestion that Clarence (i.e. Albert Victor) was the Ripper. 'I didn't agree,' said Harrison. 'But I couldn't leave the reader high and dry, so what I did was find somebody I thought was a likely candidate.'

He based his argument on the speculation that Clarence and Stephen had become homosexual lovers during or after Clarence's time in Cambridge. He thought that some of Stephen's verse indicated misogyny and some showed sadistic tendencies. He suggested that the affair was necessarily broken off, and Stephen then killed prostitutes on dates which would seem significant to his former lover: birthdays of members of the Royal Family, or pre-christian religious festivals. He suggested that two rugby songs, 'Kafoozelum' and 'They called the bastard Stephen', influenced the pattern of the murders: the former because he erroneously believed there to have been ten victims.

The only known external support for the Stephen theory comes from a letter written by Mrs Marny Hallam of Newbury to the *Sunday Times* (16 February 1975) in which she stated that her great-grandfather, a barrister, had long ago told his daughter that the authorities knew Stephen to be the Ripper.

It has been suggested that the blow to the head, which almost certainly caused Stephen's mental breakdown and death, might have caused the type of lesion in the limbic area of the brain which Joel Norris believes to be a primary cause of sexual murder (see under **Serial murder**). Also that Stowell, who undoubtedly knew **Sir William Gull**'s daughter, might indeed have learned from her that one of her father's patients was the Ripper, Stowell mistakenly thinking that she was indicating the Duke of Clarence. It is observed that, according to Harrison, Gull treated Stephen after his blow to the head. Stephen is named in the torn pages from a diary of 1896 shown by **Joseph Sickert** to **Melvyn Fairclough** and purporting to be **Abberline**'s cryptic solution to the mystery.

STEPHENSON, ROBERT DONSTON (b. 1841)

Self-styled **Dr Roslyn D'Onston**. Contemporary theorist and non-contemporaneously alleged suspect. Son of a Yorkshire seed-oil mill owner. Studied chemistry in Munich and medicine in Paris. Claimed to have fought for Garibaldi and pursued occult studies under Bulwer Lytton.

In 1863, under family pressure, he took a post with Customs in Hull, but was continually in trouble, largely because of his belief in his own superiority, and was eventually fired. He moved to London and worked as a freelance journalist, contributing especially to the *Pall Mall Gazette*, which accepted from him pieces on the Whitechapel Murders. At this period he was described by **Inspector Roots** as an excessive drinker 'who always carried drugs to sober him and stave off delirium tremens'. He may conceivably be the Robert Stephenson and/or Robert Stevenson (of approximately the same age) charged at Thames Magistrates Court with assault in June 1887, and indecent assault on 30 October 1888. During the 1890s his interest in Black Magic appears to have waned, and in 1904 he published *The Patristic Gospels*, a serious exercise in comparative Biblical studies. His subsequent career remains unknown.

In November 1888 he was a patient sharing a private ward in the London Hospital with a Dr Evans, who was nightly visited by **Dr Morgan Davies**. On one of these visits he saw the graphic and over-excited re-enactment of the Ripper's supposed M.O. that persuaded him that Davies was the Ripper. He became fully convinced when, allegedly, he learned (erroneously) from **W. T. Stead** that the Ripper habitually sodomised his victims, as Davies's mime indicated.

Stephenson told his story to an unemployed ironmongery assistant named George Marsh, and the two passed themselves off to each other as 'private detectives' investigating Dr Davies. They signed agreements to share whatever reward money they might gain, Marsh later claiming that he only did so to procure a sample of Stephenson's handwriting. On Christmas Eve 1888, Marsh went to Scotland Yard and told Inspector Roots about Stephenson, whom he described as a habitual drinker, perpetually fuddled, though never hopelessly intoxicated. On Boxing Day Stephenson gave his story to Scotland Yard, expressing some contempt for Marsh.

In 1890, Stephenson was living in Southsea with Mabel Collins, novelist and editor of *Lucifer*, the journal of the Theosophical Society. The two met Baroness Vittoria Cremers (d. 1937) and shortly went into business with her as the Pompadour Cosmetics Company in Baker Street. On one occasion, according to what Cremers told journalist Bernard O'Donnell in the late 1920s, she went into Stephenson's room and found several blood-encrusted ties in a black enamelled deed-box. Stephenson, unaware of this discovery, subsequently told her a variant of the story he had been peddling in 1888, with the additional claim that the Ripper concealed the organs he stole under his neckties. A further variant of the story was published in the *East Anglian Daily Times* by Pierre Girouard in 1929. He ascribed it to 'Baroness K . . .' (obviously Vittoria Cremers) whom he had met some years previously in London. He added the details that Stephenson (whom he named only as 'Dr H') had been struck off the register for some malfeasance; that he lived in the Harrow Road at the time of the murders; that he made his living by selling rare perfumes and giving lectures on the occult. He also claimed that the Baroness' revelation of her discovery to the chiefs of a society to which she and the doctor both belonged led to his being sent to the USA, where George Dougherty, formerly of Pinkerton's Agency and the New York Police, confirmed that he died in a New York hospital and confessed his guilt.

In 1920 the ties were in **Aleister Crowley**'s possession at his Abbey of Thelema in Cefalù, Sicily. They were seen there by model Betty May whose husband was a disciple of Crowley's and died at the 'abbey'. She told O'Donnell in 1925 that Crowley said they belonged to Jack the Ripper, a magician known to Crowley, who gave them to him. Crowley said he was 'a well-known surgeon of his day . . . he had attained the highest powers of magic and could make himself invisible'. In later writings he named this man as Stephenson, and asserted that the purpose of the murders was to kill women and extract certain organs ritually in sites that would form a calvary cross on the map, whereafter the murderer would have the gift of invisibility and be enabled to escape with ease from subsequent murder sites.

When Betty May's 'memoirs' (essentially the articles O'Donnell had written in 1925 on her time at Cefalù) were published as *Tiger Woman: My Story*, Crowley noted in the margin of his copy next to the neckties anecdote 'Victoria [*sic*] Cremers' story'.

In 1987 **Melvin Harris** came to the conclusion that Stephenson was the Ripper. He based this on the method of listing attributes he believed the Ripper needed, including: demonstrable presence in Whitechapel in 1888; sufficient strength to commit the crimes; a genteel appearance to lull prostitutes' suspicions. He believed that Stephenson uniquely satisfied all requirements, and claimed that the murders stopped because he underwent a 'religious conversion', for which the only evidence adduced is the publication of *The Patristic Gospels* in 1904. He also claimed that Stephenson's and Marsh's visits to Scotland Yard were deliberate and successful efforts to throw the police off the scent, by making Stephenson appear to be one of the familiar cranks who turn up with demonstrably false accusations or confessions in all notorious criminal cases. The theory has not persuaded any other known researchers.

STEVENS, FREDERICK
Fellow-lodger of Annie Chapman's at **Crossingham's**. Told the *Star* on 8 September 1888 that he had drunk a pint of beer with her at 12.30 a.m. that morning, and she did not finally leave the lodging-house until 1.00 a.m.

STEVENS, WILLIAM
Witness at Annie Chapman's inquest. A printer who lodged at **Crossingham's**, he saw Chapman in the lodging house kitchen at 12.10 a.m., where she picked up a piece of envelope that was beside the fireplace, transferred some pills from a broken pill-box into it, and left the kitchen.

STOCKLEY, CHIEF INSPECTOR JAMES (1863–1954)
Warrant no. 70995. Perhaps the longest-living policeman engaged on the Ripper case. Joined Metropolitan Police, 1885, at Leman Street Station, H. Division. Chief Inspector by the time of his retirement in 1911. Set up as a private detective, including among his clients Miss Florence Pratt, the Singer sewing machine heiress. On her death in 1934 she left him her fortune of £1,000,000. The will was contested, but Stockley enjoyed a very comfortable old age in a Devon cottage on £5,000 a year interest from the bequest. His part in the Ripper enquiry was small, but it was reported that he used various disguises – as loafer, costermonger, chimney sweep and itinerant musician.

STOKES, MRS ELIZABETH
Witness at Elizabeth Stride's inquest. Sister of earlier witness, **Mrs Mary Malcolm**, according to whom she was the murder victim.

Mrs Stokes and Mrs Malcolm were two of the four daughters and four sons of a publican named Perrin from Colerne, near Chippenham, Wilts. Elizabeth Perrin's first husband was a Bath wine merchant called Watts. She claimed his family disapproved of her and persuaded him to go to America, after which they had her two children placed in someone else's care, and placed Elizabeth in Fisherton House Insane Asylum, near Salisbury. Some time after Watts's death Elizabeth was found to be sane and released. She went to Walmer in domestic service, and met her second husband, a man named Sneller who (as Mrs Malcolm had correctly stated) was stranded on St Paul's Island near New Zealand, where he died. Elizabeth was left destitute, broke down, and was committed to Peckham Lunatic Asylum. Pronounced sane by the Lunacy Commissioners, she was released, and in 1884 married Mr Stokes.

Mrs Malcolm's story, which she described as a pack of lies, had greatly embarrassed her: partly because it claimed untruly that she had been caught *in flagrante delicto* by Mr Watts and proceeded to a life of mendicancy and prostitution, partly because acquaintances of Mr Stokes accused her of bigamy.

Apart from a few parallels between her life story and Elizabeth Stride's, Mrs Stokes resembled the dead woman in her limp – caused by an adder bite in childhood. (See under **Dr Phillips** for medical report on Stride including deformed leg.)

STOWELL, DR THOMAS EDWARD ALEXANDER (1885–1970)

Theorist. Author of 'Jack the Ripper – A Solution?' in the *Criminologist*, November 1970. Original proponent of theory that **Prince Albert Victor**, Duke of Clarence, was Jack the Ripper. Also the first person to associate **Sir William Gull** by name with the case. Educ. St Thomas's Hospital. MRCS, LRCP, 1910. FRCS, 1912. Worked at hospitals in Leeds, Liverpool, Newcastle, Vienna, Harvard and Manchester. Specialised in industrial medicine, becoming Chief Medical Officer to ICI, and organising the 9th International Congress on Industrial Medicine. Honorary Dip. Indust. Disease, Buenos Aires, 1949. Honorary Dip. Indust. Health, Society of Apothecaries, 1953. Published on the etiology of Dupuytren's contracture.

In 1960 he invited **Colin Wilson** to lunch at the Athenaeum following the latter's publication of a series on the Ripper in the *Evening Standard*. Stowell wrongly deduced that Wilson also believed the Prince to be the Ripper and expounded his theory. The meeting is important as the first definitely recorded occasion when Albert Victor was proposed as the Ripper, though as Wilson has willingly admitted, his memory of the details is uncertain and includes inaccuracies, especially as at the time he, like most people, knew little or nothing about Clarence, Gull or Acland. He formed the impression that Stowell was a brain surgeon. He thought Stowell told him that he had seen Sir William Gull's papers on the invitation of Gull's daughter, Caroline Acland, following Gull's death in (possibly) the early 1930s. These contained 'confidential matters' which Caroline wondered about burning. The papers revealed that Clarence had not died of influenza in the epidemic of 1892, but in a mental home near Sandringham of 'softening of the brain' caused by syphilis. From this Stowell deduced that he was the Ripper and that the scandal had been covered up.

Wilson's memory (or Stowell's geriatric account) contained the following manifest errors: Gull died in 1890, not the early 1930s; his son-in-law

Theodore Dyke Acland did die in 1931, but Stowell, as one of his executors and trustees, needed no permission from Caroline Acland to go through his papers – nor could he have obtained it in any case, as she had died two years before her husband. Gull's papers could not have referred to Clarence's death, as Gull died two years before the Prince.

In 1970 Stowell published his piece in the *Criminologist*, with heavy editorial amendments by **Nigel Morland**. By Morland's account given to **Frank Spiering**, Stowell originally designated his suspect 'X'. Morland thought this was hackneyed, and persuaded him to change it to his own initial, 'S'. Sufficient details concerning his family were given to make it apparent that 'S' was Prince Albert Victor. Stowell argued that 'S' found himself sadistically aroused by watching deer being dressed, and in 1888, in the tertiary stage of syphilis, his warped sexual passions manifested themselves in the murder and mutilation of East End prostitutes. He speculated that he had been caught shortly after the murder of Catharine Eddowes, but escaped, only to be recaptured after Mary Jane Kelly's murder.

Stowell then claimed that 'rumour mongers' following the reports of the Ripper's alleged surgical skills had suspected Sir William Gull, and stated: 'It was said on more than one occasion that Sir Wiliam Gull was seen in the neighbourhood of Whitechapel on the night of the murder. It would not surprise me to know he was there [as the royal family doctor] for the purpose of certifying the murderer to be insane.' (**Stephen Knight** made the valid point that these rumours are unknown prior to Stowell's article.)

Stowell then retailed the **Robert James Lees** story as related in Fred Archer's *Ghost Detectives*, and attached it to Gull with the claim that Caroline Acland recalled a medium and a policeman visiting the Gull household and asking impertinent questions. He concluded with the claim that, according to Caroline Acland, Gull's diary contained an entry for November 1889: 'Informed Blank that his son was dying of syphilis of the brain.' The inference is that this was the prime source for the entire theory.

It should be noted that Stowell does not say that he saw the entry himself, and he does not say whether 'Blank' is his discreet excision of a name, or was a discreet entry in the diary itself. (Cf. **J. K. Stephen** as another patient of Gull's who has been alleged as the Ripper, though we should note that the other data on 'S' – apart from the initial – do not fit Stephen.)

Stowell's article caused an immediate worldwide sensation, and may be said to have triggered the international obsession with Jack the Ripper of the past twenty years. In November 1970, however, a letter from Stowell appeared in *The Times* saying, 'I have at no time associated His Royal Highness, the late Duke of Clarence, with the Whitechapel murderer or suggested that the murderer was of royal blood.' He designated himself 'a Royalist and a Loyalist', but was already dead by the time the letter appeared. His family destroyed his papers on the subject.

STRIDE, ELIZABETH (1843–88)
Third canonical Ripper victim (but see below). Daughter of Gustaf Ericsson and his wife Beata Carlsdotter of Stora Tumlehed farm, Torslanda, near Gothenburg, Sweden. Known as Elizabeth Gustafsdotter.

1860, moved to Carl Johan parish, Gothenburg, as domestic servant to workman Lars Frederick Olofsson. 1862, moved to Cathedral parish, Gothenburg, still giving her occupation as domestic servant. 1865, registered as prostitute; gave birth to still-born girl; twice entered hospital for venereal diseases. 1866, moved to London, subsequently telling acquaintances she had been in domestic service with the family of a (possibly foreign) gentleman living near Hyde Park. 1869, married John Thomas Stride at St Giles in the Fields church, giving her maiden name as Gustifson and address as 67 Gower Street. Elizabeth subsequently told acquaintances she and Stride kept a coffee shop in Chrisp Street, Poplar. (See under **John Thomas Stride**.) March 1877, briefly admitted to Poplar Workhouse.

In 1878, the steamer *Princess Alice* sank off Woolwich, and Stride subsequently claimed she and her husband had been employed on it; that he was drowned with two of their children in the tragedy. A News Agency report of 8 October 1888, following Elizabeth Stride's death, claimed that a woman of that name identified her husband and two children among the dead in Woolwich dockyard. Subsequent research has failed to trace any such woman in the documents of 1878 and coroner **Wynne Baxter** observed in 1888 that there was no trace of her having made any claim on the subscription fund for relatives and survivors. In fact, John Thomas Stride died in Bromley in 1884.

The marriage had apparently broken up some years previously, as **Elizabeth Tanner** stated that Elizabeth Stride had lived from time to time at 32 Flower and Dean Street (a common lodging house) since 1882. The previous year she had been treated for bronchitis in Whitechapel Workhouse Infirmary. By 1885 she was living with **Michael Kidney** at 33 Dorset Street, deserting him from time to time for the remainder of her life. In 1886 she made two claims for financial aid on the Swedish Church off the Ratcliff Highway, giving her address as Devonshire Street, Commercial Road. During 1887–8, Stride amassed eight convictions for drunkenness at Thames Magistrates Court under her own name; possibly one other under the false name **Fitzgerald**. (See also **Queen's Head**.) In April 1887 she charged Michael Kidney with assault, but failed to appear to prosecute.

All associates who appeared at her inquest knew her to be Swedish, but remarked that she spoke English without a foreign accent. Almost all had heard her *Princess Alice* disaster story, and most believed her to have had two or more children with John Stride, who had either been lost in the disaster, or were being educated south of the Thames at the expense of the Swedish Church. **Sven Olsson** finally testified that the Swedish Church knew of no such children. Michael Kidney believed her to be of superior birth and breeding, and fluent in Yiddish.

In September 1888, Stride took lodgings at 32 Flower and Dean Street, where she had not stayed for the previous three months. She was allegedly seen there by **Dr Barnardo** when he visited common lodging-houses urging prostitutes to place their children under his care.

On 29 September 1888 she cleaned rooms at 32 Flower and Dean Street, for which Mrs Tanner paid her 6d [2½p]. At 6.30 p.m. she went to the Queen's Head public house; at 7.00 p.m. she returned to the lodging house, where she borrowed a clothes brush from Charles Preston, and gave Catherine Lane a piece of velvet to look after until she came back. She left looking cheerful.

At 11.00 p.m. **J. Best** and **John Gardner** saw her leave The Bricklayers' Arms in Settles Street in company with a young Englishman of clerkly appearance, and go in the direction of Commercial Road and Berner Street. At 11.45 p.m. **William Marshall** saw her with an Englishman in Berner

Street, the two moving away in the direction of Dutfield's Yard and **Matthew Packer**'s greengrocer's shop. Packer sold half a pound of black grapes to a man accompanying Stride, at a time he variously fixed as 11.00 p.m., 11.45 p.m. and (most probably) around midnight. He then watched the pair cross the road and stand in the rain for almost half an hour facing Dutfield's Yard. **Police Constable William Smith** saw Stride standing there with a man at 12.30 a.m. **James Brown** saw a woman he was 'almost certain' was Stride at 12.45 a.m. standing with a man in Fairclough Street. But at the same time, **Israel Schwartz** saw Stride assaulted and thrown to the pavement outside Dutfield's Yard (or pushed into the Yard itself) by a young intoxicated man he had been following down Berner Street from Commercial Road. Another man, who came out of the pub at the same time, might have been an accomplice assisting by scaring Schwartz off; might equally have been a bystander who changed his mind about intervening and ran away (as did Schwartz).

About 1.00 a.m., **Louis Diemschütz** drove his horse and cart into Dutfield's Yard and found the body. It was his impression that death had been so recent that the murderer must have been hiding in the yard, and escaped while he went in to the **International Workingmen's Educational Club** to report and investigate what he believed to be a drunk woman lying behind the gates. The authors' enquiries among horse-handlers suggest that it is almost certain that the horse, whose nervousness at passing the body had drawn it to Diemschütz's attention, would have reacted unmistakeably to the presence of an additional tense man in the yard.

For Stride's injuries, see under **Dr Phillips**. Her inquest was inevitably protracted, as satisfactory evidence as to her identity was delayed by the need to investigate her own extraordinary lies about her past (see under *Princess Alice* vessel) and **Mrs Mary Malcolm**'s erroneous identification of her with **Mrs Elizabeth Stokes**. The matter was only satisfactorily settled by the appearance of Mrs Stokes herself, and the further identification made by **Police Constable Walter Stride**.

Three important witnesses do not appear to have been called to the inquest: **Mrs Mary Mortimer** (whose negative evidence of seeing and hearing nothing suspicious while she stood outside her house in Berner Street might have helped fix the time of death), **Matthew Packer** and **Israel Schwartz** (see above). Dr Phillips reported to the inquest that Stride had definitely not eaten grape skins or pips for several hours before her death, though he confirmed that stains on her handkerchief were fruit juice. This apparently conflicts with Packer's testimony to having sold grapes to her companion, and the reports in the press that some of the witnesses saw a grapestalk clutched in her left hand or dropped in the Yard after her body had been removed. (See **Louis Diemschütz, Eva Harstein**.) **Walter Dew** may offer an explanation in his recollection that detectives searching the Yard found several spat-out grape skins and seeds.

Phillips also testified that all teeth from Stride's lower left jaw were missing. Coupled with the swelling or deformity of her lower lip visible in her mortuary photograph, this might offer a reason for Stride's telling associates the false story of having been kicked in the mouth with injury to her hard palate in escaping from the *Princess Alice* disaster.

Stride's funeral was sparsely attended, and she was buried in pauper's grave no. 15509 in East London Cemetery at the expense of the parish by undertaker **Hawks**.

Walter Dew remarked that 'traces of prettiness remained in her face, and there must have been a time when she was exceedingly proud of her curly black hair'. Since Dew was twenty years younger than the corpse he described, this has always suggested that Stride was a better-looking woman than is suggested by traditional accounts of the Ripper victims as prematurely aged harridans, or the drawing of a hatchet-faced virago in *Illustrated Police News*. Discovery of Stride's mortuary photograph in 1988 confirmed that she had indeed attractive facial bone structure.

Newspapers at the time, and senior police then and subsequently (**Abberline, Anderson, Macnaghten, Smith, Swanson**), accepted without question that Stride was a Ripper victim, assuming that the murderer was alarmed by Diemschütz's approaching vehicle, and either hid or made his escape, thereupon proceeding to Mitre Square to murder Catharine Eddowes and satisfy his frustrated lust. But Walter Dew remarked that he had always suspected that Stride might not have been a Ripper victim, and **Edward Woodhall** simply asserted that she was not. The authors are impressed by the complete concurrence of the array of contemporary senior policemen, with evidence at their disposal no longer available to us. Nevertheless, we feel compelled to point out the following details differentiating Stride's murder from the other victims':

(i) No abdominal mutilations.
(ii) No extravasation of blood in neck and head region, which would indicate asphyxiation before throat-cutting.
(iii) Injuries caused by a short, broad, possibly blunt knife with a bevelled end, unlike the long narrow-bladed knife sharpened to a point used in other cases.
(iv) Position of body indicating falling on its left side, rather than on its back as in other cases.
(v) The assault witnessed by Schwartz, made by a man whose drunkenness, threatening shout of 'Lipski', and continuing ferocity in the presence of male witnesses is all quite incompatible with normal conduct of **Serial murderers**. And if Stride was not killed by the man seen by Schwartz, this leaves the extraordinary coincidence that she was attacked twice in the same place in the space of about ten minutes.

STRIDE, JOHN THOMAS (1821–84)

Husband of Elizabeth Stride. Son of a shipwright, and himself originally a ship's carpenter. Resident at Munster Street, Hampstead Road, and working as a carpenter when he married Stride at St Giles in the Fields, 1869. Entered in trade directories as proprietor of coffee house at Upper North Street, Poplar, 1870–2; then at 178 Poplar High Street, 1872–4. His movements for the last ten years of his life are unknown, though his marriage seems to have broken down by 1882. He died of heart failure in Bromley Sick Asylum, his address given as Poplar Workhouse.

STRIDE, POLICE CONSTABLE WALTER FREDERICK (b. 1858)

Witness at Elizabeth Stride's inquest, and nephew of her deceased husband. Joined Metropolitan Police, 1878; Warrant no. 62349; retired, 1902. Testified that he recognised in the mortuary photographs a woman who had married his uncle.

STUDY IN TERROR, A (1965, Great Britain)
Film directed by James Hill. Stars John Neville, Donald Houston, Robert
Morley, John Fraser. Holmes and Watson identify Ripper (Fraser) in
gory but entertaining suspenser with Barbara Windsor as victim. (Video
available.)

SUTTON, DR HENRY GOWAN

Reported to **Major Henry Smith** on the **Lusk kidney**. Senior Surgeon,
London Hospital, 1888. According to Smith, 'one of the greatest authorities living on the kidney and its diseases'. Smith said Sutton affirmed he
would 'pledge his reputation that [the Lusk kidney] had been put in spirits
within a few hours of its removal from the body'. This meant it could not
have come from a dissecting room, where the body would have had to be
held intact for a day or more to await the inquest.

SWALLOW GARDENS

Site of Frances Coles' murder. Alley running north-south between Chamber Street and Rosemary Lane (today's Royal Mint Street). Despite the
romantic names, Swallow Gardens was (and is) a dark and dismal place,
frequently used in 1888 as a public convenience; while Rosemary Lane held
'Rag Fair', the most repellently squalid of all the East End street markets.

   Frances Coles was killed in the darkest part of the alley, at the centre of
the arch. Today the alley is a footpath emerging on to a strip of waste land
between the railway and Royal Mint Street. In 1888, though (as today) a
wall divided the alley from an unused half of the railway arch, it was a
thoroughfare which could accept some wheeled traffic, and there were
houses and shops leading from the railway to Rosemary Gardens.

SWANSON, CHIEF INSPECTOR DONALD SUTHERLAND
(1848–1924)

In charge of Whitechapel Murders investigation, 1 September to c.6 October 1888; thereafter desk officer in charge under **Dr Robert Anderson**'s
command until the end of the case. Born in Thurso, Scotland, he proved a
fine scholar and taught briefly on leaving school, before deciding a dom-
inie's was a dead-end career. Joined Metropolitan Police, 1868; Warrant
no.50282; by November 1887 had risen to Chief Inspector, CID, in the
Commissioner's Office (Scotland Yard). 1896, promoted Superintendent,
and thus senior professional working detective in the Metropolitan Police
(though this had been his effective role since **Williamson**'s retirement four
years previously). Retired, 1903.

   Papers and notebooks preserved by his grandson indicate that the cases
in which Swanson took most pride were the recovery of the Countess of
Dysart's jewels; of a stolen Gainsborough painting; the tracking and arrest
of a now forgotten confidence trickster; and a crackdown on 'rent boys'
(blackmailing homosexual prostitutes) in 1897. Contemporary newspapers,
however, were more impressed by Swanson's part in arresting the railway
murderer Percy Lefroy, in suppressing Fenian terrorists, and in preventing
the Jameson Raid in South Africa from sparking war with the Afrikaaners
earlier than 1899. Today he is certainly best known for his prominence in
the Ripper investigation, although this has only been widely recognised
since the publication of the **Swanson marginalia** in 1987.

   Swanson's contemporary, John Sweeney, called him 'One of the best

class of officers . . .' (*At Scotland Yard*, 1903). **Sir Melville Macnaghten**
called him 'a very capable officer with a synthetical turn of mind'. Certainly
Swanson's Scottish education set him apart from the bulk of policemen
coming up through the ranks.

He was a close associate of **Sir Robert Anderson**, whose will he witnessed after they had both retired. Swanson continued to send affectionate
Christmas letters to his 'old master' (in his words) until Anderson's death.
In his own retirement, he retained all his faculties and, as remembered by
his family, spent a great deal of time tying flies for his summer fishing
holidays, and reading and annotating books, especially on philosophy.

He did not, on the whole, approve of police memoirs detailing accounts
of cases and methods of investigation, and is not known to have made any
public statement on the identity of Jack the Ripper. But the *Pall Mall
Gazette* of 7 May 1895, discussing the suggestion that **W. G. Grainger** was
the Ripper, reported of the Ripper crimes: 'The theory entitled to the most
respect, because it was presumably based upon the best knowledge, was
that of Chief Inspector Swanson; the officer who was associated with the
investigation of all the murders, and Mr Swanson believed the crimes to be
the work of a man who is now dead.'

Some time later the publication of Anderson's *The Lighter Side of My
Official Life* in 1910, the retired Superintendent pencilled the **Swanson
marginalia** in his personal copy, identifying Anderson's unnamed suspect
as **Kosminski**, whom he erroneously described as having died shortly after
transfer to Colney Hatch Asylum.

SWANSON MARGINALIA, THE

Pencil notes in Swanson's hand, written in the margins and on the endpap-
ers of his personal copy of **Sir Robert Anderson**'s memoirs, *The Lighter
Side of My Official Life* (1910). The book passed to Swanson's unmarried
daughter on his death; she apparently never opened it. On her death,
c. 1980, it passed to her nephew, Mr Swanson's grandson, who tried
unsuccessfully to have the marginalia published. In 1987 he made renewed
attempts, and succeeded in having the notes printed in the *Daily Telegraph*.

Anderson's suspect is neither named nor clearly defined in his printed
text, beyond the observations that he was a poor Polish Jew from Whitechapel whose people would not hand him over to justice, and that 'the only
person who ever saw the murderer unhesitatingly identified the suspect the
instant he was confronted with him; but he refused to give evidence against
him'. Swanson continues, under the text: 'because the suspect was *also a
Jew* and also because his evidence would convict the suspect, and witness
would be the means of murderer being hanged, which he did not wish to be
left on his mind. D.S.S.'

In the margin he continues, 'And after this identification which suspect
knew, no other murder of this kind took place in London.'

On the endpaper appears:

After the suspect had been identified at the **Seaside Home** where he had
been sent by us with difficulty in order to subject him to identification
and he knew he was identified.

On suspect's return to his brother's house in Whitechapel he was
watched by police (City CID) by day and night. In a very short time the
suspect with his hands tied behind his back he was sent to Stepney
Workhouse and then to Colney Hatch and died shortly afterwards –

Kosminski was the suspect – D.S.S.

This strictly private and personal memorandum, written by a man who had retained all his faculties and had no reason to mislead anybody or anticipate that the notes would be remarked by anyone, must represent the truth as Swanson saw it in or about 1910. Yet the historical status of the document remains uncertain, given the following:

(i) It is true that Aaron Kosminski resided at his brother's house in Whitechapel. Nor could that be said of any other known inmate of Colney Hatch Asylum.

(ii) It is true that Aaron Kosminski was transferred from a workhouse infirmary to Colney Hatch Asylum.

(iii) That workhouse was not Stepney Union Workhouse. Stepney Board of Guardians sent their able-bodied paupers to Poplar Workhouse, maintained by Poplar Board of Guardians; and accepted aged and infirm paupers from Poplar in St Leonard's Street Infirmary, Bromley, maintained by Stepney Guardians. (Cf. **John Stride**.) Kosminski went to neither institution (he passed through Mile End Infirmary). Nor does anyone listed in either fit Swanson's or Anderson's description of the suspect.

(iv) Kosminski did not die shortly after transfer to Colney Hatch. He lived until 1919, and probably had approximately nine more years to live at the time when Swanson wrote these notes.

In the light of these demonstrably correct and demonstrably incorrect statements, it is not known with certainty how to assess: the doubtful statement that Kosminski was taken to the Workhouse Infirmary with his hands tied; the puzzling place and date implicit in the statement that the identification took place at the Seaside Home (see **Convalescent Police Seaside Home**); and the contradiction of Anderson's account of the order of events given in the fuller serialised version of his memoirs.

It has been objected that Swanson's story is inherently incredible, entailing the release of an identified and convictable suspect into his brother's custody instead of coercing the recalcitrant witness with a subpoena. The force of the observation cannot detract from the fact that this is the fullest account we have from one of the tiny handful of men who knew the final details of the Metropolitan Police enquiry; that its broad identification of a suspect is in support of Anderson's explicit claim that the Ripper's identity was positively ascertained; that the suspect's name is supported in the less well-informed **Macnaghten memoranda**; and that the historian's duty is to try to explain the written record, not just to dismiss the parts of it which are hard to interpret.

For further discussion, cf. **Sir Robert Anderson, Anderson's suspect, Aaron Davis Cohen, Convalescent Police Seaside Home, Aaron Kosminski**.

Less important marginalia in the volume identify 'Macnaghten. ch: constable' as the senior colleague who vexed Anderson by making undue fuss over a threatening letter, and assert that all '*head* officers of CID' at Scotland Yard knew the identity of the journalist who perpetrated the **'Dear Boss' letter**.

Paul Harrison's suggestion that the marginalia may not be genuine is completely unfounded. Their provenance is established beyond a peradventure, and the handwriting has been confirmed as Swanson's by the Home Office document examiner.

SWINBURNE, ALGERNON CHARLES (1837–1909)

Included by **Richard Whittington-Egan** in list of improbable suspects who have been proposed. Poet and critic. Educ. Eton and Balliol. Notorious for supposedly 'fleshly' poetry, as for drunken and self-indulgent life-style, until taken in hand by Theodore Watts-Dunton in 1879 and compelled to live the last thirty years of his life in healthy suburban retirement at Putney.

Since Swinburne's known sexual preference was for masochistic encounters with up-market prostitutes in St John's Wood, it is unclear why anyone should ever have accused him of sadistic encounters with downmarket prostitutes in the East End.

SZEMEREDY, ALIOS (1844–92)

Alleged suspect. Self-described as American surgeon, and subsequently as sausage-maker. Believed to have deserted from Austrian army and gone to Buenos Aires, where charges of robbery and murder were brought against him. Committed to a lunatic asylum, 1885. Spent nine days in Vienna during August 1889, registering his addresses as Springer Gasse and Circus Gasse. Declared he was going to America. On return to Vienna in 1892, he was arrested on suspicion of perpetrating murder and robbery, but committed suicide while being questioned.

Rumours in Vienna that he was the Ripper were picked up by the *Daily Graphic* in 1892, and subsequently developed at book length by **Carl Muusmann**.

T

TABRAM, HENRY SAMUEL (born c. 1843)
Husband of Martha Tabram. Foreman furniture packer, lived at east Greenwich. Short, well dressed with iron-grey hair, moustache and imperial, he separated from Martha, c. 1875, because of her drinking. He paid her 12/- [60p] a week maintenance at first, reducing it to 2/6d [12½p] because 'he had found out how she was going on'. At one point she took out a warrant against him and had him locked up. c. 1879 he discovered she was living with another man, **William Turner**, and thereafter refused to support her. He learned of her death from the newspapers and identified the body on 14 August 1888.

TABRAM, MARTHA (1849–88)
aka **Martha** or **Emma Turner**.
Alleged Ripper victim. Estranged wife of warehouseman **Henry Samuel Tabram**, Martha had for nine years lived on and off with **William Turner**, though he, too, found her drinking a disincentive to cohabitation. The pair had most recently lodged with **Mrs Mary Bousfield** at Star Place, Commercial Road, but decamped owing two weeks rent. Subsequently Martha lodged at 19 George Street, Spitalfields. On Saturday 4 August 1888, they met in Leadenhall Street, and Turner gave Martha 1/6d [7½p]. He never saw her again.

On Bank Holiday Monday, 6 August 1888, Martha went out in the evening accompanied by 'Pearly Poll' (see **Mary Ann Connolly**). Various witnesses thought they saw Martha in pubs from time to time with a soldier or soldiers. 'Pearly Poll's' story seems most likely: that she and Martha picked up two guardsmen – a corporal and a private – in **The Two Brewers** and drank with them in various public houses including the White Swan on Whitechapel High Street. Around 11.45 p.m. the party split up. 'Pearly Poll' and the corporal went into Angel Alley for intercourse leaning against the wall; Martha and the private went into **George Yard** (today's Gunthorpe Street) for a similar purpose.

At approximately 2.00 a.m. **Police Constable Barrett** on beat duty saw a young Grenadier Guardsman in Wentworth Street (at the north end of George Yard) who told him he was waiting for a 'chum who had gone off with a girl'. At 3.30 a.m. licensed cab driver **Alfred Crow** returned home to George Yard Building, a tenement converted from an old weaving factory at the northeast of George Yard. He noticed what he took to be a tramp sleeping on the first floor landing. At 4.50 a.m. **John Saunders Reeves**, another tenant of George Yard Building, came downstairs and found Martha's body in a pool of blood on the first floor landing. For the injuries, see under **Dr Killeen**. See under **Mary Ann Connolly** for 'Pearly Poll's' unhelpfulness which probably contributed to the insoluble nature of the crime.

The **Macnaghten memoranda** give a clear and reasonably accurate account of 'Pearly Poll' and the enquiry's failure to reach a satisfactory conclusion beyond the likelihood that Marth's soldier client had killed her. Since the discovery of the memoranda, most researchers have accepted Macnaghten's five as the canonical Ripper victims and dismissed Martha Tabram from consideration. **Jon Ogan**, however, points out that it was not believed for long that a bayonet was one of the weapons used to attack her; moreover, there was ample time between the last sighting of Martha alive at 11.45 p.m. and Crow's assumed sighting of her body at 3.30 a.m. in which she could have found another client and taken him to the landing.

The authors note that, *pace* Macnaghten, Martha Tabram was endorsed as a Ripper victim by the weighty opinions of **Inspector Abberline** and, it seems, **Dr Robert Anderson**.

TANNER, ELIZABETH

Witness at Elizabeth Stride's inquest. Deputy of the common lodging house at 32 Flower and Dean Street where, she said, Stride had lodged on and off for about six years. She gave familiar and generally erroneous biographical information about Stride. See under **Princess Alice** (**vessel**).

On Saturday 29 September 1888, Stride, who normally did cleaning work for local Jewish residents, had cleaned rooms in the lodging house, for which Mrs Turner paid her 6d [2½p]. At about 6.30 p.m. she was in the **Queen's Head** public house, and at 7.00 p.m. she returned to the lodging house kitchen briefly.

TCHKERSOFF, OLGA

Recently alleged suspect. Supposed immigrant from Russia, settled in England with her parents and younger sister Vera. Vera became a prostitute and died of sepsis after an illegal abortion. Olga's father died of pneumonia in the spring of 1888, and her mother took to drink and died from a fall. Olga, blaming Vera's seduction from the path of virtue for the entire chapter of misfortunes, set out to murder Mary Jane Kelly, who had persuaded Vera to join her in prostitution.

Proposed by **E. T. Woodhall**, who claims Olga revealed her story to two elderly Russian immigrants who subsequently went to live with their son in USA where their story was written up by a journalist. The bulk of Woodhall's *Jack the Ripper: or When London Walked in Terror* rests on genuine source material, luridly exaggerated and sometimes completely misunderstood. So it is likely that there is some such journalistic account somewhere in the American press which has evaded subsequent researchers. This is not the same thing as saying Olga Tchkersoff ever existed or the story is probable.

TELEVISION AND JACK THE RIPPER

Jack the Ripper has appeared in episodes of several tv series. See under series titles (in chronological order): *The Veil; Cimarron City; Thriller; The Green Hornet; Star Trek; The Avengers; The Sixth Sense; Kolchak; Fantasy Island.*

TEN BELLS, THE

Public house on the corner of Fournier Street and Commercial Street, Spitalfields. Renamed The Jack the Ripper, 1976–88. The Ten Bells has stood on the site since at least 1752 (possibly since before 1715). The present building has the mid-Victorian reconstructed exterior of the Ripper's day.

It was widely rumoured that Annie Chapman had been seen in a pub near Spitalfields Market at c. 5.00 a.m. on the morning of her murder, until (as the *East London Advertiser* reported) a man with a very ugly face wearing a skull cap poked his head round the door and summoned her out. The *Manchester Guardian*, without identifying the woman certainly, attributed the story to 'the potman at The Ten Bells'. The man's description fits **Edward McKenna**, arrested by police on 13 September 1888.

Local oral tradition strongly insists that Mary Jane Kelly was drinking in this pub on the night she was murdered, though cf. the **Horn of Plenty**.

THAIN, POLICE CONSTABLE JOHN, 96J

Witness at Mary Ann Nichols' inquest.

Passed the end of Buck's Row along Brady Street every thirty minutes on his beat. At 3.45 a.m., 31 August 1888, he was signalled by **Police Constable Neil** flashing his lamp. Thain responded with his lamp, and went and found Neil standing beside Mary Ann Nichols' body. Thain then fetched **Dr Llewellyn** and returned with him to Buck's Row. He found that Neil had been joined by two workmen (**Tomkins** and **Mumford**). Thain helped put the body on the ambulance, finding the back of the dress covered with blood, which got on his hands. The body was removed to the mortuary by **Sergeant Kerby**, Neil, and an officer from H Division. Thain waited under orders at the site until **Inspector Spratling**'s arrival, and watched **Mrs Green**'s son wash away the blood. On the spot where the deceased had lain there was congealed blood, about 6ins in diameter, and some had run toward the gutter.

Thain's cape had been left with the horse-slaughterers at Barber's Yard in Winthrop Street, but he denied having visited them, saying he sent it there by a brother officer. (But see under **Tomkins**.)

THICK, SERGEANT WILLIAM (1845–1930)

After **Abberline**, the best-known H Division detective involved in the case. His name frequently spelled Thicke in both press and official documents. We take the spelling from his signature.

Joined Metropolitan Police, 1868. Warrant no. 49889. Posted to H Division. After brief service with B Division (Chelsea) and P Division (Camberwell), he returned to H Division and spent the remainder of his career there. Nicknamed 'Johnny Upright': according to **Walter Dew** 'because he was very upright both in his walk and in his methods'. American author Jack London claimed that the nickname had been bestowed by a convicted villain in the dock. Arthur Harding, a Bethnal Green villain of the next generation, suggested that the intention was sarcastic, but obviously he may have been biased. Thick retired in 1893 and went to live in the former Dempsey Street, between Jubilee Street and Jamaica Street, Stepney. In 1902, Jack London, as an unorthodox socialist, decided to live for six weeks experiencing the destitute life of the East End by passing himself off as a stranded seaman. Thick was recommended to him as a reliable man who knew the neighbourhood and could find him reasonable digs. Chapter 2 of London's *People of the Abyss* describes his meeting Thick, his wife and daughters at Dempsey Street. Following his wife's death, Thick moved to live with his daughter and her family in Clapham. His granddaughter remembered him as very strict.

F. P. Wensley called Thick one of the finest policemen he had known. Walter Dew said he was 'a holy terror to the local law-breakers'. Newspaper reports in 1888 were impressed by his knowledge of the district; also by his striking check suits and blond moustache.

Thick's most prominent action during the Ripper investigation was the arrest of **John Pizer**, and the evidence he gave at Chapman's inquest that Pizer was locally known as **'Leather Apron'**. Constant references to him show that he was heavily engaged in working on the case throughout, and Police Printed Orders for Friday 9 November 1888 show an award of 7/- [27½p] to him, apparently on loan to J Division at the time.

THOMPSON –
Resident of 29 Hanbury Street (Annie Chapman's murder site). A carman employed by Goodson's of Brick Lane, he lived in the second floor front room with his wife and adopted daughter. (Since these Spitalfields slum-dwellers have been described by some writers as brutalised sensationalists, because windows overlooking the murder scene were let at 1d or more, the authors think it worth pointing out that the Thompsons' adopted daughter and **Sarah Cox** were being voluntarily cared for in 29 Hanbury Street, and **Mr Walker** had accepted caring responsibility for his feeble-minded son.) Mr Thompson arose and went to work at 3.30 a.m., 8 September 1888, without going into the yard. He saw nothing untoward.

THOMPSON, POLICE CONSTABLE ERNEST, 240H (1864–1900)
Discovered body of Frances Coles. Joined Metropolitan Police, 1890.

On beat duty for the first time, 13 February 1891, at 2.20 a.m., as he passed from Chamber Street into Swallow Gardens (an alley under a railway arch, leading to Royal Mint Street) he discovered a woman lying in the darkest part of the archway. Turning his lantern on her, he saw that she was bleeding profusely from her savagely cut throat, but her eyes were open, and she was still alive. At that moment he heard footsteps retreating from Swallow Gardens to Royal Mint Street. Thompson followed precisely the revised and strict Standing Orders on procedure in the case of discovering a body: he remained with the body. (The observation of life and possible consciousness may have made humanity dictate this also.) He was, however, criticised for not having given chase, and according to **F. P. Wensley** reproached himself for the rest of his life for not having raced away to arrest 'Jack the Ripper'.

In 1900 Thompson was himself murdered by Barnett Abrahams, who stabbed him when Thompson went to arrest him for causing a disturbance at a coffee-stall.

THOMSON, SIR BASIL HOME (1861–1939)
Informant. Assistant Commissioner of the Metropolitan Police, 1913–19; Director of Special Branch, 1919–21.

Son of the Archbishop of York, Educ. Eton and New College, Oxford. Called to the bar, 1886. Varied career with Colonial Office (including

Prime Ministership of Tonga) and Prison Service (respectively Governor of Cardiff, Dartmoor and Wormwood Scrubs Prisons; also Inspector of Prisons and Secretary to the Prison Commissioners). Appointed successor to **Sir Melville Macnaghten** as Head of CID, 1913. Gave himself the title 'Director of Intelligence' in 1919, with specific responsibility to deal with Bolsheviks whom, along with suffragettes, pacifists, socialists, trade unionists and assorted other groups, he saw as dangerous subversives. World War I had apparently come as something of a relief to him, he having once written that had there not been 'a European war to divert the current, we were heading for something very like revolution'. Resigned in 1921, following the absorption of his Intelligence section by what would become MI5. Books include: *Queer People* (1922); *The Criminal* (1925); *The Story of Scotland Yard* (1935); *The Scene Changes* (1939). His reputation suffered in 1925 when he was convicted of committing an act of indecency in Hyde Park with a twenty-one-year-old 'actress' named Thelma Delava.

In *The Story of Scotland Yard* he wrote: 'The belief of CID officers at the time was that [the Whitechapel Murders] were the work of an insane Russian doctor and that the man escaped arrest by committing suicide at the end of 1888.' This appears to confuse **Michael Ostrog** (the insane Russian doctor) with **M. J. Druitt** (the suicide recovered from the Thames on 31 December 1888), both contemporary suspects named in the **Macnaghten memoranda**.

See also under **Ostrog** for **Donald McCormick**'s varying account of a letter, allegedly written by Thomson toward the end of his life, and identifying **Konovalov** as the French police suspect for Jack the Ripper; in one of McCormick's accounts further asserting that Konovalov was known to the British as Mikhail Ostrog.

Cf. *Ochrana Gazette*, **William Le Queux**.

THRILLER (1961, USA)
TV series (67 × 50 min) hosted by Boris Karloff; above-average horror anthology series; episode 'Yours Truly, Jack the Ripper'; based on 1945 *Weird Tales* short story by *Psycho* author Robert Bloch; Ripper episode directed by Ray Milland.

THYNE, DR THOMAS (b. 1840)
Employed Lionel Druitt in 1879. MD (Edin.), MRCS (England). Residence and surgery, 140 The Minories.

Dr Joseph Ogilvie Taylor, Dr Thyne's junior partner of the previous ten years, suffered congestion of the lungs in 1879, and treated himself with morphine. In November he died of an accidental overdose. Lionel Druitt is listed in Medical Directories as practising at 140 The Minories in 1879, evidently assisting Dr Thyne during Taylor's indisposition, prior to Thyne's appointment of Dr John Cotman as his permanent junior partner. Census returns show that Thyne's assistants were resident at the practice.

Daniel Farson's discovery of this listing led him to speculate that **Montague John Druitt**, a cousin close to Lionel in age, might have visited him while he was in The Minories, and thus established an acquaintance with the East End.

TIME AFTER TIME (1979, USA)
Film directed by Nicholas Meyer. Stars Malcolm McDowell, David

Warner, Mary Steenburgen. Refined doctor Ripper (Warner) flees police of 1888 in time machine invented by H. G. Wells (McDowell), who pursues him to 1979 San Francisco. Attempted social comment provides memorable scene of Ripper and Wells flicking through tv channels, each showing violence. 'I belong here completely and utterly. I'm home,' says Ripper. 'Ninety years ago I was a freak. Today I'm an amateur.' An ingenious and enjoyable plot, aided immensely by Steenburgen, but all overshadowed by Miklos Rozsa score. (Video available.)

TOMKINS, HENRY

Witness at Mary Ann Nichols' inquest. Horse-slaughterer employed at Barber's Knacker's Yard, Winthrop Street. Resident at Coventry Street, Bethnal Green. Described as 'a rough looking man', testified that around 4.00 a.m., 31 August 1888, he was told of the murder by **Police Constable Thain**, and went in company with **James Mumford** and **Charles Brittain** to view the body.

This evidence appears to conflict with that of Thain, who claimed that the workmen were present at the murder site when he returned with **Dr Llewellyn**. It is possible that the inquest rightly detected an inclination on Thain's part to slope off from his beat for a chat with the slaughtermen, although he denied this.

TOUGHILL, THOMAS

Theorist. Glasgow correspondent of **Colin Wilson**. Advanced theory that **Frank Miles** was the Ripper.

TULLY, JAMES C. H.

Theorist. Retired banker, said to have studied the Ripper for more than a quarter of a century and to have plans for a book on the subject. Contributed eleven-page piece to **Peter Underwood**'s *Jack the Ripper: One Hundred Years of Mystery*. States he has two theories – one 'startling' and the other 'prosaic' – but does not divulge either.

TURNER, MARTHA or EMMA

Alternative name used by **Martha Tabram**.

TURNER, WILLIAM

Witness at Martha Tabram's inquest. A carpenter by trade, but in 1888 had, for several years, lived as a street hawker. Described as a short, dirty, slovenly dressed young man, with a pale face, light moustache and imperial. Resident at the time of the inquest at the Victoria Working Men's Home, Commercial Street.

He lived with Tabram, on and off, for ten years. He left her from time to time because of her drunkenness, reporting: 'If I gave her money she generally spent it on drink. In fact it was always drink. When she took to drink, however, I usually left her to her own resources, and I can't answer for her conduct then.'

He had left her about three weeks before her death, and last saw her in Leadenhall Street, near Aldgate pump, on Saturday 4 August 1888, when he gave her 1/6d [7½p].

TWO BREWERS, THE
Public house, where Martha Tabram and 'Pearly Poll' (see **Mary Ann Connolly**) allegedly met the guardsmen whom they took up alleys off Whitechapel High Street at 11.45 p.m., 6 August 1888. **Daniel Farson** identified this with a former pub on Duke's Shore, Limehouse (a stretch of Narrow Street, fronting the river, where boats can be beached at low tide). The Two Brewers was one of the pubs used by Dickens in creating The Six Jolly Fellowship Porters in *Our Mutual Friend*. Farson knew of it as, for many years, he ran the Waterman's (as is still locally celebrated on Waterman's Wine Bar's sign) at the other end of Duke Shore. Topography, however, makes it more likely that The Two Brewers used by Tabram and Connolly was the existing pub of that name in Brick Lane.

U

UNDERWOOD, PETER (b. 1923)
Author of entertaining *Jack the Ripper: One Hundred Years of Mystery* (1987). Biographer and writer on cinema. President of the Ghost Club, prolific author of books on ghosts, and probably Britain's best-known ghost-hunter, Peter Underwood nobly confined himself to one chapter on Ripper-related ghost sightings, and resisted the temptation to give more than a hint that **Mrs Caroline Maxwell** saw Mary Jane Kelly's ghost. His Ripper centenary offering was enlivened by his writing to known writers on the topic while he prepared his book, and so acquiring quotations from leading authorities and others on the state of Ripper research, as they saw it, at the beginning of 1987.

UNIDENTIFIED MAN SEEN BY THOMAS BOWYER
Thomas Bowyer stated that he last saw Mary Jane Kelly alive on the Wednesday previous to her death. She was in Miller's Court, talking to a man of twenty-seven or twenty-eight, with a dark moustache and 'very peculiar eyes'. His appearance was 'very smart and attention was drawn to him by his showing very white cuffs and a rather long white collar, the ends of which came down in front over his coat'.

UNIDENTIFIED MAN SEEN IN BUCK'S ROW
At Mary Ann Nichols' inquest, **Inspector Abberline** said police were 'unable to find the man who passed down Buck's Row while the doctor was examining the body'. Nothing more is known of this man, unless he was also the man mentioned by **Patrick Mulshaw** as telling him in Winthrop Street of the murder.

UNIDENTIFIED POLICE CONSTABLE IN VICINITY OF MITRE SQUARE
In the 'Aberconway' version of the **Macnaghten memoranda Sir Melville Macnaghten** wrote of the suspect **Kosminski**: 'This man in appearance strongly resembled the individual seen by the City PC near Mitre Square'. No City police constable is known to have seen anyone suspicious in the vicinity of Mitre Square on the night of Eddowes' murder. It has been surmised that Macnaghten confused the City policeman with Metropolitan Police Constable Smith (who saw Stride in Berner Street); or that Macnaghten misremembered **Mr Lawende** (who saw the probable murderer in the vicinity of Mitre Square) as a City policeman. Macnaghten shows confusion in suggesting, for example, that the murderer may have been prevented from mutilating Stride in Berner Street by the arrival of three Jews (Lawende, Levy and Harris at Mitre Square). But it is also possible that Eddowes was seen in the company of a man by an unknown City constable

after her release from Bishopsgate cells. Unfortunately the City Police files were destroyed during the Blitz.

UNIDENTIFIED WITNESSES AT MITRE SQUARE

The *Daily Telegraph* (12 November 1888) stated that 'two persons', said to have been in the Orange Market (St James's Place), had observed Catharine Eddowes at the end of the covered entry to the Square talking to a man aged about thirty with a fair moustache. The report stated that the City Police had made unsuccessful attempts to trace the man. The cutting was preserved in the **Scotland Yard files**.

The entry from St James's Place to Mitre Square was and is covered; so was Church Passage, where Eddowes had been seen talking to a man at 1.34 a.m. by **Joseph Lawende, Harry Harris** and **Joseph Hyam Levy**. Their sighting, however, was from Duke's Place, at a point which would be invisible from St James's Place. The unidentified witnesses would appear to have observed a continuation of negotiations at the Mitre Square end of Church Passage. They are said to have observed the couple closely, yet they saw nothing untoward, and if they were correct in identifying Eddowes, must surely have averted their gaze minutes before she was murdered.

There was a night fire station in the Orange Market, manned by two firemen, who, however, told **Superintendent Foster** they had seen nothing unusual nor anyone come out of Mitre Square. Like **James Blenkinsop**, these unidentified witnesses were not called to the inquest. It is extremely regrettable that the loss of City Police records during the war leaves us tantalisingly underinformed about the important witnesses in the Orange Market. The possibility exists, e.g., that one of them might be **Anderson's witness**.

V

VAN TURNEY, JULIA
or **Van Teurney, Vanturney** or **Venturney**.
Witness at Mary Jane Kelly's inquest. Laundress, resident 1 Miller's Court
(opposite Mary Jane Kelly's room). A widow, living with a man called
Harry Owen. Testified that **Joe Barnett** and Kelly lived together without
quarrelling; that he was kind to Kelly and gave her money. She stated that
Kelly had broken the window a few weeks previously when she was drunk
– something Mrs Van Turney said occurred rarely. She also revealed that
Kelly had another admirer called Joe, a costermonger who ill-used her for
living with Barnett. She had slept through the night of 8–9 November
1888, and did not hear the cry of 'Murder!' described by **Mrs Prater** and
Sarah Lewis.
　　Mrs Van Turney's name, and the report in one newspaper that she was
German, suggests that she may well have been that **'Julia'** whose residence
in 13 Miller's Court provoked Barnett's withdrawal. In this case one would
expect her to have confirmed **Maurice Lewis's** story that she had been
drinking with Kelly on the night of her murder if there were any truth in it.

VASSILI, VASSILY or **VASSILYEFF, NICOLAI** (b. 1842)
See **Nicholas Wassili**.

VEIL, THE (1958, USA)
Tv series hosted by Boris Karloff; episode 'Jack the Ripper'; apparently a
version of the **Robert Lees** story.

VELLENSWORTH, POLICE SERGEANT
He was sent to investigate **W. H. Pigott** at The Pope's Head, Gravesend.
The matter was then taken out of his hands by Superintendent Berry and
Inspector Abberline.

VENTURNEY, MRS JULIA
See **Julia Van Turney**.

VICTORIA, QUEEN (1819–1901)
The Queen's concern that her Government should do its utmost to protect
her subjects against the miscreant is well documented, but claims that she
was suspiciously over-interested in the murders, or even knew the identity
of the murderer, are ill-founded.
　　Stephen Knight made much of a memorandum dated 9 November 1888
in which the Queen referred back to her urgings at the time of 'the first
murder'. Knight wonders why she should have taken such interest when
she could not have known it would prove the first of a sequence. Though it

may be surprising that the Queen felt moved to comment on a violent crime in a notoriously violent area, the full and rarely printed content of Victoria's memorandum makes it quite clear that she had no secret knowledge and was not especially interested in the murderer's identity. She was concerned with street lighting and similar safety measures. An entry in her private journal for 4 October 1888 indicates that by the 'first murder' she meant Emma Elizabeth Smith's.

Unhappily there is no documented foundation for the delightful legend that she wrote to the Home Secretary, 'this murderer is obviously not an Englishman, and if he is, he is certainly not a gentleman'.

VIGILANCE COMMITTEES
These residents' organisations existed to support the maintenance of public order, and acted as pressure groups urging the vestries and police to take whatever actions private citizens deemed necessary. There were several in existence prior to the Whitechapel Murders, urging stricter enforcement of the licensing laws, but the scare of autumn 1888 brought them into prominence and caused new ones to be formed.

The Central Vigilance Society, with headquarters in the Adelphi, was essentially a group concerned with the suppression of drinking and vice. They pounced on the opportunity to issue a public letter on 8 October 1888 demanding that police and local authorities use to the full their powers to harass prostitutes, and urging the introduction of severer laws with more draconian deterrent penalties.

The most important of the Vigilance Committees connected with the murders was that formed at a meeting of ratepayers on 10 September 1888 in The Crown public house, Mile End Road. Sixteen of them, including a cigar-maker, a tailor, a picture frame maker and an actor, constituted themselves a committee, with **Mr George Lusk** as president, Mr B. Harris as secretary, and Mr Joseph Aarons as treasurer. They announced in the press that members would be available every morning in The Crown to receive information or suggestions from the public, and Mr Harris wrote to Scotland Yard from time to time urging the offer of a reward. Although Lusk's fear that the publicity attaching to his name brought him under surveillance by a suspicious man, and he troubled the police with the need for personal protection, this discreet gathering of respectable burghers, urging policies **Sir Charles Warren** tended to favour, was probably very much in his mind when he applauded Vigilance Committees' work in his indiscreet article in *Murray's Magazine*.

A year later, when the scare had died down, however, the original committee members allowed the organisation to fall into the hands of **Albert Bachert**, and the young professional agitator turned it into a noisy gadfly that was far less appealing to the authorities.

The Spitalfields Vigilance Committee (president J. Cohen; secretary Mr Van Gelder) was another which restricted itself to writing courteous letters to the authorities urging improvements in street lighting and rewards for information. The declining interest as the scare receded can be seen in Mr Van Gelder's plaintive report that more funds were needed in January 1889.

VIOLENIA, EMMANUEL DELBAST
Discredited witness. Vagrant, possibly boot-finisher. Described as half-

Spaniard, half-Bulgarian, of mulatto appearance. In 1888 he had walked from Manchester to London with his wife and two children, hoping to emigrate to Australia. He lodged in Hanbury Street and claimed that in the early morning of Saturday 8 September 1888 he saw a woman quarrelling with two men, one of whom had threatened to knife her. He attended an identity parade at Leman Street Police Station, and unhesitatingly picked out **John Pizer** as one of the men he had seen, adding that he knew Pizer as 'Leather Apron'. Pizer expressed immediate astonishment at Violenia's claim to know him.

Under further questioning, however, police came to mistrust Violenia, who refused to identify Annie Chapman's body. They came to the conclusion that he had pushed himself forward with false or irrelevant information in the morbid hope of seeing the body, and they dismissed him with a severe reprimand. Pizer subsequently told the press that he knew Violenia by sight, and believed him to be a boot-finisher, but there was no acquaintance between them which would cause Violenia to know any nickname by which Pizer might be known.

It has been suggested that Violenia was **Anderson's witness**. In the light of police attitudes to him, and the demonstrable fact that Pizer was not **Anderson's suspect**, this seems highly unlikely.

W

WACHSFIGURENKABINETT, DAS (WAXWORKS) (1924, Germany)
Film directed by Paul Leni. Stars Werner Krauss. Major item in the history of the horror film and distinguished by stylised sets; Ripper (Kraus) appears in last of trilogy of stories.

WALKER, –
Resident of 29 Hanbury Street (Annie Chapman's murder site). Occupied first floor back room with his son, described as feeble minded but very inoffensive.

WALKER, EDWARD
Father of Mary Ann Nichols. Locksmith, subsequently blacksmith. Grey-haired and bearded resident of 16 Maidswood Road, Camberwell, at the time of her death. She had lived with him between March and May 1883, but her drinking caused friction and she left after an argument. He last saw her in June 1886 at her brother's funeral; last heard from her when she wrote to him in the summer of 1888 from **Mr and Mrs Cowdry**'s. His answer to her letter received no reply.

WALTER, EMILY
Informant. Told the *Star* (10 September 1888) a man asked her to go with him into 29 Hanbury Street in the small hours of Saturday 8 September. She did not confess to having gone, but it is likely that she did, and provided the description police issued of a man wanted for interviewing, who might have been seen entering 29 Hanbury Street with a woman at 2.30 a.m.

WARDEN, WALLY
Alleged alias of Elizabeth Stride, by which **'One-Armed Liz'** first identified her body.

WARREN, SIR CHARLES (1840–1927)
Metropolitan Police Commissioner, 1886–8. Educ. Cheltenham, Sandhurst and Woolwich. Joined Royal Engineers, 1857. 1867, served in Palestine and conducted archaeological research, publishing three books on ancient Jerusalem. Returned to England, 1870. Posted to Africa as Special Commissioner for the Colonial Office, 1876–87, for which he received the CMG. Commanded Diamond Fields Horse in Kaffir War of 1887–8, and severely wounded. Promoted Lieutenant-Colonel, returned to England, 1880, as Chief Instructor, School of Military Engineering, Chatham. Led search in Egypt for missing expedition of Professor Edward Palmer, 1882. Dis-

covered the party had been murdered: traced their remains and secured punishment of the murderers. Awarded KCMG. 1884, participated in second expedition to relieve General Gordon (an intimate friend) at Khartoum. Then sent to restore order in Bechuanaland for which he was awarded the GCMG. Commanded troops at Suakim, before recall to England to succeed Sir Edmund Henderson as Commissioner of Metropolitan Police. Resigned following stormy two years, and returned to army career. Played controversial role in Battle of Majuba Hill during the Boer War. For the latter part of his life he threw his energies into the Boy Scout movement.

Warren was an evangelical christian: one of the new middle-class intellectual professional soldiers (like Gordon) satirised in Gilbert's 'very model of a modern major-general'. He was politically a moderate Liberal, which, coupled with his military experience, appealed to Gladstone's Home Secretary **Hugh Childers**, when Sir Edmund Henderson had outraged middle-class public opinion by failing to prevent a demonstration against unemployment on 8 February 1886 from turning into a riot in which club and shop windows were smashed in Pall Mall, St James's and Oxford Street. Warren's appointment was generally welcomed, *The Times* saying he was 'precisely the man whom sensible Londoners would have chosen to preside over the police of the Metropolis'. The *Pall Mall Gazette*, however, prophetically warned that Childers should 'allow his Commissioner a free hand, and back him up like a man . . .'. Childers did so, but Gladstone's Government fell in June 1886, and he was succeeded by the vacillating **Henry Matthews**.

Warren's decline in popularity began at the Lord Mayor's Show, 1886, when a section of the crowd got out of hand. This was followed by another riot in Clerkenwell. Furthermore, on Jubilee Day, 1887 (which Warren's men had policed to the entire satisfaction of the middle classes), Police Constable Endicott arrested a sempstress called Miss Cass in Regent Street and charged her with soliciting. Miss Cass's employer protested, and brought a private prosecution for wrongful arrest against Endicott. Warren, who believed Endicott's arrest to have been correct, handled the matter and the ensuing enquiry tactlessly, offending partisans of both Miss Cass and Endicott.

On 13 November 1887 there was a mass demonstration of the unemployed in Trafalgar Square that would be remembered as 'Bloody Sunday'. Warren called in troops to clear the square, and there was extraordinary violence in the course of which one man died. Though *The Times* praised Warren, the radical press never forgave him, and campaigned against him and the Met from then on. Some journalists who knew better linked Warren's name with the dubiously over-zealous anti-**Fenian** activities of certain officers (notably **Monro** and **Anderson**) who tried to link legitimate parliamentary Irish nationalism with American-Irish terrorism.

Warren's relations with Home Secretary Henry Matthews had become strained by now. Warren had assumed he would rule his force with military authority. He found that **James Monro** insisted on a personal fiefdom in **Monro's Secret Department**, and tried to manoeuvre similar independence in the CID. He learned that Richard Pennefather, the Receiver of Police, controlled all official expenditure and severely restricted his options. **Evelyn Ruggles-Brise**, Matthews' Private Secretary, later wrote:

Pennefather was a very able man, but disagreeable to deal with; he rubbed everybody up the wrong way. Warren was the finest man we had in Whitehall, but probably the worst appointment, because he *must* be independent, and the Commissioner of Police is held in very tight bonds by the Home Office. Matthews was an exceedingly able lawyer, but quite incapable of dealing with men; he was a regular Gallio in his attitude to Warren's complaints [i.e. he wasn't interested]. Later on he quarrelled with [Sir Edward] **Bradford**, and if you couldn't get on with Bradford you could get on with nobody.

In Sir Robert Anderson's opinion, these personality clashes were exacerbated by Home Office Permanent Under-Secretary **Godfrey Lushington**, who should have resolved them. Some of these tensions (especially between Warren and Monro) were known to some journalists, and exploited in the campaign attacking Warren.

As the Whitechapel Murders developed, the radical press, headed by the *Star*, demanded Warren's resignation, and the Conservative press ultimately followed suit. Warren was accused of introducing mindless militarism to the police; of demoralising the CID; of following Matthews' frivolous do-nothing lead. He was mocked for going out and letting the **bloodhounds** trace him through Regent's Park during their trials. When his resignation was accepted and announced on 9 November – the day that Mary Jane Kelly's body was found atrociously mutilated – it was widely assumed that this climactic murder had forced Warren out. 'Whitechapel has avenged us for Bloody Sunday,' crowed the *Star*. This erroneous belief has been widely repeated ever since.

In fact, Warren's resignation was the climax of a struggle for authority which had been going on between the Home Office and the Metropolitan Police Commissioners for fifty years. Warren had responded to press attacks on his force by publishing an article in *Murray's Magazine* on 'The Police of the Metropolis'. This was contrary to approved procedure, by which all officials were expected to clear all matter for publication with the Home Office senior civil servants. Warren can hardly have been unaware of this; but neither can he have relished the idea of seeking an imprimatur from men with whom his relations were fractious. Matthews responded to his impropriety with a reprimanding memorandum that many people felt would necessarily invite the resignation of a recipient with any pride. Certainly Warren offered his resignation at once, stating that he would never have taken up the post of Commissioner had he been told the Home Office rule applied to him. By sheer coincidence, this heated exchange had started a few days before Mary Kelly's murder, and the formalities were completed and announced on the day itself.

WARREN, N. P. (1950–)
Researcher. Author of 'A Postal Kidney' in the *Criminologist*, Spring 1989. Practising surgeon. FRCS (Eng), FRCS (Edin.). As a student, took an elective course with **Professor James Cameron**. Has contributed also to *True Detective*, *Justice of the Peace* and *Crime & Mystery Monthly*.

Warren has established conclusively that **Major Henry Smith** was correct in saying Eddowes' right kidney showed signs of Bright's Disease. He sees evidence that the Ripper had surgical skill, and believes the **Lusk kidney** to be probably Eddowes' left kidney. In addition, he has done considerable work on the Russian police and criminological background to the **Pedachenko** theory, and has identified an asylum likely to be the one where **John Sanders** was held before his transfer to Heavitree.

WASSILI, NICOLAI (1842–)
Also transcribed **Nicolas Vassili, Vassily** or **Vasilyeff**
Alleged suspect. Born Tiraspol, Province of Kherson, Ukraine. Educ. Tiraspol and University of Odessa. Inherited sufficient income to live without work. Joined the fanatical Shorn sect, an off-shoot of the self-castrating Skoptsky, who totally condemned sexual relations, even within marriage. In 1872, following the Russian Orthodox Church's vigorous attempts to suppress the sect, Wassili went into self-imposed exile in Paris, where he tried, largely unsuccessfully, to convert and reform prostitutes. He fell in love with a young woman named Madeleine whose initial reciprocation was withdrawn after conflict with his religious convictions. Her desertion turned his mind, and he started 'saving' prostitutes by killing five women, including Madeleine, in the space of two weeks. He did not mutilate abdominally; merely stabbed in the back. He was committed to an asylum (most press reports suggest in France, but the *New York World* says in Tiraspol), from which he was released on 1 January 1888, declaring his intention of coming to London. Some British papers asserted he had come to London, settling with 'the lower class of his countrymen', but disappearing after the first Whitechapel murder.

The above account is drawn from international newspapers at the time of the Whitechapel Murders, often copying each other and adding details, sometimes allegedly received from Berne, Belgium and the London immigrant community. No research has as yet unearthed accounts at the time of Wassili's alleged arrest and committal. No part of the story can be guaranteed true or false. Cf. **Konovalov**.

N. P. Warren has privately drawn the authors' attention to the many parallels between Wassili and Mrs Belloc Lowndes' protagonist in her fiction 'Ripper' classic *The Lodger*. Both pore over religious texts before wandering from dark to dawn; both are known as 'The Avenger'; both are released from asylums at the start of the years in which the murders occur. (Though cf. also **G. Wentworth Bell Smith** and **Sickert's veterinary student**.) Mrs Belloc Lowndes' father was a French barrister who would have known the Wassili story if it is based in fact.

WATKINS, POLICE CONSTABLE EDWARD
Discovered Catharine Eddowes' body. Joined City of London Police, 1871; retired, 1896. Watkins' beat along Duke Street (today's Duke's Place), Creechurch Lane, Leadenhall Street, Mitre Street, Mitre Square and St James's Place took him twelve to fourteen minutes to traverse. On 30 September 1888 he passed through Mitre Square at 1.30 a.m. and found it empty. Returning at approximately 1.44 a.m., he found the body in the southwest corner. He ran into Kearley and Tonge's warehouse opposite and sought the assistance of **George James Morris**. Morris went into Aldgate for assistance, and Watkins remained with the body until the arrival of **Police Constable Holland**.

WATKINS, KATHLEEN BLAKE
Canadian journalist. Leading staff reporter on *Toronto Mail*, using pen-name 'Kit'. In late 1891 she was sent to London, and ventured into

Whitechapel to visit the Ripper sites. At Miller's Court she met and interviewed **Elizabeth Prater** who took her to meet 'Lottie', the current occupant of Mary Jane Kelly's still bloodstained room. 'Kit' wrote several subsequent pieces on Whitechapel, in 1892, 1893, 1896 and 1909. In the last she referred to the murder of Kitty Ronan in the room formerly occupied by Elizabeth Prater.

WATTS, MRS ELIZABETH
Name, during her first marriage, of **Mrs Mary Malcolm**'s sister **Elizabeth Stokes**. Wrongly described as an alias of Elizabeth Stride by several contemporary journalists under the impression that Mary Malcolm's identification of Stride as her sister was correct.

WEBB, INSPECTOR RICHARD, J. Division (b. 1851)
Worked for Great Western Railway, and served for five years in Coldstream Guards, achieving rank of sergeant, before purchasing his discharge and joining Metropolitan Police in 1873. By 1887 he was Divisional Inspector, and posted to Bethnal Green, where he remained until his retirement in 1899. The *Police Review*, 9 February 1900, records that 'In conjunction with other officers he took a very active part in the endeavour to trace the perpetrator of the "Ripper" murders in the East End.'

WENSLEY, FREDERICK PORTER (1865–1949)
Informant. Very distinguished policeman. Joined Metropolitan Police, January 1888. Warrant no. 73224. For many years served in H Division CID, making his reputation by arresting William Seaman for the Turner Street murders of 1896, committed on Seaman's terminating his sentence for murderously assaulting a chemist named Simpkin in Berner Street in the same week as Elizabeth Stride was murdered there. Closely associated with **Benjamin Leeson** until the latter was invalided out of the force. He rose to become Chief Constable in charge of CID, the first man to have risen to acceptance by the ranks hitherto reserved for 'gentlemen'. He retired in 1929, and published his memoirs, *Detective Days* (1931).

He does not exaggerate his humble role in the Whitechapel Murders case, saying: 'Not that I had much to do with it. In common with hundreds of others I was drafted there and we patrolled the streets – usually in pairs – without any tangible result. We did, however, rather anticipate a great commercial invention. To our clumsy regulation boots we nailed strips of rubber, usually bits of old bicycle tyres, and so ensured some measure of silence when walking.'

He remarks that, 'Officially, only five (with a possible sixth) murders were attributed to Jack the Ripper'; mentions the Frances Coles murder; and describes **Police Constable Ernest Thompson**'s murder.

The memoirs are very valuable for background on **H Division**, and for Wensley's assessments of several of the policemen involved in the case.

WEST, –
Resident of **Crossingham's lodging house**. He confirmed knowing **'Leather Apron'** by sight, and having seen him hanging around Crossingham's in the weeks prior to the murders.

WEST, WILLIAM
Witness at Elizabeth Stride's inquest. Resident at 2 William Street, he was overseer of the printing office of *Arbeter Fraint* at the rear of the **International Workingmen's Educational Club**

About 12.30 a.m., 30 September 1888, he left the side entrance of the Club (in Dutfield's Yard) and went into the printing office to return some literature, before returning again to the Club. He then called his brother and a man called Louis Stanley, and together they left the Club by the front door (in Berner Street) and walked towards Fairclough Street. While returning from the printing office to the Club, he looked towards the gates and the point where the body was later found, seeing nothing unusual. He admitted, though, to being shortsighted, and did not know whether he would have seen the body if it had been there.

WEST, CHIEF INSPECTOR, ACTING SUPERINTENDENT
Officer responsible for combining enquiry into Whitechapel murders under **Abberline**.

Acting Superintendent in charge of H Division at the time of Mary Ann Nichols' and Annie Chapman's murders. The former fell within the province of J Division, despite **Police Constable Mizen**'s early arrival at the scene and the removal of the body to a mortuary on H Division's territory. The latter was entirely an H Division case, but in the absence on leave of **Inspector Reid**, head of the local CID, West reported to Scotland Yard: 'I would respectfully suggest that Inspector Abberline, Central, who is well acquainted with H Division, be deputed to take up this enquiry as I believe he is already engaged in the case of the Buck's Row murder which would appear to have been committed by the same person as the one in Hanbury Street.'

By the time of Elizabeth Stride's murder, **Arnold** was back in charge of H Division, and West had reverted to his substantive rank of Chief Inspector.

WESTCOTT, DR WILLIAM WYNN (1848–1925)
Recently alleged suspect, named in numerous newspaper articles, mainly of West Country origin, reporting theories and opinions of Ron Maber, Christopher Smith and **Andrew Holloway**. Educ. University College, London. Practised as a doctor in Martock, near Yeovil, 1871–9. 1887, took up residence in Camden and became Coroner for Central London. Retired from public life, 1918, and in 1921 went to live in Durban, South Africa, where he died.

Westcott revelled in societies which purported to initiate members in mysterious or occult lore. A Freemason, a leading member of the Society of Rosicrucians, an associate of **H. P. Blavatsky** (founder of the Theosophical Society) and Anna Kingsford (founder of a Hermetic Society). In 1887–8 Westcott joined with G. Samuel Liddell Mathers (self-styled MacGregor Mathers, 1854–1918) and Dr William Robert Woodman (1828–91) to found a Hermetic society: the Order of the Golden Dawn (originally the Isis-Urania Temple of the Golden Dawn in the Outer). This body, which at its height numbered about 200 initiates, was a pseudo-masonic society with rituals and liturgy devised by Westcott and Mathers, allegedly from secret Rosicrucian cipher manuscripts Westcott had obtained. Members also studied the occult.

It became influential in certain artistic circles in the 1890s when its

membership included Arthur Machen, Algernon Blackwood, Annie Horni-
man (the tea heiress and founder of Dublin's Abbey theatre), Florence Farr
(actress and lover of Yeats and Shaw), Constance Wilde (briefly – her
husband, Oscar, though himself a Freemason, thought the Golden Dawn
ridiculous) and, most significantly, W. B. Yeats, who drew some effective
imagery from its rites. Some peculiar attempts to raise 'spirits' and even
'evil powers' were practised, but this did not become the dominant feature
of the society until **Aleister Crowley** joined it in 1898, whereupon his
ambitions and ties to Mather hastened its dissolution.

In 1897 the authorities learned of Westcott's involvement with the
Golden Dawn, and threatened to eject him from his coroner's office.
He immediately left the Order and severed all ties with former occultist
colleagues.

The only reason for suspecting Westcott of being the Ripper appears to
be the belief that the murders were occult sacrifices. Christopher Smith has
suggested that Golden Dawn members committed the murders ritually in a
churchyard, subsequently dumping the bodies where they were discovered.
In fact, ten years later, when Crowley joined, George Cecil Jones, who
introduced him, described the Golden Dawn as 'a club like any other club,
a place to pass the time in and meet one's friends'. Ellic Howe, an authority
on the cult, said that during the period 1888–9 it was 'nothing more than a
kindergarten for would-be occultists'.

Even when the hard-core occultists Crowley and Mathers had gone their
own way into what they hoped was the practice of demonic magick, their
activities were far removed from mass murder. Mathers' most aggressive
magical action was to baptise a lot of dried peas by the names of his enemies
in order to shake them fiercely in a sieve. Crowley, more disgustingly,
baptised a frog 'Jesus Christ', flogged it and crucified it. The only dangers
to human life in associating with Crowley were from malnutrition, the
sadistic penances he inflicted on disciples (like sleeping in unheated huts on
gorse branches) and the liability of joining him in dependence on hard
drugs.

Those 'Satanic' cults believed to have carried out serial murders in
the USA over the last twenty years appear to have done so in association
with members' wishes to possess crude videos of sudden death, or with
drug-dealers' punitive killings which can be disguised as part of a
sequence of random murders. No such motive has been proposed in
Westcott's case.

While Westcott was profoundly interested in the occult, on which he
wrote sixteen books, he was not as deluded as Crowley and Mathers. Faced
with the choice between magic and his job he instantly abandoned magic.
There is no apparent psychological reason to link him with serial murder,
for occult or any other purpose.

WHITE, JERRY
Historian. Author of *Rothschild Buildings: Life in an East End Tenement
Block, 1887–1920*, an interesting and valuable account of life in Spitalfields.
It describes redevelopments in the area following the Ripper murders and
the long history of previously unsuccessful efforts, concluding: 'Within six
years, then, Jack the Ripper had done more to destroy the Flower and
Dean Street rookery than fifty years of road building, slum clearance and
unabated pressure from the Police, Poor Law Guardians, vestries and

sanitary officers.' White's observation is one reason why the Ripper is inseparable from East End social history.

WHITE, SERGEANT STEPHEN (1854–1919)

Interviewed **Matthew Packer**. Reported as the only officer in the investigation to come face to face with the Ripper. Joined Metropolitan Police, 1875. Warrant no. 59442. Posted to L Division Lambeth. Promoted Sergeant (CID) and transferred to H Division Whitechapel. Promoted Inspector, 1894. Retired, 1900.

When Matthew Packer's story of selling grapes to the man accompanying Elizabeth Stride shortly before her death broke in the *Evening News*, **Chief Inspector Moore** confirmed that White had interviewed Packer and all members of his household on 30 September 1888 and received assurances that they had seen and heard nothing unusual the previous night. White then returned to Berner Street with instructions to reinterview Packer and take him to identify the body in the Mortuary. He found Packer returning from having identified the body positively in the company of private detectives **Grand** and **Batchelor**. White extracted little useful information from Packer before the fruiterer was taken by Grand and Batchelor in a hansom cab to see **Sir Charles Warren**.

Shortly after White's death an article 'by a Scotland Yard man' appeared in the *People's Journal*. It asserted that White was one of the many policemen sent out in disguise to patrol the streets, and then presented a long passage, allegedly from 'One of White's reports on his nightly vigil':

For five nights we had been watching a certain alley just behind the Whitechapel Road. It could only be entered from where we had two men posted in hiding, and persons entering the alley were under observation by the two men. It was a bitter cold night when I arrived at the scene to take the reports of the two men in hiding. I was turning away when I saw a man coming out of the alley. He was walking quickly but noiselessly, apparently wearing rubber shoes which were rather rare in those days. I stood aside to let the man pass, and as he came under the wall lamp I got a good look at him.

He was about five feet ten inches in height, and was dressed rather shabbily though it was obvious that the material of his clothes was good. Evidently a man who had seen better days . . . His face was long and thin, nostrils rather delicate, and his hair was jet black. His complexion was inclined to be sallow, and altogether the man was foreign in appearance. The most extraordinary thing about him, however, was the extraordinary brilliance of his eyes . . . The man was slightly bent at the shoulders, though he was obviously quite young – about 33 at the most – and gave one the idea of having been a student or professional man. His hands were snow white and the fingers long and tapering.

As the man passed me at the lamp I had an uneasy feeling that there was something unusually sinister about him, and I was strongly moved to find some pretext for detaining him; but the more I thought it over, the more I was forced to the conclusion that it was not in keeping with British police methods that I should do so . . .

The man stumbled a few feet away from me, and I made that an excuse for engaging him in conversation. He turned sharply at the sound of my voice, and scowled at me in surly fashion, but he said 'Good night' and agreed with me that it was cold.

His voice was a surprise to me. It was soft and musical, with just a tinge of melancholy in it, and it was the voice of a man of culture – a voice altogether out of keeping with the squalid surroundings of the East End.

As he turned away, one of the police officers came out of the house he had been in, and walked a few paces into the darkness of the alley. 'Hello! what is this?' he cried, and then he called in startled tones for me to come.

In the East End we are used to some shocking sights but the sight I saw made the blood in my veins turn to ice. At the end of the cul-de-sac huddled against the wall, there was a body of a woman, and a pool of blood was streaming along the gutter from her body. It was clearly another of those terrible murders. I remembered the man I had seen, and started after him as fast as I could run, but he was lost to sight in the dark labyrinth of East End mean streets.

The 'Scotland Yard' man comments:

It was White's description that gave the late **Sir Robert Anderson** his conviction that the murderer was a Jewish medical student, who had taken this method of avenging himself on women of the class to which the victim belonged.

. . . Sir Robert Anderson . . . afterwards, in comparing notes with White, expressed the opinion that the murderer and his victim had entered the close during the temporary absence of the two watching policemen. The men afterwards admitted that they had gone away for not more than a minute.

White's alleged description of the murder site as a cul-de-sac off the Whitechapel Road fits no Ripper-related crime, nor did White himself appear at any Ripper-related inquest or press report as one of the first policemen at the scene of the crime.

Additionally, although Sir Robert Anderson is known to have believed the Ripper to be a poor Polish Jew, he is not known to have thought him to be a medical student, and would not have done so after receipt of the full medical report from **Dr Bond**, in whom Anderson placed great confidence, and who rejected the idea that the Ripper possessed surgical skill or anatomical knowledge. It must be noted, however, that what purports to be an official report by White has suffered extensively from journalistic licence which has inserted florid clichés and wholly unofficial discussion of intuitive suspicions.

Still, there may well be some factual kernel to the story, and some theorists have attempted to make use of it, variously favouring Mitre Square, Berner Street and Castle Alley. Considered opinion must be that the story cannot be attached with certainty to anything known about the Ripper murders and White's official involvement in the investigation. Exceptional caution is therefore strongly recommended.

WHITECHAPEL

Parish of St Mary Matfellon, where Emma Smith, Martha Tabram, Mary Ann Nichols, Alice McKenzie and Frances Coles were killed. Hence the designation of the Ripper case 'the Whitechapel Murders'.

The church of St Mary Matfellon (destroyed by enemy action in 1941) stood on the south side of Whitechapel High Street, almost opposite the junction with **Osborn Street**. It is not known what 'Matfellon' meant. Built as a chapel of ease for parishioners of St Botolph's, Aldgate, it was at one period in the Middle Ages given a coat of whitewash: hence the name of the parish. Its site is marked today by a small park with the paved outline of the old church.

When Oliver Cromwell permitted Jewish resettlement in 1652, the immigrants moved into the area in and around Jewry Street, where probably there were already some illegally settled Sephardic Jews clandestinely worshipping in a warehouse in Creechurch Lane. By the beginning of the eighteenth century the Great Synagogue and the Bevis Marks Synagogue had been built on the eastern edge of the City of London, ensuring that continued Jewish settlement centred on the adjacent parish of Whitechapel. The poor Jews' preferred occupation of trading in secondhand clothes led to the growth of a network of street markets from Royal Mint Street ('Rag Fair') to Finsbury Square. The most famous of these is Petticoat Lane, but Whitechapel Street Market still operates daily, selling a very wide range of goods in the Whitechapel Road.

By 1888, Whitechapel was universally known as the principal area of Jewish settlement in England, though increased immigration from the Russian empire meant that Jews were spreading out into the adjacent parishes of **Spitalfields**, Mile End, **St George's-in-the-East** and Stepney.

'WHITE-EYED MAN, THE'
Alleged suspect based on misreading. Advanced by **E. T. Woodhall** in *Jack the Ripper: or When London Walked in Terror*.

Woodhall claims that among several practical jokers who sprang out at women during the scare, one particularly alarming one painted his face black with white rings around his eyes. One day he was arrested and taken to Scotland Yard, where he seized a heavy ebony ruler, assaulted two very senior officials (whose rank **Sir Melville Macnaghten** makes clear) and escaped. Three weeks later his body was found in the Thames, trapped beneath a paddle-boat. The constable in Buck's Row – 'the only living person who ever saw and spoke to [the murderer]' – believed the White-Eyed Man to be the same man. The constable was himself murdered later by a man named Abrahams.

This concoction can be seen to be drawn from several sources. The 'White-Eyed Man' is an exaggeration of **Dr Holt**, whose spectacles have become white painted eyes. The escape after assaulting two officials is a misunderstanding of Melville Macnaghten's remark that the Ripper escaped arrest after 'knocking out' a Police Commissioner and nearly 'settling the hash' of one of HM Principal Secretaries of State (i.e. damaging the careers of **Warren** and **Matthews**). The police constable who was murdered by a man called Abrahams was **Ernest Thompson**, who heard footsteps which were probably those of Frances Coles' murderer.

WHITEHALL MYSTERY, THE
Unsolved crime, briefly associated by sensational press with the Ripper. On 3 October 1888 it was found that during the night somebody had executed a difficult climb over the palings protecting the building site on the Embankment where New Scotland Yard was going up, and deposited the limbless, headless torso of a woman in a remote vault of the new cellarage. The lady's arms were separately deposited in the Thames. The police never imagined there was any connection with the Whitechapel Murders, despite press

speculation. There might, however, have been some connection with the similar **Pinchin Street** and **Elizabeth Jackson** murders of the following year.

WHITTINGTON-EGAN, RICHARD ALPHONSE BERNARD BARRINGTON CANNINGTON (1924–)

Crime historian. Author of *A Case Book On Jack the Ripper* (1975). The doyen of British true-crime writers. After preliminary training in medicine, Richard Whittington-Egan went on to become a journalist and author of books on crime, ghosts, and the literature of the 1890s. For many years wrote features for *Weekend* magazine; also on the editorial board of the *Contemporary Review*.

His great contribution to Ripper studies has been his insistence on scholarly accuracy. Knowing that anything less than a pedantic respect for facts invites insubstantial theorising, he has meticulously avoided adopting any 'suspect', and instead published the first significant correction of accumulating errors. Writers on the Ripper today might be divided between those historians who understand why Whittington-Egan cried, 'Halt!' to the erection of fantastic theories on a basis of canards, suspect sources, and forced readings; and those who have not seen the point and continue to advance hypotheses under the impression that like a jackdaw's nest they can be built from any stray item that comes to hand, and offered as a contribution to historical understanding.

WILKINSON, FREDERICK WILLIAM

Witness at Catharine Eddowes' inquest. Deputy of Cooney's Lodging House, 56 Flower and Dean Street, where Eddowes and **John Kelly** had stayed.

WILL THE REAL JACK THE RIPPER?

Book by **Arthur Douglas** (1979). Though brief, this survey of the known material at the time it was written is so accurate, responsible and perspicacious as to lead the authors to regret that Mr Douglas has not written more on the subject.

WILLIAMS, WATKIN WYNN

Grandson of **Sir Charles Warren** and author of his biography (*The Life of General Sir Charles Warren*, 1941). He includes a generally unreliable account of the murders, and says, 'I cannot recall that my grandfather . . . ever stated in writing his personal views on the identity of Jack the Ripper', but goes on to say that his impression was he accepted the drowned doctor theory (**M. J. Druitt**) advanced by **Major Griffiths**.

WILLIAMSON, CHIEF CONSTABLE A. F. (1830–89)

Senior professional policeman in Metropolitan CID at time of Ripper murders. Joined Metropolitan Police, 1850. Promoted sergeant in CID, 1852. Inspector, 1863. Chief Inspector, 1867, thus becoming the effective head of the serving detective officers in the Detective Branch. Superintendent, 1870. Chief Constable, CID, 1886. Died in harness.

Williamson had worked closely with both **Anderson** and (especially) **Monro** combating the **Fenians**. Nevertheless, when **Sir Charles Warren** devised the rank of Chief Constable as an intermediary between the 'gentlemen' Commissioners and 'Other ranks' up to Superintendent, it was Monro's wish to bring in **Melville Macnaghten** over Williamson's head.

By 1888 Williamson was tired and in poor health. He contributed nothing, so far as is known, to the Ripper investigation, and greeted Macnaghten when he joined the force as deputy Chief Constable the following year with the cynical observation that in the police he would be blamed if he didn't do his job and he would be blamed if he did it.

WILSON, ADA

Recently alleged possible attempted victim. Young sempstress of 19 Maidman Street, Mile End. On 28 March 1888, when she was alone in the house, she answered a knock at the door and was confronted by a man aged about 30, 5ft 6ins in height, with sunburnt face and fair moustache. He demanded money, and when she refused he stabbed her twice in the throat and ran away, leaving her for dead. He was nearly apprehended by neighbours.

It has been suggested that this might have been an early and unsuccessful assault by the Ripper, on the grounds that the description of the assailant is similar to that of men seen with several Ripper victims, and that sempstress was (and in countries where the occupation still exists on a large scale, still is) a common self-description used by prostitutes. To this it has been objected that a clear motive of robbery is stated. In any case, the introduction of Ada Wilson is entirely speculative.

WILSON, COLIN (b. 1931)

Crime historian. Co-author with Robin Odell of *Jack the Ripper: Summing Up and Verdict* (1987). Born in Leicester, he left school at sixteen and had various jobs before winning instant celebrity with his first book, the philosophical *The Outsider*. He has since written on subjects as diverse as the occult and crime, as well as several novels. He has been a frequent broadcaster on television and radio.

Since publishing a series of articles, 'My Search for Jack the Ripper', in the *Evening Standard* in August 1960, he has written extensively on the subject: notably in his own crime compendia *Order of Assassins*, *A History of Crime*, and *The Second Mammoth Book of Murder*; in the Ripper-based novel *Ritual in the Dark*; and in his introductions to Donald Rumbelow's *The Complete Jack the Ripper* and Alexander Kelly's *Jack the Ripper: A Bibliography* . . . The collaboration with Robin Odell is his only book exclusively on the subject.

His forte is not the contribution of new information from personal research, but commentary on the work of others, reviewing the theories of both published writers and unpublished correspondents. He has described himself as 'a clearing house for theories', and his generous encouragement has, perhaps, made him seem too easily persuaded by ingenious argument in preference to historical probability (cf. **Thomas Toughill, Bruce Paley**). But he has made much interesting material available to a wider audience than it would otherwise have reached.

A tendency to repeat factual errors and perpetuate canards (cf. **General Booth, Thomas Stowell**) is a weakness which makes double-checking his statements advisable, but it is more than offset by his carefully thought-out psychological and sociological theories concerning deviant behaviour, which he believes follows patterns related to phases of social development (see **Serial murder**).

WINBERG, MISS
Alleged co-conspirator with **Dr Pedachenko**. Supposedly a tailoress who accompanied Pedachenko from Walworth in order to engage his victims in conversation and lull their suspicions. Cf. **William Le Queux, Konovalov, Rasputin**.

WINSLADE, HENRY (b. 1860)
Waterman who pulled **M. J. Druitt**'s body from the Thames. Resident at 4 Shore Street, Paxton Road, Chelsea. Some newspapers give his name incorrectly as Winslow.

WINSLOW, LYTTLETON STEWART FORBES (1843–1913)
Contemporary theorist. Educ. Rugby and Downing College, Cambridge. LLB, 1866; LLM, 1870; MB, 1870; MRCP (Lond.), 1871; DCL Oxon., 1873; LLD (Cantab.).

His father, Forbes Benignus Winslow, was a doctor specialising in lunacy with a large practice in private asylums. Winslow joined him in practice and became a leading alienist. In 1877 he was one of the doctors who secured a reprieve for the Stauntons (four young people convicted of starving a woman to death) on the grounds that the medical evidence was unsafe. Thenceforth, with his formidable mixture of medical and legal qualifications, Winslow believed himself to be the final arbiter on questions of sanity and legal responsibility.

From 1889 he convinced himself that he had identified the Ripper; would have arrested him had he been given a force of six constables to go to St Paul's Cathedral, where he believed the murderer regularly attended services; and by his efforts had frightened the man into abandoning murder and leaving the country. (See under **G. Wentworth Bell Smith** for Winslow's suspect.) His notion was fully investigated by police and found worthless, but this did not prevent Winslow from trumpeting his triumph in the press at every opportunity.

There is obvious alteration to the date of a 'Jack the Ripper' letter addressed to him which he produces in facsimile in his memoirs. The police noticed similar alteration in the written evidence of Mr. E. Callaghan which he produced in substantiation of his theory. In both cases the alteration brings irrelevant material back to the time of a murder or murders. Winslow's reliance on such fabrications effectively discredits him.

WOOD, SIMON (b. 1945)
Researcher. Editor of the now defunct magazine *Bloodhound* in which in March 1987 he published the results of an analysis using data found by Alan Neate of the Greater London Records Office – undertaken years earlier and privately circulated – of **Annie Elizabeth Crook**'s movements. This proved that in 1888 Annie Crook and **Walter Sickert** could not have been living at the addresses in Cleveland Street identified by **Stephen Knight** and **Joseph Sickert**, the buildings having been demolished in 1887.

He also showed conclusively that Annie Crook was not a Catholic and did not spend from 1888 until her death confined in one or more hospitals as claimed by Knight and Joseph Sickert. Moreover, since Wood used material that had been supplied to Stephen Knight, he demonstrated that Knight's conclusions relied more on Joseph Sickert's story than the apparent objectivity of his reseach would suggest.

WOODHALL, EDWIN THOMAS (b. 1885)
Theorist. Former policeman who wrote accounts of police work, among them his **Jack the Ripper: or When London Walked in Terror**. See under **Olga Tchkersoff, 'The White-Eyed Man'**.

WRIGHT, FRANCES
See **Mary Elizabeth Simonds**.

WRITING ON THE WALL, THE
See **Goulston Street graffito**.

X

XAVIER, MANUEL CRUZ (b. 1851)
Alleged suspect. Portuguese cattleman advanced as Mary Jane Kelly's murderer by **E. K. Larkins**.

Z

ZVERIEFF, NICHOLAS
Alleged informant. Said by **William Le Queux** to have told **Johann Nider-oest** that Jack the Ripper was **Dr Pedachenko**. Zverieff is described as an elderly anarchist and member of the Jubilee Street Club, an anarchist centre which opened in the East End of London in 1906. Outside the pages of Le Queux, no evidence is known for Zverieff's existence. Cf. **Rasputin, Konovalov**.

INDEX OF VICTIMS

INDEX OF SUSPECTS

INDEX OF POLICEMEN

INDEX OF BOOKS, WRITERS AND ARTICLES ON JACK THE RIPPER

GENERAL INDEX